African American Quotations

African American Quotations

Richard Newman

With a Foreword by Julian Bond

Oryx Press
1998

The rare Arabian Oryx is believed to have inspired the myth of the unicorn. This desert antelope became virtually extinct in the early 1960s. At that time several groups of international conservationists arranged to have 9 animals sent to the Phoenix Zoo to be the nucleus of a captive breeding herd. Today the Oryx population is over 800 and nearly 400 have been returned to reserves in the Middle East.

© 1998 by The Oryx Press
4041 North Central at Indian School Road
Phoenix, Arizona 85012-3397

∞ The paper used in this publication meets the minimum requirements of American National Standard for Information Science—Permanence of Paper for Printed Library Materials, ANSI Z39.48, 1984.

Library of Congress Cataloging-in-Publication Data
African American quotations / [compiled by] Richard Newman : with a foreword by Julian Bond.
    p. cm.
    Includes index.
    ISBN 1-57356-118-5 (alk. paper)
    1. Afro-Americans—Quotations. I. Newman, Richard, 1930– .
PN6081.3.A36 1998
081'.089'96073—dc21
                                       98-19474
                                          CIP

For
Belynda Bady

"Tell me whom you love and I'll tell you who you are."
—*Louisiana Creole Proverb*

CONTENTS

Foreword *by Julian Bond*   xi

Introduction   xiii

Quotations   1

Achievement   3
Action   5
Adolescence   8
Adversity   9
Affirmative Action   9
Africa   12
African American Studies   20
African Continuity   21
Afrocentrism   22
Age   22
Alienation   23
Ambition   23
America   24
Ancestors   34
Anger   37
Answers   37
Art   38
Artists   45
Atonement   48
Authenticity   48
Beauty of Blackness   49
Being Black in America   51
Black Consciousness   56
Black Culture   57
Black Experience   59
Black Power   59
Black Pride   60
Black Strength   63
Blackness   64
Blues   65
Books   66
Brotherhood   67

Business   68
Capitalism   70
Change   71
Chaos   72
Children   73
Christianity   76
Church   77
Civil Rights Movement   80
Class   82
Colonialism   84
Color   85
Community   86
Confederate Flag   89
Conservatives   90
Constitution   90
Courage   92
Creativity   97
Dance   99
Daring   100
Death   101
Declaration of Independence   103
Defeat   103
Democracy   104
Desegregation   106
Despair   106
Destiny   107
Dignity   107
Direction   108
Discipline   108
Dissent   109
Diversity   109
Dreams   111

CONTENTS

Drugs   114
Economics   115
Education   118
Emancipation   129
Emigration   130
Encouragement   131
Endurance   131
Equality   132
Ethnicity   133
Evil   134
Expectations   135
Experience   135
Exploitation   135
Failure   136
Faith   136
Family   137
Fate   139
Fear   140
Fighting   141
Folk Sayings   141
Folklore   143
Fourth of July   143
Freedom   144
Friends   150
Future   150
Gays and Lesbians   152
Gender   153
Genocide   155
Ghetto   155
Giving   156
Goals   156
God   159
Government   163
Growth   164
Guilt   165
Hair   165
Happiness   166
Harlem   166
Harlem Renaissance   168
Hate   169
Healing   171
Health   171
Heaven   171
Hell   172

Heritage   172
Heroes   173
History   173
Honesty   178
Hope   178
Human Nature   180
Humanism   181
Humanity   181
Humor   183
Ideals   184
Ideas   185
Identity   186
Imagination   189
Independence   189
Individuality   190
Injustice   190
Insight   191
Inspiration   191
Integration   192
Integrity   193
Intelligence   195
Invisibility   196
Islam   196
Jazz   197
Justice   200
Knowledge   202
Labor   203
Language   203
Law   206
Leadership   207
Liberation   210
Liberty   211
Life   212
Limitations   214
Literature   215
Living   216
Love   217
Lynching   221
Marriage   222
Memory   223
Men   223
Middle Passage   226
Mind   227
Misery   227

Mistakes   228
Money   228
Morality   229
Motown Sound   231
Music   231
NAACP   235
Names   236
Nationhood   237
Nonviolence   238
Opportunity   238
Oppression   240
Oral Tradition   242
Organization   242
Paris   243
Patriotism   244
Peace   245
Poetry   247
Poets   248
Politics   248
Poverty   253
Power   254
Prayer   255
Preaching   256
Prejudice   257
Prison   258
Progress   259
Protest   261
Public Life   262
Punishment   262
Purpose   262
Race   263
Race Consciousness   266
Race Relations   267
Racism   269
Radicalism   274
Ragtime   274
Rap   275
Rape   276
Reading   276
Reality   278
Rebellion   280
Reconstruction   281
Reform   282
Relationships   282

Religion   283
Reparations   286
Resistance   287
Respect   288
Responsibility   289
Retribution   289
Revolution   290
Rights   292
Rock 'n' Roll   293
Role Models   293
Sacrifice   294
Sanity   294
Segregation   295
Self-Acceptance   296
Self-Affirmation   297
Self-Confidence   299
Self-Expression   300
Self-Hate   301
Self-Knowledge   303
Self-Liberation   307
Self-Realization   *309*
Self-Reliance   312
Self-Respect   315
Selfishness   317
Separation   317
Service to the Community   318
Sex   319
Silence   321
Singing   321
Slavery   323
Solidarity   329
Soul   330
Spirit   331
Spirituality   332
Spirituals   333
Sports   343
Strategy   345
Stress   345
Struggle   346
Style   350
Success   351
Suffering   353
Survival   353
Talented Tenth   354

CONTENTS

Theater   355
Thinking   356
Time   356
Tokenism   357
Travel   357
Trouble   358
Truth   358
Twoness   360
Underground Railroad   361
Unity   361
Values   364
Victory   366

Violence   367
Vision   368
War   369
Winning   370
Wisdom   371
Women   371
Words   380
Words to Live By   381
Work   389
Writers   391
Writing   393
Youth   395

Indexes   397

Name Index   399
Subject Index   424
Occupation Index   491

FOREWORD

As I write, eight books of quotations sit handily on a shelf at my side, a ready reference for the countless occasions when someone else's words say better than I can what I want said. But none of the eight contains as many quotes from as many sources as does this volume.

My own favorite quotation is Frederick Douglass's "If there is no struggle, there is no progress." But choosing a favorite is like choosing among one's children—each is precious.

This collection of over 2,500 quotations will contain many of your favorites and will help provide the exact quotation to fit the right occasion. More importantly, this collection will acquaint the reader with a multitude of adages, aphorisms, maxims, mottoes, proverbs, and sayings from a large number of African Americans. Some of those who are quoted are well known. Others will be introduced to the reader for the first time and should inspire further inquiry into the lives and times of the women and men who so eloquently, and frequently so simply, summed up a thought or reflection in a few words.

Here a multitude speaks on a multitude of subjects, sharing opinions and framing ideas. Here the famous and the lesser known bring the values they learned from living black to the written and spoken word. Here the reader has an opportunity to learn of the great diversity of black opinion and thought.

As Ralph Ellison says in these pages, "Words are your business, boy. Not the Word. Words are everything. The key to the Rock, the answer to the Question."

This collection will be invaluable to the scholar, writer, or curious reader. You can quote me.

Julian Bond
NAACP Chairperson

INTRODUCTION

In 1985 Gerald L. Davis published a book with an unusual title, *I Got the Word in Me and I Can Preach It, You Know,* and its equally evocative subtitle, "A Study of the Performed African-American Sermon." In a literary vein, the great American novelist Toni Morrison writes, "We die, that may be the meaning of life. But we do language. That may be the measure of our lives." *African American Quotations* is a book of those words and of that language, showing how people of African descent have put words together in unique ways to create insightful ideas, provocative thoughts, and inspirational sentiments.

Africa's many ethnic groups are highly expressive cultures alive with stories, songs, proverbs, and historical recollections. Prohibited by slavery in this country from learning to read or write, African Americans continued many of these oral traditions in folk songs like the spirituals and folk tales, many using symbolic animal characters as did their African antecedents. Also, speech played a vital part in the slaves' everyday resistance to bondage. They learned "to wear the mask," that is, to disguise their true feelings, to dissemble, to say what they knew their masters wanted to hear, and to communicate secretly with each other through supposedly innocuous phrases and songs with double meanings. At the same time, in their own gatherings both religious and secular, verbal skill and oratorical ability became primary characteristics of those who emerged naturally as charismatic leaders.

So there is a long and intimate relationship between African Americans and language, from the rhythmic eloquence of the preacher to the rhymed lyrics of the rap artist. In adolescent word games like the dozens, insults are traded in a stylized ritual that sharpens the wits and teaches self-control. Like black music and dance, black speech has influenced mainstream and middle-class white America and infused the English language with a new vitality and energy. With curious transmogrifications, black speech is even working its way into non-English languages, like Japanese.

I decided to bring together a collection of African American quotations for several reasons. One is that an African American voice is often minimized or even excluded from standard reference works, trade books, and school texts. That exclusion deprives students, researchers, and readers of the wisdom, insight, and special way with words of some remarkable people; this book is meant to correct that shortcoming. In addition, many of the quotations here reflect the unique viewpoints of African Americans, perspectives created by the experiences of slavery, segregation, and racism. Black people are both insiders and outsiders in this country, and their particular vision has produced a singular understanding of American life in all its dimensions. Users of this book will be surprised, as I often was, at the power of words which reflect the light of a different surface of the American prism.

A number of these quotations became particularly meaningful to me, and I repeat them here without commentary. One is the statement of guitarist and singer B.B. King: "To be a black person and sing the blues, you are black twice." Another is the radically egalitarian questions of one of the spirituals: "Didn't my Lord deliver Daniel? And why not every man?" Another is the statement of the intrepid Harriet Tubman who, with a price on her head, ventured secretly into the antebellum South to bring out men, women, and children on the Underground Railroad: "I freed thousands of slaves. I could have freed thousands more—if they knew that they were slaves." A line from James Baldwin summarizes the point of bringing these quotations together: "My memory stammers, but my soul is a witness."

Collecting quotations I felt were striking enough to be of both refer-ence and general interest, I was struck by how many are the words of James Baldwin and Zora Neale Hurston. Baldwin's perceptions into the time in which he lived go straight to the heart as well as the head and have a timeless utility. Hurston speaks more from the black folk tradition, but her wisdom is no less profound than Baldwin's and her understanding of human nature may even run deeper. Researchers and readers will, I know, find their own appropriate and meaningful statements.

I owe debts of thanks to many. At Harvard University, I am privileged to be in the company of a number of people whose teaching, writing, and speaking are quite literally on the cutting edge of contemporary black thinking and expression. There are many quotations in this book, for example, by Cornel West and Henry Louis Gates Jr., but I believe their words are of larger importance than my own appreciation.

I have also been privileged over the years to hear some extraordinary black oratory. I have heard the powerful political speaking of Ronald Dellums, Jesse Jackson, Martin Luther King Jr., and Adam Clayton Powell Jr. The first great black preaching I heard was that of James H. Robinson of the Church of the Master in Harlem, but I have also listened to Peter Gomes, Sweet Daddy Grace, Samuel Proctor, Gardner C. Taylor, and Howard Thurman. I have not heard him in person, but I am impressed by the preaching I have heard on TV and video of Bishop T.D. Jakes.

During the preparation of this book, two close friends and long-time colleagues died. Both were deeply involved with African American language. James Melvin Washington was professor of church history at Union Theological Seminary and an active Baptist preacher. A wise and deeply human as well as brilliant man, he knew at first hand, and he appreciated, the African American genius for words, a genius reflected in his own teaching, preaching, and writing.

My dear friend Betty Shabazz was a private person who often mentioned to me her reluctance to be a public speaker. As long as she lived, however, she reminded us all not only of her own quiet courage and self-reliance, but of the message of her murdered husband, Malcolm X. Perhaps more than any other person in recent memory, Malcolm told the truth about America, and it is not accidental that many quotations from his speaking and writing are included here. Through her dignified silence and independent integrity, however, Betty Shabazz also spoke. In a June 1993 interview with the newspaper *City Sun*, she said of her life, "My soul is at peace." At her death, that statement takes on a new meaning, and I include it in this collection as a word of memorial tribute both for her and for Jim Washington.

SCOPE AND CONTENTS

Virtually all the quotations collected here are by men and women of color. There are a few intentional exceptions—John Brown, for instance—and there may be some unintentional ones. I have not included quotations by Africans or by people of African descent outside the United States. Again, there are a few exceptions, like Marcus Garvey, whose presence and impact were so vital in this country. Each speaker of a quotation is identified briefly, including birth and death dates—though these dates are notoriously unreliable—and occupation.

African American Quotations includes more than 2,500 quotations in English by more than 500 individuals from the 18th century to this year's newspapers. Entries are arranged alphabetically by subject, and then by author within each subject. If a speaker has more than one quotation, these quotations are arranged alphabetically by initial words. The speaker is listed by his or her birth name or by the person's commonly known name within the popular culture (with birth name in parentheses when known). Subject headings have been selected from standard sources and modified as appropriate to the general subject. A table of contents lists all the subject headings. *See* and *See Also* references are included.

Three indexes enable readers to locate quotations more easily. The Name Index lists each speaker by name. A Subject Index, including key words, identifies quotations by subject. The Occupations Index categorizes quotations by industry of the speaker.

It was difficult, I must say, to select quotations for this collection. The basic test was that a statement had to be arresting, striking, attention-getting, memorable. Ways of meeting that test varied. It could be a creative use of words. It could be some special discernment derived from the experience of being black in America. It could be that the speaker is a neglected figure in American history who deserves to be better known. While a good many quotations were rejected, there exist, I'm sure, a great many more that I never had the opportunity to see. If you know a quotation that you think should have been included, I invite you to send it to me for a possible revision or supplement. If you know it, please include information on the bibliographic source. My address is: Richard Newman, W.E.B. Du Bois Institute for Afro-American Research, Harvard University, 12 Quincy Street, Cambridge, MA 02138.

ACKNOWLEDGMENTS

I am indebted to a great many people for their interest, support, and friendship during the preparation of this book. I particularly appreciate Donna Sanzone, my old compatriot at G.K. Hall & Co., now with Oryx Press; and my friend Julian Bond, who was generous enough to write the foreword. I am also grateful to Donald Altschiller, Willie Bady Jr., Alisa Bierria, Kenneth Carpenter, Diane Cummins, James P. Danky, Henry Louis Gates Jr., Betty Kaplan Gubert, Lee Hancock, Marguerite Harrison, Irene Monroe, Pamela Petro, Warren Platt, and Jill M. Watts.

At Harvard, I thoroughly enjoy the collegiality of the staff of the Department of Afro-American Studies and the W.E. B. Du Bois Institute for Afro-American Research: April Yvonne Garrett, Joanne Kendall, Eva Stahl, Lisa Thompson, and Gwen White. It is a great pleasure to work with Patricia Sullivan and the wonderful editors and writers of the encyclopedia project. Elleni Amlak and Cornel West have gone beyond friendship to become family.

And there is always Belynda Bady.

Richard Newman
Boston, Massachusetts

QUOTATIONS

ACHIEVEMENT

1. I never doubted my ability, but when you hear all your life you're inferior, it makes you wonder if the other group have something you've never seen before. If they do, I'm still looking for it.

Hank Aaron, 1934–
Baseball star

2. I'm so fast I could hit you before God gets the news.

Muhammad Ali, 1942–
Boxing champion

3. I don't feel that I opened the door. I've never been a great mover and shaker of the earth. I think that those who came after me deserve a great deal of credit for what they have achieved.

Marian Anderson, 1897–1993
Singer

4. Whatever the white man has done, we have done, and done better.

Mary McLeod Bethune, 1875–1955
Educator

5. A negative attitude is a true handicap.

Crenner Bradley
Mother of Mayor Thomas Bradley

6. To struggle and battle and overcome and absolutely defeat every force designed against us is the only way to achieve.

Nannie Burroughs, 1879–1961
Activist

7. There is a use for almost everything.

George Washington Carver, 1864?–1943
Inventor

8. You are not judged by the height you have risen, but from the depth you have climbed.

Frederick Douglass, 1817?–1895
Abolitionist and Autobiographer

9. All of us may not live to see the higher accomplishments of an African empire, so strong and powerful as to compel the respect of mankind, but we in our lifetime can so work and act as to make the dream a possibility within another generation.

Marcus Garvey, 1887–1940
Nationalist leader

10. No matter what accomplishments you make, somebody helps you.

Althea Gibson, 1927–
Tennis champion

11. Our destination is to where we have never been before.

Peter J. Gomes, 1942–
Minister

12. The burden of being black is that you have to be superior just to be equal. But the glory of it is that, once you achieve, you have achieved indeed.

Jesse Jackson, 1941–
Minister and Civil rights activist

13. I never intended to become a run-of-the-mill person.

Barbara Jordan, 1936–1996
Lawyer and U.S. Congressperson

14. I made the most of my ability and I did the best with my title.

Joe Louis, 1914–1981
Boxing champion

15. You have the ability, now apply yourself.

Benjamin Mays, 1895–1984
Educator

16. The many of us who attain what we may and forget those who help us along the line, we've got to remember that there are so many others to pull along the way. The further they go, the further we all go.

Jackie Robinson, 1919–1972
Baseball star

17. We start with gifts. Merit comes from what we make of them.

Jean Toomer, 1894–1967
Novelist

18. We all have ability. The difference is how we use it.

Stevie Wonder, 1950–
Singer

19. Our ability to create has outreached our ability to use wisely the products of our inventions.

Whitney M. Young Jr., 1921–1971
Civil rights activist

ACTION

20. He who is not courageous enough to take risks will accomplish nothing in life.

Muhammad Ali, 1942–
Boxing champion

21. Everybody wants to do something to help, but nobody wants to be first.

Pearl Bailey, 1918–1990
Entertainer

22. To act is to be committed, and to be committed is to be in danger.

James Baldwin, 1924–1987
Writer and Activist

23. Talk! Talk! Talk! That will not free the slaves…. What is needed is action! Action!

John Brown, 1800–1859
Insurrectionist

24. Those who set in motion the forces of evil cannot always control them afterwards.

Charles W. Chesnutt, 1858–1932
Novelist

25. It is not light that is needed, but fire.

Frederick Douglass, 1817?–1895
Abolitionist and Autobiographer

26. Men must not only know, they must act.

W.E.B. Du Bois, 1868–1963
Intellectual and Activist

27. If we have to wait until ideological purity is achieved, we'll be waiting for Godot. I don't know about you, but I ain't got the time.

Henry Louis Gates Jr., 1950–
Scholar and Critic

28. It is a burden of black people that we have to do more than talk.

Barbara Jordan, 1936–1996
Lawyer and U.S. Congressperson

29. Nothing is going to be handed to you. You have to make things happen.

Florence Griffith Joyner, 1959–
Olympic track star

30. I don't know what to do. I know that something has to change in Birmingham. I don't know if I can raise money to get people out of jail. I do know I can go to jail with them,

Martin Luther King Jr., 1929–1968
Civil rights activist and Nobel laureate

31. It may get me crucified. I may even die. But I want it said even if I die in the struggle that "He died to make men free."

Martin Luther King Jr., 1929–1968
Civil rights activist and Nobel laureate

32. So the purpose of direct action is to create a situation so crisis-packed that it will inevitably open the doors to negotiation.

Martin Luther King Jr., 1929–1968
Civil rights activist and Nobel laureate

33. When people made up their minds that they wanted to be free and took action, then there was a change.

Rosa Parks, 1913–
Civil rights activist

34. Nothing counts but pressure, pressure, more pressure, and still more pressure through broad organized aggressive mass action.

A. Philip Randolph, 1889–1979
Labor leader

35. It's time to bring down the volume and bring up the program.

Al Sharpton, 1955–
Minister and Activist

36. Talk without effort is nothing.

Maria W. Stewart, 1803–1879
Lecturer

37. Don't you know you would help the race more by exposing the new forms of slavery just outside Tuskegee than by preaching submission?

William Monroe Trotter, 1872–1934
Journalist and Civil rights activist

38. I am above 80 years old. It is about time for me to be going. I have been 40 years a slave and 40 years free, and would be here 40 years more to have equal rights for all. I suppose I am kept here because something remains for me to do. I suppose I am yet to help break the chain.

Sojourner Truth, 1797?–1883
Abolitionist and Women's rights advocate

39. I'm trying to revive a grand yet flawed tradition, to take the best from liberalism, Populism, and the Gospel while keeping track of what happens to everyday people, the ones the Bible calls the least of these.

Cornel West, 1954–
Philosopher and Activist

40. It ain't nothing to find no starting place in the world. You just start from where you find yourself.

August Wilson, 1945–
Dramatist

41. When you hear a man talking, then, always inquire as to what he has done for humanity.

Carter G. Woodson, 1875–1950
Historian

42. My hobby is stirring up Negroes.

Malcolm X, 1925–1965
Nationalist leader

ADOLESCENCE

43. Few, if any, survive their teens. Most surrender to the vague but murderous pressure of adult conformity.

Maya Angelou, 1928–
Novelist and Poet

44. Trying to grow up is hurting, you know. You make mistakes. You try to learn from them, and when you don't, it hurts even more.

Aretha Franklin, 1942–
Singer

45. So much of growing up is an unbearable waiting.

Sonia Sanchez, 1934–
Poet

46. Since science has not yet found a cure for adolescence, the best we can do is give the only real antidote for immaturity—experience.

Thomas Sowell, 1930–
Economist

ADVERSITY

47. When you are in adversity for conscience's sake, you are not alone.

Peter J. Gomes, 1942–
Minister

48. There will always be some curve balls in your life. Teach your children to thrive in that adversity.

Jeanne Moutoussamy-Ashe, 1951–
Photographer

AFFIRMATIVE ACTION

49. Government may take race into account when it acts not to demean or insult any racial group, but to remedy any disadvantages cast on minorities by past racial prejudice.

William J. Brennan
U.S. Supreme Court Justice

50. You have to distinguish between means and ends. What's important here is the end, diversity. Affirmative action is just one means to that end.

Albert Carnesale
UCLA chancellor

51. Discrimination has a way of perpetuating itself, albeit unintentionally, because the resulting inequalities make new opportunities less accessible.

Frank M. Coffin, 1919–

52. White Anglo-Saxon males never have felt inferior as a result of their centuries of "affirmative action" and quotas in jobs from which Jews, racial minorities, and women were excluded and too often still are.

Marian Wright Edelman, 1939–
Children's Defense Fund official

53. I would never pull up the ladder that helped me climb out of racial poverty.

Brian Fair, 1960–
Author of *Notes of a Racial Caste Baby*

54. I don't think he's [President Bill Clinton] interested in reminding people of the disparities that we have in this country that were caused by race and class. It's unfortunate, because I think we need more affirmative action, not less affirmative action.

Henry Louis Gates Jr., 1950–
Scholar and Critic

55. Affirmative action is neither the real problem nor the whole solution. The challenge for public education is to rethink how they admit everyone.

Lani Guinier, 1950–
Law professor

56. When the government, by public policy, kept you out, the government has a responsibility, by public policy, to bring you in. And it needs to be just as intentional about including you as it was about excluding you.

Joseph Lowery, 1924–
Civil rights activist

57. It must be remembered that during most of the past 200 years, the Constitution as interpreted by this Court did not prohibit the most ingenious and pervasive forms of discrimination against the Negro. Now, when a state acts to remedy the effects of that legacy of discrimination, I cannot believe that the same Constitution stands as a barrier.

Thurgood Marshall, 1908–1993
U.S. Supreme Court Justice

58. I will never forget that I became chairman of the Joint Chiefs of Staff because of the [Massachusetts] 54th Regiment [in the Civil War]. I was not the first who was qualified, and I was not the first who had the potential. I was the first to come along after the government had secured our right to equal treatment and affirmative action so I could be measured by my performance and not by the color of my skin.

Colin Powell, 1937–
U.S. General

59. We have seen what the preference system that had been in place for 250 years has done to us.... It is not inappropriate for us to use affirmative action to get our youngsters in the pool.

Colin Powell, 1937–
U.S. General

60. There is still a great deal of resistance to the election of black office-seekers by whites on account of race.... This voting discrimination against black candidates, I argue, is discernible, specific, purposeful, and contemporary—and for which remedial action is warranted. The limitations of other policy alternatives require that the Supreme Court—and indeed the nation—rethink the permissability of race-based voting districts.

Keith W. Reeves
Political scientist

61. It has been 30 years, basically, since many minority students—African Americans, Native Americans, Latinos, and others—have had serious access to most American institutions of higher education—30 years, after 300 years of non-access. And 30 years is supposed to be enough for minorities to catch up and achieve full equality of opportunity?

Neil L. Rudenstein, 1935–
Educator

62. But for affirmative action laws, God knows where I would be today.

Clarence Thomas, 1948–
U.S. Supreme Court Justice

63. If you have two people running in a mile race round a track and one has a ball and chain tied around his leg for three laps, you can't take the ball and chain off for the final lap and still expect him to win.

Frank Watkins

64. The rules may be color-blind, but people are not.

Patricia Williams
Law professor

AFRICA

65. Africa is herself a mother. The mother of mankind.

Maya Angelou, 1928–
Novelist and Poet

66. Africa to me is more than a glamorous fact. It is a historical truth. No man can know where he is going unless he knows exactly where he has been and exactly how he arrived at his present place.

Maya Angelou, 1928–
Novelist and Poet

67. After centuries of slavers took her strongest sons and daughters, after years of colonialism, Africa needs her progeny to bring something to her.

Maya Angelou, 1928–
Novelist and Poet

68. Princes shall come out of Egypt; Ethiopia shall soon stretch out her hands unto God.

Anonymous
Psalms 67: 31 King James Version

69. The very invention of Africa (as something more than a geographical entity) must be understood ultimately as an outgrowth of European racialism.

Anthony Appiah, 1954–
Philosopher

70. Whatever Africans share, we do not have a traditional culture, common languages, a common religion, or conceptual vocabulary.... We do not even belong to a common race.

Anthony Appiah, 1954–
Philosopher

71. Egypt is to African American culture as Greece is to white culture.

Molefi Asante, 1942–
Educator

72. There is something a little mad about sitting in London or Versailles, looking at the map of Africa and drawing lines as though there were no people living there.

James Baldwin, 1924–1987
Writer and Activist

73. I am my mother's daughter, and the drums of Africa still beat in my heart. They will not let me rest while there's a single Negro boy or girl without a chance to prove his worth.

Mary McLeod Bethune, 1875–1955
Educator

74. We carry within us the wonders we seek without us: there is all Africa and her prodigies in us.

Sir Thomas Browne, 1605–1682
English physician and Writer

75. I hold thee fast, Africa. [Teneo te, Africa].

Julius Caesar, 100–44 B.C.
Roman general
As he slipped and fell to the ground upon landing in Africa in 47 B.C.

76. We have always been an African people, we have always maintained our own value system.

Stokely Carmichael, 1941–
Activist

77. In Africa one day, while sitting with some Africans, I saw a white person and I was so secure. For the first time in my life I felt no fear and knew exactly

why. I was in a sea of blackness; I was in a sea of security. There was nothing—absolutely nothing—that he could do to me.

John Henrik Clarke, 1915–
Historian

78. It's time for black people to stop playing the separating game of geography, of where the slave ship put us down. We must concentrate on where the slave ship picked us up.

John Henrik Clarke, 1915–
Historian

79. Wherever we are on the face of the earth, we are an African people.

John Henrik Clarke, 1915–
Historian

80. Spicy grove, cinnamon tree, / What is Africa to me?

Countee Cullen, 1903–1946
Poet and Writer

81. It has been the fashion of American writers to deny that the Egyptians were Negroes and claim that they are of the same race as themselves, This has, I have no doubt, been largely due to a wish to deprive the Negro of the moral support of Ancient greatness and to appropriate the same to the white race.

Frederick Douglass, 1817?–1895
Abolitionist and Autobiographer

82. The spell of Africa is upon me.

W.E.B. Du Bois, 1868–1963
Intellectual and Activist

83. Three things Africa has given the world, and they form the essence of African culture: beginnings, the village unit, and art in sculpture and music.

W.E.B. Du Bois, 1868–1963
Intellectual and Activist

84. Bloodshed and usurpations, the rum jug and the Bible—these will be the program of the white race in Africa, for, perhaps, a hundred years.... But, in the course of time, the people will become educated not only in the cruel and grasping nature of the white man, but in the knowledge of their power, their

priority ownership in the soil, and in the desperation which tyranny and greed never fail to breed for their own destruction.

T. Thomas Fortune, 1856–1928
Journalist

85. Africa for the Africans at home and abroad.

Marcus Garvey, 1887–1940
Nationalist leader

86. How dare anyone tell us that Africa cannot be redeemed when we have 400 million men and women with warm blood coursing through their veins?

Marcus Garvey, 1887–1940
Nationalist leader

87. I know no national boundary where the Negro is concerned. The whole world is my province until Africa is free.

Marcus Garvey, 1887–1940
Nationalist leader

88. Wake up, Ethiopia! Wake up, Africa! Let us work towards the one glorious end of a free, redeemed, and mighty nation. Let Africa be a bright star among the constellation of nations.

Marcus Garvey, 1887–1940
Nationalist leader

89. We should say to the millions who are in Africa to hold the fort, for we are coming 400 million strong.

Marcus Garvey, 1887–1940
Nationalist leader

90. When Europe was inhabited by a race of cannibals, a race of savage men, heathens and pagans, Africa was peopled with a race of cultured black men who were masters in art, science, and literature.

Marcus Garvey, 1887–1940
Nationalist leader

91. You do not know Africa. Africa has been sleeping for centuries—not dead, only sleeping.

Marcus Garvey, 1887–1940
Nationalist leader

92. It is still yesterday in Africa. It will take millions of tomorrows to rectify what has been done there.

Lorraine Hansberry, 1930–1965
Dramatist

93. From Greenland's icy mountains, / From India's coral strand, / Where Afric's sunny fountains / Roll down their golden sand; / From many an ancient river, / From many a palmy plain, / They call us to deliver / Their land from error's chain.

Reginald Heber, 1783–1826
English clergyman

94. Africa is not only our mother, but in the light of most recent science is beginning to appear as the mother of civilization.

Alain Locke, 1886–1954
Scholar and Critic

95. Even with all our scientific reevaluation, all our "New Negro" compensation, all our anti-Nordic polemics, a certain disrespect for Africa still persists widely.

Alain Locke, 1886–1954
Scholar and Critic

96. We now see that the missionary condescension of past generations in their attitude toward Africa was a pious but sad mistake. In taking it, we have fallen into the snare of our enemies and have given grievous offense to our brothers.

Alain Locke, 1886–1954
Scholar and Critic

97. The wind of change is blowing through this continent, and, whether we like it or not, this growth of national consciousness is a political fact.

Harold Macmillan, 1894–1986
British Prime Minister
Speech at Capetown, February 3, 1960, signaling colonial admission of African independence

98. Africanism is inextricable from the definition of Americaness—from its origins or through its integrated or disintegrating twentieth century self.... It is a dark and abiding presence, there for the literary imagination as both a visible and an invisible mediating force.

Toni Morrison, 1931–
Novelist and Nobel laureate

99. All roads lead to Africa.

Richard Newman, 1930–
Writer

100. Out of Africa, always something new [Semper aliquid novi Africam adferre].

Pliny the Elder, 23–79 A.D.
Roman scholar

101. Africa is a Dark Continent not merely because its people are dark-skinned or by reason of its extreme inpenetrability, but because its history is lost.

Paul Robeson, 1898–1976
Singer and Activist

102. I am a Negro with every drop of blood and every stir of my soul ... I want to be more African.

Paul Robeson, 1898–1976
Singer and Activist

103. I learned that along with the towering achievements of the cultures of ancient Greece and China there stood the culture of Africa, unseen and denied by the looters of Africa's material wealth.

Paul Robeson, 1898–1976
Singer and Activist

104. I sang the songs of my people—in many ways, especially rhythmically, still full of African turns of musical phrase and forms.

Paul Robeson, 1898–1976
Singer and Activist

105. In my music, my plays, my films I want to carry always this central idea: to be African. Multitudes of men have died for less worthy ideas; it is even more eminently worth living for.

Paul Robeson, 1898–1976
Singer and Activist

106. Like most of Africa's children in America, I had known little about the land of our fathers.

Paul Robeson, 1898–1976
Singer and Activist

107. The darkest thing about Africa is America's ignorance of it.

James H. Robinson, 1907–1972
Crossroads Africa official

108. African Americans ought to care about Africa and the Caribbean because we are much stronger together than separate. Our potential as black people is to harness our power globally.

Randall Robinson, 1941–
Trans Africa official

109. A foutra for [indifference to] the world, and worldings base! I speak of Africa and golden joys.

William Shakespeare, 1564–1616
English dramatist
Henry IV, part 2, act 5, scene 3

110. I crossed the waters to come here, and I am willing to cross them to return.

Venture Smith, 1729?–1805
Slave autobiographer

111. History informs us that we sprung from one of the most learned nations of the whole earth; from the seat, if not the parent, of science. Yes, poor despised Africa was once the resort of sages and legislators of other nations, was esteemed as the school for learning, and the most illustrious men of Greece flocked thither for instruction.

Maria W. Stewart, 1803–1879
Lecturer

112. I believe that the oppression of injured Africa has come up before the majesty of heaven.

Maria W. Stewart, 1803–1879
Lecturer

113. I am not ashamed of my African descent. Africa had great universities before there were any in England and the African was the first man industrious and skillful enough to work in iron.

Mary Church Terrell, 1863–1954
Women's club leader

114. I believe that the two or three millions of us should return to the land of our ancestors, and establish our own civilization, laws, customs.... What the black man needs is a country.

Henry McNeal Turner, 1834–1915
Minister and Militant activist

115. There is nothing wrong with affirming African humanity if we recognize that African civilizations, like European civilizations, have an ambiguous legacy—barbarism on the one hand and humanism on the other.

Cornel West, 1954–
Philosopher and Activist

116. I have been to Africa and know that it is not my home. America is; it is my country, too, and has been for generations.

John A. Williams, 1925–
Writer

117. Inside all blacks is one heartbeat that is fueled by the blood of Africa.

August Wilson, 1945–
Dramatist

118. Unfortunately, most of our information about African history comes from missionaries, travelers, and public functionaries who are not reliable sources.

Carter G. Woodson, 1875–1950
Historian

119. In hating Africa and in hating the Africans, we ended up hating ourselves without even realizing it.

Malcolm X, 1925–1965
Nationalist leader

AFRICAN AMERICAN STUDIES

120. Afro-American studies is an academic department. It is not a place for ethnic cheerleading; it is not a place for a 12-step recovery program to restore your sense of identity. It is a place where one studies an academic discipline in a fashion as rigorous as the study of mathematics or physics, English or history.

Henry Louis Gates Jr., 1950–
Scholar and Critic

121. Our generation will be remembered for our success or failure to produce the foundational tools for Afro-American Studies.

Henry Louis Gates Jr., 1950–
Scholar and Critic

122. Too many black studies programs have become segregated, ghettoized amen corners of quasi-religious feeling, propagating old religious fantasies and even inventing new ones.

Henry Louis Gates Jr., 1950–
Scholar and Critic

123. No black history becomes significant and meaningful unless it is taught in the context of world and national history. In its sealed-off black-studies centers, it will be simply another exercise in racial breast-feeding.

Roy Wilkins, 1901–1981
Civil rights activist

AFRICAN CONTINUITY

124. Music, dance, religion do not have artifacts as their end products, so they were saved. These nonmaterial aspects of African culture were impossible to eradicate. And these are the most important legacies of the African past, even to the contemporary black American blues, jazz, and the adaptation of the Christian religion, all rely heavily on African culture.

Amiri Baraka, 1934–
Poet and Writer

125. The folk literature of the American Negro has a rich inheritance from its African background. They brought with them no material possessions to aid in preserving the arts and customs of their homelands. Yet though empty-handed perforce, they carried on their minds and hearts a treasure of complex musical forms, dramatic speech, and imaginative stories, which they perpetuated through the vital art of expression. Wherever the slaves were ultimately placed, they established an enclave of African culture that flourished in spite of environmental disadvantages.

J. Mason Brewer, 1896–1975
Folklorist

126. But even with the rude transplanting of slavery that uprooted the technical elements of his former culture, the American Negro brought over as an emotional inheritance a deep-seated aesthetic endowment.

Alain Locke, 1886–1954
Scholar and Critic

AFROCENTRISM

127. Afrocentricity is simple. If you examine the phenomena concerning African people, you must give them agency. If you don't, you're imposing Eurocentrism on them.

Molefi Asante, 1942–
Educator

128. Afrocentrism, a contemporary species of black nationalism, is a gallant but misguided attempt to define an African identity in a white society perceived to be hostile…. It is misguided because—out of fear of cultural hybridization and through silence on the issue of class, retrograde views on black women, gay men, and lesbians, and a reluctance to link race to the common good—it reinforces the narrow discussions about race.

Cornel West, 1954–
Philosopher and Activist

AGE

129. How old would you be if you didn't know how old you was?

Satchel Paige, 1900?–1982
Baseball star

ALIENATION

130. Being one of a group of outcasts in society makes my sensitivity to the condition of aloneness much sharper than that of the average person. There is an isolation that every sensitive person feels; it is something all creative people recognize. And in all blacks there is an awareness of [our] isolation from the mainstream of society.

Hughie Lee-Smith, 1915–
Painter

131. If the problem of meaninglessness, or the absurd, is the root metaphor of modernity, then the African American experience of slavery and racism must be counted a major embodiment of the modern problem of alienation.

James M. Washington, 1948–1997
Minister and Academic

AMBITION

132. In my early youth a great bitterness entered my life and kindled a great ambition.

W.E.B. Du Bois, 1868–1963
Intellectual and Activist

133. The paradox in life is that one must be ambitious to be free from that ambition which corrupts and blinds and tempts and distorts.

Peter J. Gomes, 1942–
Minister

AMERICA

134. Who is this descendent of the slave masters to order a descendent of slaves to fight other people in their own country?

Muhammad Ali, 1942–
Boxing champion

135. This land which we have watered with our tears and our blood, is now our mother country and we are well satisfied to stay where wisdom abounds and the gospel is free.

Richard Allen, 1760–1831
AME Church founder

136. I had gone to Europe to reach for a place as a serious artist, but I never doubted I must return. I was—and am—an American.

Marian Anderson, 1897–1993
Singer

137. [The United States] is moving toward two societies, one black, one white, separate and unequal.

Anonymous, 1968
Kerner Commission Report

138. I am against U.S. intervention [in Vietnam] because we are deluded in supposing we have the right or the power to dictate the principles under which other people should live.

James Baldwin, 1924–1987
Writer and Activist

139. I love America more than any other country in the world, and exactly for this reason, I insist on the right to criticize her perpetually.

James Baldwin, 1924–1987
Writer and Activist

140. The making of an American begins at that point where he himself rejects all other ties, any other history, and himself adopts the vesture of his adopted land.

James Baldwin, 1924–1987
Writer and Activist

141. Negroes are Americans and their destiny is the country's destiny. They have no other experience besides their experience in this continent, and it is an experience which cannot be rejected, which yet remains to be embraced.

James Baldwin, 1924–1987
Writer and Activist

142. This country does not know what to do with its black population, now that they are no longer a source of wealth, are no longer to be bought and sold and bred like cattle.

James Baldwin, 1924–1987
Writer and Activist

143. To be born in a free society and not be born free is a lie.

James Baldwin, 1924–1987
Writer and Activist

144. Until the moment comes when we, the Americans, are able to accept the fact that my ancestors are both black and white, that on this continent we are trying to forge a new identity, that we need each other, that I am not a ward of America, I am not an object of missionary charity, I am one of the people whose forefathers built this country- until this moment comes there is scarcely any hope for the American dream.

James Baldwin, 1924–1987
Writer and Activist

145. In America, black is a country.

Amiri Baraka, 1934–
Poet and Writer

146. The children of these disillusioned colored pioneers inherited the total lot of their parents—the disappointments, the anger. To add to their misery, they had little hope of deliverance. For where does one run to when he's already in the promised land?

Claude Brown, 1937–
Writer

147. I, John Brown, am now quite certain that the crimes of this guilty land will never be purged away but with blood.

John Brown, 1800–1859
Insurrectionist

148. Behold the Mayflower anchored at Plymouth rock, the slave ship in James River. Each a parent, one of the prosperous, labor-honoring, law-sustaining institutions of the North; the other the mother of slavery, idleness, lynching, ignorance, unpaid labor, poverty, and dueling, despotism, the ceaseless swing of the whip; and the representation of good and evil in the New World, even to our day. When shall one of these parallel lines come to an end?

William Wells Brown, 1815–1884
Writer

149. I will not yield to you in affection for America, but I hate her institution of slavery. I love her, because I am identified with her enslaved millions by every tie that should bind man to his fellow man.

William Wells Brown, 1815–1884
Writer

150. There is nothing so indigenous, so completely "made in America" as we blacks.

William Wells Brown, 1815–1884
Writer

151. America's made bigger promises than almost any other country in history.

Ray Charles, 1930–
Singer

152. The Negro remains the constant and at times irritating reality that is America. He remains the essential psychological reality with which America must continuously seek to come to terms, and in so doing is formed by.

Kenneth B. Clark, 1914–
Social psychologist

153. Total liberty for black people or total destruction for America.

Eldridge Cleaver, 1935–1998
Black Panther Party leader

154. It is ironical that America with its history of injustice to the poor, especially the black man and the Indian, prides itself on being a Christian nation.

James Cone, 1938–
Theologian

155. America is a nation that lies to itself about who and what it is. It is a nation of minorities ruled by a minority of one—it thinks and acts as if it were a nation of white Anglo-Saxon Protestants.

Harold Cruse, 1916–
Scholar

156. Slavery was a bad thing, and freedom, of the kind we got with nothing to live on, was bad. Two snakes full of poison. One lying with his head pointing north, the other with his head pointing south.

Sarah Debro
Former slave

157. Ellis Island is for people who came over on ships. My people came in chains.

David Dinkins, 1927–
Politician

158. The allotments of Providence seem to make the black man of America the open book out of which the American people are to learn lessons of wisdom, power, and goodness.

Frederick Douglass, 1817?–1895
Abolitionist and Autobiographer

159. Go where you may, search where you will, roam through all the monarchies and despotism of the Old World, travel through South America, search out every abuse, and when you have found the last, lay your facts by the side of the everyday practices of this nation, and you will say with me that, for revolting barbarity and shameless hypocrisy, America reigns without a rival.

Frederick Douglass, 1817?–1895
Abolitionist and Autobiographer

160. We live here, have lived here, have a right to live here, and mean to live here.

Frederick Douglass, 1817?–1895
Abolitionist and Autobiographer

161. The meaning of America is the possibilities of the common man. It is a refutation of that widespread assumption that the real makers of the world must always be a small group of exceptional men, while most men are incapable of assisting civilization or achieving culture.

W.E.B. Du Bois, 1868–1963
Intellectual and Activist

162. Would America have been America without her Negro people?

W.E.B. Du Bois, 1868–1963
Intellectual and Activist

163. You whose nation was founded on the loftiest ideals, and who many times forgot those ideals with a strange forgetfulness, have more than a sentimental interest, more than a sentimental duty. You owe a debt to humanity for this Ethiopia of out-stretched arm.

W.E.B. Du Bois, 1868–1963
Intellectual and Activist

164. Your country? How come it's yours? Before the pilgrims landed we were here.

W.E.B. Du Bois, 1868–1963
Intellectual and Activist

165. [Black people are] the injection, the shot in the arm, that has kept America and its forgotten principles alive in the fat and corrupt years intervening between our divine conception and our near tragic present.

Duke Ellington, 1899–1974
Composer and Band leader

166. America is woven of many strands. I would recognize them and let it so remain. Our fate is to become one, and yet many. This is not prophecy, but description.

Ralph Ellison, 1914–1994
Novelist

167. Whatever else the true American is, he is also somehow black.

Ralph Ellison, 1914–1994
Novelist

168. Death has entered into America.

Louis Farrakhan, 1934–
Nation of Islam leader

169. White Man's Heaven is Black Man's Hell.

Louis Farrakhan, 1934–
Nation of Islam leader

170. The real problem is not the Negro but the Nation.

T. Thomas Fortune, 1856–1928
Journalist

171. In America, with all its evils and faults, you can still reach through the forest and see the sun. But we don't know yet whether that sun is rising or setting for our country.

Dick Gregory, 1932–
Comedian and Activist

172. Personally, I've never seen much difference between the South and the North. Down South folks don't care how close I get as long as I don't get too big. Up North folks don't care how big I get as long as I don't get too close.

Dick Gregory, 1932–
Comedian and Activist

173. Is this America?

Fannie Lou Hamer, 1917–1977
Civil rights activist

174. I, too, sing America.

Langston Hughes, 1902–1967
Poet and Writer

175. America is not like a blanket—one piece of unbroken cloth, the same color, the same texture, the same size, America is more like a quilt—many patches, many pieces, many colors, many sizes, all woven and held together by a common thread.

Jesse Jackson, 1941–
Minister and Civil rights activist

176. We are made up of America's many waters which makes us a new people, a true American people.

Jesse Jackson, 1941–
Minister and Civil rights activist

177. It is a sad feeling to be afraid of one's native country.

Harriet Jacobs, 1813–1897
Former slave autobiographer

178. America would not and could not be precisely the America it is, except for the influence, often silent, but nevertheless potent, that the Negro has exercised in its making.

James Weldon Johnson, 1871–1938
Writer and Activist

179. What the people want is very simple. They want an America as good as its promise.

Barbara Jordan, 1936–1996
Lawyer and U.S. Congressperson

180. It is a sad thing to consider that this country has given its least to those who have loved it the most.

June Jordan, 1936–
Poet and Essayist

181. The Negro was invented in America.

John O. Killens, 1916–1987
Novelist

182. How many must die before we can really have a free and true and peaceful society?

Coretta Scott King, 1927–
Civil rights activist

183. America is a great nation, but…. That "but" is a commentary of 200 and more years of chattel slavery and on 20 million Negro men and women deprived of life, liberty, and the pursuit of happiness.

Martin Luther King Jr., 1929–1968
Civil rights activist and Nobel laureate

184. America is essentially a dream, a dream as yet unfulfilled.

Martin Luther King Jr., 1929–1968
Civil rights activist and Nobel laureate

185. Some of us must bear the burden of trying to save the soul of America.

Martin Luther King Jr., 1929–1968
Civil rights activist and Nobel laureate

186. It is a curious but inevitable irony that the American temperament, so notorious for its overweening confidence and self-esteem, should be of all temperaments least reflective, and for all its self-consciousness, should know itself so ill.

Alain Locke, 1886–1954
Scholar and Critic

187. Subtly, the conditions that are molding a New Negro are molding a new American attitude.

Alain Locke, 1886–1954
Scholar and Critic

188. Together we planted the tree of liberty and watered its roots with our tears and blood, and under its branches we will stay and be sheltered.

Thomas E. Miller, 1849–1938
U.S. Congressperson

189. Let the greedy foreigners know that a part of this country belongs to us and that we assert the right to live and labor here.

James W.C. Pennington, 1807?–1870
Scholar and Minister

190. This is the red man's country by natural right, and the black man's by virtue of his suffering and toil.

Robert Purvis, 1810–1898
Abolitionist

191. My father was a slave and my people died to build this country, and I am going to stay and have a piece of it just like you.

Paul Robeson, 1898–1976
Singer and Activist

192. America is not a safe place.

Ntozake Shange, 1948–
Poet and Dramatist

193. Descended from a royal race / Benevolent and brave / On Afric's savage plains a prince / In this free land a slave.

Venture Smith, 1729?–1805
Slave autobiographer

194. It appears to me that America has become like the great city of Babylon.... She is indeed a seller of slaves and the souls of men.

Maria W. Stewart, 1803–1879
Lecturer

195. The United States is the most racially organized society in the Americas.

Ibrahim K. Sundiata, 1944–
Scholar

196. I could never live happily in Africa—or anywhere else—until I could live freely in Mississippi.

Alice Walker, 1944–
Writer

197. America is as much our country as it yours.

David Walker, 1785–1830
Abolitionist

198. The Americans say that we are ungrateful. But I ask them for heaven's sake, what we should be grateful to them for—for murdering our fathers and mothers? Or do they wish us to return thanks to them for chaining and handcuffing us, branding us, cramming fire down our throats, or for keeping us in slavery, and beating us nearly or quite to death to make us work in ignorance and miseries, to support them and their families?

David Walker, 1785–1830
Abolitionist

199. Let ho man of us budge one step, and let slaveholders come to beat us from our country. America is more our country than it is the whites—we have enriched it with our blood and tears. The greatest riches in all America have arisen from our blood and tears.

David Walker, 1785–1830
Abolitionist

200. I know this was the soil on which I was born, but I have nothing to glorify this as my country.

Augustus Washington, 1850?–?

201. The Negro is the only citizen of America that came by special invitation and special provision. The Caucasian came here against the protest of the leading citizens of the country in 1492.

Booker T. Washington, 1856–1915
Educator

202. It becomes the painful duty of the Negro to reproduce a record which shows that a large portion of the American people avow anarchy, condone murder, and defy the contempt of civilization.

Ida B. Wells, 1862–1931
Militant activist

203. The Negro is America's metaphor.

Richard Wright, 1908–1960
Novelist

204. Being here in America doesn't make you an American. I'm one of the 22 million black people who are the victims of Americanism.

Malcolm X, 1925–1965
Nationalist leader

205. I come here to make a speech, to tell you the truth. If the truth is anti-American, then blame the truth, don't blame me.

Malcolm X, 1925–1965
Nationalist leader

206. I'm not going to sit at your table and watch you eat, with nothing on my plate, and call myself a diner. Sitting at the table doesn't make you a diner.

Malcolm X, 1925–1965
Nationalist leader

207. We are not anti-American. We are anti or against what America is doing wrong in other parts of the world as well as here. And what she did in the Congo in 1964 is wrong. It's criminal. And what she did to the American public, to get the American public to go along with it, is criminal.

Malcolm X, 1925–1965
Nationalist leader

208. We didn't land on Plymouth Rock, my brothers and sisters, Plymouth Rock landed on us.

Malcolm X, 1925–1965
Nationalist leader

209. The Negro is the barometer of all America's institutions and values.

Whitney M. Young Jr., 1921–1971
Civil rights activist

ANCESTORS

210. Your ancestors took the lash, the branding iron, humiliations, and oppression because one day they believed you would come along to flesh out the dream.

Maya Angelou, 1928–
Novelist and Poet

211. Let our posterity know that we their ancestors, uncultured and un-learned, amid all trials and temptations, were men of integrity.

Alexander Crummell, 1819–1898
Minister and Scholar

212. You are the ancient builders of civilization, Before there was civilization, you were there, and when civilization was built, your fathers built it.

Louis Farrakhan, 1934–
Nation of Islam leader

213. Teach your children they are direct descendants of the greatest and proudest race who ever peopled the earth.

Marcus Garvey, 1887–1940
Nationalist leader

214. With some of us, militancy against discrimination and racial indignity is a heritage from our forebears.

William H. Hastie, 1904–1976
Lawyer and Judge

215. No matter who you are, the spirits are around us all the time. Especially the old ones that know us and have gone on before—the ancestors.

Bessie Jones
Author of *For the Ancestors*

216. To believe is to become what you believe.

June Jordan, 1936–
Poet and Essayist

217. We, today, stand on the shoulders of our predecessors who have gone before us. We, as their successors, must catch the torch of freedom and liberty passed on to us by our ancestors.

Benjamin Mays, 1895–1984
Educator

218. Our ancestors are an ever-widening circle of hope.

Toni Morrison, 1931–
Novelist and Nobel laureate

219. When I made that decision, I knew I had the strength of my ancestors with me.

Rosa Parks, 1913–
Civil rights activist

220. As a boy in Princeton I dreamed and dreamed of the land of my forefathers and mothers.... My paternal grandfather, torn from his ages-old continent, had survived the dreadful passage. My own father was the embodiment of the strength, warmth, and quiet dignity of the African people.

Paul Robeson, 1898–1976
Singer and Activist

221. My ancestors were among the first to people America.

Paul Robeson, 1898–1976
Singer and Activist

222. Sometimes the ancestors deem certain information so important that they send it to the subconscious mind without being consciously asked.

Luisah Teish
New Orleans Yoruba priest

223. Years ago I resolved that because I had no ancestors myself, I would leave a record of which my children would be proud, and which might encourage them to still higher effort.

Booker T. Washington, 1856–1915
Educator

224. The genius of our black foremothers and forefathers was to equip black folk with cultural armor to beat back the demons of hopelessness, meaninglessness, and lovelessness.

Cornel West, 1954–
Philosopher and Activist

225. I am where I am because of the bridges I have crossed. Sojourner Truth was a bridge. Harriet Tubman was a bridge. Ida B. Wells was a bridge. Madame C.J, Walker was a bridge. Fannie Lou Hamer was a bridge.

Oprah Winfrey, 1954–
Entertainer

226. They have traditions that have values of which you can boast and upon which you can base a claim for the right to share in the blessings of democracy.

Carter G. Woodson, 1875–1950
Historian

ANGER

227. Harlem had needed something to smash. To smash something is the ghetto's chronic need.

James Baldwin, 1924–1987
Writer and Activist

228. My position is that we have a good deal to be angry about, furious about. You know it's 1959 and they are still lynching Negroes in America.

Lorraine Hansberry, 1930–1965
Dramatist

ANSWERS

229. Most people think they know the answer. I am willing to admit I don't even know the question.

Arsenio Hall, 1956–
Entertainer

ANTISLAVERY
See Slavery

ART

230. African art is an attempt to capture the energy and essence of a thing.

James Baldwin, 1924–1987
Writer and Activist

231. All art is a kind of confession, more or less oblique.

James Baldwin, 1924–1987
Writer and Activist

232. Great art can only be created out of love.

James Baldwin, 1924–1987
Writer and Activist

233. Folkway is the basis of art.

Toni Cade Bambara, 1939–
Writer

234. Art is a moral power ... revealing to us a glimpse of the absolute ideal of perfect harmony.

Edward Mitchell Bannister, 1826?–1901
Painter

235. Art is the soul of a people.

Romare Bearden, 1914–1988
Artist

236. Black art has always existed. It just hasn't been looked for in the right places.

Romare Bearden, 1914–1988
Artist

237. The European traditions are not as interesting as before. Something else is waiting to get born.

Romare Bearden, 1914–1988
Artist

238. I am a man concerned with truth, not flattery, who shares a dual culture that is unwilling to deny the Harlem where I grew up or the Harlem of the Dutch masters that contributed its element to my understanding of art.

Romare Bearden, 1914–1988
Artist

239. I create racial identities so far as the subjects are Negro. But I have not created protest images because the world within the collage, if it is authentic, retains the right to speak for itself.

Romare Bearden, 1914–1988
Artist

240. I have chosen to paint the life of my people as I know and feel it—passionately and dispassionately. It is important that the artist identify with the self-reliance, hope, and courage of the people about him, for art must always go where energy is.

Romare Bearden, 1914–1988
Artist

241. If you're any kind of artist you make a miraculous journey and you can come back and make some statements in shapes and colors of where you were.

Romare Bearden, 1914–1988
Artist

242. Such devices ... as distortion of scale and proportion, and abstract coloration, are the very means through which I try to achieve a more personal expression.... It is not my aim to paint about the Negro in America as propaganda. It is precisely my awareness of the distortions required of the polemicist that caused me to paint the life of my people as I know it.

Romare Bearden, 1914–1988
Artist

243. We look too much to museums. The sun coming up in the morning is enough.

Romare Bearden, 1914–1988
Artist

244. Well, it's like jazz: you do this and then you improvise.

Romare Bearden, 1914–1988
Artist

245. Art is the material evidence that reminds us of our culture—of who we are.

Mary Schmidt Campbell
Arts administrator

246. Art must be realistic for me, whether sculpture or printmaking. I have always wanted my art to service my people—to reflect us, to relate to us, to stimulate us, to make us aware of our potential.

Elizabeth Catlett, 1919–
Artist

247. Progressive art can assist people to learn not only about the objective forces at work in the society in which they live, but also about the intensely social character of their interior lives.

Angela Davis, 1944–
Militant activist

248. Art is not simply works of art; it is the spirit that knows beauty, that has music in its soul and the color of sunsets in its handkerchief, that can dance on a flaming world and make the world dance, too.

W.E.B. Du Bois, 1868–1963
Intellectual and Activist

249. [My sculpture] ain't got much style. God don't want much style, but he gives you wisdom and he speeds you along.

William Edmondson, 1882?–1951
Sculptor

250. The Europeans who went to Africa came back with "modern" art. What is more African than a Picasso?

Duke Ellington, 1899–1974
Composer and Band leader

251. The ultimate in art is self-expression, not escape.

Duke Ellington, 1899–1974
Composer and Band leader

252. Picasso's "Les Demoiselles d'Avignon"—the signature painting in the creation of Cubism—stands as a testament to the shaping influence of African sculpture and to the central role that African art played in the creation of modernism.

Henry Louis Gates Jr., 1950–
Scholar and Critic

253. Art is a way of possessing destiny.

Marvin Gaye, 1939–1984
Singer and Composer

254. All art is a communication of the artist's ideas, sounds, thoughts.

Lionel Hampton, 1913–
Vibraphonist and Band leader

255. A classical people deserve a classical art.

Lorraine Hansberry, 1930–1965
Dramatist

256. I decided to paint to support my love of art, rather than have art support me.

Palmer Hayden, 1890?–1973
Painter

257. And the Negro dancers who will dance like flames and the singers who will continue to carry our songs to all who listen—they will be with us in even greater numbers tomorrow.

Langston Hughes, 1902–1967
Poet and Writer

258. The Lord puts pictures in my head and he means for me to paint them.

Clementine Hunter, 1885?–1988
Artist

259. The final measure of the greatness of all peoples is the amount and standard of the literature and art they have produced.

James Weldon Johnson, 1871–1938
Writer and Activist

260. It is the pure American Negro I am concerned with, aiming to show the natural beauty and dignity in that characteristic lip and that characteristic hair, bearing, and manner; and I wish to show that beauty not so much to the white man as to the Negro himself.

Sargent Johnson, 1887–1967
Sculptor

261. Being basically a designer, I am always weaving together my research and my feelings—taking from textiles, carvings and color—to press on canvas what I see and feel. As a painter, I am very dependent on design. With me design is basic.

Lois Mailou Jones, 1905–
Artist

262. Art for art's sake is an invalid concept; all art reflects the value system from which it comes.

Ron Karenga, 1941–
Educator

263. If I have achieved a degree of success as a creative artist, it is mainly due to the black experience which is our heritage— an experience which gives inspiration, motivation, and stimulation. I was inspired by the black aesthetics by which we are surrounded, motivated to manipulate form, color, space, line, and texture to depict our life, and stimulated by the beauty and poignancy of our environment.

Jacob Lawrence, 1917–
Painter

264. Being one of a group of outcasts in society makes my sensitivity to the condition of aloneness much sharper than that of the average person. There is an isolation that every sensitive person feels; it is something all creative people recognize. And in all blacks there is an awareness of [our] isolation from the mainstream of society.

Hughie Lee-Smith, 1915–
Painter

265. A painting has many meanings. I usually ask the viewer to bring to my paintings their own experiences. My meaning may not be your meaning. I like things to be a puzzle. I like contrasts. I am concerned with the ambiguities of life.

Hughie Lee-Smith, 1915–
Painter

266. By way of compensation [during slavery] some obviously artistic urges flowed even in the peasant Negro towards the channels of expression left open, those of song, graceful movement, and poetic speech.

Alain Locke, 1886–1954
Scholar and Critic

267. An art form can influence your thinking, your feeling, the way you dress, the way you walk, how you talk, what you do with yourself.

Wynton Marsalis, 1961–
Musician

268. Art is inseparable from life, and form and content are one.

Paule Marshall, 1929–
Novelist

269. Art is timeless.

Toni Morrison, 1931–
Novelist and Nobel laureate

270. They teach you there's a boundary line to music. But, man, there's no boundary line to art.

Charlie Parker, 1920?–1955
Jazz musician

271. My opinion of art is that a man should have a love for it, because it is my idea that he paints from his heart and mind.... To me it seems impossible for another to teach one of art.

Horace Pippin, 1888–1946
Painter

272. Pictures just come to my mind and I tell my heart to go ahead.

Horace Pippin, 1888–1946
Painter

273. Art is the ability to tell the truth, especially about oneself.

Richard Pryor, 1940–
Comedian

274. Art must be constantly lived.

John Rhodes

275. The most fundamental truth to be told in any art form is that America is killing us.

Sonia Sanchez, 1934–
Poet

276. It is not just in the United States but all through the Western Hemisphere that you get the black man's art form, which is the beat of Africa.

Hazel Scott, 1920–1981
Musician and Actor

277. Being an artist, I had an artist's instincts.... You can see the picture before it's taken; then it's up to you to get the camera to see.

James Van Der Zee, 1886–1983
Photographer

278. Art has a way of opening us up and allows us to be vulnerable, to deal with our ambiguities and incongruities and contradictions, so that we can grow and mature and develop.

Cornel West, 1954–
Philosopher and Activist

279. I paint in fragments of what is the total me.

Charles White, 1918–1979
Painter

280. African art has done much to influence artistic productions of all people.

Carter G. Woodson, 1875–1950
Historian

ARTISTS

281. An artist represents an oppressed people and makes revolution irresistible.

Toni Cade Bambara, 1939–
Writer

282. The artist must draw out of his soul the correct image of the world. He must use this image to band his brothers and sisters together.

Amiri Baraka, 1934–
Poet and Writer

283. The black artist's role in America is to aid in the destruction of America as he knows it.

Amiri Baraka, 1934–
Poet and Writer

284. Stripped of all else, the African American's own body became the prime artistic instrument.

James B. Barnes
Marion College official

285. I think the artist has to be something like a whale swimming with his mouth wide open, absorbing everything until he has what he really needs.

Romare Bearden, 1914–1988
Artist

286. Whatever subject the artist chooses, he must celebrate it in triumph.

Romare Bearden, 1914–1988
Artist

287. Cease to be a drudge; seek to be an artist.

Mary McLeod Bethune, 1875–1955
Educator

288. An artist's first responsibility is to himself.

Miles Davis, 1926–1991
Jazz musician

289. Technique in itself is not enough. It is important for the artist to develop the power to convey emotion.

Aaron Douglas, 1899–1979
Artist

290. The artist must say it without saying it.

Duke Ellington, 1899–1974
Composer and Band leader

291. The true artist destroys the accepted world by way of revealing the unseen, and creating that which is new and uniquely his own.

Ralph Ellison, 1914–1994
Novelist

292. Draw or die.

Minnie Evans, 1892–1987
Artist

293. Great artists suffer for the people.

Marvin Gaye, 1939–1984
Singer and Composer

294. My aim is to express in a natural way what I feel, what is in me, both rhythmically and spiritually, all that which in time has been saved up in my family of primitiveness and tradition and which is now concentrated in me.

William H. Johnson, 1901–1970
Painter

295. Let it be that black artists be referred to as "artists" whose works are accepted universally on the strength of their merits.

Lois Mailou Jones, 1905–
Artist

296. If the artist created only for himself and not for others, he would lock himself up somewhere and paint and play just for himself.

Ron Karenga, 1941–
Educator

297. You bring to a painting your own experience.

Jacob Lawrence, 1917–
Painter

298. The very idea of a black child becoming a professional artist was ludicrous. But my mother was very supportive, and I was so involved in creative work that I had the guts, and I kept at it.

Hughie Lee-Smith, 1915–
Painter

299. Without the artist we would not have anything.

Abby Lincoln, 1940–
Singer and Actor

300. The true work of art is a creation not of the hands, but of the mind and soul of the artist.

Nancy Elizabeth Prophet, 1890–1960
Sculptor

301. The Afro-American artist is ... a conjurer who works JuJu upon his oppressors; a witch doctor who frees his fellow victims from the psychic attack launched by demons of the outer and inner world.

Ishmael Reed, 1938–
Dramatist

302. The artist must elect to fight for Freedom or for Slavery.

Paul Robeson, 1898–1976
Singer and Activist

303. In a sick world, it is the first duty of the artist to get well.

Jean Toomer, 1894–1967
Novelist

304. The artist is the voice of the people.

Alice Walker, 1944–
Writer

305. An artist deals with aspects of reality different from those which a scientist sees.

Richard Wright, 1908–1960
Novelist

ATONEMENT

306. We need atonement. I can blame others for my troubles as a black man in America. But I must also report my own shortcomings to Allah.

Louis Farrakhan, 1934–
Nation of Islam leader

AUTHENTICITY

307. A lotta cats copy the Mona Lisa, but people still like to see the original.

Louis Armstrong, 1901–1971
Jazz musician

308. The problem with most debates about authenticity, of course, is that they ignore the bewildering variety of expressions that characterize contemporary black culture.

Michael Eric Dyson, 1958–
Scholar and Writer

AWARENESS
See Self-Consciousness

BEAUTY OF BLACKNESS
△ △ △ △ △ △ △ △

309. I am black but comely, O ye daughters of Jerusalem.

Anonymous
Song of Solomon 1:5a KJV

310. Look at me. I am black. I am beautiful.

Mary McLeod Bethune, 1875–1955
Educator

311. When I was a child, it did not occur to me, even once, that the black in which I was encased (I called it brown in those days) would be considered, one day, beautiful.

Gwendolyn Brooks, 1917–
Poet

312. I am black all over and proud of my beautiful black skin.

John E. Bruce, 1856–1924
Writer

313. Go home and tell your daughters they're beautiful.

Stokely Carmichael, 1941–
Activist

314. I find, in being black, a thing of beauty: a joy, a strength; a secret cup of gladness, a native land in neither time nor space, a native land in every Negro face! Be loyal to yourselves: your skin; your hair; your lips, your Southern speech, your laughing kindness, are Negro kingdoms, vast as any other.

Ossie Davis, 1917–
Actor

315. Especially do I believe in the Negro Race, in the beauty of its genius, the sweetness of its soul.

W.E.B. Du Bois, 1868–1963
Intellectual and Activist

316. You are no longer innocent, you are condemned to awareness.

Michael Eric Dyson, 1958–
Scholar and Writer

317. Who can be born black and not exult!

Mari Evans, 1923–
Poet

318. God made us his perfect creation. He made no mistake when he made us black with kinky hair.

Marcus Garvey, 1887–1940
Nationalist leader

319. The more blackness a woman has, the more beautiful she is.

Alex Haley, 1921–1992
Writer

320. Step outside yourself, then look back, and you will see how human, yet how beautiful and black you are, how very black, even when you're integrated.

Langston Hughes, 1902–1967
Poet and Writer

321. We know that we are beautiful.

Langston Hughes, 1902–1967
Poet and Writer

322. Art must discover and reveal the beauty which prejudice and caricature have overlaid.

Alain Locke, 1886–1954
Scholar and Critic

323. We live in a society where there is a very narrow conception of what is beautiful. It is usually pale, blonde, and a size seven.

Susan Taylor, 1946–
Editor and Writer

324. They think because they holds us in their infernal chains of slavery, that we wish to be white, or of their color—but they are dreadfully deceived—we wish to be just as it pleased our Creator to have made us.

David Walker, 1785–1830
Abolitionist

BEING BLACK IN AMERICA

325. Being a black man in America is like having another job.

Arthur Ashe, 1943–1993
Tennis champion

326. It is a great shock at the age of five or six to find that in a world of Gary Coopers, you are the Indian.

James Baldwin, 1924–1987
Writer and Activist

327. To be black in America is to live in a constant state of rage.

James Baldwin, 1924–1987
Writer and Activist

328. To be born in a free society and not be born free is a lie.

James Baldwin, 1924–1987
Writer and Activist

329. There are no good times to be black in America, but some times are worse than others.

David Bradley, 1950–
Writer

330. I've been in slavery all my life. Ain't nothing changed for me but the address.

James Brown, 1933–
Singer and Composer

331. Being black in America is often like playing your home games on your opponent's court.

James P. Comer, 1934–
Psychiatrist

332. Being black in America has nothing to do with skin color. To be black means that your soul, your mind and your body are where the dispossessed are.

James Cone, 1938–
Theologian

333. They came to my house following the demonstration and said, "You under arrest." I said, "All black people under arrest. I ain't even bothered."

Janet Daggett

334. Every black man dies first of all from being black. The other cause of death is barely worth putting down on the death certificate.

Ossie Davis, 1917–
Actor

335. Being a star made it possible for me to get insulted in places where the average Negro could never hope to go and get insulted.

Sammy Davis Jr., 1925–1990
Entertainer

336. We wear the mask that grins and lies.

Paul Laurence Dunbar, 1872–1906
Poet

337. I used to think that if I could go North and tell people about the plight of black folk in the state of Mississippi everything would be all right. But traveling around I found one thing for sure: it's up-South and down-South, and it's no different.

Fannie Lou Hamer, 1917–1977
Civil rights activist

338. I know the bitterness of being accused and harassed by prosecutors. I know the horror of being hunted and haunted. I have dashed across continents and oceans as a fugitive, and have matched my wits with the police and secret agents seeking to deprive me of one of the greatest blessings man can have—liberty.

Jack Johnson, 1873–1946
Boxing champion

339. To be a Negro in America is to hope against hope.

Martin Luther King Jr., 1929–1968
Civil rights activist and Nobel laureate

340. The country's creating a 51st state—the state of denial.

Joseph Lowery, 1924–
Civil rights activist

341. America is the world's greatest jailer, and we all in jails. Black spirits contained like magnificent birds of wonder.

Larry Neal, 1937–1981
Writer

342. Being black has made me sensitive to any group who finds limitations put on it.

Eleanor Holmes Norton, 1938–
Lawyer and Activist

343. After I came home from the 1936 Olympics with my four medals, it became increasingly apparent that everyone was going to slap me on the back, want to shake my hand, or have me up to their suite. But no one was going to offer me a job.

Jesse Owens, 1913–1980
Olympic track star

344. Until my mid-teens I lived in fear; fear of being shot, lynched or beaten to death—not for any wrong doing of my own.... I could have easily been the victim of mistaken identity or an act of terror by hate-filled white men.

Gordon Parks, 1912–
Photographer

345. There are men in America, and whole towns of them, too, who are not so destitute of true heroism but that they can assail a helpless woman, surround her house by night, break her windows, and drag her to prison, for the treasonable act of teaching females of color to read!

Nathaniel Paul, 1793?–1839
Minister

346. Blacks lead double lives, one you see and one you don't.

Jurgen Prochnow
Actor
MGM-United Artists' 1989 film *Dry White Season*

347. Being a black man in America is like being a spectator at your own lynching.

Ishmael Reed, 1938–
Dramatist

348. You must understand, being black is more involved than just wearing an X cap. It means being committed to furthering our race and nurturing our children.

Elizabeth Ridley
Educator

349. It is a waste of words to talk of ever enjoying citizenship in this country.

John B. Russwurm, 1799–1851
Abolitionist and Journalist

350. For the last 300 years we have had the same cultural background, the same system, the same system of beauty as white Americans. In art schools we draw from Greek casts.

Augusta Savage, 1900–1962
Sculptor

351. Our society has never lived up to anything they've said to anybody of color.

C.T. Vivian, 1924–
Minister and Civil rights activist

352. The black encounter with the absurd in racist American society yields a profound spiritual need for human affirmation and recognition. Hence, the centrality of religion and music—those most spiritual of human activities—in black life.

Cornel West, 1954–
Philosopher and Activist

353. Black people have always been America's wilderness in search of a promised land.

Cornel West, 1954–
Philosopher and Activist

354. We have so much to learn from [Alexis de] Tocqueville about acknowledging that race is in no way additive in the American past and present; it is constitutive. For Tocqueville, black people and indigenous people were in America but not of American democracy.

Cornel West, 1954–
Philosopher and Activist

355. Every step and the way you take it here on enemy ground is a lesson.

John Edgar Wideman, 1941–
Novelist

356. If you're born black in America you must quickly teach yourself to recognize the invisible barriers disciplining the space in which you may move.

John Edgar Wideman, 1941–
Novelist

357. I have never been able to discover that there was anything disgraceful in being a colored man. But I have often found it inconvenient—in America.

Bert Williams, 1876–1922
Entertainer

358. Each day when you see us black folk upon the dusty land of your farms or upon the hard pavement of your city streets, you usually take it for granted and think you know us, but our history is far stranger than you suspect, and we are not what we seem.

Richard Wright, 1908–1960
Novelist

359. Let us remember that we're not brutalized because we're Baptists. We're not brutalized because we're Methodists. We're not brutalized because we're

Muslims. We're not brutalized because we're Catholics. We're brutalized because we are black people in America.

Malcolm X, 1925–1965
Nationalist leader

360. You've been tricked!

Malcolm X, 1925–1965
Nationalist leader

BELIEVING
See Faith

BLACK CONSCIOUSNESS

361. Worldwide black consciousness is a psychological reserve that can be mobilized to achieve local ends as well as to aid others as the liberation process continues.

St. Clair Drake, 1911–1990
Sociologist

362. The black man must find himself as a black man before the can find himself as an American.

James Farmer, 1920–?
Civil rights activist

363. The black writer at the present time must forego the assimilationist tradition and redirect his art to the strivings within the race—those strivings that have been so pronounced, here, in the latter half of the twentieth century. To do so, he must write for and speak to the majority of black people, not to a sophisticated elite fashioned out of the programmed computers of America's largest universities.

Addison Gayle Jr., 1932–?
Literary critic

364. Black people have been mis-educated into confusing their interests with those of the dominant society.

Carter G. Woodson, 1875–1950
Historian

BLACK CULTURE

365. Here we have brought … a gift of story and song—soft, stirring melody in an ill-harmonized and unmelodious land.

W.E.B. Du Bois, 1868–1963
Intellectual and Activist

366. I don't recognize any white culture. I recognize no American culture which is not the partial creation of black people. I recognize no American style in literature, in dance, in music, even in assembly-line processes, which does not bear the mark of the American Negro.

Ralph Ellison, 1914–1994
Novelist

367. We are almost a nation of dancers, musicians, and poets.

Olaudah Equiano, 1745?–1801
Slave autobiographer

368. The African slave who sailed to the New World did not sail alone. People brought their culture, no matter how adverse the circumstances. And therefore part of America is African.

Henry Louis Gates Jr., 1950–
Scholar and Critic

369. From television to the op-ed pages, from the academy to the poetry slam, never before [1997] have so many black artists and intellectuals achieved so much success in so many fields.

Henry Louis Gates Jr., 1950–
Scholar and Critic

370. In those same towns where we couldn't get a hotel room or a meal in a decent restaurant—even if we could pay for it—the people treated us like kings once we got up on the stage.

Lionel Hampton, 1913–
Vibraphonist and Band leader

371. Never before have so many white Americans paid black Americans that sincerest form of flattery—imitation.

John H. Johnson, 1918–
Publisher

372. The position of the Negro in American culture is indeed a paradox. It almost passes understanding how and why a group of people can be socially despised, yet at the same time artistically esteemed and culturally influential, can be both an oppressed minority and a dominant cultural force.

Alain Locke, 1886–1954
Scholar and Critic

373. Oh ye pleasure-seeking sons and daughters of idleness, who move with measured step, listless and snail-like through the slow-winding cotillion; if ye wish to look upon the celebrity, if opt the "poetry of motion," upon genuine happiness rampant and unrestrained, go down to Louisiana and see the slaves dancing in the starlight of a Christmas night.

Solomon Northup, 1808?–1863
Enslaved free man

374. America is deeply rooted in Negro culture: its colloquialisms; its humor; its music. How ironic that the Negro, who more than any other people can claim America's culture as its own, is being persecuted and repressed; that the Negro who has exemplified the humanities in his very existence, is being regarded with inhumanity.

Sonny Rollins, 1930–
Jazz musician

375. [African American youth] pose the limit embodying both what American culture aims for and what the culture must not become. In the same way that the deaths of real cowboys, outlaws, adventurers and soldiers made images of these figures safe for general consumption, elements of the street kid figure are becoming incorporated into the general American character.

Timothy M. Simone
Writer

BLACK EXPERIENCE

376. There's a spectrum of black experience, just as there is of black views and opinions.

Henry Louis Gates Jr., 1950–
Scholar and Critic

BLACK POWER

377. Blackness has been a stigma, a curse with which we were born. Black Power means that henceforth this curse will be a badge of pride rather than of scorn.

Robert S. Browne, 1924–
Economist

378. Black Power!

Stokely Carmichael, 1941–
Activist

379. Black Power is a call for black people of this country to unite, to recognize their heritage, to build a sense of community.

Stokely Carmichael, 1941–
Activist

380. We want power. It can come only through organization, and organization comes through unity.

Alexander Crummell, 1819–1898
Minister and Scholar

381. Most men in the world are colored. A belief in humanity means a belief in colored men. The future world will, in all reasonable possibility, be what colored men make it.

W.E.B. Du Bois, 1868–1963
Intellectual and Activist

382. Do not call for black power or green power. Call for brain power.

Barbara Jordan, 1936–1996
Lawyer and U.S. Congressperson

383. I suggested [in 1966] that we use the panther as our symbol and call our political vehicle the Black Panther Party. The panther is a fierce animal, but he will not attack until he is backed into a corner; then he will strike out.

Huey Newton, 1942–
Black Panther Party leader

BLACK PRIDE

384. I had to break that [baseball home run] record. I had to do it for Jackie [Robinson] and my people and myself and for everybody who ever called me a nigger.

Hank Aaron, 1934–
Baseball star

385. I am of the African race, and in the color which is natural to them of the deepest dye; and it under a sense of the most profound gratitude to the Supreme Being of the universe.

Benjamin Banneker, 1731–1806
Inventor

386. If our people are to fight their way out of bondage, we must arm them with the sword and the shield and the buckler of pride—belief in themselves and their possibilities based on a sure knowledge of the past.

Mary McLeod Bethune, 1875–1955
Educator

387. The inspiration of the race is the race.

Edward Wilmot Blyden, 1832–1912
Scholar and Diplomat

388. Say it loud, I'm black and I'm proud!

James Brown, 1933–
Singer and Composer

389. I have always thanked God for making me a man, but Martin Delany always thanked God for making him a black man.

Frederick Douglass, 1817?–1895
Abolitionist and Autobiographer

390. I believe in pride of race and lineage and self; in pride of self so deep as to scorn injustice to other selves. Especially do I believe in the Negro Race: in the beauty of its genius, the sweetness of its soul, and its strength in that meekness which shall yet inherit this turbulent earth.

W.E.B. Du Bois, 1868–1963
Intellectual and Activist

391. The best blood in my veins is African blood, and I am not ashamed of it.

Frances Ellen Watkins Harper, 1825–1911
Writer and Orator

392. We are the star-dust folk, / Shining folk!

Fenton Johnson, 1888–1958
Poet

393. I am a Negro proud. My mother was black, as I have shown in my portrait of her, sitting with folded hands and an expression of resignation in a simple polka dot dress. In Europe they asked me if I was a Moor, an Indian, or North African. My answer has always been, "I am a Negro."

William H. Johnson, 1901–1970
Painter

394. I eschew racial pride because of my conception of what should properly be the object of pride for an individual: something that he or she has accomplished.

Randall Kennedy, 1954–
Law professor

395. We are not fighting for the right to be like you. We respect ourselves too much for that.

John O. Killens, 1916–1987
Novelist

396. When the history books are written in future generations, the historians will have to pause and say, "There lived a great people—a black people—who injected new meaning and dignity into the veins of civilization."

Martin Luther King Jr., 1929–1968
Civil rights activist and Nobel laureate

397. We are positively a unique people. Breathtaking people. Anything we do, we do big! Despite attempts to stereotype us, we are crazy, individual, and uncorralable people.

Leontyne Price, 1927–
Opera singer

398. For [the American Negro] a group tradition must supply compensation for persecution and pride of race the antidote for prejudice.

Arthur Schomburg, 1874–1938
Librarian and Book collector

399. I believe it, the Negro blood counts and counts to my advantage.

Henry O. Tanner, 1859–1937
Painter

400. You asked me if I was of your race. I am proud to say that I am of the same race that you are, I am colored, thank God for that. I have not the curse of God upon me for enslaving human beings.

Sojourner Truth, 1797?–1883
Abolitionist and Women's rights advocate

401. He who teaches his race to hate another does not love his own.

Carter G. Woodson, 1875–1950
Historian

BLACK STRENGTH

402. It takes strength to remember; it takes another kind to forget. It takes a hero to do both.

James Baldwin, 1924–1987
Writer and Activist

403. I have confidence not only in my country and her institutions, but in the endurance, capacity, and destiny of my people.

Blanche K. Bruce, 1841–1898
U.S. Senator

404. To make our way we must have firm resolve, persistence, tenacity. We must gear ourselves to work hard all the way. We can never let up. We can never have too much preparation and training. We must be a strong competitor. We must adhere staunchly to the basic principle that anything less than full equality is not enough. If we compromise on that principle our soul is dead.

Ralph Bunche, 1904–1971
Statesman

405. The most important thing … is that no Negro tolerate any ceiling on his ambition or imagination.

Charles Hamilton Houston, 1895–1950
Lawyer and Civil rights activist

406. As a people, we must remember that we are not as weak as we have allowed ourselves to be painted, and we are not as strong as we can be.

John E. Jacob, 1936–
National Urban League official

407. Throughout the struggle for racial justice I have constantly asked God to remove all bitterness from my heart and to give me the strength and courage to face any disaster that came my way.

Martin Luther King Jr., 1929–1968
Civil rights activist and Nobel laureate

408. There are two ways of exerting one's strength: one is pushing down, the other is pulling up.

Booker T. Washington, 1856–1915
Educator

BLACKNESS

409. I want to be black, to know black, to luxuriate in whatever I might be calling blackness at any particular time, but to do so in order to come out on the other side, to experience a humanity that is neither colorless nor reducible to color.

Henry Louis Gates Jr., 1950–
Scholar and Critic

410. Blackness is no longer a color; it is an attitude.

Dick Gregory, 1932–
Comedian and Activist

411. White supremacists ideology is based first and foremost on the degradation of black bodies in order to control them.... By convincing them that their bodies are ugly, their intellect is inherently underdeveloped, their culture is less civilized, and their future warrants less concern than that of other peoples.

Cornel West, 1954–
Philosopher and Activist

412. Our faces do not change. Our cheekbones remain as unaltered as the stony countenance of the sphinx.

Richard Wright, 1908–1960
Novelist

BLUES

See also Music

413. They call it stormy Monday / But Tuesday's just as bad.

Anonymous
Traditional

414. The blues is where we came from and what we experience. The blues came from nothingness, from want, from desire.

W.C. Handy, 1873–1958
Blues musician

415. I've got the St. Louis blues, / I'm as blue as I can be.

W.C. Handy, 1873–1958
Blues musician

416. Modern blues is the expression of the emotional life of the race.

W.C. Handy, 1873–1958
Blues musician

417. To be a black person and sing the blues, you are black twice.

B.B. King, 1925–
Blues musician

418. And Freedom had a name. It was called the blues.

Walter Mosley, 1952–
Writer

419. The blues is probably the only true history of America—in terms of being willing to confront the kind of things that Melville and Twain and Faulkner were pushing us toward.

Cornel West, 1954–
Philosopher and Activist

420. The most astonishing aspect of the blues is that, though replete with a sense of defeat and downheartedness, they are not intrinsically pessimistic; their burden of woe and melancholy is dialectically redeemed through sheer force of sensuality into an exultant affirmation of life, of love, of sex, of movement, of hope.

Richard Wright, 1908–1960
Novelist

BOOKS

421. Whenever I went to the library and there was a book in the adult section I wanted to read, my parents would write a note that said, "Let her take out whatever she wants." I always felt that I had freedom in my reading.

Rita Dove, 1952–
Poet

422. When you know that you don't know, you've got to read.

Solomon B. Fuller, 1872–1953
Entrepreneur

423. Books began to happen to me.

Langston Hughes, 1902–1967
Poet and Writer

424. We need a collection or list of books written by our men and women.

Arthur Schomburg, 1874–1938
Librarian and Book collector

425. Reading is a political act.

Jane Irving Tillman
Television reporter

426. Our people are just waiting to read words written about them by their own authors.

Lana Turner
Book club founder

427. Temples fall, statues decay, mausoleums perish, eloquent phrases declaimed are forgotten, but good books are immortal.

William T. Vernon, 1871–1944
Educator

428. Books were my extended family.

James M. Washington, 1948–1997
Minister and Academic

BROTHERHOOD

429. I believe that all men, black and brown and white, are brothers, varying through time and opportunity, in form and gift and feature, but differing in no essential particular, and alike in soul and the possibility of infinite development.

W.E.B. Du Bois, 1868–1963
Intellectual and Activist

430. We will never separate ourselves voluntarily from the slave population in this country; they are our brethren by ties of consanguinity, of suffering, and of wrong, and we feel that there is more virtue in suffering privations with them, than fancied advantage for a season.

James Forten, 1766–1842
Abolitionist and Businessperson

431. We must all learn to live together as brothers. Or we will all perish together as fools.

Martin Luther King Jr., 1929–1968
Civil rights activist and Nobel laureate

432. A man has to act like a brother before you can call him a brother.

Malcolm X, 1925–1965
Nationalist leader

433. We are all brothers of oppression, and today brothers of oppression are identified with each other all over the world.

Malcolm X, 1925–1965
Nationalist leader

BUSINESS

434. Black people are the last hired and the first fired.

Anonymous
Traditional

435. Buy where you can work.

Anonymous
Protest slogan

436. If you are black and the businesses are run by people who are not black, then those people come in at 9 a.m., leave at 5:00 p.m., and take their wealth to the communities in which they live.

Tony Brown, 1933–
Television producer

437. The society we seek to build among black people, then, is not a capitalist one. It is a society in which the spirit of community and humanistic love prevail.

Stokely Carmichael, 1941–
Activist

438. Successful businesses are founded on needs.

A.G. Gaston, 1892–1993
Businessperson

439. The world of business represents still virgin territory for black Americans.

Benjamin Hooks, 1925–
NAACP official

440. If [women] could go to banks and get a [business] loan, the whole face of Harlem would change.

Dorothy Pitman Hughes, 1938–
Entrepreneur

441. I was able to convince a loan company to loan me $500 on my mother's furniture, which we used as collateral. I used it to buy direct mail literature which I sent out to 20,000 names from insurance companies. Three thousand answered and sent me $2.00 each, and with $6000 I published my first edition of *Negro Digest* in November 1942.

John H. Johnson, 1918–
Publisher

442. I started saving when I was a little girl just to have candy money. When I got grown, I started saving for my future. I'd go to the bank once a month, hold out just enough to cover my expenses and put the rest into my saving account.

Osceola McCarthy, 1908–
Laundress and Philanthropist

443. America doesn't respect anything but money.

Mme. C.J. Walker, 1867–1919
Entrepreneur

CAPITALISM

444. Racism cannot be separated from capitalism.

Angela Davis, 1944–
Militant activist

445. Capitalism fails to realize that life is social. Marxism fails to recognize that life is individual.

Martin Luther King Jr., 1929–1968
Civil rights activist and Nobel laureate

446. Capitalism was built on the exploitation of black slaves, and continues to thrive on the exploitation of the poor, both black and white, both here and abroad.

Martin Luther King Jr., 1929–1968
Civil rights activist and Nobel laureate

447. The history of the capitalist era is characterized by the degradation of my people.

Paul Robeson, 1898–1976
Singer and Activist

448. [I am] one who was once a chattel slave freed by the proclamation of Lincoln and now wishes to be free from the slavery of capitalism.

George W. Woodbey, 1854–1937
Minister and Socialist

CHALLENGE
See Perseverance

CHANGE

449. In order to change a people you must first change their literature.

Noble Drew Ali, 1880–1929
Islamic leader

450. One does not fight to influence change and then leave the change to someone else to bring about.

Stokely Carmichael, 1941–
Activist

451. What the liberal really wants is to bring about change which will not in any way endanger his position.

Stokely Carmichael, 1941–
Activist

452. I was born by the river in a little old tent, and just like the river I've been running ever since. It's been a long time, but I know change is gonna come.

Sam Cooke, 1931?–1964
Singer

453. No one could have lived down here [Alabama] for 10 years and seen the fight the Negroes have put up without feeling hope for them, for the country and for mankind. If they win their fight I think it will change the face of the country the way that getting rid of slavery did.

Virginia Durr, 1903–
Civil rights activist

454. You really can change the world if you care enough.

Marian Wright Edelman, 1939–
Children's Defense Fund official

455. Every time I sit down to the typewriter, with every line I put on paper I am out to change the world.

John O. Killens, 1916–1987
Novelist

456. There is a spirit and a need and a man at the beginning of every great human advance. Each of these must be right for that particular moment of history, or nothing happens.

Coretta Scott King, 1927–
Civil rights activist

457. My parents were always philosophizing about how to bring about change. To me, people who didn't try to make the world a better place were strange.

Carol Moseley-Braun, 1947–
U.S. Senator

458. I felt that it was not until one wanted the world to be different that one could look at the world with will and emotion.

Richard Wright, 1908–1960
Novelist

CHAOS

459. Whenever there is chaos, it creates wonderful thinking. Chaos is a gift.

Septima Clark, 1898–1987
Educator and Civil rights activist

CHARACTER

See Integrity

CHILDREN

△ △ △ △ △ △ △ △

460. A white child might need a role model, but a black child needs more than that in this society. He needs hope.

Hank Aaron, 1934–
Baseball star

461. Children have never been good at listening to their elders, but they have never failed to imitate them.

James Baldwin, 1924–1987
Writer and Activist

462. There is a sanctity involved with bringing a child into this world; it is better than bombing one out of it.

James Baldwin, 1924–1987
Writer and Activist

463. No child is ever spoiled by too much attention. It is the lack of attention that spoils.

Bessie Blake

464. A vast number of black and Latino youths in the inner cities are trying desperately to make some sense of their lives, But they are caught in a crossfire between a small group of sociopaths in their midst and the larger society that ignores their potential and has written them out of the future.

Greg Donaldson
Author of *The Ville: Cops and Kids in Urban America*

465. For black folk who have too often been dismissed, stigmatized, or silenced without a hearing, we should be wary of repeating such rituals of repression on our own kids.

Michael Eric Dyson, 1958–
Scholar and Writer

466. If we really believe that our children are our future, we must develop an agenda to improve their lives and health. While it may take a village to raise a child, it takes responsible and caring adults to make a nurturing village.

Kenneth C. Edelin
Roxbury (MA) Comprehensive Community Health Center official

467. It's a spiritually impoverished nation that permits infants and children to be the poorest Americans.

Marian Wright Edelman, 1939–
Children's Defense Fund official

468. Throughout the social history of black women, children are more important than marriage in determining the woman's domestic role.

Paula Giddings, 1947–
Writer and Educator

469. Children respond to the expectations of their environment.

William Grier, 1926–
Physician
Price Cobb, 1928–
Psychiatrist

470. Children don't stop being children when they commit a crime.

William Hibbler
Judge

471. I never had a chance to play with dolls like other kids. I started working when I was six years old.

Billie Holiday, 1915–1959
Blues singer

472. If you choose to have that baby, then choose to take care of it. Kids are our future.

Michael Moses

473. Any black who strives to achieve in this country should think in terms of not only himself but also how he can reach down and grab another black child and pull him to the top of the mountain where he is.

Jesse Owens, 1913–1980
Olympic track star

474. Millions of our children are doing the right thing every day. They deserve our full support so that they stay the course. Their story goes so unreported in the media that the broader society is losing sight of the fact that our children are an asset, not a liability, to society.

Hugh Price, 1941–
National Urban League official

475. If I can inspire one of these youngsters to develop the talent I know they possess, then my monument will be in their work.

Augusta Savage, 1900–1962
Sculptor

476. If we love a child, and the child senses that we love him. he will get a concept of love that all subsequent hatred in the world will never be able to destroy.

Howard Thurman, 1899–1981
Minister

477. The Negro boy has obstacles, discouragements and temptations to battle with that are little known to those not situated as he is. When a white boy undertakes a task, it is taken for granted that he will succeed. On the other hand, people are usually surprised if the Negro boy does not fail.

Booker T. Washington, 1856–1915
Educator

478. Children who have not been captured by the cynicisms of adulthood replenish the imagination of the human community.

James M. Washington, 1948–1997
Minister and Academic

479. Children are the only future of any people.

Frances Cress Welsing, 1935–
Psychiatrist

480. Our children are in trouble because we adults are in trouble.

Camille Yarborough, 1938–
Actor

CHRISTIANITY

See also Religion

481. I love the pure, peaceable, and impartial Christianity of Christ: I therefore hate the corrupt, slaveholding, women-whipping, cradle-plundering, partial, and hypocritical Christianity of this land.

Frederick Douglass, 1817?–1895
Abolitionist and Autobiographer

482. I'm gonna make a gospel record and tell Jesus I cannot bear these burdens alone.

Aretha Franklin, 1942–
Singer

483. The first dealings we had with men calling themselves Christians exhibited the worst features of corrupt and sordid hearts, and convinced us that no cruelty is too great, no villainy and no robbery too abhorrent for even enlightened men to perform.

Henry Highland Garnet, 1815–1882
Abolitionist and Minister

484. The white Christian church never raised to the heights of Christ. It stayed within the limits of culture.

Jesse Jackson, 1941–
Minister and Civil rights activist

485. Unhappily, too many Christians, so called, take their religion not from the declarations of Christ, but from the writings of those they esteem learned.

John Marrant, 1755?–1797?
Missionary

486. Then let us start our Negro painters getting busy and supply a black Madonna and a black Christ for the training of our children.

George Alexander McGuire, 1866–1934
African Orthodox Church founder

487. I met a man named Jesus, and I had an exchange with him. I gave him my sorrows, he gave me his joy; I gave him my confusion, he gave me his peace; I gave him my despair, he gave me his hope; I gave him my hatred, he gave me his love; I gave him my torn life, he gave me his purpose.

Otis Moss, 1935–
Minister

488. The gospel of the New Testament is a life by the way of death. We cannot live by seeking to live. We can only live by the willingness—the commitment—to a form of self-death.

Gardner C. Taylor, 1918–
Minister

489. The basic contribution of prophetic Christianity, despite the countless calamities perpetrated by Christian churches, is that every individual, regardless of class, country, caste, race, or sex, should have the opportunity to fulfill his or her potentialities.

Cornel West, 1954–
Philosopher and Activist

490. The images, symbols, and attitudes of Christianity were the highest crystallization of the Negro's will to live he has made in this country.

Richard Wright, 1908–1960
Novelist

CHURCH

491. The fear that had shackled us all across the years left us suddenly when we were in that church, together.

Ralph Abernathy, 1926–1991
Civil rights activist

492. The only place blacks felt they could maintain an element of self-expression was the church.

Richard Allen, 1760–1831
AME Church founder

493. Old Satan's church is here below. Up to God's free church I hope to go.

Anonymous
Black hymn quoted by Harriet Jacobs

494. In the church, we think of ourselves as all part of God's family. That means we think of the people where we worship as brothers and sisters.

Benjamin Carson, 1951–
Surgeon

495. The black church was the creation of a black people whose daily existence was an encounter with the overwhelming and brutalizing reality of white power.

James Cone, 1938–
Theologian

496. The sickness of the church in America is intimately involved with the bankruptcy of American theology. When the church fails to live up to its appointed mission, it means that theology is partly responsible.

James Cone, 1938–
Theologian

497. There is in fact nothing to set the church apart as a leader in attacking the evils of the present social order.

Gordon Blaine Hancock, 1884–1970
Minister and Sociologist

498. I think if we're going to reclaim or recapture young people, it's going to have to be through the church or spirituality.

Bernice King, 1964–
Minister

499. I am grateful to God that, through the influence of the Negro church, the way of non-violence became an integral part of our struggle.

Martin Luther King Jr., 1929–1968
Civil rights activist and Nobel laureate

500. Never in Christian history, within a Christian country, have Christian churches been on the receiving end of such naked brutality and violence as we are witnessing here in America today.

Martin Luther King Jr., 1929–1968
Civil rights activist and Nobel laureate

501. The black church's conservative stance on women and queers, along with its failure to include gender and sexual orientation as oppressions which African Americans also face, makes the church's protests against racism merely myopic and anemic gestures for justice.

Irene Monroe, 1955–
Theologian

502. The black Holy Ghost roaring into some shack of a church, in the South, seizing the congregation with an ancient energy and power—the black church, therefore, represents and embodies the transplanted African memory.

Larry Neal, 1937–1981
Writer

503. The only thing that stands between this community and nihilism is the black church.

Eugene Rivers, 1950–
Minister

504. With the decline of the affirmative welfare state, black churches are going to be thrust into leadership roles which will be the equivalent of progressive churches in Third World countries.

Eugene Rivers, 1950–
Minister

505. The emergence of both free black preachers and independent black Baptist congregations in the 1780s was a momentous achievement for the African slave community in America. It was the closest thing to revolutionary expression available to them.

James M. Washington, 1948–1997
Minister and Academic

506. The church is the door through which we first walked in Western civilization.

Richard Wright, 1908–1960
Novelist

507. It is only when we are within the walls of our churches that we are wholly ourselves.

Richard Wright, 1908–1960
Novelist

508. Our going to church on Sunday is like placing one's ear to another's chest to hear the unquenchable murmur of the human heart.

Richard Wright, 1908–1960
Novelist

CIVIL RIGHTS MOVEMENT

509. The [Civil Rights] movement was a rushing tide, carrying everything in its path.

Johnnie Carr, 1911–
Activist

510. The civil rights movement that rearranged the social order of this country did not emanate from the halls of the Harvards and the Princetons and Cornells, It came from simple unlettered people who learned that they had the right to stand tall and that nobody can ride a back that isn't bent.

Dorothy Cotton, 1931–
Civil rights activist

511. It has a quality of hope and joy about it which I wish I could give you [Jessica Mitford]. I feel like I am in touch with the rising forces of the world and that the end of slavery and fear is in sight. I know this is just a moment, but the moment itself is so precious and after all it only takes a moment for a new world to be conceived.

Virginia Durr, 1903–
Civil rights activist

512. [The Civil Rights Movement offered America] the chance to become the Christian nation it had purported to be from its beginning—the brotherhood of man inside a political and social structure existing for the common good.

Paul Goodman, 1911–1972
Activist

513. This isn't a revolution of black against white, this is a revolution of right against wrong. And right has never lost.

Dick Gregory, 1932–
Comedian and Activist

514. We have talked long enough in this country about equal rights. We have talked for a hundred years or more. It is time now to write the next chapter, and to write it in the books of law.

Lyndon B. Johnson, 1908–1973
U.S. President

515. The civil-rights discourse was a moral discourse based on an appeal to whites to recognize their own humanity and act accordingly. The presumption that the people who hold power are moral rather than amoral is the fatal flaw of the movement; it depends so much on the good will of the oppressor....

Ron Karenga, 1941–
Educator

516. The patter of [protesters'] feet as they walked through Jim Crow barriers in the great stride toward freedom is the thunder of the marching men of Joshua. And the world rocks beneath their tread. My people, my people, listen, listen, the battle is in our hands.

Martin Luther King Jr., 1929–1968
Civil rights activist and Nobel laureate

517. The spark became a flame and it changed everything.

E.D. Nixon, 1899?–1987
Civil rights activist

518. The movement in the '60's had so much drama and impetus because the targets were so clear. The pain is still clear, but the target is amorphous. How, after all, do you march against sin?

Samuel D. Proctor, 1921–?
Minister and Educator

519. The Civil Rights Movement gave me the power to challenge any line that limits me.

Bernice Johnson Reagon, 1942–
Singer

520. They could outlaw an organization, but they couldn't outlaw the movement of a people determined to be free.

Fred Shuttlesworth, 1922–
Minister and Activist

521. Massive civil disobedience is a powerful weapon under civilized conditions where the law safeguards the citizens' right of peaceful demonstration.

Robert Williams, 1925–1996
Militant activist

522. We are not here to do you any harm. We merely want to have a word of prayer at this place where our ancestors were bought and sold as slaves, to ask God to help us end slavery in all its forms.

Andrew Young, 1932–
Civil rights activist

CIVIL WAR
See War

CLASS

523. History tells us a nation can survive for years by shifting the burdens of life to the people confined by force and violence to the bottom.

Lerone Bennett, 1928–
Historian

524. Domestic [i.e., house] slaves are often found to be traitors to their own people, for the purpose of gaining favor with their masters; and they are encouraged and trained up by them to report every plot they know of being formed about stealing anything or running away, or anything of the kind; and for which they are paid.

Henry Bibb, 1815–1854
Emigrationist

525. The American people have this to learn: that where justice is denied, where poverty is enforced, where ignorance prevails, and where any one class is made to feel that society is an organized conspiracy to oppress, rob, and degrade them, neither person nor property will be safe.

Frederick Douglass, 1817?–1895
Abolitionist and Autobiographer

526. The black bourgeoisie has lost much of its feeling of racial solidarity with the Negro masses.

E. Franklin Frazier, 1894–1962
Sociologist

527. Classism and racism have been compounded together in a crucible so it's hard to know where one starts and where one stops.

Henry Louis Gates Jr., 1950–
Scholar and Critic

528. History is the long and tragic story of the fact that privileged groups seldom give up their privileges voluntarily.

Martin Luther King Jr., 1929–1968
Civil rights activist and Nobel laureate

529. Many middle-class Negroes have forgotten their roots [and are] untouched by the agonies of struggles of their underprivileged brothers.

Martin Luther King Jr., 1929–1968
Civil rights activist and Nobel laureate

530. Black middle classes often feel as if they have to prove themselves—rather than just take their own creativity and humanity for granted.

Cornel West, 1954–
Philosopher and Activist

COLONIALISM

531. The ghettos in America are like the native reserves in South Africa. They symbolize the Negro as unacceptable, inferior, and kept apart.

Ralph Bunche, 1904–1971
Statesman

532. The dark ghettos are social, political, educational and— above all— economic colonies. Their inhabitants are subject peoples, victims of the greed, cruelty, insensitivity, guilt, and fear of their masters.

Kenneth B. Clark, 1914–
Social psychologist

533. The group I was in had the most classically cogent analysis: that blacks were, in effect, a people subjected to community imperialism or domestic colonialism, that their position was analogous to that of the Algerians vis a vis France, or that of the Angolans vis a vis Portugal, and that in order to achieve self-determination we had to engage in the struggle for liberation from the political and economic and social structures of the mainstream society.

Kathleen Cleaver, 1945–
Law professor

534. They often take the kindest white people to colonize the colored community.

Walter Mosley, 1952–
Writer

COLOR

535. Can the Ethiopian change his skin, or the leopard his spots?

Anonymous
Jeremiah 13:23a KJV

536. Color is not a human or personal reality; it is a political reality.

James Baldwin, 1924–1987
Writer and Activist

537. My skin color keeps things, literally, from being either black or white.

Toi Derricotte, 1941–
Writer

538. The mind does not take its complexion from the skin.

Frederick Douglass, 1817?–1895
Abolitionist and Autobiographer

539. He that despises a black man for the sake of his color, reproacheth his Maker.

Prince Hall, 1735?–1807
Masonic founder

540. I have seen that the world is to the strong, regardless of a little pigmentation more or less.

Zora Neale Hurston, 1891–1960
Writer and Folklorist

541. If it was so honorable and glorious to be black, why was it the yellow-skinned people among us had so much prestige?

Zora Neale Hurston, 1891–1960
Writer and Folklorist

542. Negroes are like trees. They wear all colors naturally.

Claude McKay, 1889–1948
Writer

543. We are living in a world where your color matters more than your character.

Sister Souljah, 1964–
Rap artist

COMMUNITY

❚❑❙ ❙❑❙❙❑❙ ❙❑❙❙❑❙ ❙❑❙❙❑❙ ❙❑❙

544. We all knew that what Jackie Robinson was doing was not just for himself, but for all of us.

Hank Aaron, 1934–
Baseball star

545. I suppose that regardless of what any Negro in America might do or how high he might rise in social status, he still has something in common with every other Negro.

Claude Brown, 1937–
Writer

546. The love we seek to encourage is within the black community, the only American community where men call each other "brother" when they meet.

Stokely Carmichael, 1941–
Activist

547. Let us take our painting and prints and sculptures not only to Atlanta University, to the art galleries, and to patrons of the arts who have money to buy them; let us exhibit them where Negro people meet—in the churches, in the schools and universities, in the associations and clubs and trade unions. Then let us seek inspiration in the Negro people—a principal and never-ending source.

Elizabeth Catlett, 1919–
Artist

548. The four billion dollars African Americans spend don't go to the black community.

Benjamin Chavis Jr., 1948–
Activist

549. It is time for us, who call ourselves artists, scholars, and thinkers, to rejoin the people from whom we came.

Ossie Davis, 1917–
Actor

550. I think somewhere along the line, in developing my own work and my own taste, I came to know and love the crowd.... The curtain goes up on the stage of life every time we walk into the street.

Joseph Delaney, 1904–1991
Painter

551. There is nothing more dangerous than to build a society with a large segment of people in that society who feel that they have no stake in it, who feel that they have nothing to lose. People who have a stake in their society protect that society, but when they don't have it, they unconsciously want to destroy it.

Marcus Garvey, 1887–1940
Nationalist leader

552. When I pitched headforemost into the world, I landed in the crib of negroism.

Zora Neale Hurston, 1891–1960
Writer and Folklorist

553. We were all black and we were all poor and we were all right there in place. For us, the larger community didn't exist.

Barbara Jordan, 1936–1996
Lawyer and U.S. Congressperson

554. Strangely enough, I can never be what I ought to be until you are what you ought to be.

Martin Luther King Jr., 1929–1968
Civil rights activist and Nobel laureate

555. I can well understand what Langston Hughes said ... that he would never live outside the Negro community, Because this was his life ... his sustenance.

Jacob Lawrence, 1917–
Painter

556. I had acceptance at a very early age from the community, and that does a lot. The people that accepted me didn't necessarily know about art, but they encouraged me.

Jacob Lawrence, 1917–
Painter

557. I have the people behind me, and the people are my strength.

Huey Newton, 1942–
Black Panther Party leader

558. Black men must make a special effort to become spiritual and psychological fathers to needy black children within their extended families and community.

Alvin Poussaint, 1934–
Psychiatrist

559. I am the product of the sustained indignation of a branded grandfather, the militant protest of my grandmother, the disciplined resentment of my father and mother, and the power of the mass action of the church.

Adam Clayton Powell Jr., 1908–1972
Minister and U.S. Congressperson

560. Yes, here is my homeground—here and in all Negro communities throughout the land. Here I stand.

Paul Robeson, 1898–1976
Singer and Activist

561. There was a cohesiveness about poor black communities before integration that today's middle-class black communities do not have, or do not need.

Gloria Wade-Gayles, 1967–

562. We must trust the people.

Faye Wattleton, 1944–
Planned Parenthood president

563. To do something together without a whole lot of jealousy or envy, we've got to keep our eyes on something bigger than us.

Cornel West, 1954–
Philosopher and Activist

564. They came from places called the Carolinas and the Virginias, Georgia, Alabama, Mississippi, and Tennessee. They came strong, eager, searching. The city rejected them and they filed and settled along the riverbanks and under bridges in shallow, ramshackle houses made of sticks and tarpaper.

August Wilson, 1945–
Dramatist

565. No one does it alone.

Oprah Winfrey, 1954–
Entertainer

566. The money you spend for whiskey will run a government.

Malcolm X, 1925–1965
Nationalist leader

CONFEDERATE FLAG

567. [The issue of the Confederate flag is] whether Americans such as myself … will have to suffer the indignity of being reminded time and time again that at one point in this country's history, we were human chattel, we were property, we could be traded, bought and sold.

Carol Moseley-Braun, 1947–
U.S. Senator

CONFIDENCE
See Self-Confidence

CONSCIENCE
See Integrity

CONSERVATIVES

568. The new black conservatives are first-generation middle-class persons who offer themselves as examples of how well the system works for those willing to sacrifice and work hard. Yet in familiar American fashion, genuine white peer acceptance still preoccupies—and often escapes them. In this regard they are still affected by white racism.

Cornel West, 1954–
Philosopher and Activist

CONSTITUTION

569. I would have the [pro-slavery] Constitution torn in shreds and scattered to the four winds of heaven. Let us destroy the Constitution and build on its ruins the temple of liberty.

William Wells Brown, 1815–1884
Writer

570. We know we are citizens because it is written in an amendment to the Constitution.

Septima Clark, 1898–1987
Educator and Civil rights activist

571. Men talk of the Negro problem; there is no Negro problem. The problem is whether American people have loyalty enough, honor enough, patriotism enough, to live up to their own Constitution.

Paul Laurence Dunbar, 1872–1906
Poet

572. If America has a civic religion, the First Amendment is its central article of faith.

Henry Louis Gates Jr., 1950–
Scholar and Critic

573. It is dangerous for white America to insist that basic American documents be read by the black, poor, and oppressed, because such people are just naive enough to go out and do what the founding fathers said oppressed people should do.

Dick Gregory, 1932–
Comedian and Activist

574. [African Americans were] the foremost proponents of freedom and justice in the nation, demanding of the Constitution more than its slave-holding creators dared to dream, wresting it toward an integrity that the Fathers would not give it.

Vincent Harding, 1931–
Scholar and Writer

575. In the view of the Constitution, in the eyes of the law, there is in this country no superior, dominant ruling class of citizens.

John Marshall Harlan
U.S. Supreme Court justice dissent in Plessy v. Ferguson, May 18, 1896

576. When that document was completed on the 17th of September in 1787, I was not included in that "We the people." I felt somehow for years that George Washington and Alexander Hamilton just left me out by mistake. But through the process of amendment, interpretation, and court decision, I have finally been included in "We the people." My faith in the Constitution is whole; it is complete, it is total.

Barbara Jordan, 1936–1996
Lawyer and U.S. Congressperson

577. I do not believe that the meaning of the Constitution was forever "fixed" at the Philadelphia Convention.... The government they devised was defective from the start, requiring several amendments, a civil war, and momentous social transformation to attain the system of constitutional government, and its respect for the individual freedoms and human rights, we hold as fundamental today.

Thurgood Marshall, 1908–1993
U.S. Supreme Court Justice

578. If the First Amendment means anything, it means that the state has no business telling a man, sitting alone in his own house, what books he may read or what films he may watch.

Thurgood Marshall, 1908–1993
U.S. Supreme Court Justice

579. While the Union survived the Civil War, the Constitution did not.

Thurgood Marshall, 1908–1993
U.S. Supreme Court Justice

COURAGE

580. Don't let anything stop you. There will be times when you'll be disappointed, but you can't stop.

Sadie T.M. Alexander, 1898–1989
Lawyer and Activist

581. One isn't necessarily born with courage, but one is born with potential. Without courage, we cannot practice any other virtue with consistency.

Maya Angelou, 1928–
Novelist and Poet

582. We wanted something for ourselves and for our children, so we took a chance with our lives.

Unita Blackwell, 1933–
Civil rights activist

583. Records are made to be broken.

Jim Brown, 1936–
Athlete and Actor

584. That old flag never touched the ground, boys.

William H. Carney, 1840?–1908
Civil War soldier

585. As long as I can stand it, God, I'll keep on keeping on.

Ray Charles, 1930–
Singer

586. Brothers, we have striven to regain the precious heritage we received from our fathers.... I am resolved that it is better to die than to be a white man's slave, and I will not complain if by dying I save you.

Joseph Cinque, 1817?–?
Amistad Revolt leader

587. I knew we had no aviators, neither men nor women, and I knew the race needed to be represented, so I thought it my duty to risk my life to learn aviation and encourage flying among men and women of our race.

Bessie Coleman, 1892–1926
Aviator

588. The reason I became a ballerina of the Metropolitan Opera was because I couldn't be topped. You don't get there because, you get there in spite of.

Janet Colins, 1923–
Prima ballerina

589. Decide that you want it more than you are afraid of it.

Bill Cosby, 1937–
Actor

590. If you want to be the best, Baby, you've got to work harder than anybody else.

Sammy Davis Jr., 1925–1990
Entertainer

591. Let the colored man stand his ground. There is far more honor in dying like a free man than living like a slave.

T. Thomas Fortune, 1856–1928
Journalist

592. If you must bleed, let it all come at once—rather die freemen, than live to be slaves.

Henry Highland Garnet, 1815–1882
Abolitionist and Minister

593. Lose not courage, lose not faith, go forward.

Marcus Garvey, 1887–1940
Nationalist leader

594. Most of us who aspire to be tops in our fields don't really consider the amount of work required to stay tops.

Althea Gibson, 1927–
Tennis champion

595. I dared to speak when I should have been silent.

Lani Guinier, 1950–
Law professor

596. I've lost the title two times, but I knew the only thing that would stop me was if I quit on myself. You have to face your challenges and give your all.

Evander Holyfield, 1962–
Boxing champion

597. I was born in the slum, but the slum was not born in me. And it wasn't born in you, and you can make it. Wherever you are tonight, you can make it. Hold your head high, stick your chest out. You can make it. It gets dark sometimes, but the morning comes. Don't you surrender.

Jesse Jackson, 1941–
Minister and Civil rights activist

598. The greatest inventions in the world had hundreds of failures before the answers were found.

Michael Jordan, 1961–
Basketball star

599. There are a million excuses for not paying the price.

Michael Jordan, 1961–
Basketball star

600. Ask any athlete: we all hurt at times. I'm asking my body to go through several different tasks. To ask it not to ache would be too much.

Jackie Joyner-Kersee, 1962–
Olympic champion

601. It may get me crucified. I may even die. But I want it said even if I die in the struggle that "He died to make men free."

Martin Luther King Jr., 1929–1968
Civil rights activist and Nobel laureate

602. The ultimate measure of a man is not where he stands in moments of comfort and convenience, but where he stands at times of challenge and controversy.

Martin Luther King Jr., 1929–1968
Civil rights activist and Nobel laureate

603. We are entering deeper nights of social disruption in our country, We have the resources to solve our problem. But the question is, do we have the will?

Martin Luther King Jr., 1929–1968
Civil rights activist and Nobel laureate

604. The only way for a fighter to get back in shape is to fight his way back.

Sugar Ray Leonard, 1956–
Boxing champion

605. It's a very lonely thing to be one of the first.

Arthur Mitchell, 1883–1968
U.S. Congressperson

606. I believe, deep in my heart, that the dark tinge of my skin is the thing that has been my making. For, you see, I have had to work 100 per cent harder to realize my ambition.

Archibald Motley Jr., 1891–1981
Artist

607. I had felt for a long time, that if I was ever told to get up so a white person could sit, that I would refuse to do.

Rosa Parks, 1913–
Civil rights activist

608. I was frightened, but I believed we needed help to get us more jobs and better education.

Rosa Parks, 1913–
Civil rights activist

609. I will not be a silent congressman.

Adam Clayton Powell Jr., 1908–1972
Minister and U.S. Congressperson

610. Keep the faith, Baby!

Adam Clayton Powell Jr., 1908–1972
Minister and U.S. Congressperson

611. I will stand my ground. Somebody must die in this cause. I may be doomed to the stake and the fire or to the scaffold tree, but it is not for me to falter.

Sojourner Truth, 1797?–1883
Abolitionist and Women's rights advocate

612. When rungs were missing, I learned to jump.

William Warfield, 1929–?
Singer

613. Most of our problems can be solved. Some of them will take brains, and some of them will take patience, but all of them will have to be wrestled with like an alligator in the swamp.

Harold Washington, 1922–1987
Politician, Mayor of Chicago

CREATIVITY

614. Only as a part of the mass can we recognize its needs as to our artistic contribution.

Elizabeth Catlett, 1919–
Artist

615. I've always told the musicians in my band to play what they know and then play above that. Because then anything can happen, and that's where great art and music happens.

Miles Davis, 1926–1991
Jazz musician

616. I contend that the Negro is the creative voice of America, is creative America, and it was a happy day in America when the first unhappy slave was landed on its shores. There, in our tortured induction into this land of liberty, we built its most graceful civilization.

Duke Ellington, 1899–1974
Composer and Band leader

617. It's not that the cultural cutting edge has been influenced by black creativity; it's that black creativity, it so often seems today, is the cultural cutting edge.

Henry Louis Gates Jr., 1950–
Scholar and Critic

618. Often, what we write, the music we write, and the pictures we paint are dialogues with our deepest consciousness.

Marita Golden, 1950–
Writer and Educator

619. This is one of the glories of man, the inventiveness of the human mind and the human spirit: whenever life doesn't seem to give an answer, we create one.

Lorraine Hansberry, 1930–1965
Dramatist

620. Everything that IS was once IMAGINED!

Ted Joans, 1928–
Poet

621. I don't think anybody steals anything; all of us borrow.

B.B. King, 1925–
Blues musician

622. We can only reflect our own experience, but we would hope that we would be understood by others, universally beyond the source.

Jacob Lawrence, 1917–
Painter

623. In flavor of language, flow of phrase, accent of rhythm in prose, verse and music, color and tone of imagery, idiom and timbre of emotion and symbolism, it is the ambition and promise of Negro artists to make a distinctive contribution.

Alain Locke, 1886–1954
Scholar and Critic

624. I realized by using the high notes of the chords as a melodic line, and by the right harmonic progression, I could play what I heard inside me. That's when I was born.

Charlie Parker, 1920?–1955
Jazz musician

625. If you have but one wish, let it be for an idea.

Percy Sutton, 1920–
Politician

626. And so our mothers and grandmothers have, more often than not anonymously, handed on the creative spark, the seed of the flower they themselves never hoped to see.

Alice Walker, 1944–
Writer

CULTURE
See Black Culture

DANCE

627. There is a purifying process in dancing.

Katherine Dunham, 1910–?
Dancer

628. Black dance embodied a resistance to the confinement of the body solely to wage work.

Tera W. Hunter
Writer

629. Dance is vulnerability; it's about giving your love, light, generosity.

Judith Jamison, 1943–
Dancer

630. Once you've danced, you always dance.

Judith Jamison, 1943–
Dancer

631. The influence which the Negro has exercised on the art of dancing in this country has been almost absolute.

James Weldon Johnson, 1871–1938
Writer and Activist

632. Dance is our Negritude. It's us and we shouldn't try to deny that.

Spike Lee, 1957–
Filmmaker

633. We must never forget that dance is the cradle of Negro music.

Alain Locke, 1886–1954
Scholar and Critic

634. The dance is strong magic. The dance is a spirit. It turns the body to liquid steel. It makes it vibrate like a guitar. The body can fly without wings. It can sing without voice. The dance is strong magic.

Pearl Primus, 1919–1994
Dancer

635. Dance is the fist with which I fight the sickening ignorance of prejudice.

Pearl Primus, 1919–1994
Dancer

636. Americans will be amazed to find how many of the modern dance steps are relics of the African heritage.

Paul Robeson, 1898–1976
Singer and Activist

637. The Afro-American approach to dance, which was uprooted from Africa, is at the very core of the dance in America.

Tevis Williams
Journalist

DARING

638. If we do not now dare everything, the fulfillment of that prophecy, re-created from the Bible in song by a slave, is upon us: "God gave Noah the rainbow sign / No more water, the fire next time."

James Baldwin, 1924–1987
Writer and Activist

639. I gloried in the danger and the wild and free life of the plains.

Nat "Deadwood Dick, the cowboy adventurer" Love, 1854–?
Cowboy

DEATH

640. We've been to hell and back again. And death cannot have the final word.

Ossie Davis, 1917–
Actor

641. Help us to hope that the seeming Shadow of this Death is to our human blindness but the exceeding brightness of a newer greater life.

W.E.B. Du Bois, 1868–1963
Intellectual and Activist

642. When I am dead wrap the mantle of the Red, Black, and Green around me for in the new life I shall rise ... to lead the millions up the heights of triumph with the colors that you well know.

Marcus Garvey, 1887–1940
Nationalist leader

643. Brother, brother, there are too many of us dying.

Marvin Gaye, 1939–1984
Singer and Composer

644. Death is a slave's freedom.

Nikki Giovanni, 1943–
Poet

645. Sometimes the strong die, too.

Louis Gossett Jr.
Actor

646. If physical death is the price I must pay to free my white brothers and sisters from the permanent death of the spirit, then nothing could be more redemptive.

Martin Luther King Jr., 1929–1968
Civil rights activist and Nobel laureate

647. It is a terrible thing to kill a man, no matter what the reason.

Nat "Deadwood Dick, the cowboy adventurer" Love, 1854–?
Cowboy

648. In slavery, black folks said they ain't got time to die.

Joseph Lowery, 1924–
Civil rights activist

649. We have slumbered and slept too long already; the night is far spent; the night of death approaches.

Maria W. Stewart, 1803–1879
Lecturer

650. I am not going to die. I'm going home like a shooting star.

Sojourner Truth, 1797?–1883
Abolitionist and Women's rights advocate

651. If I never see you again, I'll see you in the Kingdom.

Harriet Tubman, 1820?–1913
Abolitionist

652. Cease, gentle music! the solemn gloom of night / Now seals the fair creation from my sight.

Phillis Wheatley, 1753?–1784
Poet

653. You can't make me do nothing but die.

Richard Wright, 1908–1960
Novelist

654. If I die or am killed before making it back to the States, you may rest assured that what I've already set in motion will never be stopped.

Malcolm X, 1925–1965
Nationalist leader

655. It is a blessing to die for a cause because you can so easily die for nothing.

Andrew Young, 1932–
Civil rights activist

DECISIONS
See Opportunity

DECLARATION OF INDEPENDENCE

656. The Declaration of Independence is a dishonest document.

John Hope Franklin, 1915–
Historian

DEFEAT

657. The encountering [of defeats] may be the very experience which creates the vitality and the power to endure.

Maya Angelou, 1928–
Novelist and Poet

658. Defeat is not bitter unless you swallow it.

Joe Clark, 1939–
Educator

DEGRADATION
See Oppression

DEMOCRACY

659. We will build a democratic America in spite of undemocratic Americans.
Shirley Chisholm, 1924–
Politician

660. If this nation is not truly democratic, then she must die.
Alexander Crummell, 1819–1898
Minister and Scholar

661. [During Reconstruction] it was the black man that raised a vision of democracy in America such as neither American nor European conceived in the eighteenth century and they have not even accepted in the twentieth century, and yet a conception which every clear-sighted man knows is true and inevitable.
W.E.B. Du Bois, 1868–1963
Intellectual and Activist

662. Privilege is anathema to democracy.
Nikki Giovanni, 1943–
Poet

663. In a racially divided society, majority rule may become majority tyranny.
Lani Guinier, 1950–
Law professor

664. America must begin the struggle for democracy at home.
Martin Luther King Jr., 1929–1968
Civil rights activist and Nobel laureate

665. Democracy itself is obstructed and stagnated to the extent that any of its channels are closed.
Alain Locke, 1886–1954
Scholar and Critic

666. The Negro question is too often put forward merely as the Negro question. It is just as much, and often more seriously, the question of democracy. The position of the Negro in American society is its one great outstanding anomaly.

Alain Locke, 1886–1954
Scholar and Critic

667. A child born to a black mother in a state like Mississippi—born to the dumbest, poorest sharecropper —by merely drawing its first breath in the democracy has exactly the same rights as a white baby born to the wealthiest person in the United States, It's not true, but I challenge anyone to say it's not a goal worth working for.

Thurgood Marshall, 1908–1993
U.S. Supreme Court Justice

668. It is not the fear of Negro supremacy in the South that causes the southern election of officers to suppress the Negro vote, but it is the fear of the rule of majority regardless of race. The master class does not want to surrender to the rule of the people.

Thomas E. Miller, 1849–1938
U.S. Congressperson

669. The very advantages of a democracy make disfranchisement therein the worst of tyrannies.

William Pickens, 1881–1954
Editor and Civil rights activist

670. If the majority rules, then the earth belongs to colored people.

Charles V. Roman, 1864–1934
Physician

671. A democratic way of life occurs when we are every day reaffirming the rights of ordinary, everyday people.

Cornel West, 1954–
Philosopher and Activist

672. I have a deep, existential confidence in the rightness of radical democracy.

Cornel West, 1954–
Philosopher and Activist

673. Our tragicomic times require more democratic concepts of knowledge and leadership which highlight human fallibility and mutual accountability; notions of individuality and contested authority which stress dynamic traditions; and ideals of self-realization within participatory communities.

Cornel West, 1954–
Philosopher and Activist

DESEGREGATION

674. Along with the fight to desegregate schools, we must desegregate the entire cultural statement of America, we must desegregate the minds of the American people.

John O. Killens, 1916–1987
Novelist

DESPAIR

675. We must delve into the depths where neither liberals nor conservatives dare to tread, into the murky waters of despair and dread that now flood the streets of black America.

Cornel West, 1954–
Philosopher and Activist

DESTINY

676. The "nuclear" irony of American history and the American social political and economic system is that the destiny of the enslaved and disadvantaged Negro determines the destiny of the nation.

Kenneth B. Clark, 1914–
Social psychologist

677. The Lord who told me to take care of my people meant me to do it just as long as I live, and so I do what he told me.

Harriet Tubman, 1820?–1913
Abolitionist

DIGNITY

678. [Rosa Parks] sat down with dignity so that all black people could stand up with pride.

Michael Eric Dyson, 1958–
Scholar and Writer

679. Human dignity is more precious than prestige.

Claude McKay, 1889–1948
Writer

680. Ours is the truest dignity of man, the dignity of the undefeated.

Ethel Waters, 1896?–1977
Singer and Actor

DIRECTION

681. We proceeded in an easterly direction, and all busied themselves in searching for gold; but my errand was of a different character: I had come to discover what I suspected to be a pass [now Beckwourth Pass through the Sierra Nevada Mountains].

Jim Beckwourth, 1798–1866
Mountain man

682. Where do we go from here?

Martin Luther King Jr., 1929–1968
Civil rights activist and Nobel laureate

683. It's pretty hard for the Lord to guide you if you haven't made up your mind which way you want to go.

Mme. C.J. Walker, 1867–1919
Entrepreneur

DISCIPLINE

684. I cannot imagine a writer who is not continually reaching, who contains no discontent that what he or she is producing is not more than it is. so primarily, I suppose, discipline is the foundation of the profession, and that holds regardless of anything else.

Mari Evans, 1923–
Poet

685. It doesn't matter what you are trying to accomplish. It's all a matter of discipline.

Wilma Rudolph, 1940–1994
Olympic track star

DISCRIMINATION
See Segregation

DISSENT

686. Human salvation lies in the hands of the creatively maladjusted.

Martin Luther King Jr., 1929–1968
Civil rights activist and Nobel laureate

687. We must encourage creative dissenters. We must demonstrate, teach, and preach, until the foundations of our nation are shaken.

Martin Luther King Jr., 1929–1968
Civil rights activist and Nobel laureate

DIVERSITY

688. We Americans have a chance to become someday a nation in which all racial stocks and classes can exist in their own selfhoods, but meet on a basis of respect and equality and live together socially, economically, and politically.

Shirley Chisholm, 1924–
Politician

689. Cultural pluralism: it's the air we breathe; it's the ground we stand on.

Ralph Ellison, 1914–1994
Novelist

690. Anglo-American regional culture is simply not universal. We're helping to create a new cultural consciousness, one that's pluralistic and diverse.

Henry Louis Gates Jr., 1950–
Scholar and Critic

691. Each of us helplessly and forever contains the other—male and female, female and male, white and black, black and white. We are a part of each other.

Henry Louis Gates Jr., 1950–
Scholar and Critic

692. Pluralism isn't supposed to be about policing the boundaries; it's supposed to be about breaking boundaries down, acknowledging the fluid and interactive nature of all our identities.

Henry Louis Gates Jr., 1950–
Scholar and Critic

693. The teaching of literature is the teaching of values, is the teaching of an aesthetic and political order in which none of the members of the black community, the minority community of color, or the women's community, were ever able to discover the reflection or representation of their images or hear the resonances of their cultural voices.

Henry Louis Gates Jr., 1950–
Scholar and Critic

694. Future leaders, those who would lead the nation, must know that the flag is red, white and blue but the nation is not red, white and blue. It is red and yellow and brown and black and white.

Jesse Jackson, 1941–
Minister and Civil rights activist

695. Integration is an opportunity to participate in the beauty of diversity.

Martin Luther King Jr., 1929–1968
Civil rights activist and Nobel laureate

696. We have a right to a diversity of voices. We are diverse. We don't have to all agree on everything.

Jill Nelson
Writer

697. We must protect each other's rights and existence. The minorities of this city [New York] are the majority of this city.

Al Sharpton, 1955–
Minister and Activist

DOING THE RIGHT THING
See Morality

DREAMS

698. I have a dream. This dream must, alas, be disentangled from whatever nightmare controls this fearfully White Republic.

James Baldwin, 1924–1987
Writer and Activist

699. Though there are whites and blacks among us who hate each other, we will not; there are those who are betrayed by greed, by guilt, by blood lust, but not we; we will set our faces against them, and join hands and walk together into that dazzling future when there will be no white or black. This is the dream of all liberal men, a dream not at all dishonorable, but, nevertheless, a dream. For, let us join hands on this mountain as we may, the battle is elsewhere.

James Baldwin, 1924–1987
Writer and Activist

700. The dream is real, my friends. The failure to make it work is the unreality.

Toni Cade Bambara, 1939–
Writer

701. Little dreams stay home. Big dreams go to New York.

David Dinkins, 1927–
Politician

702. If you don't dream, you might as well be dead.

George Foreman, 1949–
Boxing champion

703. If you are committed to pursuing your dreams, you must expect that you will run up against those who feel you can't do the job.

Mary Futrell, 1940–
Educator

704. Poor people are allowed the same dreams as everyone else.

Kimi Gray

705. The dream is the truth.

Zora Neale Hurston, 1891–1960
Writer and Folklorist

706. It is one of the blessings of this world that few people see visions and dream dreams.

Zora Neale Hurston, 1891–1960
Writer and Folklorist

707. Exercise the right to dream. You must face reality—that which is. But then dream of the reality that ought to be, that must be.

Jesse Jackson, 1941–
Minister and Civil rights activist

708. I have a dream that one day in the red hills of Georgia the sons of former slaves and the sons of former slave owners will be able to sit down together at the table of brotherhood.

Martin Luther King Jr., 1929–1968
Civil rights activist and Nobel laureate

709. Man is what his dreams are.

Benjamin Mays, 1895–1984
Educator

710. In one hand I have a dream, and in the other I have an obstacle. Tell me, which one grabs your attention?

Henry Parks, 1916–
Businessperson

711. You can't just sit there and wait for people to give you that golden dream, you've got to get out there and make it happen for yourself.

Diana Ross, 1944–
Singer

712. I learned to dream that I could be more than I was permitted to be in the segregated society around me.

Percy Sutton, 1920–
Politician

713. We are the first generation of black people in four hundred years who can live our dreams.

Susan Taylor, 1946–
Editor and Writer

714. As long as one has a dream in his heart, he cannot lose the significance of living.

Howard Thurman, 1899–1981
Minister

715. A dream is the bearer of a new possibility, the enlarged horizon, the great hope.

Howard Thurman, 1899–1981
Minister

716. This is the first miracle, a man becomes his dreams; then it is that the line between what he does and is and his dream melts away.

Howard Thurman, 1899–1981
Minister

717. Dreams was one [of] the reasons you got up the next day.

Sherley Anne Williams, 1944–
Writer

718. Dream the biggest dream for yourself. Hold the highest vision of life for yourself.

Oprah Winfrey, 1954–
Entertainer

DRUGS

719. Drugs were dumped in the ghetto more than a generation ago, and we all know why.... We are now undergoing the most savage aspect of this genocidal detail, which will be halted only when genocide is perceived as suicide.

James Baldwin, 1924–1987
Writer and Activist

720. We have a generation enslaving itself to drugs, young men and women doing to our race what slavery couldn't.

Lucille Clifton, 1935–
Poet

721. Dope never helped anybody sing better or play music better or do anything better. All dope can do is kill you—and kill you the long, slow, hard way.

Billie Holiday, 1915–1959
Blues singer

722. The most deadly thing about cocaine is that it separates you from your soul.

Quincy Jones, 1933–
Musician and Business executive

723. There is a new Ku Klux Klan out there called Killer Crack and Cocaine, and the new lynch mob is sweeping all through the black neighborhood.

Joseph Lowery, 1924–
Civil rights activist

724. Blood may be thicker than water, but it is not thicker than crack cocaine.

Dorothy Riley, 1937–
Educator

725. When a person is a drug addict, he's not the criminal; he's a victim of the criminal. The criminal is the man who brings drugs into the country.

Malcolm X, 1925–1965
Nationalist leader

ECONOMICS

726. As long as Negroes are hemmed into racial blocs of prejudice and pressure, it will be necessary for them to bank together for economic betterment.

Mary McLeod Bethune, 1875–1955
Educator

727. What we mean by integration is not to be with them, but to have what they have.

Julian Bond, 1940–
Civil rights activist

728. I basically believed that, ultimately, a sharing society would have to come into being to have any society at all, because capitalism is without humanity, without heart, and without concern for people.

John Henrik Clarke, 1915–
Historian

729. As long as you are a consumer, you are a beggar. You must become a producer. We must learn from the lessons of the Japanese.

Camille Cosby, 1945–
Philanthropist

730. Marshal some of our purchasing power and start producing some of the things we are already spending money for. You spent $400 million last year just for toothpaste.

Louis Farrakhan, 1934–
Nation of Islam leader

731. There can be no overproduction of anything as long as there are hungry mouths to be fed. It does not matter if the possessors of these hungry mouths are too poor to buy the bread. If they are hungry, there is no overproduction.

T. Thomas Fortune, 1856–1928
Journalist

732. Racially speaking, we oppose segregation, but economically speaking it forms the basis of our professional and business life.

Gordon Blaine Hancock, 1884–1970
Minister and Sociologist

733. When a Negro buys from the Negro grocer, he not only gets a loaf of bread but helps to make a place of employment for some aspiring Negro. His dollar does double duty.

Gordon Blaine Hancock, 1884–1970
Minister and Sociologist

734. Could slavery exist long if it did not sit on a commercial throne?

Frances Ellen Watkins Harper, 1825–1911
Writer and Orator

735. We Negroes of America are tired of a world divided superficially on the basis of blood and color, but in reality on the basis of poverty and power—the rich over the poor, no matter what their color.

Langston Hughes, 1902–1967
Poet and Writer

736. Despite the strength of a $350 million market, African Americans seem reluctant to show that strength with a well-organized boycott.

Julianne Malvreaux, 1953–
Economist

737. There is no other American community in which the huge bulk of local business, from the smallest to the largest, is operated by outsiders.

Claude McKay, 1889–1948
Writer

738. The study of economic oppression led me to realize that Negroes were not alone but were part of an unending struggle for human dignity the world over.

Pauli Murray, 1910–1985
Lawyer and Minister

739. We have made no radical changes in the economic servitude of the black masses.

Adam Clayton Powell Jr., 1908–1972
Minister and U.S. Congressperson

740. Do you ask what we can do? Unite and build a store of your own…. Do you ask where is the money? We have spent more than enough for nonsense.

Maria W. Stewart, 1803–1879
Lecturer

741. At the bottom of education, at the bottom of politics, even at the bottom of religion, there must be for our race economic independence.

Booker T. Washington, 1856–1915
Educator

742. The Southern mortgage system is the curse of the Negro. It is the mortgage system which blinds him, robs him of independence, allures him, and winds him deeper and deeper in its meshes each year 'til he is lost and bewildered.

Booker T. Washington, 1856–1915
Educator

743. Standing ground for a race, as for an individual, must be laid in intelligence, industry, thrift, and property.

Booker T. Washington, 1856–1915
Educator

744. In the final analysis, lynching and mob violence, disfranchisement, unequal distribution of school funds, the Ku Klux Klan and all other forms of

racial prejudice are for one great purpose—that of keeping the Negro in the position where he is economically exploitable.

Walter White, 1893–1955
Civil rights activist

745. Economic advancement must be the next big move in the life of African Americans.

Eddie N. Williams, 1933–
Joint Center for Political and Economic Studies official

746. In the first place, we need to obtain economic independence. You may talk about rights and all that sort of thing. the people who own this country will rule this country. They always have done so and they always will.

Carter G. Woodson, 1875–1950
Historian

EDUCATION

747. All education is self-acquired, since no one can educate another.

Charles G. Adams, 1936–
Minister

748. I try to learn as much as I can because I know nothing compared with what I need to know.

Muhammad Ali, 1942–
Boxing champion

749. [Mother] said that I must always be intolerant of ignorance, but understanding of illiteracy. That some people, unable to go to school, were more educated and more intelligent than college professors.

Maya Angelou, 1928–
Novelist and Poet

750. A mind is a terrible thing to waste.

Anonymous
United Negro College Fund motto

751. We want education that teaches us our true history and our role in the present-day society.

Anonymous
Black Panther Party Platform

752. Education is indoctrination if you're white, subjugation if you're black.

James Baldwin, 1924–1987
Writer and Activist

753. An educator in a system of oppression is either a revolutionary or an oppressor.

Lerone Bennett, 1928–
Historian

754. There should be no "Negro History Corner" or "Negro History Week." There should be an integration of African American culture in all of its diversity throughout the curriculum.

Janice Hall Benson
Psychologist

755. Going to school wasn't a requirement in our house. It was a sacrament.

Julia Boyd, 1949–
Psychotherapist

756. In the long run, there has to be something like equal opportunity for all kids to get a good education in this country. Better-off people will always have an advantage, but equal opportunity should be a goal, an aspiration.

Albert Carnesale
UCLA chancellor

757. If you can't teach me, don't criticize me.

Sonya Carson, 1934?–
Teenage parent

758. Education is the key to unlock the golden door of freedom.

George Washington Carver, 1864?–1943
Inventor

759. We are the only racial group within the United States ever forbidden by law to read and write.

Alice Childress, 1920–1994
Writer

760. [Frederick Douglass] was a graduate from a particular institution, with his diploma written on his back.

Charles P. Chipman
Author of *Negroes in Our History*

761. An education ... about ourselves would empower black women because it would help us understand the source of our powerlessness. And, understanding is always the first step towards change.

Johnnetta Cole, 1936–
Educator

762. The first sign of an educated person is that she asks more questions than she delivers answers.

Johnnetta Cole, 1936–
Educator

763. I have proven that children labeled "untouchable" can learn.

Marva Collins, 1940–
Educator

764. I know most of you can't spell your name. You don't know the alphabet, you don't know how to read.... I promise you that you will. None of you has ever failed. School may have failed you.

Marva Collins, 1936–
Educator

765. Personal experience is important in any scholarly activity, but it cannot substitute for scientific research.

James Cone, 1938–
Theologian

766. Educate your sons and daughters, send them to school, and show them that beside the cartridge box, the ballot box, and the jury box, you have also the knowledge box.

Frederick Douglass, 1817?–1895
Abolitionist and Autobiographer

767. A little learning, indeed, may be a dangerous thing, but the want of learning is a calamity to any people.

Frederick Douglass, 1817?–1895
Abolitionist and Autobiographer

768. Education must not simply teach work—it must teach life.

W.E.B. Du Bois, 1868–1963
Intellectual and Activist

769. Either the United States will destroy ignorance or ignorance will destroy the United States.

W.E.B. Du Bois, 1868–1963
Intellectual and Activist

770. Public education for all at public expense was, to the South, a Negro idea.

W.E.B. Du Bois, 1868–1963
Intellectual and Activist

771. This the American black man knows: his fight is a fight to the finish. Either he dies or he wins. There can be no compromise. This is the last great battle of the West.

W.E.B. Du Bois, 1868–1963
Intellectual and Activist

772. If southern whites found the prospect of an educated slave so threatening, education must hold the promise of liberation.

Audrey Edwards
Publisher

Craig K. Polite, 1947–
Publisher

773. Once I had a professor say to me, "You know, you have as much education as a lot of white people. " I said, "Doctor, I have more education than most white people."
Joycelyn Elders, 1933–
U.S. Surgeon General

774. Dropouts [from school] are living critics of their environment, of our society, and of our educational system.
Ralph Ellison, 1914–1994
Novelist

775. Education is all a matter of building bridges.
Ralph Ellison, 1914–1994
Novelist

776. Education is the jewel casting brilliance into the future.
Mari Evans, 1923–
Poet

777. The white side has been in control of virtually everything, so they're the ones who need educating on what justice and equality mean.
John Hope Franklin, 1915–
Historian

778. Education in the past has been too much inspiration and too little information.
E. Franklin Frazier, 1894–1962
Sociologist

779. To secure the blessings of liberty, we must secure the blessings of learning.
Mary Futrell, 1940–
Educator

780. To see your enemy and know him is part of the complete education of man.
Marcus Garvey, 1887–1940
Nationalist leader

781. You can be educated in some vision and feeling as well as in mind.

Marcus Garvey, 1887–1940
Nationalist leader

782. Generally, standardized tests don't serve African American children well at all.

Judith Griffin

783. When a griot dies, it is as if a library has burned to the ground.

Alex Haley, 1921–1992
Writer

784. Although you are deprived of the means of education; yet you are not deprived of the means of meditation.

Prince Hall, 1735–1807
Masonic founder

785. The struggle to get an education was the best part of my education.

Gordon Blaine Hancock, 1884–1970
Minister and Sociologist

786. When a school child remains unchallenged, he or she will shut down and lose interest in learning altogether.

Bessie Hogan

787. Many of our institutions apparently are not trying to make men and women of their students at all. They are doing their best to produce spineless Uncle Toms, uninformed, and full of mental and moral evasions.

Langston Hughes, 1902–1967
Poet and Writer

788. It is hard to apply oneself to study when there is no money to pay for food and lodging.

Zora Neale Hurston, 1891–1960
Writer and Folklorist

789. Education remains the key to both economic and political empowerment. that is why the schools charged with educating African Americans have, perhaps, the greatest, the deepest challenge of all.

Barbara Jordan, 1936–1996
Lawyer and U.S. Congressperson

790. I only went through tenth grade, but you'll see all kinds of textbooks around me. The more popular I become, the more I miss education. whether you play blues or whatever, don't let people keep you like you were.

B.B. King, 1925–
Blues musician

791. The function of education is teach one to think intensively and to think critically. Intelligence plus character—that is the goal of true education.

Martin Luther King Jr., 1929–1968
Civil rights activist and Nobel laureate

792. Nothing in the world is more dangerous than sincere ignorance and conscientious stupidity.

Martin Luther King Jr., 1929–1968
Civil rights activist and Nobel laureate

793. Schooling is what happens inside the walls of the school, some of which is educational. Education happens everywhere, and it happens from the moment a child is born—and some people say before—until it dies.

Sara Lawrence-Lightfoot, 1944–
Writer and Academic

794. The combined opposition cannot prevent us from advancing so long as we have the road to books and schools open to us.

Benjamin Lee, 1841–1926
Educator

795. Education meant the death of the institution of slavery in this country, and the slave owners took good care that their slaves got none of it.

Nat "Deadwood Dick, the cowboy adventurer" Love, 1854–?
Cowboy

796. As a black child, just attending school is almost an act of sedition.

Miriam Makeba, 1932–
Singer

797. Your knowledge, your education is your husband. Your husband may leave you, but what you have in your mind will never leave you.

Miriam Makeba, 1932–
Singer

798. Our purpose is to educate as well as to entertain.

Curtis Mayfield, 1942–
Songwriter and Singer

799. If you can't go to Morehouse, go to Harvard.

Benjamin Mays, 1895–1984
Educator

800. The mind is like the body. If you don't work actively to protect its health, you can lose it, especially if you're a black man, 19 years old and wondering, as I was, if you were born into the wrong world.

Nathan McCall

801. I learned quickly that education was the best vehicle to begin overturning a status quo that historically repressed and marginalized our race.

Kweisi Mfume
NAACP official

802. If you can't count, they can cheat you. If you can't read, they can beat you.

Toni Morrison, 1931–
Novelist and Nobel laureate

803. The education and training of our children must not be limited to the "Three Rs" only. It should instead include the history of the black nation, the knowledge of civilizations of man and the universe, and all sciences.

Elijah Muhammad, 1897–1975
Nation of Islam leader

804. It is hard to apply oneself to study. We have been to their schools and gone as far as they allowed us to go.

Elijah Muhammad, 1897–1975
Nation of Islam leader

805. Our kids hear terrible things about themselves. They hear they are incapable of learning.

Aynim Palmer

806. In order to be a truly knowledgeable person, one has got to be engaged in serious, systematic learning.

Benjamin Payton, 1932–
Educator

807. There is one sin that slavery committed against me which I can never forgive. It robbed me of my education. The injury is irreparable.

James W.C. Pennington, 1807?–1870
Scholar and Minister

808. The army provides an educational system that is better than the public schools in many cities.

Alvin Poussaint, 1934–
Psychiatrist

809. Literacy not only affects members of the "underclass," but reaches into the centers of higher education.

Ishmael Reed, 1938–
Dramatist

810. I assume that if the students are in my class, they're here to learn. I emphasize hard work, It's hard work that separates so-called geniuses from the also-rans.

Abdulalim Sahibs

811. More and more African American parents have concluded that the nation's public schools are failing to meet their children's needs.

Charlene Solomon

812. One may receive the information, but miss the teaching.

Jean Toomer, 1894–1967
Novelist

813. For colored people to acquire learning in this country makes tyrants quake and tremble in their sandy foundation.

David Walker, 1785–1830
Abolitionist

814. The black man must be given the training necessary to offset the influences of slavery.

Booker T. Washington, 1856–1915
Educator

815. Does ignorance produce more taxable property than intelligence? Are jails and courts and chain gangs less costly than schoolhouses? Is an ignorant citizen more valuable than an intelligent citizen?

Booker T. Washington, 1856–1915
Educator

816. Education is the sole and only hope of the Negro race in America.

Booker T. Washington, 1856–1915
Educator

817. The first thing to do is to get into every school, private, public, or otherwise, Negro literature and history. We aren't trying to displace other literature but trying to acquaint all children with Negro history and literature.

Booker T. Washington, 1856–1915
Educator

818. The great problem confronting us, as race, is, what to do with the education we have in our heads.

Booker T. Washington, 1856–1915
Educator

819. How can you teach book learning to people who are hungry and without proper shelter and know nothing about good living?

Booker T. Washington, 1856–1915
Educator

820. I plead for industrial education and development for the Negro, not because I want to cramp him, but because I want to free him. I want to see him enter the all-powerful business and commercial world.

Booker T. Washington, 1856–1915
Educator

821. Never get to the point where you will be ashamed to ask anybody for information. The ignorant man will always be ignorant if he fears that by asking another for information he will display ignorance. Better once display your ignorance of a certain subject than always know nothing of it.

Booker T. Washington, 1856–1915
Educator

822. No schoolhouse has been opened for us that has not been filled.

Booker T. Washington, 1856–1915
Educator

823. The schools in the country districts in the South rarely last over three months and a half in a year, and are usually held in a church, a wreck of a log cabin, or under a bush arbor.

Booker T. Washington, 1856–1915
Educator

824. We must do something and we must do it now. We must educate the white people out of their 250 years of slave history.

Ida B. Wells, 1862–1931
Militant activist

825. History shows that just as thorough education in the belief in the inequality of the races has brought the world to the cat-and-dog stage of religious and racial strife, so may thorough education in the equality of the races bring about a reign of brotherhood through an appreciation of all races, creeds, and colors.

Carter G. Woodson, 1875–1950
Historian

826. The mere imparting of information is not education. Above all things, the effort must result in making a man think and do for himself.

Carter G. Woodson, 1875–1950
Historian

827. Real education means to inspire people to live more abundantly, to learn to live with life as they find it and make it better.

Carter G. Woodson, 1875–1950
Historian

828. The same educational process which inspires and stimulates the oppressor with the thought that he is everything and has accomplished everything worthwhile, depresses and crushes at the same time the spark of genius in the Negro by making him feel that his race does not amount to much and never will measure up to the standards of other peoples.

Carter G. Woodson, 1875–1950
Historian

829. Education is our passport to the future, for tomorrow belongs to the people who prepare for it today.

Malcolm X, 1925–1965
Nationalist leader

EGYPT
See Africa

EMANCIPATION

830. [Slaves] were set free without a dollar, without a foot of land, and without the wherewithal to get the next meal even, and this too by a great Christian nation.

H.C. Bruce, 1836–?
Writer

831. I stand here tonight to advance in my humble way, the unrestricted and complete Emancipation of every slave in the United States whether claimed by loyal or disloyal masters.

Frederick Douglass, 1817?–1895
Abolitionist and Autobiographer

832. When the Russian serfs had their chains broken and were given their liberty, the government of Russia—aye, the despotic government of Russia—gave to these poor emancipated serfs a few acres of land on which they would live and earn their bread. But when you turned us loose, you gave us no acres. You turned us loose to the sky, to the storm, to the whirlwind, and, worst of all, you turned us loose to the wrath of our infuriated masters.

Frederick Douglass, 1817?–1895
Abolitionist and Autobiographer

833. The nation has not yet found peace from its sin; the freedman has not yet found his promised land.

W.E.B. Du Bois, 1868–1963
Intellectual and Activist

834. After the coming of freedom there were two points upon which practically all the people on our place were agreed … that they must change their names, and that they must leave the old plantation for at least a few days or weeks in order that they might really feel sure that they were free.

Booker T. Washington, 1856–1915
Educator

EMIGRATION

835. I believe that the Negroid race has been free long enough now to begin to think for himself and plan for better conditions than he can lay claim to in this country or ever will. There is no manhood future in the United States for the Negro.… I believe that two or three millions of us should return to the land of our ancestors, and establish our own nation.

Henry McNeal Turner, 1834–1915
Minister and Militant activist

EMPLOYMENT
See Work

ENCOURAGEMENT

836. The people in the church did not contribute one dime to help me with my education. But they gave me something far more valuable. They gave me encouragement.

Benjamin Mays, 1895–1984
Educator

ENDURANCE

837. "Seek first the Kingdom of God and its righteousness and all these other things will be added unto you." This means endurance now, liberty later.

James Cone, 1938–
Theologian

ENTREPRENEURSHIP
See Business

EQUALITY

838. The American Negro demands equality—political equality, industrial equality, and social equality; and he is never going to rest satisfied with anything else.

W.E.B. Du Bois, 1868–1963
Intellectual and Activist

839. Colored Americans, in their fight for equality, must disabuse white people's minds of the opinion that the only equality the Negro desires is the association of white people.

Jessie Fauset, 1882–1961
Writer

840. If we are not struggling for equality, in heaven's name for what are we living?

John Hope, 1868–1936
Educator

841. The only way to get equality is for two people to get the same thing at the same time at the same place.

Thurgood Marshall, 1908–1993
U.S. Supreme Court Justice

842. Equality is the heart and essence of democracy, freedom, and justice.

A. Philip Randolph, 1889–1979
Labor leader

843. If the great laboring masses of people, black and white, are kept forever snarling over the question as to who is superior or inferior, they will take a long time to combine for achievement of a common benefit.

A. Philip Randolph, 1889–1979
Labor leader

844. The Negro struggle has hardly run its course; and it will not stop moving until it has been utterly defeated or won substantial equality. But I fail to see how the movement can be victorious in the absence of radical programs for full employment, the abolition of slums, the reconstruction of our education system, new definitions of work and leisure.

Bayard Rustin, 1910–1977
Civil rights activist

845. The real radical is that person who has a vision of equality and is willing to do those things that will bring reality closer to that vision.

Bayard Rustin, 1910–1977
Civil rights activist

846. God is just. When he created man he made him in his image and never intended one should misuse the other. All men are born free and equal in his sight.

Susie King Taylor, 1848–1912
Former slave and Army nurse

847. The wisest among my race understand that the agitation of questions of social equality is the extremist folly.

Booker T. Washington, 1856–1915
Educator

ETHNICITY

848. W.E.B. Du Bois predicted that the problem of the 20th century would be the color line ... the problem of the 21st century will be that of ethnic difference.

Henry Louis Gates Jr., 1950–
Scholar and Critic

EVIL

849. I have seen the devil by day and by night, and have seen him in you and in me, in the eyes of the cop and the sheriff and the deputy, the landlord, the housewife, the football player, in the eyes of some junkies, eyes of preachers, governors, wardens, orphans, presidents, and in the eyes of my father, and in my mirror.

James Baldwin, 1924–1987
Writer and Activist

850. It is not a persuasive argument than an evil should continue because it has existed in the past.

William H. Hastie, 1904–1976
Lawyer and Judge

851. I am on the thin side of evil and trying not to break through.

Toni Morrison, 1931–
Novelist and Nobel laureate

852. The purpose of evil was to survive it.

Toni Morrison, 1931–
Novelist and Nobel laureate

853. A devil is a mental attitude born out of false pride and self-exalting lies.

Herbert Muhammad, 1928–
Nation of Islam leader

854. The major struggle I've had through my years of reading and writing is coming to terms with the problem of evil, undeserved harm, and unjustified suffering. And the major form of evil in American civilization is white supremacy.

Cornel West, 1954–
Philosopher and Activist

EXPECTATIONS

855. No one rises to low expectations.

Les Brown, 1945–
Motivational speaker

856. You have to expect things of yourself before you can do them.

Michael Jordan, 1961–
Basketball star

EXPERIENCE

857. Experience, which destroys innocence, also leads one back to it.

James Baldwin, 1924–1987
Writer and Activist

EXPLOITATION

858. I cannot tolerate black exploitation of black people any more than I can tolerate it from white people.

Louis Farrakhan, 1934–
Nation of Islam leader

FAILURE

859. I felt that, should I fail, it would be ascribed to the fact that I was Colored.

Frances Coppin, 1837–1913
Educator and Civic leader

860. Failure is not a fatal disease.

Earl G. Graves Jr., 1935–
Publishing executive

861. Treat failure as practice shots.

Deborah McGriff, 1949–
Educator

862. Failure is another stepping stone to greatness.

Oprah Winfrey, 1954–
Entertainer

FAITH

863. A person without faith has no future.

Michael J. Cheatham

864. The language of faith is crucial because it affords human beings the privilege of intimacy with the ultimate.

Michael Eric Dyson, 1958–
Scholar and Writer

865. As I reflect down the vistas of the past, as I think about all the problems and all the experiences I have had; without a faith in God, a faith in prayer, and a disposition of loyalty to God, I don't know what I would have done.

C.L. Franklin, 1918–1984
Minister

866. Here lies the dust of a poor hell-deserving sinner, who ventured into eternity trusting wholly on the merits of Christ for salvation.

Lemuel Haynes, 1753–1833
Minister and Writer

867. To believe is to become what you believe.

June Jordan, 1936–
Poet and Essayist

FAMILY

868. It was the Lord who knew of the impossibility every parent in that room faced: how to prepare the child for the day when the child would be despised and how to create in the child—by what means?—a stronger antidote to this poison than one had found for oneself.

James Baldwin, 1924–1987
Writer and Activist

869. The function of the family is to celebrate the triumphs and heroes of the black struggle and to remember the defeats.

Janice Hall Benson
Psychologist

870. Family faces are ... mirrors. Looking at people who belong to us, we see the past, present, and future.

Gail Lumet Buckley, 1937–
Writer

871. No one family form— nuclear, extended, single-parent, matrilineal, fictive, residential, nonresidential—necessarily provides an environment better for humans to live or raise children in.

Johnnetta Cole, 1936–
Educator

872. My only recollections of my own mother are of a few hasty visits made in the night on foot, after the daily tasks were over.

Frederick Douglass, 1817?–1895
Abolitionist and Autobiographer

873. Of my father I know nothing. Slavery had no recognition of fathers, as none of families.

Frederick Douglass, 1817?–1895
Abolitionist and Autobiographer

874. If you are a parent, recognize that it is the most important calling and rewarding challenge you have. What you do every day, what you say and how you act, will do more to shape the future of America than any other factor.

Marian Wright Edelman, 1939–
Children's Defense Fund official

875. They have forgotten the struggle.... and they have forgotten the road over which we have come, and they are not teaching it to their children.

Alex Haley, 1921–1992
Writer

876. The true accolade was not only my father saying he was pleased, but that my grandmother would have been proud of me.

William H. Hastie, 1904–1976
Lawyer and Judge

877. What I most remember was an abiding sense of comfort and security. I got plenty of mothering, not only from Pop and my brothers and sisters when they were home, but from the whole of our close-knit community.

Paul Robeson, 1898–1976
Singer and Activist

878. It is the family that gives us a deep private sense of belonging. Here we first begin to have our self defined for us.

Howard Thurman, 1899–1981
Minister

879. A man must be at home somewhere before he can feel at home everywhere.

Howard Thurman, 1899–1981
Minister

FATE

880. We are all puppets in the hands of fate and seldom see the strings that move us.

Charles W. Chesnutt, 1858–1932
Novelist

881. Fate is determined by what one does and what one doesn't do.

Ralph Ellison, 1914–1994
Novelist

FATHERS
See Family

FEAR

882. Never, never let a person know you're frightened.

Maya Angelou, 1928–
Novelist and Poet

883. To defend one's self against fear is simply to insure that one will, one day, be conquered by it; fears must be faced.

James Baldwin, 1924–1987
Writer and Activist

884. I was afraid because I was ignorant.

Tawana Brawley
Crime subject

885. Lord, make me so uncomfortable that I will do the very thing I fear.

Ruby Dee, 1923–
Actor

886. Most fear stems from sin: to limit one's sins assuredly limits one's fears, thereby bringing more peace to one's spirit.

Marvin Gaye, 1939–1984
Singer and Composer

887. Fear causes people to do the easy thing, the quickest thing.

Evander Holyfield, 1962–
Boxing champion

888. When I dare ... to use my strength in the service of my vision, then it becomes less and less important whether I am afraid.

Audre Lorde, 1934–1992
Writer

889. Fear is a two-edged sword that sometimes cuts the wielder.

Jackie Robinson, 1919–1972
Baseball star

890. To be afraid is to be behave as if the truth were not true.

Bayard Rustin, 1910–1997
Civil rights activist

891. He who fears is literally delivered to destruction.

Howard Thurman, 1899–1981
Minister

892. Fear is a noose that binds until it strangles.

Jean Toomer, 1894–1967
Novelist

FIGHTING

893. Sometimes it's worse to win a fight than to lose.

Billie Holiday, 1915–1959
Blues singer

894. Fighting is a game where everybody is the loser.

Zora Neale Hurston, 1891–1960
Writer and Folklorist

FOLK SAYINGS

895. All I HAVE to do is be black and die.

Anonymous
Traditional

896. The blacker the berry, the sweeter the juice.
Anonymous
Traditional

897. Every shut-eye ain't sleep and every good-bye ain't gone.
Anonymous
Traditional

898. Jesus! No man works like him. He builds a platform in the air and calls the saints from everywhere.
Anonymous
Traditional

899. Mothers raise their daughters and let their sons grow up.
Anonymous
Traditional

900. Romance without finance don't stand a chance.
Anonymous
Traditional

901. This world ain't no friend to grace.
Anonymous
Traditional

902. We ain't what we want to be, we ain't what we're gonna be, but thank God we ain't what we was.
Anonymous
Traditional

903. What goes around, comes around.
Anonymous
Traditional

FOLKLORE

904. Nothing has been done in Negro folklore when the greatest cultural wealth of the continent was disappearing without the world ever realizing it had ever been.

Zora Neale Hurston, 1891–1960
Writer and Folklorist

FOURTH OF JULY

905. What to the American Slave is your Fourth of July? I answer: a day that reveals to him, more than all other days of the year, the gross injustice and cruelty to which he is the constant victim. To him, your celebration is a sham, your boasted liberty an unholy license, your national greatness, swelling vanity; your sounds of rejoicing are empty and heartless; your denunciation of tyrants, brass-fronted impudence; your shouts of liberty and equality, hollow mockery; your prayers and hymns, your sermons and thanksgiving, with all your religious parade and solemnity, are to him mere bombast, fraud, deception, impiety, and hypocrisy, a thin veil to cover up crimes which would disgrace a nation of savages.

Frederick Douglass, 1817?–1895
Abolitionist and Autobiographer

906. The Fourth of July—memorable in the history of our nation as the great day of independence to its countrymen—had no claim upon our sympathies. They made a flag and threw it to the heavens and bid it float forever; but every star in it was against us.

Henry McNeal Turner, 1834–1915
Minister and Militant activist

FREEDOM

907. All human beings are born free and equal in dignity and rights.

Anonymous
Universal Declaration of Human Rights, 1948, Article 1

908. In Mississippi there is a town called Freedom; in Washington there is a Department called Justice.

Anonymous
Civil Rights Movement saying

909. There is no way to freedom; freedom is the way.

Anonymous
Civil Rights Movement saying

910. What do we want? Freedom! / When do we want it? Now!

Anonymous
Civil Rights Movement chant

911. Every man has a place in the world, but no man has the right to designate that place.

Pearl Bailey, 1918–1990
Entertainer

912. Black freedom will make white freedom possible. Indeed, our freedom, which we have been forced to buy at so high a price, is the only hope of freedom that they have.

James Baldwin, 1924–1987
Writer and Activist

913. Freedom is the fire which burns away illusion.

James Baldwin, 1924–1987
Writer and Activist

914. A man is either free or he is not. There cannot be any apprenticeship for freedom.

Amiri Baraka, 1934–
Poet and Writer

915. When people seek freedom, they are always impatient.

Ralph Bunche, 1904–1971
Statesman

916. Here we stand on the edge of the twenty-first century and still we are not free.

Johnnetta Cole, 1936–
Educator

917. A man is free when he can determine the style of his existence in an absurd world.

James Cone, 1938–
Theologian

918. A man is free when he sees himself for what he is and not as others define him.

James Cone, 1938–
Theologian

919. We are all foot soldiers on the march to freedom, here and everywhere.

David Dinkins, 1927–
Politician

920. Who would be free themselves must strike the blow.

Frederick Douglass, 1817?–1895
Abolitionist and Autobiographer

921. Freedom always entails danger.

W.E.B. Du Bois, 1868–1963
Intellectual and Activist

922. Freedom is a state of mind: a spiritual unchoking of the wells of human power and superhuman love.

W.E.B. Du Bois, 1868–1963
Intellectual and Activist

923. The most rewarding freedom is freedom of the mind.

Amy Jacques Garvey, 1896–1973
Nationalist leader

924. Radicalism is a label that is always applied to the people who are endeavoring to get freedom.

Marcus Garvey, 1887–1940
Nationalist leader

925. Freedom without organization is chaos. I want to put freedom into music the way I conceive it. It is free, but it's organized freedom.

Dizzy Gillespie (John Birks Gillespie), 1917–1993
Jazz musician

926. The free man is the man with no fears.

Dick Gregory, 1932–
Comedian and Activist

927. It may be that God himself has written upon both my heart and brain a commission to use time, talent and energy in the cause of freedom.

Frances Ellen Watkins Harper, 1825–1911
Writer and Women's rights advocate

928. No man may make another free. Freedom was something internal. The outside signs were just signs and symbols of the man inside. All you could do was to give the opportunity for freedom and the man himself must make his own emancipation.

Zora Neale Hurston, 1891–1960
Writer and Folklorist

929. Freedom, in the larger and higher sense, every man must gain for himself.

Martin Luther King Jr., 1929–1968
Civil rights activist and Nobel laureate

930. Freedom is not free.

Martin Luther King Jr., 1929–1968
Civil rights activist and Nobel laureate

931. What we are seeing now is a freedom explosion....The deep rumbling of discontent that we hear today is the thunder of the disinherited masses, rising from dungeons of oppression to the bright hills of freedom.

Martin Luther King Jr., 1929–1968
Civil rights activist and Nobel laureate

932. When we let freedom ring, when we let it ring from every village and every hamlet, from every state and every city, we will be able to speed up that day when all of God's children, black men and white men, Jews and gentiles, Protestants and Catholics, will be able to join hands and sing in e words of the old Negro spiritual, "Free at last! Free at last! Thank God almighty, we are free at last!"

Martin Luther King Jr., 1929–1968
Civil rights activist and Nobel laureate

933. The fact that I was now free gave me a new born courage to face the world and what the future might hold for me.

Nat "Deadwood Dick, the cowboy adventurer" Love, 1854–?
Cowboy

934. What would have happened when Patrick Henry said, "Give me liberty or give me death," if one of his slaves had stood up and said, "Me, too!"

Otis Moss, 1935–
Minister

935. I was determined to achieve the total freedom that our history lessons taught us we were entitled to, no matter what the sacrifice.

Rosa Parks, 1913–
Civil rights activist

936. My mother believed in freedom and equality even though we didn't know it for reality during our life in Alabama.

Rosa Parks, 1913–
Civil rights activist

937. Freedom is never given; it is won.

A. Philip Randolph, 1889–1979
Labor leader

938. Hunger and lack of freedom always go hand in hand.

Paul Robeson, 1898–1976
Singer and Activist

939. The song of freedom must prevail.

Paul Robeson, 1898–1976
Singer and Activist

940. Who ever walked behind anyone to freedom? If we can't go hand·in hand, I don't want to go.

Hazel Scott, 1920–1981
Pianist

941. I grew up like a neglected weed, ignorant of liberty, having no experience of it. Now that I've been free, I know what a dreadful condition slavery is.

Harriet Tubman, 1820?–1913
Abolitionist

942. I was free, but there was no one to welcome me to the land of freedom. I was a stranger in a strange land.

Harriet Tubman, 1820?–1913
Abolitionist

943. Sometimes you've got to let everything go, purge yourself. I did that, I had nothing, but I had my freedom.....Whatever is bringing you down, get rid of it, Because you'll find that when you're free, your true creativity, your true self comes out.

Tina Turner, 1939–
Singer

944. In the end, freedom is a personal and lonely battle and one faces down fears of today so that those of tomorrow might be engaged.

Alice Walker, 1944–
Writer

945. We must and shall be free I say, in spite of you. You may do your best to keep us in wretchedness and misery, to enrich you and your children, but God will deliver us from under you.

David Walker, 1785–1830
Abolitionist

946. The white man who would close shop or factory against the black man seeking an opportunity to earn an honest living is but half free.

Booker T. Washington, 1856–1915
Educator

947. In every human breast God has implanted a principle which we call love of freedom; it is impatient of oppression, and pants for deliverance; and by the leave of our modern Egyptians, I will assert that the same principle lives in us.

Phillis Wheatley, 1753?–1784
Poet

948. Either we must attain freedom for the whole world or there will be no world left for any of us.

Walter White, 1893–1955
Civil rights activist

949. Freedom is heavy. You got to put your shoulder to freedom. Put your shoulder to it and hope your back hold up.

August Wilson, 1945–
Dramatist

950. The only thing that can free you is the belief that you can be free.

Oprah Winfrey, 1954–
Entertainer

951. Liberty is to come to the Negro, not as a bequest, but as a conquest.

Carter G. Woodson, 1875–1950
Historian

FRIENDS

952. No person is your friend who demands your silence or denies your right to grow.

Alice Walker, 1944–
Writer

953. Surround yourself only with people who are going to lift you higher.

Oprah Winfrey, 1954–
Entertainer

FUTURE

954. We need leadership that thinks about the future and asks us to invest ourselves.

Anita DeFrantz
Lawyer and Athlete

955. I'll wrassle me up a future or die trying.

Zora Neale Hurston, 1891–1960
Writer and Folklorist

956. Facing the rising sun of our new day begun, / Let us march on 'til victory is won.

James Weldon Johnson, 1871–1938
Writer and Activist

957. America is too engrossed with the present to have anything but empty and boastful claims upon the future.

Alain Locke, 1886–1954
Scholar and Critic

958. There is no future for a people who deny their past.

Adam Clayton Powell Jr., 1908–1972
Minister and U.S. Congressperson

959. A large number of our young people are not being prepared for the future. They are losing faith in the promise of America.

Colin Powell, 1937–
U.S. General

960. There is so much to be done, and we are the ones to get it done. You can play a role in your community. Volunteer to be a tutor. Become a mentor.... We have to help our kids one at a time.

Colin Powell, 1937–
U.S. General

961. Nothing the future brings can defeat a people who have come through 300 years of slavery and humiliation and privation with heads high and eyes clear and straight.

Paul Robeson, 1898–1976
Singer and Activist

962. Our future lies chiefly in our own hands.

Paul Robeson, 1898–1976
Singer and Activist

963. Instead of always looking at the past, I put myself ahead twenty years and try to look at what I need to do now in order to get there then.

Diana Ross, 1944–
Singer

964. When I look at the future, it's so bright it burns my eyes.

Oprah Winfrey, 1954–
Entertainer

GAYS AND LESBIANS

965. Our churches sometimes promote these irrational feelings and behaviors. Like the idea that gay or lesbian people can't take good care of children.

Joycelyn Elders, 1933–
U.S. Surgeon General

966. There are in the military gay and lesbian and bisexual people of African American descent already. We have come over a path that with tears has been watered.

Elias Farajaje-Jones
DC Coalition of Black Gay Men representative

967. It is very important for anxious and paranoid heterosexuals to realize that the world is filled with perfectly capable, well-adjusted, competent homosexuals. Homosexuality is not a deviation, it is a variation. And people need to know that.

Peter J. Gomes, 1942–
Minister

968. I was wearing makeup and eyelashes when no men were wearing that.

Little Richard (Richard Penniman), 1935–
Entertainer

969. I am a black lesbian and I am your sister.

Audre Lorde, 1934–1992
Writer

970. When I see a white, gay man who is a national bank executive and owns a home and cottage, do I see someone from my community as a black, femme, lesbian writer, filmmaker, and artist? Do I need to?

Roberta M. Munroe
Journalist

971. I just don't see why everyone has to be labeled. I just don't think words like homosexual or gay do anything for anybody.

Bruce Nugent, 1906–1987
Artist and Writer

GENDER

972. You have to be able—be willing—to teach your son, just as you would teach your daughter, what it is to respect another human being.

Andrea Thompson Adam, 1944–
Los Angeles Commission on Assaults Against Women official

973. It is one of the facts of life that there are two sexes, which fact has given the world most of its beauty, cost it not a little of its anguish, and contains the hope and glory of the world.

James Baldwin, 1924–1987
Writer and Activist

974. The emotional, sexual, and psychological stereotyping of females begins when the doctor says, "It's a girl."

Shirley Chisholm, 1924–
Politician

975. Of my two "handicaps," being female put many more obstacles in my path than being black.

Shirley Chisholm, 1924–
Politician

976. We are free to say that in respect to political rights, we hold women to be justly entitled to all we claim for men.

Frederick Douglass, 1817?–1895
Abolitionist and Autobiographer

977. The future woman must have a life work and economic independence. she must have the right of motherhood at her own discretion.
W.E.B. Du Bois, 1868–1963
Intellectual and Activist

978. For black and white women, gendered identity was reconstructed and represented in very different, indeed antagonistic, racialized contexts.
Evelyn Brooks Higginbotham, 1945–
Scholar

979. Sojourner Truth's famous and haunting question "Ain't I a woman?" laid bare the racialized configuration of gender under a class rule that compelled and expropriated women's physical labor and denied them the legal right to their own bodies and sexuality.
Evelyn Brooks Higginbotham, 1945–
Scholar

980. The invocation of cultural excuses for gender subordination and abuse is not only a distortion of community mores, it is a manipulative excuse for illegal behavior.
Anita Hill, 1956–
Law professor

981. Slavery is terrible for men, but it is far more terrible for women. Superadded to the burden common to all, they have wrongs and sufferings and mortifications peculiarly their own.
Harriet Jacobs, 1813–1887
Former slave autobiographer

982. It's important not only for a little black girl growing up to know, yeah, you can become an astronaut because here's Mae Jemison. But it's important for older white males who sometimes make decisions on those careers of those little black girls.
Mae Jemison, 1956–
Astronaut

983. Feminism is the political theory and practice that struggles to free all women: women of color, working-class women, poor women, disabled women, lesbians, old women—as well as white, economically privileged, heterosexual women. Anything less than this vision of total freedom is not feminism, but merely female self-aggrandizement.

Barbara Smith, 1946–
Writer and Publisher

984. My race and my gender have never been an issue for me, I have been blessed in knowing who I am and I am part of a great legacy.

Oprah Winfrey, 1954–
Entertainer

GENOCIDE

985. Genocide is the logical conclusion of racism.

James Cone, 1938–
Theologian

GHETTO

986. [The ghetto is] a kind of concentration camp, and not many people survive it.

James Baldwin, 1924–1987
Writer and Activist

987. New solutions [to urban problems] must not follow the pattern of the last 30 years, where government support was the primary vehicle for change. The future will depend largely on job creation in inner-city neighborhoods. The inner city must be transformed into a stable community providing opportunities for those coming off of welfare. There must also be major investments in all forms of education, whether public, private, or parochial.

Floyd Flake
Minister

988. We cannot be satisfied as long as the Negro's basic mobility is from a smaller ghetto to a larger one.

Martin Luther King Jr., 1929–1968
Civil rights activist and Nobel laureate

989. The streets had been my stomping ground, my briar patch. the place I'd fled from with all my might, the place always snatching me back.

John Edgar Wideman, 1941–
Novelist

GIVING

990. Having been given, I must give.

Paul Robeson, 1898–1976
Singer and Activist

GOALS

991. Racism is not an excuse to not do the best you can.

Arthur Ashe, 1943–1993
Tennis champion

992. My people, all they want is a place where they can be people, a place where they can stand up and be part of that place, just being natural to the place without worrying how someone may be coming along to take that place away from them.

Sidney Bechet, 1897–1959
Jazz musician

993. Strive to make something of yourself; then strive to make the most of yourself.

Alexander Crummell, 1819–1898
Minister and Scholar

994. If a slave has a bad master, his ambition is to get a better one; when he does get a better, he aspires to have the best; and when he gets the best, he aspires to be his own master.

Frederick Douglass, 1817?–1895
Abolitionist and Autobiographer

995. Our strength is that with the total society saying to us, " NO, NO, NO, NO," we continue to move toward our goal.

Ralph Ellison, 1914–1994
Novelist

996. Up, you mighty race. You can accomplish what you will.

Marcus Garvey, 1887–1940
Nationalist leader

997. I am old enough to know that victory is often a thing deferred, and rarely at the summit of courage .... What is at the summit of courage, I think, is freedom. The freedom that comes with the knowledge that no earthly thing can break you.

Paula Giddings, 1947–
Writer and Educator

998. Greatness is not measured by what a man or woman accomplishes, but the opposition he or she has to overcome to reach his or her goals.

Dorothy Height, 1912–
National Council of Negro Women official

999. I always had something to shoot for each year: to jump one inch farther.

Jackie Joyner-Kersee, 1962–
Olympic champion

1000. Did you ever have a goal and still not know where you're going? I knew I wasn't going to stay where I was, but I wasn't sure just where I was going.

Joe Louis, 1914–1981
Boxing champion

1001. The tragedy in life doesn't lie in not reaching your goal. The tragedy lies in having no goal to reach.

Benjamin Mays, 1895–1984
Educator

1002. I knew that whatever I set my mind to do, I could do.

Wilma Rudolph, 1940–1994
Olympic track star

1003. When I was in the third grade I wanted to be president. I can still remember the stricken look on my teacher's face when I announced it in class. By the time I was in the fourth grade I had decided to be the president's wife instead. It never occurred to be I could be neither because I was black.

Michelle Wallace, 1952–
Journalist

1004. I decided that for the rest of my life, I was going to make the world a better place, to fight for justice. Also to be able to read and write the way James Brown danced and the way Aretha Franklin sang.

Cornel West, 1954–
Philosopher and Activist

1005. It is impossible for a people to rise above their aspirations. If we think we cannot, we almost certainly cannot. Our greatest enemy is our defeatist attitude.

Robert Williams, 1925–1996
Militant activist

1006. Everything the Negro does has to do with his image of himself and his aspirations. It involves human as well as racial fulfillment.

Hale Woodruff, 1900–1980
Painter

1007. In the ghettoes the white man has built for us, he has forced us not to aspire to greater things, but to view life as survival.

Malcolm X, 1925–1965
Nationalist leader

GOD

1008. People see God every day; they just don't recognize him.

Pearl Bailey, 1918–1990
Entertainer

1009. God is a means of liberation and not a means to control others.

James Baldwin, 1924–1987
Writer and Activist

1010. Only the Lord saw the midnight tears.

James Baldwin, 1924–1987
Writer and Activist

1011. Our creator is the same and never changes despite the names given him by people here and in all parts of the world.

George Washington Carver, 1864?–1943
Inventor

1012. We are one of the few peoples on the face of the earth who do not worship a God that reflects us.

Camille Cosby, 1945–
Philanthropist

1013. Remember that in a contest with oppression, the Almighty has no attribute which can take sides with oppressors.

Frederick Douglass, 1817?–1895
Abolitionist and Autobiographer

1014. Surely, Thou too art not white, O Lord, a pale bloodless, heartless thing?

W.E.B. Du Bois, 1868–1963
Intellectual and Activist

1015. God is always capable of making something out of nothing.

Louis Farrakhan, 1934–
Nation of Islam leader

1016. The Spirit of the Consciousness of the Presence of God is the source of all supply. It can and it will and it actually does satisfy every good desire.

Father Divine, 1879–1965
Religious leader

1017. With sincere wishes to you, declaring that you and all concerned might be even as I Am, this leaves ME Well, Healthy, Joyful, Peaceful, Lively, Loving, Successful, Prosperous, and Happy in Spirit, Body, and Mind and in every organ, muscle, sinew, joint, limb, vein, and bone and even in every ATOM, fiber, and cell of MY BODILY FORM.

Father Divine, 1879–1965
Religious leader

1018. We have gradually won our way back into the confidence of the God of Africa, and he shall speak with the voice of thunder, that shall shake the pillars of a corrupt and unjust world, and once more restore Ethiopia to her ancient glory.

Marcus Garvey, 1887–1940
Nationalist leader

1019. Holy ground is not a place of pilgrimage: it is where you are when God finds you.

Peter J. Gomes, 1942–
Minister

1020. The one thing more than anything else that I wish for you is to discover that you are not alone, and that the stranger in the fire with you is God. That discovery is the discovery of God in your life and work, and I could wish no greater discovery for you—here and now—than that, and when you have discovered that, you have discovered everything.

Peter J. Gomes, 1942–
Minister

1021. Gangway! Gangway for de Lawd, God Jehovah.

Richard B. Harrison, 1864–1935
Actor

1022. Sometimes God has to get you alone by yourself so he can talk to your head.

T.D. Jakes
Evangelist

1023. God discovered that man when Moses killed the Egyptian brutally beating a defenseless Hebrew slave. It was then that God summoned an angel to go down and get that man's name and address, for I can use him.

Vernon Johns
Minister

1024. We've got some difficult days ahead. But it doesn't matter with me now. Because I've been to the mountaintop. And I don't mind. Like anybody, I would like to live a long life. Longevity has its place. But I'm not concerned about that now. I just want to do God's will. And he's allowed me to go up to the mountain. And I've looked over. And I've seen the promised land.

Martin Luther King Jr., 1929–1968
Civil rights activist and Nobel laureate

1025. Erase the white gods from your hearts. We must go back to our own native church to our own God.

George Alexander McGuire, 1866–1934
African Orthodox Church founder

1026. We poor creatures have need to believe in God, for if God Almighty will not be good to us some day, why were we born? When I heard of his delivering his people from bondage, I know it means the poor African.

Polly
Slave

1027. We have tried all the courts of the land with no avail; now let us try the courts of Heaven, with an unshakable confidence in Him, with patience to wait until change comes.

Reverdy C. Ransom, 1861–1959
Minister

1028. God revealed himself ... with all the suddenness of a flash of lightning, showing ... that he pervaded the universe and that there was no place where God was not.

Sojourner Truth, 1797?–1883
Abolitionist and Women's rights advocate

1029. Every race of people since time began who have attempted to describe God by words or painting, or by carvings, have conveyed the idea that the God who made them and shaped their destinies was symbolized in themselves, and why should not the Negro believe that he resembles God as much as other people?

Henry McNeal Turner, 1834–1915
Minister and Militant activist

1030. We have as much right biblically and otherwise to believe that God is a Negro as white people have to believe that God is a fine-looking, symmetrical, and ornamental white man.

Henry McNeal Turner, 1834–1915
Minister and militant activist

1031. I think it pisses God off if you walk by the color purple in a field somewhere and don't notice it.

Alice Walker, 1944–
Writer

1032. If a person is to be freed from his frustrations and insecurities, he must surrender to something larger than himself.

Herman Watts
Minister

1033. All my work is about intimacy—God in all those places of intimacy and pain and contradiction.

Renita Weems
Seminary professor

1034. What God has intended for you goes far beyond anything you can imagine.

Oprah Winfrey, 1954–
Entertainer

GOODNESS
See Morality

GOVERNMENT

1035. In a great city, City Hall must be a beacon to the people's aspirations, not a barrier.

Thomas Bradley, 1917–
Politician

1036. To change the character of the government at this point is neither possible nor desirable. All that is necessary to be done is to make the government consistent with itself, and render the rights of the states consistent with the sacred rights of human nature.

Frederick Douglass, 1817?–1895
Abolitionist and Autobiographer

1037. A government which can protect and defend its citizens from wrong and outrage and does not is vicious. A government which would do it and cannot is weak.

Frances Ellen Watkins Harper, 1825–1911
Writer and Orator

1038. A government which has the power to tax a man in peace, draft him in war, should have power to defend his life in the hour of peril.

Frances Ellen Watkins Harper, 1825–1911
Writer and Orator

1039. This administration [of New York City Mayor Rudolph Giuliani] is like the Rocky Mountains. The higher up you go, the whiter it gets.

Al Sharpton, 1955–
Minister and Activist

1040. Creative federalism stresses local initiative, local solutions to local problems. But where the obvious needs for action to meet an urban problem are not being fulfilled, the federal government has a responsibility.

Robert C. Weaver, 1907–1997
U.S. Secretary of Housing

1041. Do not think you [President Bill Clinton] can balance the budget on the backs of the poor and working people and have a conversation on race on the side.

Cornel West, 1954–
Philosopher and Activist

1042. The American people are not aware of what is really happening.

Frank Wills, 1948–
Watergate security guard

GROWING UP
See Adolescence

GROWTH

1043. It takes a deep commitment to change and an even deeper commitment to grow.

Ralph Ellison, 1914–1994
Novelist

1044. Whenever we stop growing, we start deteriorating.

Louis Farrakhan, 1934–
Nation of Islam leader

1045. Growth always involves the risk of failure.

Howard Thurman, 1899–1981
Minister

1046. Growing is the reward of learning.

Malcolm X, 1925–1965
Nationalist leader

GUILT

1047. I won't allow that word [guilt] in my life, and I've forgotten how to spell it.

Diahann Carroll, 1935–
Singer

HAIR

1048. Hair still works on the minds of many anglicized Africans.

Tony Brown, 1933–
Television producer

1049. The day I looked at myself with a natural was the first time I liked what I saw.

Marita Golden, 1950–
Writer and Educator

1050. We teach you to love the hair that God gave you.

Malcolm X, 1925–1965
Nationalist leader

HAPPINESS

1051. Happiness is like perfume; you can't pour it on somebody else without getting a few drops on yourself.

James Van Der Zee, 1886–1983
Photographer

HARLEM

1052. The subtle, insidious wine of New York will begin to intoxicate.

Paul Laurence Dunbar, 1872–1906
Poet

1053. Stories are legion of African American and African pilgrims progressing to Manhattan then plunging headlong into the ultimate symbolic black cultural space—the city within a city, the "Mecca of the New Negro."

Henry Louis Gates Jr., 1950–
Scholar and Critic

1054. Harlem was like a great magnet for the Negro intellectual, pulling him from everywhere.

Langston Hughes, 1902–1967
Poet and Writer

1055. I was in love with Harlem long before I got there.

Langston Hughes, 1902–1967
Poet and Writer

1056. Melting pot Harlem—Harlem of honey and chocolate and caramel and rum and vinegar and lemon and lime and gall. Dusky dream Harlem running into a nightmare tunnel where the subway from the Bronx keeps right on downtown, where the money from the clubs goes right on back downtown, where the jazz is drained to Broadway.

Langston Hughes, 1902–1967
Poet and Writer

1057. [Harlem] is known as being exotic, colorful, and sensuous: a place where life wakes up at night.

James Weldon Johnson, 1871–1938
Writer and Activist

1058. Harlem is the largest plantation in this country.

John O. Killens, 1916–1987
Novelist

1059. Each group has come [to Harlem] with its own separate motives and for its own special ends, but their greatest experience has been the finding of one another.

Alain Locke, 1886–1954
Scholar and Critic

1060. Harlem is the precious fruit in the Garden of Eden, the big apple.

Alain Locke, 1886–1954
Scholar and Critic

1061. Without pretense to their political significance, Harlem has the same role to play for the New Negro as Dublin had for the New Ireland or Prague for the New Czechoslovakia.

Alain Locke, 1886–1954
Scholar and Critic

1062. Harlem is the queen of the black belt, drawing Aframericans together into a vast humming hive.

Claude McKay, 1889–1948
Writer

1063. It was loving the City that distracted me and gave me ideas. Made me think I could speak in its loud voice and make the sound human.

Toni Morrison, 1931–
Novelist and Nobel laureate

1064. Harlem! Praised. Reviled. Criticized. Ridiculed. Denounced. A lovable hodge-podge of conflicting colors, contradictory movements, extremes in everything, leavened by the saving grace of the good old-fashioned belly laugh. a teeming international city, a gridiron of brick cubicles rescued from obscurity by the blacks.

George Schuyler, 1895–1977
Journalist

HARLEM RENAISSANCE

1065. For the Afro-American in the 1920s, being a "New Negro" was being "modern." And being a "New Negro" meant, largely, not being an "Old Negro," disassociating oneself from the symbols and legacy of slavery—being urbane, assertive, militant.

Nathan Huggins, 1927–1989
Historian

1066. The Negro was in vogue.

Langston Hughes, 1902–1967
Poet and Writer

1067. It is a social disservice to blunt the fact the Negro of the Northern centers has reached a stage where tutelage, even of the most interested and well-intentioned sort, must give place to new relationships, where positive self-direction must be reckoned with in ever-increasing measure.

Alain Locke, 1886–1954
Scholar and Critic

1068. Negro life is not only founding new centers, but finding a new soul.

Alain Locke, 1886–1954
Scholar and Critic

1069. Negro life is seizing upon its first chances of group expression and self-determination.

Alain Locke, 1886–1954
Scholar and Critic

HATE

1001 1000000 1000001 1000001 1001

1070. You lose a lot of time, hating people.

Marian Anderson, 1897–1993
Singer

1071. Hatred, which could destroy so much, never failed to destroy the man who hated.

James Baldwin, 1924–1987
Writer and Activist

1072. I imagine one of the reasons people cling to their hates so stubbornly is because they sense, once the hate is gone, they will be forced to deal with pain.

James Baldwin, 1924–1987
Writer and Activist

1073. My life, my real life, was in danger, and not from anything other people might do but from the hatred I carried in my own heart.

James Baldwin, 1924–1987
Writer and Activist

1074. Remember, to hate, to be violent, is demeaning. It means you're afraid of the other side of the coin—to love and be loved.

James Baldwin, 1924–1987
Writer and Activist

1075. When our thoughts—which bring actions—are filled with hate against anyone, Negro or white, we are in a living hell. That is as real as hell ever will be.

George Washington Carver, 1864?–1943
Inventor

1076. The price of hating other human beings is loving oneself less.

Eldridge Cleaver, 1935–1998
Black Panther Party leader

1077. I used to hate. But as I've matured in the word of God, I now see that hatred has no place here.

Louis Farrakhan, 1934–
Nation of Islam leader

1078. Hate is consuming and weakening. Hateful thinking breeds negative actions.

Marcus Garvey, 1887–1940
Nationalist leader

1079. There is no sense in hate: it comes back to you; therefore make your history so laudable, magnificent, and untarnished that another generation will not seek to repay your seeds for the sins inflicted upon their fathers.

Marcus Garvey, 1887–1940
Nationalist leader

1080. I never learned hate at home, or shame. I had to go to school for that.

Dick Gregory, 1932–
Comedian and Activist

1081. When a man is despised and hated by other men and all around are the instruments of violence in behalf of such attitudes, then he may find himself resorting to hatred as a means of salvaging a sense of self, however fragmented.

Howard Thurman, 1899–1981
Minister

HEALING

1082. As soon as healing takes place, go out and heal somebody else.

Maya Angelou, 1928–
Novelist and Poet

HEALTH

1083. Health is a human right, not a privilege to be purchased.

Shirley Chisholm, 1924–
Politician

1084. A person cannot succeed in anything without a good, sound body—a body that is as able to stand up against hardships, that is able to endure.

Booker T. Washington, 1856–1915
Educator

HEAVEN

1085. There is no heaven or hell in the sense that they are places one goes after death. The heaven or hell to which one goes is right there in the span of years that we spend in this body on earth.

Adam Clayton Powell Jr., 1908–1972
Minister and U.S. Congressperson

1086. Heaven is where you'll be when you are OK right where you are.

Sun Ra, 1914–1993
Musician

HELL

1087. If hell is what we are taught it is, then there will be more Christians there than all the days in creation.

Marcus Garvey, 1887–1940
Nationalist leader

HERITAGE

1088. I had a heritage, rich, and nearer than the tongue which gave it voice. My mind resounded with the words and my blood raced to the rhythm.

Maya Angelou, 1928–
Novelist and Poet

1089. I hope that when my life ends, I would have added a little beauty, perception, and quality for those who follow.

Jacob Lawrence, 1917–
Painter

1090. Children are begging to know who they are. Up until 14, a child needs to have a strong background in his or her heritage before he or she goes out into the world.

Jackie Turnage

1091. Let us not sell our birthright for a thousand worlds, which indeed would be as dust upon the balance.

Phillis Wheatley, 1753?–1784
Poet

1092. We must recapture our heritage and our ideals if we are to liberate ourselves from the bonds of white supremacy. We must launch a cultural revolution to unbrainwash an entire people.

Malcolm X, 1925–1965
Nationalist leader

HEROES

1093. What has suddenly happened is that the white race has lost its heroes. Worse, its heroes have been revealed as villains and its greatest heroes as arch-villains.

Eldridge Cleaver, 1935–1998
Black Panther Party leader

1094. One day the South will recognize its real heroes.

Martin Luther King Jr., 1929–1968
Civil rights activist and Nobel laureate

HISTORY

1095. If you want Negro history you will have to get it from somebody who wore the shoe, and by and by, one to the other, you will get a book.

Anonymous
Former slave

1096. He had no future in the past, because once you leave, you cannot really go back.

James Baldwin, 1924–1987
Writer and Activist

1097. I want American history taught. Unless I'm in the book, you're not in it either. History is not a procession of illustrious people. It's about what happens to a people. Millions of anonymous people is what history is about.

James Baldwin, 1924–1987
Writer and Activist

1098. People are trapped in history and history is trapped in them.

James Baldwin, 1924–1987
Writer and Activist

1099. Which of us has overcome his past?

James Baldwin, 1924–1987
Writer and Activist

1100. History, as taught in our schools, has been a celebration of the white, male, Protestant founding fathers rather than the great mix of people in the American drama.

Mary Frances Berry, 1938–
Historian

1101. History is a clock that people use to tell their time of day. It is a compass they use to find themselves on the map of human geography. It tells them where they are and what they are.

John Henrik Clarke, 1915–
Historian

1102. We are never, absolutely, never to forgive and forget what happened to us.

John Henrik Clarke, 1915–
Historian

1103. Black America must never forget the price paid for today's progress and promise.

Johnnetta Cole, 1936–
Educator

1104. The black man's one great and present hope is to know and understand his Afro-American history.

Harold Cruse, 1916–
Scholar

1105. The story of America is incomplete without history from the bottom up.

Donald DeVore
Amistad Research Center official

1106. If the house is to be set in order, one cannot begin with the present; he must begin with the past.

John Hope Franklin, 1915–
Historian

1107. Racial segregation, discrimination, and degradation are no unantici-pated accidents in this nation's history. They stem logically and directly from the legacy that the founding fathers bestowed upon contemporary America.

John Hope Franklin, 1915–
Historian

1108. American history is a myth and can only be accepted when read with blinders that block out the facts.

Dick Gregory, 1932–
Comedian and Activist

1109. There is black history untold in the memories of the hundreds of thousands of grandmothers, grandfathers, great-aunts.

Alex Haley, 1921–1992
Writer

1110. A people must face its history squarely in order to transcend it.

John O. Killens, 1916–1987
Novelist

1111. Western man wrote "his" history as if it were the history of the entire human race.

John O. Killens, 1916–1987
Novelist

1112. More than anything else, it is important to study history.

B.B. King, 1925–
Blues musician

1113. Sometimes history takes things into its own hands.

Thurgood Marshall, 1908–1993
U.S. Supreme Court Justice

1114. All great people glorify their history and look back upon their early attainments with a spiritual vision.

Kelly Miller, 1863–1939
Educator

1115. I had no idea that history was being made. I was just tired of giving in.

Rosa Parks, 1913–
Civil rights activist

1116. The story of the historical Negro will never be completely known until every book, pamphlet and manuscript on the subject has been found and recorded in bibliographic form.

Dorothy Porter, 1904–1995
Librarian and Bibliographer

1117. The course of history can be changed but not halted.

Paul Robeson, 1898–1976
Singer and Activist

1118. The American Negro must remake his past in order to make his future.

Arthur Schomburg, 1874–1938
Librarian and Book collector

1119. History must restore what slavery took away. For it is the social damage of slavery that the present generation must repair and offset.

Arthur Schomburg, 1874–1938
Librarian and Book collector

1120. Though it is orthodox to think of America as the one country where it is unnecessary to have a past, what is a luxury for the nation as a whole becomes a prime social necessity for the Negro.

Arthur Schomburg, 1874–1938
Librarian and Book collector

1121. We seem lately to have come at least to realize what the true scientific attitude requires, and to see that the race issue has been a plague on both our historical houses, and that history cannot be properly written with either bias or counterbias.

Arthur Schomburg, 1874–1938
Librarian and Book collector

1122. Don't nobody try to tell me to keep quiet and undo my history.

Nate Shaw

1123. History is one long version of "Up from Slavery."

Ibrahim K. Sundiata, 1944–
Scholar

1124. History and experience should not be ignored.

Roy Wilkins, 1901–1981
Civil rights activist

1125. The achievements of the Negro properly set forth will crown him as a factor in early human progress and a maker of modern civilization.

Carter G. Woodson, 1875–1950
Historian

1126. We have a wonderful history behind us .... It reads like the history of a people in a heroic age .... We are going back to that beautiful history and it is going to inspire us to greater achievements.

Carter G. Woodson, 1875–1950
Historian

1127. History is a people's memory, and without a memory, man is demoted to the lower animals.

Malcolm X, 1925–1965
Nationalist leader

1128. Of all our studies, history is the best qualified to reward our research.

Malcolm X, 1925–1965
Nationalist leader

HOME
See Family

HONESTY

1129. This was my weakness [during the U.S. Senate Judiciary committee hearings on Supreme Court nominee Clarence Thomas]—I assumed a level of honesty in the questioning that did not exist.

Anita Hill, 1956–
Law professor

1130. Just be honest. You may only become rich in reputation, but they will record you as a success.

Isaac Murphy, 1856?–1896
Thoroughbred jockey

HOPE

1131. When I used to live in the Brewster Projects, I always thought it would be fantastic to have a phone. I would dream about a phone.

Florence Ballard, 1943–1976
Singer

1132. Hope is delicate suffering.

Amiri Baraka, 1934–
Poet and Writer

1133. Let not the shining thread of hope become so enmeshed in the web of circumstances that we lose sight of it.

Charles W. Chesnutt, 1858–1932
Novelist

1134. In His good time America shall rend the Veil and the prisoner shall go free.

W.E.B. Du Bois, 1868–1963
Intellectual and Activist

1135. Malcolm is gone and Martin is gone, and it up to all of us to nourish the hope they gave us.

Lena Horne, 1917–
Entertainer

1136. It is easy to be hopeful in the day when you can see the things you wish on.

Zora Neale Hurston, 1891–1960
Writer and Folklorist

1137. Keep hope alive!

Jesse Jackson, 1941–
Minister and Civil rights activist

1138. Where there is hope there is life, where there is life there is possibility, and where there is possibility, change can occur.

Jesse Jackson, 1941–
Minister and Civil rights activist

1139. Black folks need to blow out the dim lamp of poverty and turn on the beacon light of hope.

T.J. Jemison, 1918–
Minister

1140. In the middle of the 20th century, the Negro is the new white hope.

John O. Killens, 1916–1987
Novelist

1141. Hope is a song in a weary throat.

Pauli Murray, 1910–1985
Lawyer and Minister

1142. What's happened is that hope has died and secular liberals can't speak to the death of hope.

Eugene Rivers, 1950–
Minister

1143. Rob a people of their sense of history and you take away hope.

Wyatt T. Walker, 1929–
Minister and Civil rights activist

1144. I am a prisoner of hope.

Cornel West, 1954–
Philosopher and Activist

HUMAN NATURE

1145. At its heart, human nature is not random.

Alisa Bierria, 1974–
Philosopher

1146. The world changes, but men are always the same.

Richard Wright, 1908–1960
Novelist

HUMANISM

1147. All the western nations have been caught in a lie, the lie of their pretended humanism.

James Baldwin, 1924–1987
Writer and Activist

1148. Humanism starts not with identity but with the ability to identify with others. It asks what we have in common with others while acknowledging the internal diversity among ourselves. It is about the priority of a shared humanity.

Henry Louis Gates Jr., 1950–
Scholar and Critic

HUMANITY

1149. I speak to the black experience, but I am always talking about the human condition—about what we can endure, dream, fail at, and still survive.

Maya Angelou, 1928–
Novelist and Poet

1150. It is a terrible, an inexorable, law that one cannot deny the humanity of another without diminishing one's own: in the face of one's victim, one sees oneself. Walk through the streets of Harlem and see what we, this nation, have become.

James Baldwin, 1924–1987
Writer and Activist

1151. The workings of the human heart are the profoundest mystery of the universe. One moment they make us despair of our kind, and in the next, we see in them the reflection of the divine image.

Charles W. Chesnutt, 1858–1932
Novelist

1152. You don't have to teach people to be human. You have to teach them how to stop being inhuman.

Eldridge Cleaver, 1935–1998
Black Panther Party leader

1153. I try to say [in art] that the story of mankind, no matter what ethnic nor racial variety, is one story; we are all part of that story, which in a deeper sense of life is a reflection in time of the eternal.

Allan Rohan Crite, 1910–
Artist

1154. [Negroes] must eventually surrender race "solidarity" and the idea of American Negro culture to the concept of world humanity, above race and nation. This is the price of Liberty. This is the cost of Oppression.

W.E.B. Du Bois, 1868–1963
Intellectual and Activist

1155. We are concerned not only about the Negro poor, but the poor all over America and all over the world.

Coretta Scott King, 1927–
Civil rights activist

1156. When a white man in Africa by accident looks into the eyes of a native and sees the human being (which it is his chief preoccupation to avoid), his sense of guilt, which he denies, fumes up in resentment and he brings down the whip.

Doris Lessing, 1919–
Novelist and Writer

1157. Humility is probably the greatest power that one can study, to understand that you didn't create anything. God created it all.

Melba Moore, 1945–
Singer

1158. If the Negro is to be a man, full and complete, he must take part in everything that belongs to manhood. If he omits a single duty, responsibility, or privilege, to that extent he is limited and incomplete.

Henry McNeal Turner, 1834–1915
Minister and Militant activist

1159. More and more we must learn to think not in terms of race or color or language or religion or of political boundaries, but in terms of humanity. Above all races and political boundaries there is humanity.

Booker T. Washington, 1856–1915
Educator

1160. I think one of the problems on the left is that we tend to get so caught up at times in our own ideology and our own analysis and jargon that we don't actually relate to people as human beings who we know are catching hell but who have a very different language, a very different tradition.

Cornel West, 1954–
Philosopher and Activist

1161. Man is a promise that he must never break.

Richard Wright, 1908–1960
Novelist

1162. We have to keep in mind at all times that we are not fighting for integration, nor are we fighting for separation. We are fighting for recognition as free humans in this society.

Malcolm X, 1925–1965
Nationalist leader

HUMOR

1163. If you want to feel humor too exquisite and subtle for translation, sit invisibly among a gang of Negro workers.

W.E.B. Du Bois, 1868–1963
Intellectual and Activist

1164. We couldn't escape, so we developed a style of humor which recognized the basic artificiality, the irrationality, of the actual arrangement.

Ralph Ellison, 1914–1994
Novelist

1165. The black man bringing gifts and particularly the gift of laughter ... is easily the most anomalous, the most inscrutable figure of the century.

Jessie Fauset, 1882–1961
Writer

1166. Humor is laughing at what you haven't got when you ought to have it.

Langston Hughes, 1902–1967
Poet and Writer

1167. Here come de judge!

Pigmeat Markham (Dewey Markham), 1904–1981
Comedian

1168. If Negroes can lift clowning to artistry, they can thumb their noses at superior people who rate them as a clowning race.

Claude McKay, 1889–1948
Writer

1169. America is such a paradoxical society, hypocritically paradoxical, that if you don't have some humor, you'll crack up.

Malcolm X, 1925–1965
Nationalist leader

IDEALS

1170. I considered cash money as the smallest part of my resources. I had faith in a living God, faith in myself, and a desire to serve.

Mary McLeod Bethune, 1875–1955
Educator

1171. No matter how far a person can go, the horizon is still way beyond you.

Zora Neale Hurston, 1891–1960
Writer and Folklorist

1172. The motto I taught my boys was "Aim at the Sun!" If you do not bring it down, you will shoot higher than if you had aimed at the earth.

Rebecca Steward

1173. Our ideals of freedom, democracy, and equality must be invoked to invigorate all of us, especially the landless, propertyless, and luckless.

Cornel West, 1954–
Philosopher and Activist

1174. You don't have to be born with a silver spoon in your mouth to end up at the end of the golden rainbow.

Dianne Wilkerson, 1955–
Politician

IDEAS

1175. Every new idea is an impossibility until it is born.

Ronald H. Brown, 1941–1997?
Politician

1176. Individual ideas, like breaths, are waiting to be drawn from unlimited supply.

Margaret Danner, 1915–
Poet

1177. Ideas rise with new morning, but never die.

Frank Marshall Davis, 1905–
Poet and Journalist

1178. You can kill a man, but you can't kill an idea.

Medgar Evers, 1926–1963
Civil rights activist

1179. Ideas are the glory of man alone. No other creature can have them.

Matthew Henson, 1866–1955
Explorer

1180. In the great market place of public opinion, where the vital living questions of the age are to be decided, is continually being fought out the mighty battle of ideas.

William Henry Lewis, 1868–1948
Athlete and Lawyer

1181. Let's trace the birth of an idea. It's born as rampant radicalism, then it becomes progressivism, then liberalism, then it becomes moderate, conservative, outmoded, and gone.

Adam Clayton Powell Jr., 1908–1972
Minister and U.S. Congressperson

IDENTITY

1182. While there is a place for racial identities in a world shaped by racism ... if we are to move beyond racism we shall have, in the end, to move beyond current racial identities.

Anthony Appiah, 1954–
Philosopher

1183. By means of what the white man imagines the black man to be, the black man is enabled to know who the white man is.

James Baldwin, 1924–1987
Writer and Activist

1184. The Negro must preserve his identity. Unity and harmony of sentiment and feeling are the levers that must of necessary overturn American caste-prejudice.

John E. Bruce, 1856–1924
Writer

1185. I've never understood why people find it so hard to recognize the real person inside of me.

RuPaul Charles, 1960–
Entertainer

1186. You're born naked, the rest is drag.

RuPaul Charles, 1960–
Entertainer

1187. I do not feel inhibited or bound by what I am. That does not mean that I have never had bad scenes relating to being black and / or a woman, it means that other people's craziness has not managed to make me crazy.

Lucille Clifton, 1935–
Poet

1188. The fact is that American whites, as a whole, are just as much in doubt about their nationality, their cultural identity, as are Negroes.

Harold Cruse, 1916–
Scholar

1189. God made us in his own image, and he had some purpose when he thus created us; then why should we seek to destroy our identity?

Marcus Garvey, 1887–1940
Nationalist leader

1190. My grandfather was colored, my father is Negro, and I am black.

Henry Louis Gates Jr., 1950–
Scholar and Critic

1191. Too often in this country we speak of race as something that blacks have, of sexual orientation as something that gays and lesbians have, of gender as something that women have, of ethnicity as something that so-called ethnics have, and assume that if you don't fall into any of these categories, then you don't have to worry about any of those things.

Henry Louis Gates Jr., 1950–
Scholar and Critic

1192. You define your self by your work, by your morality, by who you love, the children you father, the money you've raised, the books you published, the paintings you painted.

Henry Louis Gates Jr., 1950–
Scholar and Critic

1193. Once you know who you are, you don't have to worry any more.

Nikki Giovanni, 1943–
Poet

1194. She knows who she is because she knows who she isn't.

Nikki Giovanni, 1943–
Poet

1195. If you let the world define you, you are dead, and that is all there is to it. If you let the spirit define you, you have a life that even death itself cannot intimidate or extinguish.

Peter J. Gomes, 1942–
Minister

1196. [African Americans'] reading and writing [in literary societies] was motivated by a desire to expand ideas of liberty and justice and to communicate an identity that was black, American, and above all, human.

Elizabeth McHenry
Scholar

1197. In my music, my plays, my films I want to carry always the central idea: to be African. Multitudes of men have died for less worthy ideals, it is even more eminently worth living for.

Paul Robeson, 1898–1976
Singer and Activist

1198. The black man's history—when you refer to him as the black man you go way back, but when you refer to him as a Negro, you can only go as far back as the Negro goes. And when you go beyond the shores of America, you can't find a Negro.

Malcolm X, 1925–1965
Nationalist leader

1199. The Muslim's X symbolized the true African family name that he could never know. For me, my X replaced the white slavemaster name of "Little" which some blue-eyed devil named Little had imposed upon my paternal forebears. The receipt of my X meant that forever after, in the Nation of Islam, I would be known as Malcolm X. Mr. Muhammad taught that we should keep X until God Himself returned and gave us a Holy Name from his own mouth.

Malcolm X, 1925–1965
Nationalist leader

IMAGINATION

1200. A man who has no imagination has no wings.

Muhammad Ali, 1942–
Boxing champion

INDEPENDENCE

1201. It's easy to be independent when you've got money. But to be independent when you haven't got a thing, that's the Lord's test.

Mahalia Jackson, 1911–1972
Gospel singer

1202. You need self-independence. Not servants, not workers or another one. You need now to turn and go work for yourself.

Elijah Muhammad, 1897–1975
Nation of Islam leader

INDIVIDUALITY

1203. It is impossible to raise and educate a race in the mass. All revolutions and improvements must start with individuals.

J.W.E. Bowen, 1855–1933
Minister

1204. If a man is not faithful to his own individuality, he cannot be loyal to anything.

Claude McKay, 1889–1948
Writer

1205. There is something about democratic individuality which is very different from rugged, ragged, rapacious individualism.

Cornel West, 1954–
Philosopher and Activist

INJUSTICE

1206. The bones of injustice have a peculiar way of rising from the tombs to plague and mock the iniquitous.

Marcus Garvey, 1887–1940
Nationalist leader

1207. Injustice anywhere is a threat to justice everywhere.

Martin Luther King Jr., 1929–1968
Civil rights activist and Nobel laureate

INSIGHT

1208. I do not say that the only person who can write of England must be an Englishman, or that only the Japanese should write of Japan, but I would insist that if a person is writing of a group to which he is socially and culturally alien, he must have some extraordinary gifts of insight.

W.E.B. Du Bois, 1868–1963
Intellectual and Activist

INSPIRATION

1209. Lift up yourselves. Take yourselves out of the mire and hitch your hopes to the stars.

Marcus Garvey, 1887–1940
Nationalist leader

1210. I have been in Sorrow's kitchen and licked out all the pots. Then I have stood of the peaking mountains wrapped in rainbows, with a harp and a sword in my hands.

Zora Neale Hurston, 1891–1960
Writer and Folklorist

1211. Inspiration! Who can sing thy force? / Or who describe the swiftness of thy course?

Phillis Wheatley, 1753?–1784
Poet

1212. Stretch your mind and fly.

Whitney M. Young Jr., 1921–1971
Civil rights activist

INTEGRATION

1213. Integration and education are not synonymous.

James Baldwin, 1924–1987
Writer and Activist

1214. Integration is irrelevant.

Stokely Carmichael, 1941–
Activist

1215. I'm not interested in a curriculum of inclusion. What we need is a curriculum of liberation.

John Henrik Clarke, 1915–
Historian

1216. The goal [was] to establish the presence of people of African descent in every field of endeavor.... The problem was when we did integrate Lexington or Scarsdale, we missed what it was like back home.

Henry Louis Gates Jr., 1950–
Scholar and Critic

1217. I hear that melting-pot stuff a lot, and all I can say is that we haven't melted.

Jesse Jackson, 1941–
Minister and Civil rights activist

1218. Integration comes after liberation. A slave cannot integrate with his master.

John O. Killens, 1916–1987
Novelist

1219. The combination of integrationist policies and crack did more damage to the black community [in the 1980s] than anything since the imposition of Jim Crow laws in the 1870s.

Jefferson Morley, 1958–
Reporter

1220. Integration means self-destruction, death, and nothing else.

Elijah Muhammad, 1897–1975
Nation of Islam leader

1221. Integration without preparation only leads to frustration.

Leon Sullivan, 1922–
Minister and Entrepreneur

1222. In our onslaught upon what we term separate institutions, we too frequently lose sight of the fact that to our church, association, and school we are at this hour chiefly indebted for whatever preparation we have made for the great battle of today.

William S. Whipper, 1805–1885
Abolitionist

INTEGRITY

1223. I will die before I will sell out my people for the white man's money.

Muhammad Ali, 1942–
Boxing champion

1224. This fact of nature [skin color] offers no clue to the character or quality of the person underneath.

Marian Anderson, 1897–1993
Singer

1225. I'm a fighter; nobody has ever bought me or bossed me.

Shirley Chisholm, 1924–
Politician

1226. I prefer to be true to myself, even at the hazard of incurring the ridicule of others, rather than to be false, and incur my own abhorence.

Frederick Douglass, 1817?–1895
Abolitionist and Autobiographer

1227. As a splendid palace deserted by its inmates looks like a ruin, so does a man without character, all his material belongings notwithstanding.

Mohandas K. Gandhi, 1869–1948
Indian nationalist leader

1228. How can I give up when in every part of the world I see my people being exploited and treated as if they're dregs of the earth? I could never do it. I could never compromise my conscience. What would I tell my God?

Marcus Garvey, 1887–1940
Nationalist leader

1229. There is counterfeit gold and counterfeit silver, counterfeit bills, and counterfeit men.

Lemuel Haynes, 1753–1833
Minister and Writer

1230. Young people, do not compromise your principles for anyone. Don't let any college or institution turn you into a "Negro." Always remember who you are and give back to the community.

Queen Mother Moore (Audley Moore), 1898–1997
Nationalist leader

1231. I'm coming out 100 percent real. I ain't compromising anything.

Tupac Shakur, 1971–1996
Rap artist

1232. Character, not circumstances, makes the man.

Booker T. Washington, 1856–1915
Educator

1233. Being your own man does not mean taking advantage of anyone else.

Flip Wilson, 1933–
Comedian

INTELLIGENCE

1234. The color of the skin is in no way connected with strength of the mind or intellectual powers.

Benjamin Banneker, 1731–1806
Inventor

1235. The foremost enemy of the Negro intelligentsia has been isolation.

Lorraine Hansberry, 1930–1965
Dramatist

1236. I understand the vocation of the intellectual as trying to turn easy answers into critical questions and ask these critical questions to those with power.

Cornel West, 1954–
Philosopher and Activist

1237. Muffle your rage. Get smart instead of muscular.

Roy Wilkins, 1901–1981
Civil rights activist

INVISIBILITY

1238. I am an invisible man.... I am a man of substance, of flesh and bone, fiber and liquids—and I might even be said to possess a mind. I am invisible, understand, simply because people refuse to see me.

Ralph Ellison, 1914–1994
Novelist

ISLAM

1239. Elijah Muhammad has been able to do what generations of welfare workers and committees and resolutions and reports and housing projects and playgrounds have failed to do: to heal and redeem drunkards and junkies, to convert people who have come out of prison and keep them out, to make men chaste and women virtuous, and to invest both the male and the female with a poise and serenity that hang about them like an unfailing light.

James Baldwin, 1924–1987
Writer and Activist

1240. They call the brothers and sisters in prison a lost community that can't be redeemed, but the teachings of the honorable Elijah Muhammad change the lives of men and women so that they become outstanding citizens. The worst one out there is the best one if we can get to his mind.

Muhammad Rodney

JAZZ

1☐0☐ 0☐00☐0☐ 0☐00☐0☐ 0☐00☐0☐ 0☐0

1241. Man if you gotta ask, you'll never know.

Louis Armstrong, 1901–1971
Jazz musician

1242. We all do "do, re, mi," but you have to find the other notes yourself.

Louis Armstrong, 1901–1971
Jazz musician

1243. The European musical scale cannot transcribe—cannot write down, does not understand of notes or the price of [jazz].

James Baldwin, 1924–1987
Writer and Activist

1244. Jazz came into existence as an exceedingly laconic description of black circumstances: and as a way, by describing these circumstances, of overcoming them.

James Baldwin, 1924–1987
Writer and Activist

1245. The music called jazz began ... not only to redeem a history unwritten and despised, but to checkmate the European notion of the world.

James Baldwin, 1924–1987
Writer and Activist

1246. You could remove the white elements—the French quadrilles, the Mexican military rhythms, the Italian melodies—and the music would still recognizably be jazz. But if you removed the black elements—the emphasis on improvisation, the polyphony, the complex rhythms, not to mention the all-important attitude that music was part of daily life—the remainder would not be jazz.

Laurence Bergreen
Writer

1247. Jazz functions better underground.

Roy Brooks

1248. If you wanted to get into jazz, you had to go downtown where the pimps, prostitutes, hustlers, gangsters, and gamblers supported the music. If it wasn't for them, there wouldn't be no jazz! They supported the club owners who bought the music. It wasn't the middle-class people who said, "Let's go hear Charlie Parker tonight."

Betty Carter, 1930–
Singer

1249. Forget the rules. You have to play all 12 notes of your solo anyway.

John Coltrane, 1926–1967
Tenor saxophonist

1250. The thing to judge in any jazz artist is, does the man project, and does he have ideas?

Miles Davis, 1926–1991
Jazz musician

1251. If jazz means anything at all … it means the same thing it meant to musicians 50 years ago—freedom of expression.

Duke Ellington, 1899–1974
Composer and Band leader

1252. It is an American idiom with African roots, a trunk of soul with limbs reaching in every direction.

Duke Ellington, 1899–1974
Composer and Band leader

1253. [Jazz] is the only music that is able to describe the present period in the history of the world.

Duke Ellington, 1899–1974
Composer and Band leader

1254. In a Harlem cabaret / Six long-headed jazzers play.

Langston Hughes, 1902–1967
Poet and Writer

1255. Jazz to me is one of the inherent expressions of Negro life in America: the eternal tom-tom beating in the Negro soul—the tom-tom of revolt against weariness in a white world, a world of subway trains, and work, work, work; the tom-tom of joy and laughter, sand pain swallowed in a smile.

Langston Hughes, 1902–1967
Poet and Writer

1256. Jazz is the nobility of the race put into sound.

Wynton Marsalis, 1961–
Musician

1257. Jazz is the ancestral down-home voice at its highest level of refinement.

Albert Murray, 1916–
Writer and Critic

1258. Jazz tells us what we African Americans have done with our experience on these shores.

Albert Murray, 1916–
Writer and Critic

1259. What a terrible revenge by the culture of the Negroes on that of the whites.

Ignacy Paderewski, 1860–1941
Polish composer and Pianist

1260. Jazz is an important expression of the 20th century: black experience in America, the nobility of the race put into sound. I was determined to achieve the total freedom that our history lessons taught us we were entitled to, no matter what the sacrifice.

Rosa Parks, 1913–
Civil rights activist

1261. Jazz is a very democratic musical form. It comes out of a communal experience. We take our respective instruments and collectively create a thing of beauty.

Max Roach, 1925–
Drummer

1262. Jazz is not just music, it's a way of life, it's a way of being, a way of thinking. I think that the Negro in America is jazz. Everything he does—the slang he uses, the way he walks, the way he talks, his jargon, the new inventive phrases we make up to describe things—all that to me is jazz just as much as the music we play.

Nina Simone, 1933–
Pianist and Singer

1263. Jazz takes all the elements in our culture and puts them into perspective.

Billy Taylor, 1921–
Musician

JUSTICE

1264. The Negro question will trouble the American government and the American conscience until a substantial effort is made to settle it upon the principles of justice.

Charles W. Chesnutt, 1858–1932
Novelist

1265. To demand freedom is to demand justice. When there is no justice in the land, a man's freedom is threatened.

James Cone, 1938–
Theologian

1266. I say at once, in peace and war, I am content with nothing for the black man short of equal and exact justice.

Frederick Douglass, 1817?–1895
Abolitionist and Autobiographer

1267. The Negro does not want love. He wants justice.

E. Franklin Frazier, 1894–1962
Sociologist

1268. Don't be deceived; there is no justice but strength.

Marcus Garvey, 1887–1940
Nationalist leader

1269. And how can I get justice from a judge who honestly does not know that he is prejudiced?

Dick Gregory, 1932–
Comedian and Activist

1270. A man must be willing to die for justice. Death is an inescapable reality and men die daily, but good deeds live forever.

Jesse Jackson, 1941–
Minister and Civil rights activist

1271. Anyone can convict a Negro in the South.

Claude Rains
Actor
Warner Brothers' 1937 film, *They Won't Forget*

1272. No justice, no peace!

Al Sharpton, 1955–
Minister and Activist

1273. We must now refocus the views of the public on the issue of justice rather than the issues of aimless harmony.

Al Sharpton, 1955–
Minister and Activist

1274. The answer to injustice is not to silence the critic, but to end the injustice.

Richard Wright, 1908–1960
Novelist

1275. We want justice by any means necessary.

Malcolm X, 1925–1965
Nationalist leader

KEEPING ON
See Perseverance

KNOWLEDGE

∿∿∿∿∿∿

1276. Nothing is more powerful and liberating than knowledge.

William H. Gray III, 1941–
U.S. Congressperson

1277. Knowledge is power, and power is the key to changing things.

Jill Nelson
Writer

1278. The realization of ignorance is the first act of knowing.

Jean Toomer, 1894–1967
Novelist

1279. The prime condition of slavery was to keep closed every avenue to knowledge. The Negro had no estate, no family life. His sole inheritance was his body.

Booker T. Washington, 1856–1915
Educator

LABOR

1280. The labor movement traditionally has been the only haven for the disposed, the despised, the neglected, the downtrodden, and the poor.
A. Philip Randolph, 1889–1979
Labor leader

1281. White and black workers ... cannot be organized separately as the fingers on my hand. They must be organized together, as the fingers on my hand when they are doubled up in the form of a fist.
A. Philip Randolph, 1889–1979
Labor leader

LANGUAGE

1282. These women heal us by telling our stories, by embodying emotion that our everydays can't hold.
Elizabeth Alexander
Poet

1283. Every legend contains its residuum of truth, and the root function of language is to control the universe by describing it.
James Baldwin, 1924–1987
Writer and Activist

1284. For the horrors of the American Negro's life there has been almost no language.
James Baldwin, 1924–1987
Writer and Activist

1285. The power of the white world is threatened whenever a black man refuses to accept the white world's definitions.

James Baldwin, 1924–1987
Writer and Activist

1286. My mama taught me the power of the word, the importance of the resistance tradition, and the high standards our community has regarding verbal performance.

Toni Cade Bambara, 1939–
Writer

1287. The language of the academy is most important to me because it provides a critical vocabulary to explore the complex features of American and African American thought and life.

Michael Eric Dyson, 1958–
Scholar and Writer

1288. America is a melting pot. We all want to qualify for the best possible jobs. In order to compete, we must be able to master the English language and use it properly.

Myrlie Evers-Williams
NAACP official

1289. For centuries African Americans have been forced to develop coded ways of communicating to protect them from danger. Allegories and double meanings, words redefined to mean their opposites ("bad" meaning "good," for instance) ... have enabled blacks to share messages only the initiated understood.

Henry Louis Gates Jr., 1950–
Scholar and Critic

1290. The very large questions of obscenity and the First Amendment [surrounding rap lyrics] cannot even be addressed until those who would answer them become literate in the vernacular traditions of African Americans.

Henry Louis Gates Jr., 1950–
Scholar and Critic

1291. Language today is not able to articulate the rights of the poor.

Evelyn Brooks Higginbotham, 1945–
Scholar

1292. I think all the artists who use the black vernacular in this society understand that, to white minds, the black vernacular has always been associated with the idea of being stupid. I guess I feel that part of my mission as an artist—this is what binds me culturally to an Ice Cube and even a Snoop Doggy Dog—is understanding the beauty and aesthetic complexity in the vernacular.

Bell Hooks, 1961–
Feminist and Critic

1293. I have the map of Dixie on my tongue.

Zora Neale Hurston, 1891–1960
Writer and Folklorist

1294. Good poetry and successful revolution change our lives. And you cannot compose a good poem or wage a revolution without changing consciousness. And you cannot alter consciousness unless you attack the language that you share with your enemies and invent a language that you share with your allies.

June Jordan, 1936–
Poet and Essayist

1295. Maybe our forefathers couldn't keep their language together when they were taken away from Africa, but this, the blues, was a language we invented to let people know we had something to say.

B.B. King, 1925–
Blues musician

1296. Black people's grace has been with what they do with language.

Toni Morrison, 1931–
Novelist and Nobel laureate

1297. What a triumphal journey we have made from those dark days when we were beaten and chained in an attempt to prevent us from learning to read and write. Here we are, the ones who energize language today, who reinvent and enrich the very tongues of those who wish to silence us.

Elizabeth Nunez

1298. The patterns of what's called "speaking black" have been preserved in the black church, where great preachers shift in and out of vernacular and standard English. That's part of the magic of the African American oral tradition.

Geneva Smitherman, 1940–
Linguist

1299. We have kids in the inner cities who are verbal geniuses, but we call them deficient in school and attempt to eradicate a part of their identity.

Geneva Smitherman, 1940–
Linguist

1300. Perhaps the most striking characteristic of slavery was the secretiveness it imposed upon the slave nature with regard to himself, his thoughts, desires and purposes. To the slave, language became in very truth an instrument for the concealment of thought rather than its expression.

Albion W. Tourgee, 1838–1905
Novelist

1301. We must understand that we will be charged heavily in the workplace of we don't have a grasp of standard English.

Hilda Vest, 1933–
Educator

LAW

1302. Black people know what white people mean when they say law and order.

Fannie Lou Hamer, 1917–1977
Civil rights activist

1303. It may be true that the law cannot make a man love me, but it can keep him from lynching me, and I think that's pretty important.

Martin Luther King Jr., 1929–1968
Civil rights activist and Nobel laureate

1304. One has not only a legal but a moral responsibility to disobey unjust laws.

Martin Luther King Jr., 1929–1968
Civil rights activist and Nobel laureate

1305. You can't legislate integration, but you can certainly legislate desegregation. You can't legislate morality, but you can regulate behavior. You can't make a man love me, but the law can restrain him from lynching me.

Martin Luther King Jr., 1929–1968
Civil rights activist and Nobel laureate

1306. Human society could not exist one hour except on the basis of law which holds the baser passions of men in restraint.

Kelly Miller, 1863–1969
Educator

1307. A man's respect for law and order exists in precise relationship to the size of his paycheck.

Adam Clayton Powell Jr., 1908–1972
Minister and U.S. Congressperson

1308. I have firmly believed all along that the law was on our side and would, when we appealed to it, give us justice. I feel shorn of that belief and utterly discouraged, and just now, if it were possible, would gather my race in my arms and fly away with them.

Ida B. Wells, 1862–1931
Militant activist

LEADERSHIP

1309. What we need are mental and spiritual giants who are aflame with a purpose.... We're a race ready for crusade, for we've recognized that we're a race on this continent that can work out its own salvation.

Nannie Burroughs, 1883–1961
Activist

1310. Far too often we become cowards when faced with individuals who have strong leadership abilities, individuals who often do not want social revolution as much as they want personal power.

Shirley Chisholm, 1924–
Politician

1311. Our leadership is just we ourself.

Claudette Colvin, 1940–
Civil rights activist

1312. And we will know him [Malcolm X] then for what he was and is—a Prince, our own black shining Prince!—who didn't hesitate to die, because he loved us so.

Ossie Davis, 1917–
Actor

1313. We cannot have perfection. We have few saints. But we must have honest men or we die. We must have unselfish, far-seeing leadership or we fail.

W.E.B. Du Bois, 1868–1963
Intellectual and Activist

1314. Most of our leaders are picked by the very enemy we are trying to get free of. Our leaders are not connected to the black masses.

Louis Farrakhan, 1934–
Nation of Islam leader

1315. Leadership means everything—pain, blood, death.

Marcus Garvey, 1887–1940
Nationalist leader

1316. Our leader will not be a white man with a black heart, nor a black man with a white heart, but a black man with a black heart.

Marcus Garvey, 1887–1940
Nationalist leader

1317. We're looking for moral leadership. We're looking for a president who's not afraid to talk about race in a public forum. The entire country is running from this problem.

Lani Guinier, 1950–
Law professor

1318. The people are our teachers.

Prathia Hall

1319. When leaders have fulfilled their functions, it's time for them to retire.

Nathan Hare, 1934–
Sociologist

1320. We have allowed our civilization to outrun our culture, and so we are in danger now of ending up with guided missiles in the hands of misguided men.

Martin Luther King Jr., 1929–1968
Civil rights activist and Nobel laureate

1321. The white establishment is skilled in flattering and cultivating emerging leaders. It presses its own image on them, and finally, from imitation of manners, dress, and style of living, a deeper strain of corruption develops. This kind of Negro leader acquires the white man's contempt for the ordinary Negro.... Ultimately, he changes from the representative of the Negro to the white man into the white man's representative to the Negro.

Martin Luther King Jr., 1929–1968
Civil rights activist and Nobel laureate

1322. The leadership is there. If you go out and work with your people, then the leadership will emerge.

Bob Moses
Civil rights activist

1323. This generation had no [Frederick] Douglass, no [Adam Clayton] Powell, no [Martin Luther] King, no Malcolm [X] to break things down for them.

Susan Taylor, 1946–
Editor and Writer

1324. [Much leadership is] too hungry for status to be angry, too eager for acceptance to be bold, too self-invested in advancement to be defiant.

Cornel West, 1954–
Philosopher and Activist

1325. Only a visionary leadership that can motivate "the better angels of our nature," as Lincoln said, and active possibilities for a freer, more efficient, and stable America ... deserves cultivation and support.

Cornel West, 1954–
Philosopher and Activist

1326. We need leaders—neither saints nor sparkling television personalities—who can situate themselves within a larger historical narrative of this country and our world, who can grasp the complex dynamics of our peoplehood and imagine a future grounded in the best of our past, yet who are attuned to the frightening obstacles that now perplex us.

Cornel West, 1954–
Philosopher and Activist

LEARNING
See Education

LIBERATION

1327. We have to create an art for liberation and for life.

Elizabeth Catlett, 1919–
Artist

1328. We shall never secure emancipation from the tyranny of the white oppressor until we have achieved it in our own souls.

W.E.B. Du Bois, 1868–1963
Intellectual and Activist

1329. The liberation of Afro-Americans ... ultimately lies in an understanding, appreciation, and assertion of his Afro-American and African cultural heritage.

E.U. Essien-Udom

1330. The next great liberation movement will come from the same place the last one came from, and so many before it: from below.

James Goodman
Scholar

1331. Liberation means you don't have to be silenced.

Toni Morrison, 1931–
Novelist and Nobel laureate

1332. God will not suffer us always to be oppressed. Our sufferings will come to an end, in spite of all the Americans this side of eternity.

David Walker, 1785–1830
Abolitionist

1333. There can be no true black political liberation without religious and cultural liberation.

Gayraud Wilmore
Minister and Academic

LIBERTY

1334. Liberty exists in the very idea of man's creation. It was his even before he comprehended it. He was created in it, endowed with it, and it can never be taken away.

Frederick Douglass, 1817?–1895
Abolitionist and Autobiographer

1335. The cost of liberty is less than the price of repression.

W.E.B. Du Bois, 1868–1963
Intellectual and Activist

1336. Liberty is a spirit sent from God and like its great Author is no respecter of persons.

Henry Highland Garnet, 1815–1882
Abolitionist and Minister

1337. History teaches us that grave threats to liberty often come in times of urgency, when constitutional rights seem too extravagant to endure.

Thurgood Marshall, 1908–1993
U.S. Supreme Court Justice

1338. I would fight for my liberty so long as my strength lasted, and if the time came for me to go, the Lord would let them take me.

Harriet Tubman, 1820?–1913
Abolitionist

LIFE

⟁ ⟁ ⟁ ⟁ ⟁ ⟁ ⟁ ⟁

1339. People say I had a full life, but I ain't dead yet. I'm just getting started.

Muhammad Ali, 1942–
Boxing champion

1340. Life is preparation. What does that mean? Live! And you will find out.

Barbara Bady, 1931–
Poet

1341. A man without ambition is dead. A man with ambition but no love is dead. A man with ambition and love for his blessings here on earth is ever so alive.

Pearl Bailey, 1918–1990
Entertainer

1342. One is responsible to life. It is the small beacon in that terrifying darkness from which we come and to which we shall return.

James Baldwin, 1924–1987
Writer and Activist

1343. The wretched of the earth do not decide to become extinct; they resolve, on the contrary, to multiply: life is their weapon against life, life is all that they have.

James Baldwin, 1924–1987
Writer and Activist

1344. I want to see how life can triumph.

Romare Bearden, 1914–1988
Artist

1345. Life is a marvelous, transitory adventure.

Nikki Giovanni, 1943–
Poet

1346. There has to be more than this, and there is, and you can have it if you turn around and claim a place for God in your life.

Peter J. Gomes, 1942–
Minister

1347. The great are those who in their lives fought for life.

Stephen Henderson, 1925–
Educator

1348. Life for me ain't been no crystal stair.

Langston Hughes, 1902–1967
Poet and Writer

1349. Life is exquisitely a time-thing, like music.

E.E. Just, 1883–1941
Marine biologist

1350. I don't believe that life is supposed to make you feel good, or to make you feel miserable either. Life is just supposed to make you feel.

Gloria Naylor, 1950–
Writer

1351. Life doesn't give you all the practice races you need.

Jesse Owens, 1913–1980
Olympic track star

1352. My soul is full of concern and love, and I understand the meaning of my own life and the lives of others.

Betty Shabazz, 1934?–1997
Educator

1353. A man's life is a single statement.

Howard Thurman, 1899–1981
Minister

1354. Brother, life is water that is being drawn off.

Jean Toomer, 1894–1967
Novelist

LIMITATIONS

1355. If you know whence you came, there is really no limit to where you can go.

James Baldwin, 1924–1987
Writer and Activist

1356. People mistake their limitations for high standards.

Jean Toomer, 1894–1967
Novelist

LITERACY
See Education

LITERATURE

▽▨◁▽◁▽◁▽◁▽◁▽◁▽◁▽◁▽

1357. We are at the commencement [1901] of a "negroid" renaissance ... that will have as much importance in literary history as the much spoken of and much praised Celtic and Canadian renaissance.

William Stanley Braithwaite, 1878–1962
Poet and Anthologist

1358. In the next phase of Afro-American writing, a literature of celebration must be created—not a celebration of oppression, but a celebration of survival in spite of it.

John Henrik Clarke, 1915–
Historian

1359. In literacy lay freedom for the black slave.... No group of slaves anywhere, at any other period of history, has left such a large repository of testimony about the horror of becoming the legal property of another human being.

Henry Louis Gates Jr., 1950–
Scholar and Critic

1360. Our history and individuality as a people not only provide material for masterly treatment, but would seem to make a Race Literature a necessity as an outlet for unnaturally suppressed inner lives which our people have been compelled to lead.

Victoria Earle Matthews, 1861–1907
Writer

1361. Each person has a literature inside them.

Anna Deavere Smith, 1950–
Actor

1362. After several years' work, suddenly it was as if a door opened and I knew without a doubt that I was inside. I knew literature. And that was my joy.

Jean Toomer, 1894–1967
Novelist

1363. Literature should not be judged good or bad according to its imitation of the styles and taste of Europeans, but according to its presentation of the styles and traditions stemming from Africa and Afro-American culture.

Darwin T. Turner, 1931–
Scholar

LIVING

1364. The day I no longer go on stage will be the day I die.

Josephine Baker, 1906–1975
Entertainer

1365. The measure of a man is in the lives he's touched.

Erin Banks

1366. The seven wonders of the world I have seen, and many places I have been. Take my advice, folks, and see Beale Street first.

Henry Chase

1367. Living in the inner city is the same as living in the suburbs or surviving in the world. You have to know who you are, set goals in life, and maintain a self-image.

Marva Collins, 1936–
Educator

1368. The best lessons, the best sermons are those that are lived.

Yolanda King, 1955–
Actor

1369. It isn't how long one lives, but how well. Jesus died at 33; Joan of Arc at 19; Byron and Burns at 33; Marlowe at 29; Shelley at 30; Dunbar before 35 ... and Martin Luther King Jr. at 39.

Benjamin Mays, 1895–1984
Educator

1370. The best way to live in this world is to live above it.

Sonia Sanchez, 1934–
Poet

1371. To know is to exist; to exist is to be involved, to move about, to see the world with my own eyes.

Alice Walker, 1944–
Writer

LOVE

1372. Love is like a virus. It can happen to anybody at any time.

Maya Angelou, 1928–
Novelist and Poet

1373. Love does not begin and end the way we seem to think it does. Love is a battle, love is a war; love is growing up.

James Baldwin, 1924–1987
Writer and Activist

1374. Love is love.

James Baldwin, 1924–1987
Writer and Activist

1375. The human heart is limited and capable of loving and caring for but a few people. If this were not so, we'd all be saints.

Romare Bearden, 1914–1988
Artist

1376. I love you for your brownness/And the rounded darkness of your breast.

Gwendolyn Bennett, 1902–1981
Painter

1377. I leave you love. Love builds. It is positive and helpful. It is more beneficial than hate, Injuries quickly forgotten quickly pass away. Personally and racially, our enemies must be forgiven. Our aim must be to create a world of fellowship and justice where no man's skin color or religion is held against him. "Love they neighbor" is a precept which could transform the world if it were universally practiced.

Mary McLeod Bethune, 1875–1955
Educator

1378. Love is a special word, and I use it only when I mean it. You say the word too much and it becomes cheap.

Ray Charles, 1930–
Singer

1379. If you love 'em in the morning with their eyes full of crust; if you love 'em at night with their hair full of curlers, chances are, you're in love.

Miles Davis, 1921–1991
Jazz musician

1380. There is no god but Love and work is his prophet.

W.E.B. Du Bois, 1868–1963
Intellectual and Activist

1381. Love is indescribable and unconditional. I could tell you a thousand things that it is not, but not one that it is.

Duke Ellington, 1899–1974
Composer and Band leader

1382. Unconditional love not only means I am with you, but also I am for you, all the way, right or wrong.

Duke Ellington, 1899–1974
Composer and Band leader

1383. Most of us love from our need to love, not because we find someone deserving.

Nikki Giovanni, 1943–
Poet

1384. Baby, where did our love go?

Brian Holland; Lamont Dozier; Eddie Holland
Motown Records songwriters

1385. Or maybe the purpose of being here, wherever we are, is to increase the durability and the occasions of love among and between peoples.

June Jordan, 1936–
Poet and Essayist

1386. Be loving enough to absorb evil.

Martin Luther King Jr., 1929–1968
Civil rights activist and Nobel laureate

1387. What is needed is a realization that power without love is reckless and abusive. and love without power is sentimental and anemic.

Martin Luther King Jr., 1929–1968
Civil rights activist and Nobel laureate

1388. Love is a rock against the wind.

Etheridge Knight, 1931–
Poet

1389. Love is like playing checkers. You have to know which man to move.

Moms Mabley (Jackie Mabley), 1897–1975
Comedian

1390. Is this love that I'm feeling?

Bob Marley, 1946–?
Reggae singer

1391. I wish I woulda knowed more people. If I woulda knowed more, I woulda loved more.

Toni Morrison, 1931–
Novelist and Nobel laureate

1392. Love is or it ain't. Thin love ain't love at all.

Toni Morrison, 1931–
Novelist and Nobel laureate

1393. Lonliness is a constant companion to loving.

Bettye J. Parker-Smith

1394. Learn me the way to teach the word of love / For that's the pure intelligence above.

Ann Plato, 1820–?
Poet

1395. The opposite of love was not hate but indifference.

Bill Russell, 1934–
Basketball star

1396. I'm private. But there were some public things I had to do because of his [Malcolm X's] commitment to the cause. I loved him and he loved the people.

Betty Shabazz, 1934?–1997
Educator

1397. Through a love experience I discovered the reality of the soul.

Jean Toomer, 1894–1967
Novelist

1398. Love stretches your heart and makes you big inside.

Margaret Walker, 1915–
Writer

1399. Great men cultivate love.

Booker T. Washington, 1856–1915
Educator

1400. Love means exposing yourself to the pains of being hurt, deeply hurt by someone you trust.

Renita Weems
Seminary professor

1401. Love is a funny thing. It just sneaks up on you all kinds of ways.

Sarah E. Wright, 1928–
Writer

1402. If you think we are here to tell you to love the white man, you have come to the wrong place.

Malcolm X, 1925–1965
Nationalist leader

LYNCHING

1403. Mob law is the most forcible expression of an abnormal public opinion; it shows the society is rotten to the core.

T. Thomas Fortune, 1856–1928
Journalist

1404. Lynching is a practical demonstration of racial hysteria; it is actualized through fear, a guilty conscience, or a retributive foreboding.

Amy Jacques Garvey, 1896–1973
Nationalist leader

1405. I think something is dreadfully wrong with this country when any person, any person in this free country would be subjected to this.... And from my standpoint, as a black American, it is a high tech lynching.

Clarence Thomas, 1948–
U.S. Supreme Court Justice

1406. No one can say, who has any respect for the truth, that the United States is a civilized nation, especially if we take the daily papers and inspect them for a few moments and see the deeds of horror.

Henry McNeal Turner, 1834–1915
Minister and Militant activist

1407. No savage nation can exceed the atrocities which are often heralded through the country and accepted by many as an incidental consequence. Men are hung, shot, and burnt by bands of murderers who are most invariably represented as the most influential and respectable citizens, while the evidence of guilt of what is charged against the victims is never established in any court.

Henry McNeal Turner, 1834–1915
Minister and Militant activist

1408. In slave times the Negro was kept subservient and submissive by the frequency and severity of the scourging, but, with freedom, a new system of intimidation came in vogue; the Negro was not only whipped and scourged, he was killed.

Ida B. Wells, 1862–1931
Militant activist

1409. Nowhere in the civilized world, save the United States, do men go out in bands, to hunt down, shoot, hang to death, a single individual.

Ida B. Wells, 1862–1931
Militant activist

1410. Surely the humanitarian spirit of this country which reaches out to denounce the treatment of Russian Jews, the Armenian Christians, the laboring poor of Europe, the Siberian exiles, and the native women of India will not longer refuse to lift its voice on this subject [lynching].

Ida B. Wells, 1862–1931
Militant activist

MARRIAGE

1411. You must polish your marriage every day.

Elleni Amlak, 1959–
Designer

1412. Mom and Pop were just a couple of kids when they got married. He was 18, she was 16, and I was three.

Billie Holiday, 1915–1959
Blues singer

1413. Real marriage is the sacrificing of your ego, not for the other person, but for the relationship.

Oprah Winfrey, 1954–
Entertainer

MEMORY

1414. There is no Dream but Deed, there is no Deed but Memory.

W.E.B. Du Bois, 1868–1963
Intellectual and Activist

1415. The great difficulty lies in trying to transpose last night's moment to a day which has no knowledge of it.

Zora Neale Hurston, 1891–1969
Writer and Folklorist

1416. History is a people's memory and without a memory man is demoted to the level of the lower animals.

Malcolm X, 1925–1965
Nationalist leader

MEN

1417. Am I not a man and a brother?

Anonymous
Abolitionist motto

1418. That marvelously mocking, salty authority with which black men walked was dictated by the tacit and shared realization of the price each had paid to be able to walk at all.

James Baldwin, 1924–1987
Writer and Activist

1419. The strong men keep a-comin' on / The strong men gittin' stronger.

Sterling A. Brown, 1901–1989
Scholar and Writer

1420. Some of the most unforgettable women in the world … are men.

RuPaul Charles, 1960–
Entertainer

1421. Black men are not going to cringe before anyone but God.

Marcus Garvey, 1887–1940
Nationalist leader

1422. Black men, you were once great; you shall be great again.

Marcus Garvey, 1887–1940
Nationalist leader

1423. Black males have long intrigued the western imagination, whether as gods or kings in much of classical antiquity or devils or sambos since the high Middle Ages…. Tragically, every African American male who walks down any street in America carries with him the hidden heritage of this negative cultural and psychological legacy.

Henry Louis Gates Jr., 1950–
Scholar and Critic

1424. Women who accuse men, particularly powerful men, of harassment are often confronted with the reality of the men's sense that they are more important than women, as a group.

Anita Hill, 1956–
Law professor

1425. If men could become pregnant, abortion would be a sacrament.

Florynce Kennedy, 1916–?
Lawyer and Feminist

1426. There [in the old West] a man's work was to be done, and a man's life to be lived, and when death was to be met [the black cowboy] met it like a man.

Nat "Deadwood Dick, the cowboy adventurer" Love, 1854–?
Cowboy

1427. There ain't nothing' an old man can do but bring me a message from a young one.

Moms Mabley (Jackie Mabley), 1897–1975
Comedian

1428. A woman is a woman until the day she dies, but a man's a man only as long as he can.

Moms Mabley (Jackie Mabley), 1897–1975
Comedian

1429. All the good men are either dead or Men waiting to be born.

Gloria Naylor, 1950–
Writer

1430. We have survived the Middle Passage and we have survived slavery. We have survived the deadly arbitrariness of Jim Crow and the hatefulness of northern discrimination. But now we face a danger more covert, more insidious, more threatening and potentially more final even than these: the apparently sly conspiracy to do away with black men as a troublesome presence in America.

William Strickland

1431. We must cherish our old men. We must revere their wisdom, appreciate their insight, love the humanity of their words.

Alice Walker, 1944–
Writer

1432. God made us men long before men made us citizens.

Charles T. Walker, 1858–1921
Minister

1433. Treat us like men, and there is no danger but we will all live in peace and happiness together.

David Walker, 1785–1830
Abolitionist

MENTAL SLAVERY
See Slavery

MIDDLE PASSAGE

1434. We may as well die in trying to be free as be killed and eaten.
Joseph Cinque, 1817?–?
Amistad Revolt leader

1435. Death was more preferable than life, and a plan was concerted amongst us, that we might burn and blow up the ship, and to perish all together in the flames.
Ottaban Cugoano, 1747?–?

1436. When I recovered a little I found some black people about me.... I asked them if we were not to be eaten by those white men with horrible looks, red faces, and loose hair.
Olaudah Equiano, 1745?–1801
Slave autobiographer

MILITANCY
See Race Consciousness

MILITARY
See War

MIND

1437. The mind is and always will be our primary business.

Benjamin Mays, 1895–1984
Educator

1438. It is the mind that makes the body.

Sojourner Truth, 1797?–1883
Abolitionist and Women's rights advocate

MISERY

1439. The white man's happiness cannot be purchased by the black man's misery.

Frederick Douglass, 1817?–1895
Abolitionist and Autobiographer

1440. Envy and pride are the leading lines to all the misery that mankind has suffered from the beginning of the world to this day.

John Marrant, 1755–1797?
Missionary

MISTAKES

1441. Mistakes are a fact of life / It is the response to the error that counts.

Nikki Giovanni, 1943–
Poet

1442. Every man got a right to his own mistakes. Ain't no man that ain't made any.

Joe Louis, 1914–1981
Boxing champion

MONEY

1443. Where there is money there is fighting.

Marian Anderson, 1897–1993
Singer

1444. Money, it turned out, was exactly like sex: you thought of nothing else if you didn't have it, and thought of other things if you did.

James Baldwin, 1924–1987
Writer and Activist

1445. Money is a great dignifier.

Paul Laurence Dunbar, 1872–1906
Poet

1446. The important thing is not how much money a person makes; it is what he does with it that matters.

A.G. Gaston, 1892–1993
Businessperson

1447. Everything costs a lot of money when you haven't got any.

Joe Louis, 1914–1981
Boxing champion

1448. I don't like money actually, but it quiets my nerves.

Joe Louis, 1914–1981
Boxing champion

1449. The lack of money is the root of all evil.

Reverend Ike (Frederick J. Eikerenkoetter), 1936–
Religious leader

1450. Money is in abundance; where are you?

Reverend Ike (Frederick J. Eikerenkoetter), 1936–
Religious leader

MORALITY

1451. I try to do the right thing at the right time. They may just be little things, but usually they make the difference between winning and losing.

Kareem Abdul Jabbar, 1947–
Basketball star

1452. I really didn't do the things that people reported, but then there were some others that they didn't know about.

Josephine Baker, 1906–1975
Entertainer

1453. Never shirk one simple duty: / Earn your honors, earn your rest.

Walter H. Brooks, 1851–1945
Minister

1454. It is easy to do right out of fear, but it is better to do right because right is right.

Louis Farrakhan, 1934–
Nation of Islam leader

1455. We should not be the first to destroy God's world.

Jesse Jackson, 1941–
Minister and Civil rights activist

1456. Life's most persistent and urgent question is, what are you doing for others?

Martin Luther King Jr., 1929–1968
Civil rights activist and Nobel laureate

1457. When evil men plot, good men must plan. When evil men burn and bomb, good men must build and bind. When evil men shout ugly words of hatred, good men must commit themselves to the glories of love.

Martin Luther King Jr., 1929–1968
Civil rights activist and Nobel laureate

1458. I will always protest against the double standard of morals.

Mary Church Terrell, 1863–1954
Women's club leader

1459. The highest test of the civilization of any race is its willingness to extend a helping hand to the less fortunate. A race, like an individual, lifts itself up by lifting others up.

Booker T. Washington, 1856–1915
Educator

MOTHERS
See Family

MOTOWN SOUND

1460. We thought of the neighborhoods we were raised in and came up with a six-word definition [of the Motown Sound]: rats, roaches, struggle, talent, guts, love.

Berry Gordy Jr., 1929–
Music executive

MULTICULTURALISM
See Diversity

MUSIC

1461. I was just born to swing, that's all.

Lil Hardin Armstrong, 1898–1971
Jazz musician

1462. All music is folk music. I ain't never heard no horse sing.

Louis Armstrong, 1901–1971
Jazz musician

1463. Before my time the name was levee camp music, then in New Orleans we called it ragtime. The fantastic music you hear on radio today, used to hear it way back in the old sanctified churches where the sisters would shout till their petticoats fell down. Nothin' new. Old soup warmed over.

Louis Armstrong, 1901–1971
Jazz musician

1464. We [Armstrong and Joe Oliver] never had to look at each other when we played, both thinking the same thing.
Louis Armstrong, 1901–1971
Jazz musician

1465. We were poor and everything like that, but music was all around you. Music kept you rollin'.
Louis Armstrong, 1901–1971
Jazz musician

1466. You see we colored people have our own music that is part of us. It's a product of our souls. It's been created by the suffering and miseries of our race. Some of the melodies made up by slaves of the old days and others were handed down down from the days before we left Africa.
Louis Armstrong, 1901–1971
Jazz musician

1467. There are three different strains in the black music revolution today—classical jazz (such as Wynton Marsalis), avant jazz (such as Anthony Braxton), and the fusion of Hip-Hop and jazz (such as the compositions of Steve Coleman).
Anthony Davis, 1951–
Composer and Musician

1468. You need controlled freedom.
Miles Davis, 1926–1991
Jazz musician

1469. There is no true American music but the wild sweet melodies of the Negro slave.
W.E.B. Du Bois, 1868–1963
Intellectual and Activist

1470. I am now satisfied that the future music of this continent must be founded upon what are called the Negro melodies. This can be the foundation of a serious and original school of composition to be developed in the United States.
Anton Dvorak, 1841–1904
Czech composer

1471. It don't mean a thing if it ain't got that swing.

Duke Ellington, 1899–1974
Composer and Band leader

1472. Music is my mistress, and she plays second fiddle to no one.

Duke Ellington, 1899–1974
Composer and Band leader

1473. The music of my race is something that is going to live, something which posterity will honor in a higher sense than merely that of music of the ballroom.

Duke Ellington, 1899–1974
Composer and Band leader

1474. Musically, we were changing the way that we spoke, to reflect the way that we felt.

Dizzy Gillespie (John Birks Gillespie), 1917–1993
Jazz musician

1475. The spirit hits me and I just keep going and don't stop. The more I play, the more I can invent, the more ideas come to me.

Lionel Hampton, 1913–
Vibraphonist and Band leader

1476. I always joked that I didn't ask to sing and dance, but it's true. When I open my mouth, music comes out.

Michael Jackson, 1958–
Entertainer

1477. Maybe fifty years after I'm dead my music will be appreciated.

Scott Joplin, 1868?–1917
Composer and Pianist

1478. I'm just doing stuff. Letting the people know what American folk music is, unwritten music, made up by the people.

Huddie Ledbetter, 1885–1949
Blues singer

1479. Reggae is the spontaneous sound of a local revolutionary impulse.

Michael Manley, 1924–
Jamaican statesman

1480. One of the guiding philosophies of music is to find your own voice.

Thelonious Monk, 1917–1982
Bebop composer and Pianist

1481. There are no wrong notes.

Thelonious Monk, 1917–1982
Bebop composer and Pianist

1482. Music is your own experience, your thoughts, your wisdom. If you don't live it, it won't come out of your horn.

Charlie Parker, 1920?–1955
Jazz musician

1483. Music is the greatest communication in the world. Even if people don't understand the language that you're singing in, they still know good music when they hear it.

Lou Rawls, 1937–
Singer

1484. I hear my way through the world.

Paul Robeson, 1898–1976
Singer and Activist

1485. I heard my people singing—in the glow of parlor coal stove and on summer porches sweet with lilac air, from choir loft and Sunday morning pews—and my soul was filled with their harmonies.

Paul Robeson, 1898–1976
Singer and Activist

1486. The Negro has a field all to himself in musical expression. His enemies will listen to his music when they will hear nothing else.

J.A. Rogers, 1880–1966
Historian

1487. I like rap because it's a creative art form that's developed by our young people.

Betty Shabazz, 1934?–1997
Educator

1488. I learned to take music apart and analyze the notes and put it back together again.

Sarah Vaughan, 1924?–1990
Singer

1489. [Music is] about movement, the rhythm of life.

Cornel West, 1954–
Philosopher and Activist

1490. I'm convinced that we are only an extension of African civilization, and all this music is really African music.

Randy Weston, 1926–
Pianist

1491. Blacks and whites were making efforts to change things, and music helped bridge the gaps.

Mary Wilson

NAACP

1492. The NAACP ... through the years, the oldest, largest, most consulted, most feared, most respected and most effective civil rights organization, has been a beacon in the continuing struggle for freedom.

Benjamin Hooks, 1925–
NAACP official

NAMES

1493. The name means everything.

Noble Drew Ali, 1880–1929
Islamic leader

1494. I was not only hunting for my liberty, but also hunting for my name.

William Wells Brown, 1815–1884
Writer

1495. A new master might often change a slave's name and this indicated that the slave had absolutely no rights.

William Wells Brown, 1815–1884
Writer

1496. It is certain that all Africans are not Negroes, nor are all who are Negroes, African. Why should the race name of millions of African descent in America be derived from color only?

James C. Embry

1497. The good news is that God changes names.

T.D. Jakes
Evangelist

1498. You diminish a person's humanity when you call him out of his name.

Cornel West, 1954–
Philosopher and Activist

NATIONHOOD

1499. Before you have a God, you must have a Nationality.
Noble Drew Ali, 1880–1929
Islamic leader

1500. We do not want a Nation, we are a Nation.... We are unconscious captives until we realize this.
Amiri Baraka, 1934–
Poet and Writer

1501. We are a nation within a nation as the Poles in Russia, the Hungarians in Austria, the Welsh, Irish, and Scotch in the British Dominion.
Martin R. Delany, 1812–1885
Emigrationist

1502. We must have a nationality before we can become anybody.
John Mercer Langston, 1829–1897
Educator and U.S. Congressperson

1503. I felt so tall within, I felt the power of a nation within me.
Sojourner Truth, 1797?–1883
Abolitionist and Women's rights advocate

1504. When I left the house of bondage I left everything behind. I wasn't going to keep nothing of Egypt on me, and so I went to the Lord and asked him to give me a new name. And he gave me Sojourner because I was to travel up and down the land showing the people their sins and being a sign unto them. I told the Lord I wanted two names because everybody else had two, and the Lord gave me Truth, because I was to declare the truth to the people.
Sojourner Truth, 1797?–1883
Abolitionist and Women's rights advocate

NONVIOLENCE

1505. There is never time in the future in which we will work out our salvation. The challenge is in the moment, the time is always now.

James Baldwin, 1924–1987
Writer and Activist

1506. Nonviolence is a powerful and just weapon. It is a weapon unique in history, which cuts without wounding, and ennobles the man who wields it. It is a sword that heals.

Martin Luther King Jr., 1929–1968
Civil rights activist and Nobel laureate

1507. Nonviolent resistance is not a method for cowards; it does resist.

Martin Luther King Jr., 1929–1968
Civil rights activist and Nobel laureate

OPPORTUNITY

1508. When I was young, the world was white, everywhere, forever. But it is certainly not white in the same way for any young black person today.

James Baldwin, 1924–1987
Writer and Activist

1509. In these strenuous times, we are likely to become morbid and look constantly upon the dark side of life, and spend entirely too much time considering and brooding over what we can't do, rather than what we can do, and instead of growing morose and despondent over opportunities that are shut from us, let us rejoice at the many unexplored fields in which there is unlimited fame and fortune to the successful explorer.

George Washington Carver, 1864?–1943
Inventor

1510. Every intersection in the road of life is an opportunity to make a decision.

Duke Ellington, 1899–1974
Composer and Band leader

1511. Take advantage of every opportunity; where there is none, make it for yourself.

Marcus Garvey, 1887–1940
Nationalist leader

1512. A race is distinguished by its great men, but where there is no opportunity for development, it is impossible to tell what the race can do.

James Walker Hood, 1831–1918
AME Zion bishop

1513. Failure to recognize possibilities is the most dangerous and common mistake one can make.

Mae Jemison, 1956–
Astronaut

1514. One chance is all you need.

Jesse Owens, 1913–1980
Olympic track star

1515. It is time for blacks to begin to shift from a war-time to a peace-time identity, from fighting for opportunity to the seizing of it.

Shelby Steele, 1946–
Writer and Editor

1516. I had to make my own living and my own opportunity.... Don't sit down and wait for the opportunities to come; you have to get up and make them.

Mme. C.J. Walker, 1867–1919
Entrepreneur

1517. We should not permit our grievances to overshadow our opportunities.
Booker T. Washington, 1856–1915
Educator

OPPRESSION
▽//△\▽//△\▽//△\▽//△\▽//△\▽

1518. The root of oppression is loss of memory.
Paula Gunn Allen

1519. There are two things over which you have complete domination, authority, and control—your mind and your mouth.
Molefi Asante, 1942–
Educator

1520. In the face of one's victim one sees oneself.
James Baldwin, 1924–1987
Writer and Activist

1521. The basic error of white comments about their own oppression is the assumption that they know the nature of their enslavement. This cannot be so, because if they really knew, they would liberate themselves by joining the revolution of the black community. They would destroy themselves and be born again as beautiful black people.
James Cone, 1938–
Theologian

1522. Only as we rise ... do we encounter opposition.
Frederick Douglass, 1817?–1895
Abolitionist and Autobiographer

1523. Today I see more clearly than yesterday that back of the problem of race and color lies a greater problem which both obscures and implements it: and that is the fact that so many civilized persons are willing to live in comfort even if the price of this is poverty, ignorance, and disease of the majority of their fellow men.

W.E.B. Du Bois, 1868–1963
Intellectual and Activist

1524. After a period of time, the oppressed man begins imitating the behavior of the oppressor.

Dick Gregory, 1932–
Comedian and Activist

1525. In order to perpetuate itself, every oppression must corrupt or distort those various sources of power within the culture of the oppressed that can provide energy for change.

Audre Lorde, 1934–1992
Writer

1526. You are confined by your own system of oppression.

Toni Morrison, 1931–
Novelist and Nobel laureate

1527. In theory, the Emancipation Proclamation had been a wonderful thing. But in 1915 in Alabama, it was only a theory. The Negro had been set free to work 18 hours a day, free to see all his labor add up to a debt at the year's end, free to be chained to the land he tilled, but could never own any more than if he were still a slave.

Jesse Owens, 1913–1980
Olympic track star

1528. It is inconceivable that American Negroes would fight with those who have oppressed them for generations against the Soviet Union. which in a generation, has raised our people to full human dignity.

Paul Robeson, 1898–1976
Singer and Activist

1529. You can't hold a man down without staying down with him.

Booker T. Washington, 1856–1915
Educator

1530. When you control a man's thinking you do not have to worry about his actions. You do not have to tell him not to stand here or go yonder. He will find his "proper place" and will stay in it. You do not need to send him to the back door. He will go without being told. In fact, if there is no back door, he will cut one for his special benefit. His education makes it necessary.

Carter G. Woodson, 1875–1950
Historian

ORAL TRADITION

1531. The earliest instruction was imparted orally, a system still extant in Africa and the Orient. It trains the mind to listen.

Arthur Schomburg, 1874–1938
Librarian and Book collector

ORGANIZATION

1532. If we must have justice, we must be strong; if we must be strong, we must come together; if we must come together, we can only do so through the system of organization.

Marcus Garvey, 1887–1940
Nationalist leader

1533. No organization can do everything. Every organization can do something.

A. Philip Randolph, 1889–1979
Labor leader

1534. True liberation can be acquired and maintained only when the Negro people possess power; and power is the product and flower of organization— organization of the masses, the masses in the mills and mines, on the farms, in the factories, in churches, in fraternal organizations, in homes, colleges, women's clubs, student groups, trade unions, tenants' leagues, in cooperative guilds, political organizations, and civil rights associations.

A. Philip Randolph, 1889–1979
Labor leader

PARENTS
See Family

PARIS

1535. I have only two loves, Paris and my own country.

Josephine Baker, 1906–1975
Entertainer

1536. Paris is the dance, and I am the dancer.

Josephine Baker, 1906–1975
Entertainer

1537. For Paris is, according to its legend, the city where everyone loses his head, and his morals, lives through at least one historie d'amour, ceases, quite, to arrive anywhere on time, and thumbs his nose at the Puritans—the city, in brief, where all become drunken on the fine old air of freedom.

James Baldwin, 1924–1987
Writer and Activist

1538. I went away to Paris and found myself.

James Baldwin, 1924–1987
Writer and Activist

1539. The only reason I stay in Paris is because I can work.

Sidney Bechet, 1897–1959
Jazz musician

1540. From the day I set foot in France, I became aware of the working of a miracle within me.... I recaptured for the first time since childhood the sense of being just a human being.

James Weldon Johnson, 1871–1938
Writer and Activist

1541. To live in Paris is to allow one's sensibilities to be nourished by physical beauty.

Richard Wright, 1908–1960
Novelist

PATRIOTISM

1542. I have a deep and abiding belief in my country and her security.

Chappie James (Daniel James), 1920–1973
U.S. General

1543. The black man cannot protect a country, if the country doesn't protect him.

Henry McNeal Turner, 1834–1915
Minister and Militant activist

1544. A man who loves a country that hates him is a human dog and not a man.

Henry McNeal Turner, 1834–1915
Minister and Militant activist

1545. You're not supposed to be so blind with patriotism that you can't face reality. Wrong is wrong no matter who does it or says it.

Malcolm X, 1925–1965
Nationalist leader

PEACE

1546. Let a Secretary of Peace be appointed.
Benjamin Banneker, 1731–1806
Inventor

1547. The entire world will be living on borrowed time until peace is finally made secure, and if that is to be accomplished, it will be only the UN that can do it.
Ralph Bunche, 1904–1971
Statesman

1548. Peace, it's wonderful! Aren't you glad?
Father Divine, 1879–1965
Religious leader

1549. If you cannot find peace within yourself, you will never find it anywhere else.
Marvin Gaye, 1939–1984
Singer and Composer

1550. We defeat oppression with liberty. We cure indifference with compassion. We remedy social injustice with justice. And if our journey embodies these lasting principles, we find peace.
Patricia Roberts Harris, 1924–1985
U.S. Secretary of Health, Education, and Welfare

1551. I hope never to be at peace. I hope to make my life manageable, and I think it's fairly manageable now. But, Oh, I would never accept peace. That means death.
Jamaica Kincaid, 1949–
Writer

1552. True peace is not merely the absence of tension; it is the presence of justice.

Martin Luther King Jr., 1929–1968
Civil rights activist and Nobel laureate

1553. My soul is at peace.

Betty Shabazz, 1934?–1997
Educator

1554. For the advancement of peace and unity I shall pity the faults of my fellow man and praise his virtues, forgive his injuries and proclaim his favors, hide his stains and display his perfections, hoping that he will be likewise charitable toward my own shortcomings.

Carter G. Woodson, 1875–1950
Historian

1555. You cannot separate peace from freedom because no one can be at peace until he has his freedom.

Malcolm X, 1925–1965
Nationalist leader

PERSEVERANCE
See Courage

PLURALISM
See Diversity

POETRY

1556. Poetry is music made less abstract.

Amiri Baraka, 1934–
Poet and Writer

1557. Poetry is not a luxury. It is a vital necessity of our existence. It forms the quality of the light within which we predicate our hopes and dreams toward survival and change, first made into language, then into idea, then into more tangible action.

Audre Lorde, 1934–1992
Writer

1558. Poetry is the way we help give name to the nameless so it can be thought.

Audre Lorde, 1934–1992
Writer

1559. Poetry is a part of prayer, a part of the way we express love to each other. It transforms the heart.

Schyleen Qualls, 1949–
Poet and Actor

1560. Poetry is more like improvisational jazz, where each person plays the note that she hears.

Alice Walker, 1944–
Writer

1561. The poetry of a people comes from the deep recesses of the unconscious, the irrational, and the collective body of our ancestral memories.

Margaret Walker, 1915–
Writer

POETS

1562. Yet do I marvel at this curious thing / To make a poet black and bid him sing.

Countee Cullen, 1903–1946
Poet

1563. I know why the caged bird sings.

Paul Laurence Dunbar, 1873–1906
Poet

1564. O black and unknown bards of long ago / How came your lips to touch the sacred fire?

James Weldon Johnson, 1871–1938
Writer and Activist

POLITICS

1565. The decisions that are made about who goes to Stanford and who goes to San Quentin are made outside the control of the black community.

Walter Allen

1566. If you postulate an either-or choice between Africa and the West, there is no place for you in the real world of politics.

Anthony Appiah, 1954–
Philosopher

1567. A black liberal is a contradiction in terms.

Belynda B. Bady, 1961–
Entrepreneur

1568. Say it loud, I'm black and I'm proud!

James Brown, 1933–
Singer and Composer

1569. I did not run on the basis of race, but I will not run away from it. I am proud of who I am and I am proud of this [Democratic] Party, for we are truly America's last best hope to bridge the division of race, region, religion, and ethnicity.

Ronald H. Brown, 1941–1997
Politician

1570. There was a time when I was a picketer across the street. Then I decided I didn't want to be there outside of policy-making. I wanted to be inside, fighting right there on their turf.

Yvonne Brathwaite Burke, 1932–
Politician

1571. The act of registering to vote … marks the beginning of political modernization by broadening the base of participation. It also does something the existentialists talk about: it gives one a sense of being. The black man who goes to register is saying to the white man, "No."

Stokely Carmichael, 1941–
Activist

1572. Everyone is represented in Washington by a rich and powerful lobby, it seems. But there is no lobby for the people.

Shirley Chisholm, 1924–
Politician

1573. Our children, our jobless men, our deprived, rejected, and starving fellow citizens must come first. For this reason, I intend to vote No on every money bill that comes to the floor of this House that provides any funds for the Department of Defense.

Shirley Chisholm, 1924–
Politician

1574. I can't help having a political life. And I guess this is related to my background, growing up in the South where to be black was to be political.

Angela Davis, 1944–
Militant activist

1575. You can believe that almost any black who holds office or aspires to office is obliged to have a view on controversial black figures. I'd like to be asked about controversial white figures for a change.

David Dinkins, 1927–
Politician

1576. The Republican Party is the ship; all else is the sea.

Frederick Douglass, 1817?–1895
Abolitionist and Autobiographer

1577. The Supreme Court has surrendered.... It has destroyed the Civil Rights Bill and converted the Republican party into a party of money rather than a party of morals.

Frederick Douglass, 1817?–1895
Abolitionist and Autobiographer

1578. As Negro voting power increased, Congress got an improved sense of hearing.

W.E.B. Du Bois, 1868–1963
Intellectual and Activist

1579. May God write us down as asses if ever again we are found putting our trust in either the Republican or Democratic parties.

W.E.B. Du Bois, 1868–1963
Intellectual and Activist

1580. We formed our own [Mississippi Freedom Democratic Party] because the whites would not let us register.

Fannie Lou Hamer, 1917–1977
Civil rights activist

1581. His [Michael Dukakis's] foreparents came to America in immigrant ships. My foreparents came to America in slave ships. But whatever the original ships, we are both in the same boat tonight.

Jesse Jackson, 1941–
Minister and Civil rights activist

1582. If you don't vote, you are irrelevant to the process. If you do not have integrity, you are a coward. Only by engaging, engaging, engaging, engaging can you make things happen.

Jesse Jackson, 1941–
Minister and Civil rights activist

1583. If American women would increase their voting turnout by 10 percent, I think we would see an end to all of the budget cuts in programs benefiting women and children.

Coretta Scott King, 1927–
Civil rights activist

1584. There are more Negroes in jail with me than there are on the voting rolls.

Martin Luther King Jr., 1929–1968
Civil rights activist and Nobel laureate

1585. It's going to be up to us to challenge the Democrats and the Republicans on the issue of democracy.

Melvin H. King
Activist and Politician

1586. It is important for women, and especially African American women, to become involved and to hold public office.

Constance Baker Motley, 1921–
Lawyer and Judge

1587. I do not care so far as I am personally concerned whether you give me my seat or not. I will go back to my people and come here again.

Pinckney B.S. Pinchback, 1837–1921
U.S. Senator

1588. In politics, as in other things, there is no such thing as one getting something for nothing. The payoff may involve compromises of various types that may strike at the ideals and principles one has held dear all his life.

A. Philip Randolph, 1889–1979
Labor leader

1589. African Americans ought to care about Africa and the Caribbean because we are much stronger together than separate. Our potential as black people is to harness our power globally.

Randall Robinson, 1941–
Trans Africa official

1590. For [the American Negro] a group tradition must supply compensation for persecution, and pride of race the antidote for prejudice.

Arthur Schomburg, 1874–1938
Librarian and Book collector

1591. I got into heated arguments with sisters or brothers who claimed that the oppression of black people was only a question of race. I argued that there were black oppressors as well as white ones. That's why you've got blacks who support Nixon or Reagan or other conservatives. Black folks with money have always tended to support candidates who they believed would protect their financial interests.

Assata Shakur

1592. All politicians have baggage. It's just that some politicians get skycaps to carry their baggage. I have to carry my own.

Al Sharpton, 1955–
Minister and Activist

1593. I am for Negro suffrage in every rebel state. If it be just, it should not be denied; if it be necessary, it should be adopted; if it be punishment to traitors, they deserve it.

Thaddeus Stevens

1594. There's only one party ideologically in this country, and it represents racism, hatred, and fascism.

William Strickland

1595. When poor people feel they make a difference they vote. There's no apathy; there's disappointment.

Dorothy Tillman, 1947–
Civil rights activist

1596. The fundamental issue of black identity—the affirmation of African humanity and ability—is a precondition for any black progressive politics.

Cornel West, 1954–
Philosopher and Activist

1597. The real servant of the people, then, will give more attention to those to be served than to the use that somebody may want to make of them.

Carter G. Woodson, 1875–1950
Historian

1598. Nonvoting is a fruitless temper tantrum.

Bruce Wright, 1918–
Judge

POVERTY

1599. If you think poor, you are poor.

Wally Amos, 1937–
Athlete and Entrepreneur

1600. I was born poor, I lived poor, and I'm going to die poor.

Arthur Crudup, 1905–1974
Blues musician

1601. To be a poor man is hard, but to be a poor race in a land of dollars is the very bottom of hardships.

W.E.B. Du Bois, 1868–1963
Intellectual and Activist

1602. When you're poor, you grow up fast.

Billie Holiday, 1915–1959
Blues singer

1603. The gap between black and white is greater [in 1997] than at any time since 1954. But it is not as great as the gap between haves and have-nots. Some will go to Yale and the others will go to jail. Americans are comfortable talking about black and white. We're not as comfortable talking about haves and have-nots.

Jesse Jackson, 1941–
Minister and Civil rights activist

1604. Congress has wearied on the war on poverty and decided to wage war against poor people instead.

Hugh Price, 1941–
National Urban League official

POWER

⚞ ⚞ ⚞ ⚞ ⚞ ⚞ ⚞ ⚞

1605. There is a soul force in the universe, which, if we permit it, will flow through us and produce.

Mohandas K. Gandhi, 1869–1948
Indian nationalist leader

1606. The only protection against injustice in man is power— physical, financial, and scientific.

Marcus Garvey, 1887–1940
Nationalist leader

1607. My message is about changing our way of thinking about women and abuses of power.

Anita Hill, 1956–
Law professor

1608. There is nothing essentially wrong with power. The problem is American power is unequally distributed.

Martin Luther King Jr., 1929–1968
Civil rights activist and Nobel laureate

1609. There is a strong moralistic strain in the Civil Rights Movement that would remind us that power corrupts, forgetting that the absence of power also corrupts.

Bayard Rustin, 1910–1997
Civil rights activist

1610. The love of power is one of the greatest human infirmities, and with it comes the usurping influence of despotism, the mother of slavery.

William S. Whipper, 1805–1885
Abolitionist

1611. Power in defense of freedom is greater than power on behalf of tyranny.

Malcolm X, 1925–1965
Nationalist leader

PRAYER

1612. Every man prays in his own language, and there is no language that God does not understand.

Duke Ellington, 1899–1974
Composer and Band leader

1613. Don't pray when it rains if you don't pray when the sun shines.

Satchel Paige, 1900?–1982
Baseball star

1614. Prayer is an attempt to count the stars of our souls.

James M. Washington, 1948–1997
Minister and Academic

1615. Through precept and example, [my mother] taught me that prayer is a conversation with God. That was the reigning assumption of the African American Christian community that nurtured me.

James M. Washington, 1948–1997
Minister and Academic

PREACHING

1616. We may be debarred entrance to many pulpits (as some of us now are) and stand at the door or on the street corner in order to preach to men and women. No difference when or where, we must preach a whole gospel.

Julia A.J. Foote, 1823–1901
Minister

1617. If a man may preach, because the Saviour died for him, why not the woman? Seeing he died for her also. Is he not a whole Saviour instead of a half one?

Jarena Lee, 1783–1853?
Minister

1618. I'm going to preach whether you get saved or not.

Joseph Lowery, 1924–
Civil rights activist

PREJUDICE

1619. The prejudiced people can't insult you because they're blinded by their own ignorance.

Pearl Bailey, 1918–1990
Entertainer

1620. Race prejudice is the devil unchained.

Charles W. Chesnutt, 1858–1932
Novelist

1621. Up to the age of 31, I had been hurt emotionally, spiritually, and physically as much as 31 years can bear.... and still I was entire, complete, functional and my mind was sharp, my reflexes were good, and I was not bitter. But under the mental corrosion of race prejudice in Los Angeles, I had become bitter and saturated with hate.

Chester Himes, 1909–1984
Writer

1622. The ignorant are always prejudiced and the prejudiced are always ignorant.

Charles V. Roman, 1864–1934
Physician

1623. Prejudice is not so much dependent upon natural antipathy as upon education.

David Ruggles, 1810–1849
Journalist and Abolitionist

PRIDE
See Black Pride

PRISON

1624. There are literally thousands of people imprisoned solely because of their race and poverty.

Benjamin Chavis Jr., 1948–
Activist

1625. It frightens me that our young black men have a better chance of going to jail than of going to college.

Johnnie J. Cochran
Lawyer

1626. Jails and prisons are designed to break human beings, to convert our population into specimens in a zoo—obedient to our keepers, but dangerous to each other.

Angela Davis, 1944–
Militant activist

1627. Most people are unaware of the fact that jail and prison are two entirely different institutions. People in prison have already been convicted. Jails are primarily for pretrial confinement.... More than half of the jail population have never been convicted of anything.

Angela Davis, 1944–
Militant activist

1628. Every prisoner is not a criminal, just as every criminal is not in prison.

Michael Eric Dyson, 1958–
Scholar and Writer

1629. Unfortunately the prisons of our land often reproduce the pathology that they seek to eliminate.

Michael Eric Dyson, 1958–
Scholar and Writer

1630. I have never been constrained except that I made the prison.

Mari Evans, 1923–
Poet

1631. I was accused of robbing a gas station of $70.... I agreed to confess in return for a light county jail sentence.... They tossed me into the penitentiary with one to life. That was in 1960 [10 years ago]. I was 18 years old. I've been here ever since.

George Jackson, 1941–1971
Prisoner and Activist

1632. In every state, more and more prisons are being built and even more are on the drawing board. Who are they for? They certainly aren't planning to put white people in them.

Assata Shakur

1633. The kitchenette is our prison, our death sentence without trial.

Richard Wright, 1908–1960
Novelist

1634. I was in prison before entering here.... The solitude, the long moments of meditative contemplation, have given me the key to my freedom.

Malcolm X, 1925–1965
Nationalist leader

1635. In our prisons there are hundreds, perhaps even thousands of people I would call political prisoners.

Andrew Young, 1932–
Civil rights activist

PROGRESS

1636. I stand before you today as the elected leader of the greatest city of a great nation, to which my ancestors were brought, chained and whipped, in the hold of a slave ship. We have not finished the journey toward liberty and justice, but surely we have come a long way.

David Dinkins, 1927–
Politician

1637. I believe that we could go much farther and much faster without a great calamity the white leadership seems to fear so strongly.

Gordon Blaine Hancock, 1884–1970
Minister and Sociologist

1638. The line of progress is never straight. For a period of movement may follow a straight line and then it encounters obstacles and the path bends.

Martin Luther King Jr., 1929–1968
Civil rights activist and Nobel laureate

1639. From 1863, when slavery was abolished in this country, down to the present time [1907] history reveals to us the fact that the Negro race, though spurned on every hand, has made the most rapid progress, under the most trying circumstances, of any race on the globe.

W.A. Luis, 1948–
Educator

1640. If you always do what you always did, you will always get what you always got.

Moms Mabley (Jackie Mabley), 1897–1975
Comedian

1641. There is no short cut to utopia.

Claude McKay, 1889–1948
Writer

1642. There is no power on earth that can permanently stay our progress.

Booker T. Washington, 1856–1915
Educator

1643. Though the line of progress may seem at times to waver, now advancing, now retreating, now on the mountains, now in the valley, now in the sunshine, now in the shadow, the aim has ever been forward, and we have gained more than we have lost.

Booker T. Washington, 1856–1915
Educator

1644. We are crawling up, working up, yea, bursting up, often through oppression, unjust discrimination and prejudice; but through them all we are coming up.

Booker T. Washington, 1856–1915
Educator

1645. I will never say that progress is being made. If you stick a knife in my back nine inches and pull it out six inches, there's no progress. You pull it all the way out, that's not progress. The progress is healing the wound that's below.

Malcolm X, 1925–1965
Nationalist leader

PROTEST

1646. You've got to rattle your cage door. You've got to let them know that you're in there, and that you want out.

Florynce Kennedy, 1916–?
Lawyer and Feminist

1647. We are four millions, out of 30 millions who inhabit this country, and we have rights as well as privileges to maintain and we must assert our manhood in their vindication.

Pinckney B.S. Pinchback, 1837–1921
U.S. Senator

PUBLIC LIFE

1648. Public life deteriorates due to class polarization, racial balkanization, and especially a predatory market culture.

Cornel West, 1954–
Philosopher and Activist

PUNISHMENT

1649. There is scarcely a single fact more worthy of indelible record than the utter inefficiency of human punishments to cure human evils.

William S. Whipper, 1805–1885
Abolitionist

PURPOSE

1650. I believe I was born to help my people to be free.

Muhammad Ali, 1942–
Boxing champion

1651. I wasn't concerned about the hardships because I always felt I was doing what I had to do, what I wanted to do, and what I was destined to do.

Katherine Dunham, 1910–
Dancer

1652. The time for cynicism is over—and it is you who will help to shape the end of cynicism. It is you—if you will summon the courage—who will forge new initiatives in finance, technology, medicine, and management that will put all Americans back to work and at the same time give America a better shot at feeding the hungry, sheltering the homeless, healing the sick, and caring for the children.

Myrlie Evers-Williams
NAACP official

1653. One God! One Aim! One Destiny!

Marcus Garvey, 1887–1940
Nationalist leader

1654. Man cannot live without some knowledge of the purpose of life. If he can find no purpose in life, he creates one in the inevitability of death.

Chester Himes, 1909–1984
Writer

1655. I believe we are here on the planet earth to live, grow up and do what we can do to make this world a better place for all people to enjoy freedom.

Rosa Parks, 1913–
Civil rights activist

RACE

1656. I know one race, the human race.

Osceola Adams, 1890–1933
Actor

1657. None of us is responsible for the complexion of his skin. This fact of nature offers no clue to the character or quality of the person underneath.

Marian Anderson, 1897–1993
Singer

1658. I think it is clear enough that a biologically rooted conception of race is both dangerous in practice and misleading in theory: African unity, African identity need securer foundations than race.

Anthony Appiah, 1954–
Philosopher

1659. The Pan-Africanists responded to their experience of racial discrimination by accepting the racialism it presupposed.

Anthony Appiah, 1954–
Philosopher

1660. What we in the academy can contribute—even if only slowly and only marginally—is a disruption of the discourse of "racial" and "tribal" differences.

Anthony Appiah, 1954–
Philosopher

1661. Being black is not inherently a problem, unless you're in a world of white supremacy. You cannot have a conversation of race that does not deal with what created white supremacy.

Kathleen Cleaver, 1945–
Law professor

1662. Ashamed of my race? And of what race am I? I am many in one.

Joseph S. Cotter, 1861–1949
Teacher and Writer

1663. The history of the world is the history, not of individuals, but of groups, not of nations, but of races, and he who ignores or seeks to override the race idea in human history ignores and overrules the central thought of all history.

W.E.B. Du Bois, 1868–1963
Intellectual and Activist

1664. Has the God who made the white man and the black left any record declaring us a different species? Are we not sustained by the same power, supported by the same food, hurt by the same wounds, wounded by the same wrongs, pleased with the same delights, and propagated by the same means? And should we not then enjoy the same liberty, and be protected by the same laws?

James Forten, 1766–1842
Abolitionist and Businessperson

1665. Race designation is a political designation.

Jesse Jackson, 1941–
Minister and Civil rights activist

1666. The fact that race matters ... does not mean that the salience and consequences of racial distinctions are good or that race must continue to matter in the future. Nor does the brute sociological fact that race matters dictate what one's response to that fact should be.

Randall Kennedy, 1954–
Law professor

1667. The racial differences we see today may be a late (and trivial) development in human evolution.

Douglas Preston

1668. No American is an expert on race. Each of us has our own experience, and sometimes it is intense enough to make us think that we know the subject thoroughly. When we recognize that we do not, we will have taken the first step toward learning.

David K. Shipler
Author of A *Country of Strangers*

1669. In my body were many bloods, some dark blood, all blended in the fire of six or more generations. I was, then, either a new type of man or the very oldest.

Jean Toomer, 1894–1967
Novelist

1670. How difficult it is sometimes to know where the black begins and the white ends.

Booker T. Washington, 1856–1915
Educator

1671. To talk about race in America is to explore the wilderness inside ourselves and to come to terms with a history that we'd rather conceal.

Cornel West, 1954–
Philosopher and Activist

RACE CONSCIOUSNESS
 ▯▯▮ ▯▯▮▮▯ ▯▯▮▮▯ ▯▯▮▮▯ ▯▮▯

1672. The world is white no longer, and it will never be white again.
James Baldwin, 1924–1987
Writer and Activist

1673. I belong to this race, and when it is down I belong to a down race; when it is up I belong to a risen race.
Frances Ellen Watkins Harper, 1825–1911
Writer and Orator

1674. All blacks are militant in their guts, but militancy is expressed in different ways.
Barbara Jordan, 1936–1996
Lawyer and U.S. Congressperson

1675. I must attribute my motivation and my desire to be an artist to the people of the black community.
Jacob Lawrence, 1917–
Painter

1676. If a cat had kittens in an oven, would you call them biscuits?
Queen Mother Moore (Audley Moore), 1898–1997
Nationalist leader

1677. One of the great tasks of Negro writers of the future will be to show the Negro to himself; it will be, paraphrasing the language of James Joyce, to forge in the smithy of our souls the uncreated conscience of our race.
Richard Wright, 1908–1960
Novelist

1678. You wouldn't be in this country if some enemy hadn't kidnapped you and brought you here. On the other hand, some of you think you came here on the Mayflower.
Malcolm X, 1925–1965
Nationalist leader

RACE PRIDE
See Black Pride

RACE RELATIONS
∧∘ ∧ ∘∧ ∘∧ ∘∧ ∘∧ ∘∧ ∘∧ ∘∧

1679. As long as you keep a person down, some part of you has to be down there to hold him down, so it means you cannot soar as you otherwise might.
Marian Anderson, 1897–1993
Singer

1680. In order to get beyond racism, we must first take account of race.
Harry Blackmun
U.S. Supreme Court Justice

1681. The eyes of the world are focused on this [race] problem, on what happens in the United States. This has a tremendous effect on the United States' image abroad.
Ralph Bunche, 1904–1971
Statesman

1682. We have talked at each other and about each other for a long time. It's high time we all began talking with each other.
Bill Clinton, 1946–
U.S. President

1683. It is ironic that virtually every Martin Luther King Jr. Boulevard in America is a street of abandoned buildings, abandoned businesses, abandoned people, abandoned dreams. Those who honor King's name need to think about fulfilling the promise of his dream to those who have been forsaken in our inner cities.
James P. Danky, 1947–
Librarian and Bibliographer

1684. The problem of the 20th century is the problem of the color line—the relations of the darker to the lighter races of men in Asia, Africa, in America, and the islands of the sea.

W.E.B. Du Bois, 1868–1963
Intellectual and Activist

1685. There is an historical circumstance, known to few, that connects the children of the Puritans with these Africans of Virginia in a very singular way. They are our brethren, as being lineal descendents from the Mayflower, the fated womb of which, in her first voyage, sent forth a brood of Pilgrims on Plymouth Rock, and, in a subsequent one, spawned slaves upon the Southern soil—a monstrous birth, but with which we have an instinctive sense of kindred, and so we are stirred by an irresistable impulse to attempt their rescue, even at the cost of blood and ruin. The character of our sacred ship, I fear, may suffer a little by this revelation, but we must let her white progeny offset her dark one, and two such portents never sprang from an identical source before.

Nathaniel Hawthorne
Novelist

1686. Why can't we all just get along?

Rodney King, 1965–
Los Angeles police victim

1687. Those who become inoculated with the virus of race hatred are more unfortunate than the victim of it.

Kelly Miller, 1863–1939
Educator

1688. By and large ... the Aframerican is not a particularly sadistic fellow, despite his long and intimate association with Caucasians.

George Schuyler, 1895–1977
Journalist

1689. To be black and marginally comfortable, I have to accept a gradual change of the oppressive status quo: act dumb enough not to threaten white people, but appear intelligent enough to be useful and worthy of their liberal investment.

Judy Simmons
Journalist

1690. We are a country of strangers, and we are having a great deal of difficulty with our differences, because ultimately, we lack the ability to look at specific human beings.

Anna Deavere Smith, 1950–
Actor

1691. The social problems of urban life in the United States are, in large measure, the problems of racial inequality.

William Julius Wilson
Sociologist

1692. I believe there are some sincere white people. But I think they should prove it.

Malcolm X, 1925–1965
Nationalist leader

RACISM

1693. I'm not going to help nobody against something Negroes don't have. If I'm going to die, I'll die right here fighting you. If I'm going to die, you're my enemy. My enemy is the white people, not Viet Congs or Chinese or Japanese. You're my foes when I want freedom. You're my foes when I want equality. You're my foes when I want justice. You won't even stand up for me in America for my religious beliefs and you want me to go somewhere and fight, while you won't even stand up for me here at home.

Muhammad Ali, 1942–
Boxing champion

1694. AIDS isn't the heaviest burden I have had to bear ... being black is the greatest burden I've had to bear. No question about it, race has always been my biggest burden, having to live as a minority in America.

Arthur Ashe, 1943–1993
Tennis champion

1695. Every black man, whatever his style, had been scarred, as in some tribal rite; and every white man, though white men, mostly, had no style, had been maimed.

James Baldwin, 1924–1987
Writer and Activist

1696. Black people will never gain full equality in this country. Even those Herculean efforts that we hail as successful will produce no more that temporary "peaks of progress," short-lived victories that slide into irrelevance as racial patterns adapt in ways that maintain white dominance. This is a hard to accept fact that all history verifies. We must acknowledge it, not as a sign of submission, but as an act of ultimate defiance.

Derrick Bell, 1930–
Law professor

1697. We misunderstand racism completely if we do not understand that racism is mask for a much deeper problem involving not the victims of racism but the perpetrators.

Lerone Bennett, 1928–
Historian

1698. Once, we thought that segregation and racism were the same thing, and that, when segregation was done away with, racism would be done away with, too.

Julian Bond, 1940–
Civil rights activist

1699. Racism systematically verifies itself anytime the slave can only be free by imitation of his master.

H. Rap Brown, 1943–
Militant activist

1700. I believe racism has killed more people than speed, heroin, or cancer, and will continue to kill until it's no more.

Alice Childress, 1920–1994
Writer

1701. We and the Native Americans were the only citizens or aliens legally forbidden to enter libraries, concert halls, theaters, and public schools.

Alice Childress, 1920–1994
Writer

1702. The struggle of racism all along has been a struggle to regain the essential manhood lost after the European expansion into the broader world and the attempt to justify the slave trade.

John Henrik Clarke, 1915–
Historian

1703. I see racism as such being even more dangerous in the latter nineties than it was in the fifties and sixties. For one thing, it is more structurally entrenched in the economic system and so the globalization of capitol has led to racism structures that are often not recognized as racism.

Angela Davis, 1944–
Militant activist

1704. The struggle is much more difficult now because racism is more entrenched and complicated.

Angela Davis, 1944–
Militant activist

1705. You degrade us and then ask why we are degraded. You shut our mouths and ask why we don't speak. You close your colleges and seminaries against us and then ask why we don't know.

Frederick Douglass, 1817?–1895
Abolitionist and Autobiographer

1706. People have been sitting on my neck or my head for a century, and when I get a piece of my neck out, they start this reverse discrimination cry.

John Hope Franklin, 1915–
Historian

1707. The last vestige of racism in the West will be intellectual racism.

Henry Louis Gates Jr., 1950–
Scholar and Critic

1708. [African Americans] are treated worse than aliens among a people whose language we speak, whose religion we profess, and whose blood flows and mingles in our veins.

Frances Ellen Watkins Harper, 1825–1911
Writer and Orator

1709. Until my singing made me famous, I'd lived so far inside the colored people's world that I didn't have to pay attention every day to the way some white people in this country act toward a person with a darker skin.

Mahalia Jackson, 1911–1972
Gospel singer

1710. White America cannot save itself if it prevents us from being saved.

James Weldon Johnson, 1871–1938
Writer and Activist

1711. Racism is a sickness unto death.

Martin Luther King Jr., 1929–1968
Civil rights activist and Nobel laureate

1712. Racism in America is much more complex than either the conscious conspiracy of a power elite or the simple delusion of a few ignorant bigots. It is part of our common experience, therefore a part of our common culture.

Charles Lawrence

1713. Race has become metaphorical, a way of referring to and disguising forces, events, classes, and expressions of social decay and economic division far more threatening to the body politic than biological "race" ever was.

Toni Morrison, 1931–
Novelist and Nobel laureate

1714. Before the summer project last year [1964] we watched five Negroes murdered in two counties in Mississippi with no reaction from the country. We couldn't get the news out. Then we saw that when three civil rights workers were killed, and two of them were white, the whole country reacted, went into motion. There's a deep problem behind that, and I think if you can begin to understand what that problem is—why you don't move the same way when a Negro is killed the same way you move when a white person is killed—then maybe you can begin to understand this country in relation to Vietnam, and the Third World, the Congo and Santo Domingo.

Bob Moses
Civil rights activist

1715. Why does such a birth ["out of wedlock"] become pathological when it occurs in the maternity ward in Lincoln hospital in the South Bronx, say, rather than within the pastel walls of an alternative birthing center?

Adolph Reed, 1947–
Writer and Critic

1716. They will never let me play a part in which a Negro is on top.

Paul Robeson, 1898–1976
Singer and Activist

1717. For those of you who are tired of hearing about racism, imagine how much more tired WE are of constantly experiencing it.

Barbara Smith, 1946–
Writer and Publisher

1718. Racism makes the absurd assumption that one race is the quintessential embodiment of the entire species.

James M. Washington, 1948–1997
Minister and Academic

1719. The Negro race is the only race that has ever come in contact with the European race that has proved itself able to withstand its atrocities and oppression. All others like the Indians who they could not make subservient to their use they have destroyed.

Joseph Wilson, 1836–1891
Historian

1720. When you've taught a man to hate himself, you've really got it and gone.

Malcolm X, 1925–1965
Nationalist leader

1721. Every black person who rises is subject to a greater degree of criticism and more than any other segment of the population.

Coleman Young, 1923–1997
Politician, Mayor of Detroit

RADICALISM

1722. We need more radicalism among us before we can speak as becomes a suffering, oppressed, and persecuted people.

Charles Lenox Remond, 1810–1873
Abolitionist

RAGTIME

See also Music

1723. In Paris they call [ragtime] American music.

James Weldon Johnson, 1871–1938
Writer and Activist

1724. Out of this ragtime came the fragmentary outlines of the menace to old Europe, the domination of America, the emergence of Africa, the end of confidence and any feeling of security, the nervous excitement, the beginning of modern times.

J.B. Priestly, 1894–
English writer

RAP

See also Music

1725. White kids wanted to be black, black kids wanted to be like those in the video. MTV executives said, "Let's kill rap and hip hop, it's bringing people together."
Chuck D.
Rap artist

1726. 2 Live Crew is engaged in heavy-handed parody, turning the stereotypes of black and white American culture on their heads. These young artists are acting out, to lively dance music, a parodic exaggeration of the age-old stereotypes of the oversexed black female and male.
Henry Louis Gates Jr., 1950–
Scholar and Critic

1727. Rap is the most positive thing for black kids because it gives information and talks about society, about black history.
Ice Cube (O'Shea Jackson), 1969–
Rap artist

1728. Before you can understand what I mean, you have to know how I lived or how the people I'm talking to live.
Tupac Shakur, 1971–1996
Rap artist

1729. Black rap music recovers and revises elements of black rhetorical style, some from black preaching and black rhythmic drumming.
Cornel West, 1954–
Philosopher and Activist

RAPE

1730. What happened to me happens to hundreds of thousands of women every day.

Tawana Brawley
Crime subject

1731. You know, Mrs. Stowe, slave women can't help themselves.

Eliza Buick

1732. Rape was an insurrectionary act.... I wanted to send waves of consternation throughout the white race.

Eldridge Cleaver, 1935–1998
Black Panther Party leader

1733. Nobody in this section of the country believes the old threadbare lie that Negro men rape white women. If Southern white men are not careful, they will over-reach themselves and public sentiment will have a reaction; a conclusion will then be reached which will be very damaging to the moral reputation of their women.

Ida B. Wells, 1862–1931
Militant activist

READING

1734. We are the only racial group within the United States ever forbidden by law to read and write.

Alice Childress, 1920–1994
Writer

1735. I had often seen my master and Dick employed in reading; and I had a great curiosity to talk to the books as I thought they did, and so to learn how all things had a beginning. For that purpose I have often taken up a book, and have talked to it, and then put my ears to it, when alone, in hopes it would answer me; and I have been very much concerned when I found it remained silent.

Olaudah Equiano, 1745?–1801
Slave autobiographer

1736. It often requires more courage to read some books than it does to fight a battle.

Sutton E. Griggs, 1872–1930
Novelist and Minister

1737. Father could read a little, and he helped us all with our ABC's, but it is hard work learning to read and write without a teacher, and there was no school a black child could attend at that time.

Nat "Deadwood Dick, the cowboy adventurer" Love, 1854–?
Cowboy

1738. One of the joys of reading is the ability to plug into the shared wisdom of mankind.

Ishmael Reed, 1938–
Dramatist

1739. In the old days, in my mother's time, I heard colored people had to pray in secret and learn to read in secret. The white man didn't want us to learn.... A book was a precious thing.

Rose Smith

1740. If you can't read, you can't lead.

Leon Sullivan, 1922–
Minister and Entrepreneur

1741. I cannot read a book but I can read the people.

Sojourner Truth, 1797?–1883
Abolitionist and Women's rights advocate

1742. Reading had changed forever the course of my life.

Malcolm X, 1925–1965
Nationalist leader

REALITY

❚❒❚ ❚❒❚❒❚ ❚❒❚❒❚ ❚❒❚❒❚ ❚❒❚

1743. If one is lucky, a solitary fantasy can totally transform one million realities.

Maya Angelou, 1928–
Novelist and Poet

1744. The price one pays for pursuing any profession, or calling, is an intimate knowledge of its ugly side.

James Baldwin, 1924–1987
Writer and Activist

1745. You cannot fix what you cannot face.

James Baldwin, 1924–1987
Writer and Activist

1746. Our future expectations must be turned into present realities.

James Cone, 1938–
Theologian

1747. In the beginning was not the shadow but the act, and the province of Hollywood is not actual, but illusion.

Ralph Ellison, 1914–1994
Novelist

1748. We need something we don't yet have: a way of speaking about black poverty that doesn't falsify the reality of black advancement; a way of speaking about black advancement that doesn't distort the enduring realities of black poverty.

Henry Louis Gates Jr., 1950–
Scholar and Critic

1749. It is naive to think that [Martin Luther] King's dream is going to be totally realized in 25 years in light of 350 years of slavery, segregation, and institutionalized racism.

William H. Gray III, 1941–
U.S. Congressperson

1750. Because I and my reality did not comport with what they accepted as their reality, I and my reality had to be reconstructed by the Senate committee members with assistance from the press and others.

Anita Hill, 1956–
Law professor

1751. The fact that we are black is our ultimate reality.

Ron Karenga, 1941–
Educator

1752. One never knows, do one?

Fats Waller, 1904–1943
Pianist and Composer

1753. What you see is what you get.

Flip Wilson, 1933–
Comedian

1754. We are not what we seem.

Richard Wright, 1908–1960
Novelist

REBELLION

1755. Remember Denmark Vesey, remember Nathaniel Turner, remember Shields Green and Copeland, who followed noble John Brown, and fell as glorious martyrs for the cause of the slave.

Frederick Douglass, 1817?–1895
Abolitionist and Autobiographer

1756. Who would be free themselves must strike the blow.

Frederick Douglass, 1817?–1895
Abolitionist and Autobiographer

1757. I have nothing more to offer that what General Washington would have had to offer had he been taken by the British and put to trial by them. I have adventured my life in endeavoring to obtain the liberty of my countrymen, and am a willing sacrifice to their cause; and I beg, as a favor, that I may be immediately led to execution, I know that you have pre-determined to shed my blood, why then all this mockery of a trial?

Gabriel Prosser, 1775?–1800
Insurrectionist

1758. I heard a loud noise in the heavens, and the Spirit instantly appeared to me and said the Serpent was loosened, and Christ had laid down the yoke he had borne for the sins of men and that I should take it on and fight against the Serpent, for the time was fast approaching when the first should be last and the last first.

Nat Turner, 1800?–1831
Prophet and Insurrectionist

1759. Remember that ours is not a war for robbery, or to satisfy our passions; it is a struggle for freedom.

Nat Turner, 1800?–1831
Prophet and Insurrectionist

1760. The riots in Los Angeles and in other cities shocked the world. They shouldn't have. Many of us have watched our country—including our government—neglect the problems, indeed the people of our inner cities for years—

even as matters reached a crisis stage.... For years, they have been crying out for help. For years, their cries have not been heard.

Maxine Waters, 1938–
Politician

1761. [At Martin Luther King's assassination], the first time since the Civil War, the United States government had to bring out the National Guard to protect the White House.

Cornel West, 1954–
Philosopher and Activist

RECONSTRUCTION

1762. The unending tragedy of Reconstruction is the utter inability of the American mind to grasp its real significance, its national and worldwide implications. It was vain for [Sen. Charles] Sumner and [Rep. Thaddeous] Stevens to hammer in the ears of the people that this problem involved the very foundations of American democracy, both political and economic.

W.E.B. Du Bois, 1868–1963
Intellectual and Activist

1763. It is a heritage of which they would be proud to know how their fathers and grandfathers handled their brief day of power during the Reconstruction period.

Ida B. Wells, 1862–1931
Militant activist

REFORM

1764. The pleas of crying soft and sparing never answered the purpose of a reform and never will.

David Ruggles, 1810–1849
Journalist and Abolitionist

1765. We have many reformers, few transformers.

Jean Toomer, 1894–1967
Novelist

RELATIONSHIPS

1766. There are roads out of the secret place within us along which we must all move as we go to touch others.

Romare Bearden, 1914–1988
Artist

1767. To understand how any society functions you must understand the relationship between the men and the women.

Angela Davis, 1944–
Militant activist

1768. The person who seeks to change another person in a relationship basically sets the stage for a great deal of conflict.

Wesley Snipes, 1962–
Actor

RELIGION

∧ ∧ ∧ ∧ ∧ ∧ ∧ ∧

1769. In the year 2000, Moors will come into their own.

Noble Drew Ali, 1880–1929
Islamic leader

1770. When the fire comes, I will be the water.

Noble Drew Ali, 1880–1929
Islamic leader

1771. If you deny us your [Methodist] name, you cannot seal up the Scriptures from us, and deny us a name in heaven.

Richard Allen, 1760–1831
AME Church founder

1772. If God can forgive you and me, surely we ought to be able to forgive someone who merely burned down the church. He did not burn down the church. He just burned down the building.

Alfred Baldwin

1773. Testimony is an integral part of the black religious tradition. It is the occasion where the believer stands before the community of faith in order to give account of the hope that is in him or her.

James Cone, 1938–
Theologian

1774. My chief problem has been that of reconciling a Christian upbringing with a pagan inclination.

Countee Cullen, 1903–1946
Poet

1775. I am not a prophet, I am not a messenger, but I am a warner.

Louis Farrakhan, 1934–
Nation of Islam leader

1776. If we can put the names of our faiths aside for the moment and look at principles, we will find a common thread running through all the great religious expressions.

Louis Farrakhan, 1934–
Nation of Islam leader

1777. The wheel is real.

Louis Farrakhan, 1934–
Nation of Islam leader

1778. I have food for every mind. I have food for every soul.

Father Divine, 1879–1965
Religious leader

1779. I never said I was God, but you can't prove to me I'm not!

Sweet Daddy Grace, 1881–1960
Religious leader

1780. If you sin against God, grace can save you, but if you sin against grace, God cannot save you.

Sweet Daddy Grace, 1881–1960
Religious leader

1781. Why should the devil have all the fun?

Sweet Daddy Grace, 1881–1960
Religious leader

1782. Let not the fashions of the world divert your minds from eternity.

Lemuel Haynes, 1753–1833
Minister and Writer

1783. There is no parallel instance of an oppressed race thus sustained by the religious sentiment alone.

Thomas Wentworth Higginson, 1823–1911
Abolitionist and Civil War officer

1784. You can only ordain a man to be what he already is.

T.D. Jakes
Evangelist

1785. I prayed earnestly that God would give me above all things a religion like the one I had heard about from the old slaves and seen demonstrated in their lives.

Charles H. Mason, 1866–1961
Church of God in Christ founder

1786. Happy am I!

Solomon Lightfoot Michaux, 1884–1968
Evangelist

1787. I am a devout musician.

Charlie Parker, 1920–1955
Jazz musician

1788. I believe in hearing the inaudible and touching the intangible and seeing the invisible.

Adam Clayton Powell Jr., 1908–1972
Minister and U.S. Congressperson

1789. Religion without humanity is a poor human stuff.

Sojourner Truth, 1797?–1883
Abolitionist and Women's rights advocate

1790. When you meet an American Negro who's not a Methodist or a Baptist, some white man's been tampering with his religion.

Booker T. Washington, 1856–1915
Educator

1791. The absurdities of racism insinuate themselves in conscious and unconscious ways in the lives of black people. Religion has been a central way for us to maintain our sanity.

James M. Washington, 1948–1997
Minister and Academic

1792. Institutional religion has had its potentially sharp prophetic edge dulled by its overt or silent complicity in maintaining the status quo.

James M. Washington, 1948–1997
Minister and Academic

1793. Religion is the form in which America first allowed our personalities to be expressed.

Richard Wright, 1908–1960
Novelist

REPARATIONS

~·~·~·~·~·~·~·~

1794. Ever since 1950 I've been on the trail fighting for reparations. They owe us more than they could ever pay. They stole us from our mothers and fathers and took our names away from us. They worked us free of charge 18 hours a day, seven days a week under the lash for centuries.

Queen Mother Moore (Audley Moore), 1898–1997
Nationalist leader

1795. Every family shall have a plot of not more than forty acres of tillable ground.

William T. Sherman, 1820–1891
U.S. General
Special Field Orders, Savannah, GA, Jan. 16, 1865

1796. Reparations will not level the playing field … but they will further the process. Reparations through tax abatement would be a specific acknowledgement of a specific wrong in a specific place.

Ibrahim K. Sundiata, 1944–
Scholar

RESISTANCE

▽╱△▽╱△▽╱△▽╱△▽╱△▽╱△▽

1797. Deny the existence of resistance [to slavery] and one negates the dynamic, the soul, the reality of history.

Herbert Aptheker, 1915–
Historian

1798. In the act of resistance, the rudiments of freedom are already present.

Angela Davis, 1944–
Militant activist

1799. The doctrine that submission to violence is the best cure for violence did not hold good as between slaves and overseers. He was whipped oftener who was whipped easiest.

Frederick Douglass, 1817?–1895
Abolitionist and Autobiographer

1800. We refuse to allow the impression to remain that we assent to inferiority, are submissive under oppression, and apologize before insults.

W.E.B. Du Bois, 1868–1963
Intellectual and Activist

1801. We both knew the end was near. You don't challenge the system like that without knowing the price to be paid.

Myrlie Evers-Williams
NAACP official

1802. I'm sick and tired of being sick and tired.

Fannie Lou Hamer, 1917–1977
Civil rights activist

1803. My colored brethren, if you have not swords, I say to you, sell your garments and buy one.... They said that they cannot take us back to the South, but I say under the present law [Fugitive Slave Law of 1850] they can; and now I say unto you, let them only take your dead bodies.

John Jacobs
National Urban League official

1804. Negroes have straightened their backs in Albany [Georgia] and once a man straightens his back you can't ride him anymore.

Martin Luther King Jr., 1929–1968
Civil rights activist and Nobel laureate

1805. If we must die—let it not be like hogs / Hunted and penned in an inglorious spot.

Claude McKay, 1889–1948
Writer

1806. I ask you, had you not rather be killed than be a slave to a tyrant, who takes the life of your mother, wife, and dear little children?

David Walker, 1785–1830
Abolitionist

1807. I felt that one had better die fighting against injustice than to die like a dog or rat in a trap. I had already determined to sell my life as dearly as possible if attacked. I felt if I could take one lyncher with me, this would even up the score a little bit.

Ida B. Wells, 1862–1931
Militant activist

RESPECT

1808. I had to fight hard against loneliness, abuse, and the knowledge that any mistake I made would be magnified because I was the only black man out there. Many people resented my impatience and honesty, but I never cared about acceptance as much as I cared about respect.

Jackie Robinson, 1919–1972
Baseball star

RESPONSIBILITY

1809. Let us realize too that even we disenfranchised have our duties.

W.E.B. Du Bois, 1868–1963
Intellectual and Activist

1810. None of us are responsible for our birth. Our responsibility is the use we make of life.

Joshua Henry Jones, 1886–1934
Novelist and Newspaperperson

RETRIBUTION

1811. A bill is coming in that I fear America is not prepared to pay.

James Baldwin, 1924–1987
Writer and Activist

1812. God wields national judgment on national sins.

Frances Ellen Watkins Harper, 1825–1911
Writer and Orator

1813. [White plantation owners] were a proud and selfish people ... and I believe ... that God finally sent the boll weevil to humble them.... Thanks to the boll weevil, a lot of those thieving plantation owners died out.

Mahalia Jackson, 1911–1972
Gospel singer

REVOLUTION

1814. We have the longest revolutionary heritage of any people on the face of the earth.

John Henrik Clarke, 1915–
Historian

1815. We need a revolution inside of our own minds.

John Henrik Clarke, 1915–
Historian

1816. The French Revolution did not spread from France to the West Indies, but from the West Indies to France.

W.E.B. Du Bois, 1868–1963
Intellectual and Activist

1817. We are not born revolutionaries. Revolutionaries are forged through constant struggle and the study of revolutionary ideas and experiences.

James Forman, 1929–?
Civil rights activist

1818. If they take my life, it won't stop the revolution.

Nikki Giovanni, 1943–
Poet

1819. You can jail a revolutionary, but you can't jail the revolution.

Fred Hampton, 1948–1969
Black Panther Party leader

1820. The problem is we have to find some way ... to encourage the white liberal to stop being a liberal— and become an American radical.... The conditions of our people dictate what can only be called revolutionary attitudes.

Lorraine Hansberry, 1930–1965
Dramatist

1821. It is as radical for a black American in Mississippi to claim his full rights under the Constitution and the law as it is for a white American in any state to advocate the overthrow of the existing national government.

James Weldon Johnson, 1871–1938
Writer and Activist

1822. Revolution accelerates evolution.

Kelly Miller, 1863–1939
Educator

1823. When reform becomes impossible, revolution becomes imperative.

Kelly Miller, 1863–1939
Educator

1824. Each of you tramps who read these lines, avail yourselves of those little methods of warfare which Science has placed in the hands of the poor man, and you will become a power in this or any other land. Learn the use of explosives!

Lucy Parsons, 1853–1942
Anarchist

1825. I'm not a movie star, I'm a revolutionary.

Geronimo Pratt (Elmer Pratt), 1948–
Militant activist

1826. We are the advance guard of a massive moral revolution for jobs and freedom.

A. Philip Randolph, 1889–1979
Labor leader

1827. You and I are living at a time when there's a revolution going on, a worldwide revolution. It goes beyond Mississippi, it goes beyond Alabama, it goes beyond Harlem.... What is it revolting against? ... An international Western power structure.

Malcolm X, 1925–1965
Nationalist leader

RIGHTS

1828. As the agitation which culminated in the abolition of African slavery in this country covered a period of 50 years, so may we expect that before the rights conferred upon us by the [Civil] war amendments are fully conceded, a full century will have passed away.

T. Thomas Fortune, 1856–1928
Journalist

1829. We have waited for more than 340 years for our Constitutional and God-given rights.

Martin Luther King Jr., 1929–1968
Civil rights activist and Nobel laureate

1830. The only way to make sure people you agree with can speak is to support the rights of people you don't agree with.

Eleanor Holmes Norton, 1938–
Lawyer and Activist

1831. An insignificant right becomes important when it's assailed.

William Pickens, 1881–1954
Editor and Civil rights activist

1832. I started with this idea in my head, "There's two things I've got a right to—death or liberty."

Harriet Tubman, 1820?–1913
Abolitionist

1833. We have built up your country. We have worked in your fields, and garnered your harvests for 250 years! Do we ask you for compensation for the tears you have caused, and the hearts you have broken, and the lives you have curtailed, and the blood you have spilled? We are willing to let the dead past bury the dead, but we ask you, now, for our RIGHTS.

Henry McNeal Turner, 1834–1915
Minister and Militant activist

ROCK 'N' ROLL

∧ ⌒ ∧ ⌒ ∧ ⌒ ∧ ⌒ ∧ ⌒ ∧ ⌒ ∧

See also Music

1834. Rock 'n' roll introduced black culture to white American youth ... and introduced the possibility of interracialism.

Julian Bond, 1940–
Civil rights activist

ROLE MODELS

1835. I don't want to be a role model just because I am a model. I would like to be a role model for doing something that's worthy, for doing something for the community, for giving something back.

Naomi Campbell, 1970–
Model

1836. Why do I have to be an example for your kid? You be an example for your own kid.

Bob Gibson, 1935–?
Baseball star

1837. Youth are looking for something; it's up to adults to show them what is worth emulating.

Jesse Jackson, 1941–
Minister and Civil rights activist

1838. I realize that I am a role model.... The best thing for me and other athletes is to stay out of trouble.

Shaquille O'Neal, 1972–
Basketball star

1839. Role models can be black. Role models can be white.
Colin Powell, 1937–
U.S. General

RULES FOR LIVING
See Words to Live By

SACRIFICE

1840. To increase abiding satisfaction for the mass of our people, someone must sacrifice something of his own happiness.
W.E.B. Du Bois, 1868–1963
Intellectual and Activist

1841. I am in the hand of God and at your disposal. My life is not dear unto me, but I am ready to be offered at any moment.
David Walker, 1785–1830
Abolitionist

SANITY

1842. Perhaps to be sane in this country is the best evidence of insanity.
Addison Gayle Jr., 1932–?
Literary critic

SATISFACTION
See Self-Realization

SCHOOLS
See Education

SEGREGATION

⟁ ⟁ ⟁ ⟁ ⟁ ⟁ ⟁ ⟁

See also Racism

1843. Does segregation of children in public schools solely on the base of race, even though the physical facilities and other "tangible" factors may be equal, deprive the children of the minority group of equal educational opportunities? We believe that it does.

Anonymous
Brown v. Board of Education of Topeka May 17, 1954

1844. Sometimes I feel discriminated against, but it does not make me angry. It merely astonishes me. How can any deny themselves the pleasure of my company?

Zora Neale Hurston, 1891–1960
Writer and Folklorist

1845. Segregation was wrong when it was forced by white people, and I believe it is still wrong when it is requested by black people.

Coretta Scott King, 1927–
Civil rights activist

1846. Weren't no sign that said black or white; it was an imagination line.

E.D. Nixon, 1899?–1987
Civil rights activist

SELF-ACCEPTANCE

1847. You cannot belong to anyone else until you belong to yourself.

Pearl Bailey, 1918–1990
Entertainer

1848. Your crown has been bought and paid for. All you must do is put it on your head.

James Baldwin, 1924–1987
Writer and Activist

1849. I would like to be finished with shame, to know that I love myself and my own people.

Toi Derricotte, 1941–
Writer

1850. Be as you are and hope that it's right.

Dizzy Gillespie (John Birks Gillespie), 1917–1993
Jazz musician

1851. We build our temples for tomorrow, strong as we know how, and we stand on top of the mountain, free within ourselves.

Langston Hughes, 1902–1967
Poet and Writer

1852. I am somebody!

Jesse Jackson, 1941–
Minister and Civil rights activist

1853. I have simply tried never to forget the soil from which I sprang.

Paul Robeson, 1898–1976
Singer and Activist

1854. All my limitations are self-imposed, and my liberation can only come from true self-love.

Max Robinson, 1939–
Journalist

1855. I just run. I don't know why I run so fast.

Wilma Rudolph, 1940–1994
Olympic track star

1856. Having God for my friend and portion, what have I to fear? As long as it is the will of God, I rejoice that I am as I am.

Maria W. Stewart, 1803–1879
Lecturer

1857. You've got to love yourself enough, not only so that others will be able to love you, but that you'll be able to love others.

Cornel West, 1954–
Philosopher and Activist

1858. If I did not want others to violate my life, how could I voluntarily violate it myself?

Richard Wright, 1908–1960
Novelist

SELF-ACTUALIZATION
See Self-Realization

SELF-AFFIRMATION

1859. No one can figure out your worth but you.

Pearl Bailey, 1918–1990
Entertainer

1860. To those who have suffered in slavery I can say I, too, have suffered.... To those who have battled for liberty, brotherhood, and citizenship I can say I, too, have battled.

Frederick Douglass, 1817?–1895
Abolitionist and Autobiographer

1861. You can love Mozart, Picasso, even play ice hockey, and still be black as the ace of spades.

Henry Louis Gates Jr., 1950–
Scholar and Critic

1862. "Sing loud!" my father always told me, "just in case someone is listening."

Patti LaBelle, 1946–
Singer

1863. We have been raised to fear the yes in ourselves.

Audre Lorde, 1934–1992
Writer

1864. Anyone who puts his hand on you, do your best to see that he doesn't put it on anybody else.

Malcolm X, 1925–1965
Nationalist leader

SELF-AWARENESS
See Self-Knowledge

SELF-CONFIDENCE

1865. Unless we start to believe in ourselves, we will never convince anyone to believe in us. It is time to believe in ourselves, it is time to start believing in Africa.

Ronald H. Brown, 1941–1997
Politician

1866. I need to keep thinking and analyzing, and have that transformed onto a piece of paper. Besides, if we as African American women don't write our own books, then other folks will continue to define us.

Johnnetta Cole, 1936–
Educator

1867. If you have no confidence in self, you are twice defeated in the race of life. With confidence, you have won even before you have started.

Marcus Garvey, 1887–1940
Nationalist leader

1868. I made a lot of mistakes out of the ring, but I never made any in it.

Jack Johnson, 1873–1946
Boxing champion

1869. If you don't have confidence, you'll always find a way not to win.

Carl Lewis, 1961–
Olympic track star

1870. Literary societies provided the literal and psychological space where their membership might develop the confidence to speak for themselves rather than be spoken for.

Elizabeth McHenry
Scholar

SELF-CONSCIOUSNESS
See Self-Knowledge

SELF-DEFINITION
See Self-Confidence

SELF-DETERMINATION
See Self-Liberation

SELF-EXPRESSION

See also Self-Realization

1871. There are two things over which you have complete domination, authority, and control—your mind and your mouth.
Molefi Asante, 1942–
Educator

1872. We younger Negro artists who create now intend to express our individual dark-skinned selves without fear or shame. If white people are pleased, we are glad. If they are not, it doesn't matter.
Langston Hughes, 1902–1967
Poet and Writer

SELF-FULFILLMENT
See Self-Realization

SELF-HATE

1873. He [James Baldwin's stepfather] claimed to be proud of his blackness, but it had also been the cause of much humiliation and it had fixed bleak boundaries to his life.

James Baldwin, 1924–1987
Writer and Activist

1874. My life, my real life, was in danger, and not from anything other people might do but from the hatred I carried in my own heart.

James Baldwin, 1924–1987
Writer and Activist

1875. Who among us has not at some point in time succumbed to the propaganda, looked in a mirror, and felt ourselves to be wanting?

Marcia Ann Gillespie, 1940–
Editor

1876. We must take control of ourselves and come out of our own black racism. We must believe in ourselves, in our God, to lead us out of this forest where they are performing genocide.

Nettie Jones, 1941–
Writer

1877. Black on black crime is the result of self-hatred. Self-hatred is a result of our oppression. We can't get back at the folks who oppress us so we attack ourselves.

Joseph Lowery, 1924–
Civil rights activist

1878. The Negro wants to be a white man. He processes his hair. Acts like a white man. He wants to integrate with the white man, but he cannot integrate with himself or his own mind.

Elijah Muhammad, 1897–1975
Nation of Islam leader

1879. A system of oppression draws much of its strength from the acquiescence of its victims who have accepted the dominant image of themselves and are paralyzed by a sense of helplessness.

Pauli Murray, 1910–1985
Lawyer and Minister

1880. Self-hate is a form of mental slavery that results in poverty, ignorance and crime.

Susan Taylor, 1946–
Editor and Writer

1881. It is impossible to grow up in America, no matter what color you are, and not have some white supremacy in you.

Cornel West, 1954–
Philosopher and Activist

1882. Hated by whites and being an organic part of the culture that hated him, the black man grew in turn to hate in himself that which others hated in him.

Richard Wright, 1908–1960
Novelist

1883. America's greatest crime against the black man was not slavery or lynchings, but that he was taught to wear a mask of self-hate and self-doubt.

Malcolm X, 1925–1965
Nationalist leader

1884. Who taught you to hate the texture of your hair? Who taught you to hate the color of your skin? … Who taught you to hate your self?

Malcolm X, 1925–1965
Nationalist leader

SELF-HELP
See Self-Realization

SELF-IDENTITY
See Self-Knowledge

SELF-KNOWLEDGE

1885. I brought to Shakespeare, Bach, Rembrandt, to the stones of Paris, to the cathedral at Chartres, and to the Empire State Building, a special attitude. These were not really my creations, they did not contain my history; I might search in them in vain forever for any reflection of myself. I was an interloper; this was not my heritage.

James Baldwin, 1934–1987
Writer and Activist

1886. In America, the color of my skin had stood between myself and me.

James Baldwin, 1924–1987
Writer and Activist

1887. Like snowflakes, the human pattern is never cast twice.

Alice Childress, 1920–1994
Writer

1888. Don't ever forget that we are aware of the universal misery of our time and world and are trying in our various ways to contribute that which is relatively sane.

Beauford Delaney, 1902?–1979
Painter

1889. Herein lies the tragedy of the age; not that men are poor ... not that men are wicked ... but that men know so little of men.

W.E.B. Du Bois, 1868–1963
Intellectual and Activist

1890. I sit with Shakespeare and he winces not. Across the color line I move arm in arm with Balzac and Dumas, where smiling men and welcoming women glide in gilded halls. From out of the caves of evening that swing between the strong-limbed earth and the tracery of stars, I summon Aristotle and Aurelius and what soul I will, and they come all graciously with no scorn nor condescension. So, wed with Truth, I dwell above the veil. Is this the life you grudge us, O knightly America?

W.E.B. Du Bois, 1868–1963
Intellectual and Activist

1891. You are no longer innocent, you are condemned to awareness.

Michael Eric Dyson, 1958–
Scholar and Writer

1892. We are blinded by the night, we are blinded by the mystery of history, we are blinded by the destiny of time.

C.L. Franklin, 1918–1984
Minister

1893. If you escape from people too often, you wind up escaping from yourself.

Marvin Gaye, 1939–1984
Singer and Composer

1894. A man without knowledge of himself and his heritage is like a tree without roots.

Dick Gregory, 1932–
Comedian and Activist

1895. Depression and grief are hatred turned on the self.

William Grier, 1926–
Physician

1896. The thing that makes you exceptional, if you are at all, is inevitably that which must also make you lonely.

Lorraine Hansberry, 1930–1965
Dramatist

1897. What has reduced them [the poor Africans among us] to their present pitiful abject state? Is it any distinction the God of nature hath made in their formation? Nay, but being subjected to slavery, by the cruel hands of oppressors they have been forced to view themselves as a rank of being far below others.

Lemuel Haynes, 1753–1833
Minister and Writer

1898. We search for the meaning of life in the realities of our experiences, in the realities of our dreams, our hopes, our memories.

Chester Himes, 1909–1984
Writer

1899. What if there is no me like the statue?

Zora Neale Hurston, 1891–1960
Writer and Folklorist

1900. It is not a sign of weakness, but a sign of high maturity, to rise to the level of self-criticism.

Martin Luther King Jr., 1929–1968
Civil rights activist and Nobel laureate

1901. It's when you're down that you learn about your faults.

Claude McKay, 1889–1948
Writer

1902. When you want something in life, you have to focus.

Roslyn McMillan
Writer

1903. The slave master will not teach you the knowledge of self, as there would not be a master-slave relationship any longer.

Elijah Muhammad, 1897–1975
Nation of Islam leader

1904. I stumbled upon James Baldwin. In *Go Tell it on the Mountain* I found for the first time the story of my life.

Richard Perry, 1944–
Writer

1905. When nobody speaks your name, or even knows it, you, knowing it, must be the first to speak it.

Marlon Riggs, 1957–1994
Director

1906. Ego has always been a paradox—it is the point from which you see, but it also makes you blind.

Bill Russell, 1934–
Basketball star

1907. I freed thousands of slaves. I could have freed thousands more, if they had known they were slaves.

Harriet Tubman, 1820?–1913
Abolitionist

1908. I have fought and kicked and fasted and prayed and cursed and cried myself to the point of existing. It has been like being born again, literally. Just knowing has meant everything to me. Knowing has pushed me out into the world, into college, into places, into people.

Alice Walker, 1944–
Writer

1909. No one can hate their source and survive.

Alice Walker, 1944–
Writer

1910. The longer I live and the more I study the question, the more I am convinced that it is not so much the problem of what you will do with the Negro, as what the Negro will do with you and your civilization.

Booker T. Washington, 1856–1915
Educator

1911. The two basic challenges presently confronting Afro-Americans are self-image and self-determination. The former is the perennial human attempt to define who and what one is, the issue of self-identity, The latter is the political struggle to gain significant control over the major institutions that regulate people's lives. These challenges are abstractly distinguishable, yet concretely inseparable.

Cornel West, 1954–
Philosopher and Activist

1912. I do not deal in happiness. I deal in meaning.
Richard Wright, 1908–1960
Novelist

SELF-LIBERATION

1913. When I thought of slavery, with its democratic whips, its republican chains, its evangelical bloodhounds, and its religious slaveholders—when I thought of all this paraphernalia of American democracy and religion behind me, I was encouraged to press forward, my heart was strengthened and I forgot that I was tired and hungry.
William Wells Brown, 1815–1884
Writer

1914. After the firing on Fort Sumter I concluded that I would emancipate myself.
Blanche K. Bruce, 1841–1898
U.S. Senator

1915. We shall never secure emancipation from the tyranny of the white oppressor until we have achieved it in our own soul.
W.E.B. Du Bois, 1868–1963
Intellectual and Activist

1916. The moment the slave resolves that he will no longer be a slave, his fetters fall. He frees himself and shows the way to others. Freedom and slavery are mental states.
Mohandas K. Gandhi, 1869–1948
Indian nationalist leader

1917. The first dying to be done by the black man will be done to make himself free.
Marcus Garvey, 1887–1940
Nationalist leader

1918. We have to liberate ourselves.

Marcus Garvey, 1887–1940
Nationalist leader

1919. When I liberate others, I liberate myself.

Fannie Lou Hamer, 1917–1977
Civil rights activist

1920. I do not know whether the bird you are holding is dead or alive, but what I do know is that it is in your hands. It is in your hands.

Toni Morrison, 1931–
Novelist and Nobel laureate

1921. The runaway Negro was the vanguard, the first hero in the struggle to free his race.

William Pickens, 1881–1954
Editor and Civil rights activist

1922. The Negro peoples should not place their problems for solution down at the feet of their white sympathetic allies which has been and is the common fashion of the old school Negro leadership, for, in the final analysis, the salvation of the Negro, like the workers, must come from within.

A. Philip Randolph, 1889–1979
Labor leader

1923. Salvation for a race, nation, or class must come from within. Freedom is never granted; it is won. Justice is never given; it is exacted, Freedom and justice must be struggled for by the oppressed of all lands and races, and the struggle must be continuous.

A. Philip Randolph, 1889–1979
Labor leader

1924. Free people have a right to self-determination and self defense.

Betty Shabazz, 1934?–1997
Educator

1925. A necessary act of liberation within myself was to acknowledge the beauty of the black, black woman.

Alice Walker, 1944–
Writer

1926. Our liberation begins when the truth of our own experiences is admitted to ourselves.

Alice Walker, 1944–
Writer

1927. We must recapture our heritage and our ideals if we are to liberate ourselves from the bonds of white supremacy. We must launch a cultural revolution to unbrainwash an entire people.

Malcolm X, 1925–1965
Nationalist leader

SELF-REALIZATION

See also Self-Expression

1928. Champions aren't made in gyms. Champions are made from something they have deep inside them—a desire, a dream, a vision. They have to have last-minute stamina, they have to be a little faster, they have to have the skill and the will. But the will must be stronger than the skill.

Muhammad Ali, 1942–
Boxing champion

1929. I don't have to be what you want me to be. I'm free to be who I want to be.

Muhammad Ali, 1942–
Boxing champion

1930. This life is not real. I conquered the world and it did not bring me satisfaction.

Muhammad Ali, 1942–
Boxing champion

1931. I'm black, male, at the bottom of the social heap. I'm castrated in drag. But I'm also freed. There's a sort of cultural Judgment Day going on. Everybody's been forced to come out of the closet, in all kinds of ways, not just sexually.... Every time I bat my eyelashes it's a political act.

RuPaul Charles, 1960–
Entertainer

1932. The greatest gift is not being afraid to question.

Ruby Dee, 1923–
Actor

1933. Let us not try to be the best or worst of others, but let us make the effort to be the best of ourselves.

Marcus Garvey, 1887–1940
Nationalist leader

1934. When a school child remains unchallenged, he or she will shut down and lose interest in learning altogether.

Bessie Hogan

1935. In my early days I was a sepia Hedy Lamar. Now I'm black and a woman, singing my own way.

Lena Horne, 1917–
Entertainer

1936. I had a way of life inside me and I wanted it with a want that was twisting me.

Zora Neale Hurston, 1891–1960
Writer and Folklorist

1937. We can go on talking about racism and who treated whom badly, but what are you going to do about it? Are you going to wallow in that, or are you going to create your own agenda?

Judith Jamison, 1943–
Dancer

1938. My inner life is mine, and I shall defend and maintain its integrity against all the powers of hell.

James Weldon Johnson, 1871–1938
Writer and Activist

1939. Your cultural center, the lifestyle of your people, is the most important single mechanism in your life, and you must be in control of it at all times.

Elma Lewis, 1929–
Arts director

1940. Our poets have now stopped speaking for the Negro—they speak as Negroes. Where formerly they spoke to others and tried to interpret, they now speak to their own and try to express.

Alain Locke, 1886–1954
Scholar and Critic

1941. We have been to their schools and gone as far as they allowed us to go.

Elijah Muhammad, 1897–1975
Nation of Islam leader

1942. My father ... believed that the mere act of seeking the kingdom brought all things unto you.

Adam Clayton Powell Jr., 1908–1972
Minister and U.S. Congressperson

1943. More and more African American parents have concluded that the nation's public schools are failing to meet their children's needs.

Charlene Solomon

1944. Guided by my heritage of a love of beauty and a respect for strength— in search of my mother's garden, I found my own.

Alice Walker, 1944–
Writer

1945. Everyone has a gift; you let it take you as far as it can.

Lynette Woodard, 1959–
Basketball star

1946. Men can starve from a lack of self-realization as they can from a lack of bread.

Richard Wright, 1908–1960
Novelist

SELF-REFLECTION
See Self-Knowledge

SELF-RELIANCE

∿∿∿∿∿

1947. Nothing can dim the light which shines from within.

Maya Angelou, 1928–
Novelist and Poet

1948. A ghetto can be improved in one way only: out of existence.

James Baldwin, 1924–1987
Writer and Activist

1949. In America the Negro stands alone as a race. No people has borne opposition like him, and no race has been so much imposed upon. Whatever progress he makes, it must be mainly by his own efforts.

William Wells Brown, 1815–1884
Writer

1950. "Moses, my servant, is dead. Therefore arise and go over Jordan." There are no deliverers. They're all dead. We must arise and go over Jordan. We can take the promised land.

Nannie Burroughs, 1883–1961
Activist

1951. The black man should act and do for himself, just like the white man under like circumstances would be justified in doing—self-reliance as the principle of black nationality.

Martin R. Delany, 1812–1885
Emigrationist

1952. Every people should be the originators of their own designs, the projectors of their own schemes, and creators of the events that lead to their destiny—the consummation of their own desires.

Martin R. Delany, 1812–1885
Emigrationist

1953. Out of the depths we have cried unto the deaf and dumb masters of the world. Out of the depths we cry to our own sleeping souls.

W.E.B. Du Bois, 1868–1963
Intellectual and Activist

1954. There is in this world no such force as the force of a man determined to rise.

W.E.B. Du Bois, 1868–1963
Intellectual and Activist

1955. Stand on your own two feet, and fight like hell for your place in the world.

Amy Jacques Garvey, 1896–1973
Nationalist leader

1956. Black men and black men alone hold the key to the gateway leading to their freedom.

Marcus Garvey, 1887–1940
Nationalist leader

1957. A large part of the SNCC (Student Nonviolent Coordinating Committee during the Civil Rights Movement) work was psychological: to get people to believe that they could at first organize, and then proceed to make a difference in their own lives.

Charles Hamilton Houston, 1895–1950
Lawyer and Civil rights activist

1958. We can't rely on anyone but ourselves to define our existence, to shape the image of ourselves.

Spike Lee, 1957–
Filmmaker

1959. Learning to take hold of one's life is very difficult in a culture that values property over life.

Haki Madhubuti, 1942–
Poet

1960. The day has arrived that you will have to help yourselves or suffer the worst.

Elijah Muhammad, 1897–1975
Nation of Islam leader

1961. I had to constantly overcome the disadvantages of having no academic training by inventing my own way of doing things.

Gordon Parks, 1912–
Photographer

1962. We wish to plead our own cause. Too long have others spoken for us.

John B. Russwurm, 1799–1851
Abolitionist and Journalist

1963. I found, while thinking about the far-reaching world of the creative black women, that often the truest answer to a question that really matters can be found very close.

Alice Walker, 1944–
Writer

1964. I think there is no more serious or important time in a young person's life than when he leaves home for the first time to enter school, or any line of business, and I think I can judge pretty accurately what a person is going to amount to by the way he acts during the first one or two years that he is absent from home.

Booker T. Washington, 1856–1915
Educator

1965. To those of my race who underestimate the importance of cultivating friendly relations with the Southern white man, who is their next-door neighbor, I would say, "Cast down your bucket where you are"—cast it down in making friends in every manly way of the people of all races by whom we are surrounded.

Booker T. Washington, 1856–1915
Educator

1966. Let the Negro depend on no party, but on himself for his salvation.

Ida B. Wells, 1862–1931
Militant activist

1967. You can't base your life on other people's expectations.

Stevie Wonder, 1950–
Singer

1968. Tell 'em, sir, we are rising.

Richard R. Wright, 1855?–1947
Educator and Entrepreneur

His response, as a child in Georgia, to Gen. O.O. Howard's question, "When I shall return home, what shall I tell the people of the North of the colored people of the South?"

SELF-RESPECT

1969. I am primarily interested in the Negro's self-respect. If the masses of Negroes can save their self-respect and remain free from hate, so much the better for their moral development.

E. Franklin Frazier, 1894–1962
Sociologist

1970. Deal with yourself as an individual worthy of respect and make everyone else deal with you the same way.

Nikki Giovanni, 1943–
Poet

1971. I love myself when I am laughing.

Zora Neale Hurston, 1891–1960
Writer and Folklorist

1972. You were born with a silver spoon in your mouth. I was born with an iron hoe in my hand.

Kelly Miller, 1863–1939
Educator

1973. If you're not feeling good about you, what you're wearing outside doesn't mean a thing.

Leontyne Price, 1927–
Opera singer

1974. Already the Negro sees himself against a reclaimed background, in a perspective that will give pride and self-respect ample score, and make history yield for him the same values that the treasured past of any people affords.

Arthur Schomburg, 1874–1938
Librarian and Book collector

1975. Unless we learn the lesson of self-appreciation and practice it, we shall spend our lives imitating other people and deprecating ourselves.

Aida Overton Walker, 1880–1914
Singer and Dancer

1976. Any time there is a self-loving, self-respecting, and self-determining black man or woman, he or she is one of the most dangerous folks in America. Because it means you are free enough to speak your mind, you're free enough to speak the truth.

Cornel West, 1954–
Philosopher and Activist

SELF-UNDERSTANDING
See Self-Knowledge

SELFISHNESS

1977. We are so selfish we spoil everything we do.
Lemuel Haynes, 1753–1833
Minister and Writer

1978. Man is terribly selfish, and he will take his chances for keeping things as they are in his favor rather than yield to any sacrifice of his position as an exploiter and self-styled superior of his victims.
Carter G. Woodson, 1875–1950
Historian

SEPARATION

1979. Segregation is no longer the law, but too often separation is still the rule. And we cannot forget one stubborn fact that has not yet been said as clearly as it should: there is still discrimination in America.
Bill Clinton, 1946–
U.S. President

1980. That separateness led to inequality was the great theme of the civil rights era. That inequality leads to separateness is the unavoidable conclusion of its aftermath.
Henry Louis Gates Jr., 1950–
Scholar and Critic

1981. When people ask why a separate black [lawyers'] organization is needed at this late date, the answer is simple. It's not that late.
Thurgood Marshall, 1908–1993
U.S. Supreme Court Justice

1982. In all things that are purely social we can be as separate as the fingers, yet one as the hand in all things essential to mutual progress.

Booker T. Washington, 1856–1915
Educator

SERVICE TO THE COMMUNITY

1983. Service is the rent you pay for room on this earth.

Shirley Chisholm, 1924–
Politician

1984. This means that each black person had to decide what he was going to do and the choice should be made in favor of service to people.

James Forman, 1929–?
Civil rights activist

1985. Imagine what a harmonious world it could be if every single person, both young and old, shared a little of what he is good at doing.

Quincy Jones, 1933–
Musician and Business executive

1986. Everybody can be great because everybody can serve.

Martin Luther King Jr., 1929–1968
Civil rights activist and Nobel laureate

1987. The rich man who achieves a degree of greatness achieves it not because he hoards his wealth, but because he gives it away in the interest of good causes.

Benjamin Mays, 1895–1984
Educator

1988. If we can finally succeed in translating the idea of leadership into that of service, we may soon find it possible to lift the Negro to a higher level. Under leadership we have come to the ghetto; by service within the ranks, we may work our way out of it.

Carter G. Woodson, 1875–1950
Historian

SEX

1989. People do not understand the difference between sex, love, consent, power. Our society, in general, doesn't teach us these things.

Rhonda Brinkley, 1956–
Rosa Parks Sexual Assault Crisis Center, LA, representative

1990. When Harriet goes to bed with a man, she always takes her wet blanket with her.

Anatole Broyard, 1920–1990
Literary critic

1991. They have Jim Crow theater laws and Jim Crow streetcar laws, but what they need are Jim Crow bedroom laws.

Oscar De Priest, 1871–1951
U.S. Congressperson

1992. I can't see anything wrong with sex between consenting anybodies.

Marvin Gaye, 1939–1984
Singer and Composer

1993. It's been a special plight for the black woman. I remember my uncles and some of my aunts—and that's why it tickled me when you talked about integration. Because I'm very black, but I remember some of my aunts was as white as anybody here— and blue-eyed and some green-eyed— and my grandfather didn't do it, you know.

Fannie Lou Hamer, 1917–1977
Civil rights activist

1994. Please get over the notion that your particular "thing" is something that only the deepest, saddest, the most nobly tortured can know. It ain't. It's just one kind of sex—that's all. And, in my opinion, the universe turns regardless.
Lorraine Hansberry, 1930–1965
Dramatist

1995. In the core of the heart of the American race problem the sex factor is rooted; rooted so deeply that it is not always recognized when it shows on the surface.
James Weldon Johnson, 1871–1938
Writer and Activist

1996. I want kids to understand that safe sex is the way to go. Sometimes we think that only gay people can get [HIV] , or that it's not going to happen to me. Here I am. And I'm saying it can happen to anybody, even Magic Johnson.
Magic Johnson, 1960–
Basketball star

1997. I am appalled at the ethical bankruptcy of those who preach a "right to life" that means, under present social policies, a bare existence in utter misery for many poor women and their children.
Thurgood Marshall, 1908–1993
U.S. Supreme Court Justice

1998. The moral standard of the whites is written in the flesh and blood of three million of our race.
William Pickens, 1881–1954
Editor and Civil rights activist

1999. One million mulattos are facts which no arguments can demolish.
John S. Rock, 1825–1866
Physician and Lawyer

2000. If we can't preserve the privacy of our right to procreate, I can't imagine what rights we will be able to protect.
Faye Wattleton, 1944–
Planned Parenthood president

2001. True chivalry respects all womanhood, and no one who reads the record, as it is written in the faces of the million mulattos in the South, will for a minute conceive that the southern white man had a very chivalrous regard for the honor due the women of his own race or respect for the womanhood which circumstances placed in his power.

Ida B. Wells, 1862–1931
Militant activist

SILENCE

2002. You don't always have to have something to say.

Sammy Davis Jr., 1925–1990
Entertainer

2003. Silence kills the soul; it diminishes the possibilities to rise and fly and explore.

Marlon Riggs, 1957–1994
Director

SINGING

2004. Singing is my way of opening my arms and heart and letting what's in me come out.

Jenny Burton

2005. I sing to people about what matters. I sing to the realists, people who accept it like it is. I express problems, there are tears when it's sad and smiles when it's happy. It seems simple to me, but to some, feelings take courage.

Aretha Franklin, 1942–
Singer

2006. I sing about life.

Marvin Gaye, 1939–1984
Singer and Composer

2007. I don't know how to sing black, and I don't know how to sing white, either. I know how to sing. Music is not a color to me. It's an art.

Whitney Houston
Singer

2008. Lift ev'ry voice and sing / Till earth and heaven ring.

James Weldon Johnson,1871–1938
Writer and Activist
J. Rosamond Johnson, 1873–1954
Musician

2009. Singing is not a luxury, it is a requirement.

Bernice Johnson Reagon, 1942–
Singer

2010. Never sing a song unless you mean it from your heart.

Ruby Lee Reeves

2011. It's singing with soul that counts.

Sarah Vaughan, 1924?–1990
Singer

2012. When I was a honky-tonk entertainer, I used to work from nine until unconscious. I was just a young girl, and when I tried to sing anything but the double-meaning songs, they'd say, "Oh, my God, Ethel, get hot!"

Ethel Waters, 1896?–1977
Singer and Actor

SLAVE REVOLTS
See Rebellion

SLAVERY

2013. The soul of one man cannot by human law be made the property of another. The owner of a slave is the owner of a living corpse, but he is not the owner of a man.

John Quincy Adams
U.S. President

2014. Vile habits acquired in a state of servitude are not easily thrown off.

Richard Allen, 1760–1831
AME Church founder

2015. We have had a recent arrival from the land of chains and whips, where the image of the Divine Being is bought and sold. But, thank the good Lord! when he arrived at our office, we, at once, recognized him as a man and a brother.

Jehiel C. Beman, 1789–1858
Minister

2016. This was a southern auction, at which the bones, muscles, sinews, blood, and nerves of a young lady of 16 were sold for 500 dollars; her moral character for 200; her improved intellect for 100; her Christianity for 400; and her chastity and virtue for 300 dollars more, And this, too, in a city thronged with churches, whose tall spires look like so many signals pointing to heaven, and whose ministers preach that slavery is a God-ordained institution.

William Wells Brown, 1815–1884
Writer

2017. When I was a child, my owner saw what he considered to be a good business deal and immediately accepted it. He traded me off for a horse.

George Washington Carver, 1864?–1943
Inventor

2018. Even the good part was awful.

Lucille Clifton, 1935–
Poet

2019. The truth is that the historical and current condition of you and yours is rooted in [slavery], is shaped by it, is bound to it, and is the reality against which all else must be gauged.

Johnnetta Cole, 1936–
Educator

2020. I had much rather starve in England, a free woman, than to be a slave for the best man that ever breathed upon the American continent.

Ellen Craft, 1826?–1891
Escaped slave

2021. Behold the practical operation of this internal slave trade—the American slave trade, sustained by American politics and American religion. Here you will see men, women, and children reared like swine for the market.

Frederick Douglass, 1817?–1895
Abolitionist and Autobiographer

2022. It is not color, but crime, not God, but man, that afforded the true explanation of the existence of slavery [and] what man can make, man can unmake.

Frederick Douglass, 1817?–1895
Abolitionist and Autobiographer

2023. No man can put a chain about the ankle of his fellowman, without at last finding the other end of it about his own neck.

Frederick Douglass, 1817?–1895
Abolitionist and Autobiographer

2024. There is not a man beneath the canopy of heaven who does not know that slavery is wrong for him.

Frederick Douglass, 1817?–1895
Abolitionist and Autobiographer

2025. Thus the very crimes of slavery become slavery's best defense. By making the enslaved a character fit only for slavery, they excuse themselves for refusing to make the slave a freeman.

Frederick Douglass, 1817?–1895
Abolitionist and Autobiographer

2026. I am not ashamed of my grandparents for having been slaves. I am only ashamed of myself for having at one time been ashamed.

Ralph Ellison, 1914–1994
Novelist

2027. The sugar they raised was excellent; nobody tasted blood in it.

Ralph Waldo Emerson, 1803–1882
Philosopher

2028. It seems almost incredible that the advocates of liberty should conceive of the idea of selling a fellow creature to slavery.

James Forten, 1766–1842
Abolitionist and Businessperson

2029. I would say the slavery issue must be addressed by every American, but it is more than the slavery issue.... It is the categorial sense that blacks were inferior.

John Hope Franklin, 1915–
Historian

2030. Let not the 12 million Negroes be ashamed of the fact that they are the grandchildren of slaves. There is no dishonor in being slaves. There is dishonor in being slaveholders.

Mohandas K. Gandhi, 1869–1948
Indian nationalist leader

2031. We have outgrown slavery, but our minds are still enslaved to the thinking of the master race. Now take the kinks out of your mind, instead of out of your hair.

Marcus Garvey, 1887–1940
Nationalist leader

2032. The real slave needs no chains.

Dick Gregory, 1932–
Comedian and Activist

2033. When will all races and classes of men learn that men made in the image of God will not be the slaves of another image?

Sutton E. Griggs, 1872–1930
Novelist and Minister

2034. Slavery is gone, but the spirit of it still remains.

Francis J. Grimke, 1850–1937
Minister

2035. Slavery was the central and determining phenomenon shaping the first centuries of American history.

Thomas Holt, 1942–
Scholar

2036. Alas! and am I born for this? / To wear the slavish chain?

George M. Horton, 1800?–1880?
Slave poet

2037. It is essentially this triumph of the human spirit over adversity that is the great story of Afro-American slavery.

Nathan Huggins, 1927–1989
Historian

2038. You never knew what it is to be a slave; to be entirely unprotected by law or custom; to have the laws reduce you to the condition of a chattel, entirely subject to the will of another. You never exhausted your ingenuity in avoiding the snares, and eluding the power of a hated tyrant; you never shuddered at the sound of his footsteps, and trembled within hearing of his voice.

Harriet Jacobs, 1813–1897
Former slave autobiographer

2039. All men are equal in his sight, / The bond, the free, the black, the white; / He made them all, them freedom gave, / He made the man, man made the slave.

James N. Mars, 1790–?
Former slave and Writer

2040. Our brethren in the South should not be called slaves but prisoners of war.

William C. Nell, 1816–1874
Historian and Abolitionist

2041. There was not a day throughout the 10 years I belonged to Epps that I did not consult with myself upon the project of escape.

Solomon Northup, 1808?–1863
Enslaved free man

2042. Slavery was the worst days ever seen in the world. There was things past telling, but I got the scars on my body to show 'til this day.

Mary Reynolds
Former slave

2043. Slavery denies essential self-determination.

Ibrahim K. Sundiata, 1944–
Scholar

2044. I have lived on through all that has taken place these 40 years in the antislavery cause, and I have pleaded with all the force I had that the day might come that the colored people might own their own soul and body. Well, the day has come, although it came through blood. It makes no difference how it came—it did come.

Sojourner Truth, 1797?–1883
Abolitionist and Women's rights advocate

2045. Every time I saw a white man I was afraid of being carried away.... Slavery is the next thing to hell.

Harriet Tubman, 1820?–1913
Abolitionist

2046. I have heard their groans and sighs, and seen their tears, and I would give every drop of blood in my veins to free them.

Harriet Tubman, 1820?–1913
Abolitionist

2047. I had too much sense to be raised, and, if I was, I would never be of any service to any one as a slave.

Nat Turner, 1800?–1831
Prophet and Insurrectionist

2048. As a black man, my labors will be antislavery labors.

Samuel Ringgold Ward, 1817–1866?
Abolitionist

2049. From some of the things that I have said one may get the idea that some of the slaves did not want freedom. That is not true, I have never seen one who did not want to be free, or one who would return to slavery.

Booker T. Washington, 1856–1915
Educator

2050. The slavery of antebellum times has passed away, but there is a moral slavery existing in the South which will take a long time to pass away.

Booker T. Washington, 1856–1915
Educator

2051. That which was 300 years being woven into the warp and woof of our democratic institutions could not be effaced by a single battle, magnificent as was that battle, that which for centuries had bound master and slave, yea, North and South, to a body of death, could not be blotted out by four years of war, could not be atoned for by shot and sword, nor blood and tears.

Booker T. Washington, 1856–1915
Educator

2052. We must turn away from the memories of the slave past.

Booker T. Washington, 1856–1915
Educator

2053. While bodily slavery is dead, commercial slavery is far from dead.

Booker T. Washington, 1856–1915
Educator

2054. What I came through in life, if I go down into myself for it, I could make a book.

J. White
Former slave

SOLIDARITY

See also Unity

2055. In Africa you never say, "I am my brother's keeper." You just keep him.
John Henrik Clarke, 1915–
Historian

2056. We come out of a collective society and are forced to live in an individual society.
John Henrik Clarke, 1915–
Historian

2057. I am of the common herd.
Oscar De Priest, 1871–1951
U.S. Congressperson

2058. The only thing that links me to this land is my family, and the painful consciousness that here there are three million of my fellow creatures, groaning beneath the iron rod of the worst despotism that could be devised.
Frederick Douglass, 1817?–1895
Abolitionist and Autobiographer

2059. All of our Mercedes Benzes and Halston frocks will not hide our essential failure as a generation of black "haves" who did not protect the black future during our watch.
Marian Wright Edelman, 1939–
Children's Defense Fund official

2060. What could be more absurd and ridiculous than that one group of individuals who are trying to throw off the yolk of oppression themselves, so as to get relief from conditions which handicap and injure them, should favor laws and customs which impede the progress of another unfortunate group and hinder them in every conceivable way.
Mary Church Terrell, 1863–1954
Women's club leader

2061. Those are the same stars and that is the same moon that look down upon your brothers and sisters [in slavery], and which they see as they look up to them.

Sojourner Truth, 1797?–1883
Abolitionist and Women's rights advocate

2062. The large majority of the Negroes who have put on the finishing touches of our best colleges, however, are all but worthless in the uplift of their people.

Carter G. Woodson, 1875–1950
Historian

SOUL

2063. My memory stammers, but my soul is a witness.

James Baldwin, 1924–1987
Writer and Activist

2064. Invest in the human soul. Who knows, it might be a diamond in the rough.

Mary McLeod Bethune, 1875–1955
Educator

2065. Soul is a way of life, but it is always the hard way.

Ray Charles, 1930–
Singer

2066. My soul has grown deep like the rivers.

Langston Hughes, 1902–1967
Poet and Writer

2067. If a man can reach the latter days of his life with his soul intact, he has mastered life.

Gordon Parks, 1912–
Photographer

SPEECH
See Language

SPIRIT

2068. You can't regiment spirit, and it is the spirit that counts.

Romare Bearden, 1914–1988
Artist

2069. A spirit of steadfast determination, exaltation in the face of trials—it is the very soul of our people that has been formed through all the long and weary years of our march toward freedom.

Paul Robeson, 1898–1976
Singer and Activist

2070. The most sacred place isn't the church, the mosque, or the temple, it's the temple of the body. That's where spirit lives.

Susan Taylor, 1946–
Editor and Writer

2071. If you want to accomplish the goals of your life, you have to begin with the spirit.

Oprah Winfrey, 1954–
Entertainer

2072. We are a [civil rights] movement, not an organization. And we move when the spirit says move.

Andrew Young, 1932–
Civil rights activist

SPIRITUALITY

2073. Our emphasis [as an African people] was not on religion, but rather on spirituality; and spirituality is higher than religion.

John Henrik Clarke, 1915–
Historian

2074. I sometimes realize that there is something on the earth that is free of everything but what created it, and that is the one thing I have been trying to find.

Ornette Coleman, 1930–
Saxophone player

2075. The problems we face as a nation are indeed, at the root, spiritual.

Louis Farrakhan, 1934–
Nation of Islam leader

2076. To spiritually regulate oneself is another form of the higher education that fits man for a nobler place in life.

Marcus Garvey, 1887–1940
Nationalist leader

2077. I will not let prejudice or any of its attendant humiliations and injustices bear me down to spiritual defeat.

James Weldon Johnson, 1871–1938
Writer and Activist

2078. I never thought that a lot of money or fine clothes—the finer things of life—would make you happy. My concept of happiness is to be fulfilled in a spiritual sense.

Coretta Scott King, 1927–
Civil rights activist

2079. All classes of people under social pressure are permeated with a common experience; they are emotionally welded as others cannot be. With them, even ordinary living has epic depth and lyric intensity, and this, their material handicap, is their spiritual advantage.

Alain Locke, 1886–1954
Scholar and Critic

SPIRITUALS

2080. Angel done changed my name / Done changed my name from natural to grace.

Anonymous
Traditional

2081. Come by here, my Lord / Come by here.

Anonymous
Traditional

2082. Death is going to lay his cold icy hands on me.

Anonymous
Traditional

2083. Deep river, / My home is over Jordan.

Anonymous
Traditional

2084. Didn't my Lord deliver Daniel? / And why not every man?
Anonymous
Traditional

2085. Do Lord, do Lord, do remember me / Way beyond the blue.
Anonymous
Traditional

2086. Dry bones going to rise again / Rise and hear the word of the Lord.
Anonymous
Traditional

2087. Every time I feel the spirit / Moving in my heart / I will pray.
Anonymous
Traditional

2088. Everybody talkin' about heaven ain't going there.
Anonymous
Traditional

2089. Ezekiel saw the wheel / Away up in the middle of the air.
Anonymous
Traditional

2090. Free at last, free at last / Thank God Almighty, I'm free at last.
Anonymous
Traditional

2091. Give me that old-time religion / It's good enough for me.
Anonymous
Traditional

2092. Go down, Moses / Way down in Egypt land / Tell old Pharaoh / Let my people go.
Anonymous
Traditional

2093. Go tell it on the mountain / Over the hills and everywhere / That Jesus Christ is born.

Anonymous
Traditional

2094. Good news, the chariot's coming

Anonymous
Traditional

2095. The gospel train is coming / I hear it just at hand.

Anonymous
Traditional

2096. He died for you, He died for me / He died to set the whole world free.

Anonymous
Traditional

2097. He's got the whole world in his hands.

Anonymous
Traditional

2098. Hush, O, hush / Somebody's calling my name.

Anonymous
Traditional

2099. I ain't going to grieve my Lord no more / The Bible tells me so.

Anonymous
Traditional

2100. I found free grace and dying love / I'm new born again.

Anonymous
Traditional

2101. I hold my brother with a trembling hand / I would not let him go.

Anonymous
Traditional

2102. I know you by your daily walk / There's a meeting here tonight.
Anonymous
Traditional

2103. I never intend to die in Egypt land.
Anonymous
Traditional

2104. I want to be ready / To walk in Jerusalem just like John.
Anonymous
Traditional

2105. I woke up this morning / With my mind stayed on freedom.
Anonymous
Traditional

2106. If anybody asks you what's the matter with me / Just tell him I say I'm running for my life.
Anonymous
Traditional

2107. If you get there before I do / Look out for me, I'm coming too.
Anonymous
Traditional

2108. If you want to find Jesus / Go in the wilderness.
Anonymous
Traditional

2109. I'm a-rolling in Jesus' arms / On the other side of Jordan.
Anonymous
Traditional

2110. I'm a-rolling through an unfriendly world / O, sisters, won't you help me to pray?
Anonymous
Traditional

2111. I'm going to eat at the welcome table / Some of these days.
Anonymous
Traditional

2112. I'm going to lay down my sword and shield / Down by the riverside.
Anonymous
Traditional

2113. I'm working on the building for my Lord.
Anonymous
Traditional

2114. In that great getting-up morning / Fare you well! Fare you well!
Anonymous
Traditional

2115. It's me, it's me, O Lord / Standing in the need of prayer.
Anonymous
Traditional

2116. I've been 'buked and I've been scorned / I've been talked about sure as you're born.
Anonymous
Traditional

2117. I've been in the storm so long / O, give me a little time to pray.
Anonymous
Traditional

2118. John saw, O, John saw / John saw the holy number.
Anonymous
Traditional

2119. Joshua fit the battle of Jericho / And the walls came tumblin' down.
Anonymous
Traditional

2120. Just above my head / I hear freedom in the air.

Anonymous
Traditional

2121. Keep a-inchin' along / Master Jesus is coming by and by.

Anonymous
Traditional

2122. King Jesus is my only friend.

Anonymous
Traditional

2123. Let the church roll on.

Anonymous
Traditional

2124. Let us break bread together / On our knees.

Anonymous
Traditional

2125. Listen to the lambs all a-crying / I want to go to heaven when I die.

Anonymous
Traditional

2126. Look what a wonder Jesus had done / Sinner believe.

Anonymous
Traditional

2127. Lord, I want to be a Christian / In-a my heart.

Anonymous
Traditional

2128. Lord, I want to be in that number / When the saints go marching in.

Anonymous
Traditional

2129. Mary and Martha just long gone / To ring those charming bells.

Anonymous
Traditional

2130. Mary set her table / In spite of all; her foes / King Jesus sat at the center place / And cups did overflow.

Anonymous
Traditional

2131. Members, don't get weary / For the work's most done.

Anonymous
Traditional

2132. Michael, row the boat ashore / Hallelujah!

Anonymous
Traditional

2133. My Lord, what a mourning / When the stars begin to fall.

Anonymous
Traditional

2134. No more auction block for me / Many thousand gone.

Anonymous
Traditional

2135. Nobody knows the trouble I see / Nobody knows like Jesus.

Anonymous
Traditional

2136. O, didn't it rain, children! / Didn't it rain!

Anonymous
Traditional

2137. O, freedom, O, freedom / O, freedom over me / And before I'll be a slave / I'll be buried in my grave / And go home to my Lord and be free.

Anonymous
Traditional

2138. O, Lord, O, my Lord, O, my good Lord / Keep me from sinking down.

Anonymous
Traditional

2139. O, Lord, write my name / The angels in heaven going to write my name.

Anonymous
Traditional

2140. O, Mary, don't you weep, don't you mourn / Pharaoh's army got drownded.

Anonymous
Traditional

2141. O, stand the storm / It won't be long.

Anonymous
Traditional

2142. O, walk together, children / There's a great camp meeting in the promised land.

Anonymous
Traditional

2143. O, won't you come and go with me / I'm bound for the promised land.

Anonymous
Traditional

2144. O, you got to walk that lonesome valley / You got to walk it by yourself.

Anonymous
Traditional

2145. One of these days about twelve o'clock / This old world's going to reel and rock.

Anonymous
Traditional

2146. Ride on, King Jesus / No man can hinder me.

Anonymous
Traditional

2147. Rock-a my soul / In the bosom of Abraham.

Anonymous
Traditional

2148. Run to Jesus / Shun the danger / I don't expect to stay much longer here.

Anonymous
Traditional

2149. Slavery's chain done broke at last / Going to praise God till I die.

Anonymous
Traditional

2150. Sometimes I feel like a motherless child / A long way from home.

Anonymous
Traditional

2151. Soon I will be done with the troubles of the world / Going home to live with God.

Anonymous
Traditional

2152. Steal away, steal away / Steal away to Jesus.

Anonymous
Traditional

2153. Sweep it clean, ain't going to tarry here.

Anonymous
Traditional

2154. Swing low, sweet chariot / Coming for to carry me home.

Anonymous
Traditional

2155. There is a balm in Gilead / To heal the sin-sick soul.

Anonymous
Traditional

2156. There's a star in the east on Christmas morn / Rise up, shepherd, and follow.

Anonymous
Traditional

2157. There's no hiding place down there.

Anonymous
Traditional

2158. There's no more slavery in the Kingdom.

Anonymous
Traditional

2159. This may be the last time / I don't know.

Anonymous
Traditional

2160. This old world is not my home / Come on sinner and go with me.

Anonymous
Traditional

2161. 'Tis the old ship of Zion / She has landed many a thousand / And will land so many more.

Anonymous
Traditional

2162. Wade in the water, children / God's going to trouble the water.

Anonymous
Traditional

2163. We are climbing Jacob's ladder / Soldier of the cross.

Anonymous
Traditional

2164. Were you there when they crucified my Lord? / Were you there?

Anonymous
Traditional

2165. When the storm of life is raging / Stand by me.

Anonymous
Traditional

2166. Who lock, who lock the lion's jaw? / God lock, God lock the lion's jaw.

Anonymous
Traditional

2167. You got a right, I got a right / We all got a right to the tree of life.

Anonymous
Traditional

2168. You shall reap just what you sow / On the mountains, in the valleys / You shall reap just what you sow.

Anonymous
Traditional

SPORTS

2169. I'm the greatest.

Muhammad Ali, 1942–
Boxing champion

2170. I keep telling myself, don't get cocky. Give your services to the press and the media, be nice to the kids, throw a baseball into the stands once in a while.

Vida Blue, 1949–
Baseball star

2171. You ever hear of cycles? Basketball is now in its black cycle.

Wilt Chamberlain, 1936–
Basketball star

2172. In the field of sports you are more or less accepted for what you do rather than what you are.

Althea Gibson, 1927–
Tennis champion

2173. It's hard being black. You ever been black? I was black once—when I was poor.

Larry Holmes, 1949–
Boxing champion

2174. Money lets you live better. It doesn't make you play better.

Reggie Jackson, 1946–
Baseball star

2175. It's too late for me.

Buck Leonard, 1907–1997
Baseball star
Greatest first baseman in the Negro Leagues when the major leagues were integrated

2176. At the beginning of the World Series of 1947, I experienced a completely new emotion when the National Anthem was played. This time, I thought, it is being played for me, as much as for anyone else.

Jackie Robinson, 1919–1972
Baseball star

2177. I enjoy out-thinking another man and out-maneuvering him, but I still don't like to fight.

Sugar Ray Robinson, 1920–1989
Boxing champion

2178. In sports, especially professional sports, your accomplishments only stand up on their own when you retire.

Darryl Strawberry, 1962–
Baseball star

STRATEGY

2179. Minority groups must predicate their survival on strategy, even as majorities predicate theirs on strength.

Gordon Blaine Hancock, 1884–1970
Minister and Sociologist

STRENGTH
See Black Strength

STRESS

2180. Afflictions are the best blessings in disguise.

Anonymous
Afro-American Encyclopedia 1869

2181. This depthless alienation from oneself and one's people is, in sum, the American experience.

James Baldwin, 1924–1987
Writer and Activist

2182. Black people have been traumatized and psychologically wounded. This is something we cannot discuss enough at this historical moment.

Bell Hooks, 1961–
Feminist and Critic

2183. It's not the load that breaks you down, it's the way you carry it.

Lena Horne, 1917–
Entertainer

2184. The test of character is the amount of strain it can bear.

Charles Hamilton Houston, 1895–1950
Lawyer and Civil rights activist

STRUGGLE

2185. Don't buy where you can't work.

Anonymous
Harlem protest slogan

2186. We're in a struggle for the soul of this country. We're in a struggle for America's moral center.

Harry Belafonte, 1927–
Singer and Civil rights activist

2187. I have always been confident that the Negro will win this struggle [for justice] but it is not the Negro really, but the nation that must win it.

Ralph Bunche, 1904–1971
Statesman

2188. Truth is that transcendent reality disclosed in the people's historical struggle for liberation, which enables them to know that their fight for freedom is not futile.

James Cone, 1938–
Theologian

2189. If there is no struggle, there is no progress. Those who profess to favor freedom, and yet deprecate agitation, are men who want crops without plowing up the ground. They want rain without thunder and lightning. They want the ocean without the awful roar of its many waters. This struggle may be a moral one, or it may be a physical one, or it may be both moral and physical, but it must be a struggle. Power concedes nothing without a demand.

Frederick Douglass, 1817?–1895
Abolitionist and Autobiographer

2190. There must always be the continuing struggle to make the increasing knowledge of the world bear some fruit in increasing understanding and in the production of human happiness.

Charles R. Drew, 1904–1950
Physician and Inventor

2191. If I die, it will be in a good cause. I've been fighting for America just as much as the soldiers in Vietnam.

Medgar Evers, 1926–1963
Civil rights activist

2192. And so our struggle continues as still we rise to beat back the snarling dogs of segregation.

Myrlie Evers-Williams
NAACP official

2193. Look for me in the whirlwind or storm, look for me all around you, for, with God's grace, I shall come and bring with me countless millions of black slaves who have died in America and the West Indies and the millions in Africa to aid you in the fight for Liberty, Freedom, and Life.

Marcus Garvey, 1887–1940
Nationalist leader

2194. Since 1619 Negroes have tried every method of communication, of transformation of their situation from petition to the vote, everything. There isn't anything that hasn't been exhausted.

Lorraine Hansberry, 1930–1965
Dramatist

2195. Every try will not succeed. If you live, your business is trying.

John O. Killens, 1916–1987
Novelist

2196. The issues in the 1950s were very simple, whether you sit in a restaurant or whether you can vote.... Now we have to find a way to simplify very complicated issues, and we haven't been able to do it yet.

Joseph Lowery, 1924–
Civil rights activist

2197. We are ready, willing, and able to grapple with the issues that face America today. We are going to go one day at a time, one block at a time, one life at a time.

Kweisi Mfume
NAACP official

2198. One ought to struggle for its own sake. One ought to be against racism and sexism because they are wrong, not because one is black or one is female.

Eleanor Holmes Norton, 1938–
Lawyer and Activist

2199. The battles that count aren't the ones for gold medals. The struggle within yourself—the invisible, inevitable battles inside all of us—that's where it's at.

Jesse Owens, 1913–1980
Olympic track star

2200. There was only one thing I could do—hammer relentlessly, continually, crying aloud, even if in a wilderness, and force open, by sheer muscle power, every closed door.

Adam Clayton Powell Jr., 1908–1972
Minister and U.S. Congressperson

2201. I am not a part-time struggler. I'm in the movement for the liberation of African people full time, seven days a week, 24 hours per day, for life.

Queen Mother Moore (Audley Moore), 1898–1997
Nationalist leader

2202. By fighting for their rights now, American Negroes are helping to make America a moral and spiritual arsenal of democracy. Their fight against the poll tax, against lynch law, segregation, and Jim Crow, their fight for economic, political, and social equality thus becomes part of the global war for freedom.

A. Philip Randolph, 1889–1979
Labor leader

2203. If Negroes secure their goals, immediate and remote, they must win them, and to win them they must fight, sacrifice, suffer, go to jail, and, if need be, die for them.

A. Philip Randolph, 1889–1979
Labor leader

2204. I am a radical and I am going to stay one until my people get free to walk the earth.

Paul Robeson, 1898–1976
Singer and Activist

2205. Songs of liberation—who can lock them up? The spirit of freedom— who can jail it? A people's unity—what lash can beat it down? Civil rights— what doubletalk can satisfy our need?

Paul Robeson, 1898–1976
Singer and Activist

2206. It is of no use for us to sit with our hands folded, hanging our heads like bulrushes, lamenting our wretched condition; but let us make a mighty effort and arise; and if no one will promote or respect us, let us promote and respect ourselves.

Maria W. Stewart, 1803–1879
Lecturer

2207. As long as one black American survives, the struggle for equality with other Americans must also survive. This is a debt we owe to those blameless hostages we leave to the future, our children.

Alice Walker, 1944–
Writer

2208. We never stopped believing that we were part of something good that has never happened before.

Harold Washington, 1922–1987
Politician, Mayor of Chicago

2209. The Negro must, without yielding, continue the grim struggle for integration and against segregation; for his own physical, moral, and spiritual well-being; and for that of white America and the world at large.

Walter White, 1893–1955
Civil rights activist

2210. If it costs me my life in the morning I will tell you tonight that the time has come for the black man to die fighting.

Malcolm X, 1925–1965
Nationalist leader

2211. The system that we enjoy in the United States is a system born of struggle. Yes, it's also a system which was built on the inhumanity of human slavery. But somehow those very slaves who at one point in our history created the cheap labor force which enabled that system to take off and thereby made industrialization possible—those same slaves and their children's children came back again in the [19] fifties and sixties and humanized that system.

Andrew Young, 1932–
Civil rights activist

STYLE

2212. For years we've been hanging our maid's uniforms in the same closet as our tiaras and fox stoles. Black style is nothing if not inconsistent.

Bonnie Allen
Fashion editor

2213. The majestic splendor of the black woman's body [is] ebony magic that, after all is said and done, never fails to keep us going in high style.

Bonnie Allen
Fashion editor

2214. Life is what your creator gave you for free. Style is what you do with it.

Mae Jemison, 1956–
Astronaut

2215. God created black people and black people created style.

George C. Wolfe, 1954–
Dramatist and Producer

SUCCESS

2216. Success is not the key to happiness. Happiness is the key to success. If you love what you are doing, you will be successful.

Herman Cain, 1948–
Business executive

2217. Most people search high and wide for the keys to success. If they only knew, the key to their dreams lies within.

George Washington Carver, 1864?–1943
Inventor

2218. There are so many privileges and immunities denied us as citizens, which we are entitled to enjoy equally with others, that we would be discouraged at the prospect of the long fight we have before us to secure them, if we did not stop to reflect that, by our history as well as the history of others, they only succeed who refuse to fail and who fight all the time for theirs whatever the obstacles. I feel that way about it now at the age of 75 as I did at the age of 21. I want all the young and the old people of the race to feel about it in the same way.

T. Thomas Fortune, 1856–1928
Journalist

2219. No matter where you go to school, there are many ways to fail and only a few ways to excel.

Jesse Jackson, 1941–
Minister and Civil rights activist

2220. If you have achieved any level of success, then pour it into someone else. Success is not success without a successor.

T.D. Jakes
Evangelist

2221. We surround ourselves with images of success to hide our secret fears.

T.D. Jakes
Evangelist

2222. If you can somehow think and dream of success in small steps, every time you make a step, every time you accomplish a small goal, it gives you confidence to go on from there.

John H. Johnson, 1918–
Publisher

2223. The guy who takes a chance, who walks the line between the known and the unknown, who is unafraid of failure, will succeed.

Gordon Parks, 1912–
Photographer

2224. It is better for us to succeed, though some die, than for us to fail, though all live.

William Pickens, 1881–1954
Editor and Civil rights activist

2225. Racism exists in some form or other everywhere. The key to succeeding in a workplace where you are the only black person is to hold strong to your internal power.

Andrea D. Pinkney

2226. There are no secrets to success. Don't waste time looking for them. Success is the result of perfection, hard work, learning from failure, loyalty to those for whom you work, and persistence.

Colin Powell, 1937–
U.S. General

2227. What success I achieved in the theater is due to the fact that I have always worked just as hard when there were 10 people in the house as when there were thousands, just as hard in Springfield, Illinois, as on Broadway.

Bojangles Robinson (William Robinson), 1878–1949
Dancer

2228. Anytime you see somebody more successful than you are, they are doing something you aren't.

Malcolm X, 1925–1965
Nationalist leader

2229. Every black person who rises is subject to a greater degree of criticism than any other segment of the population.

Coleman Young, 1923?–
Politician, Mayor of Detroit

SUFFERING

2230. To live is to suffer; to survive is to find some meaning in the suffering.

Roberta Flack, 1939–
Singer

2231. This is the cross that we must bear for the redemption of our people.

Martin Luther King Jr., 1929–1968
Civil rights activist and Nobel laureate

2232. I do not know which of our afflictions God intends that we overcome and which he means for us to bear.

Jean Toomer, 1894–1967
Novelist

SURVIVAL

2233. Someone was hurt before you; wronged before you; hungry before you; beaten before you; humiliated before you; raped before you; yet, someone survived.

Maya Angelou, 1928–
Novelist and Poet

2234. We must change in order to survive.

Pearl Bailey, 1918–1990
Entertainer

2235. It's impossible to eat enough if you're worried about the next meal.

James Baldwin, 1924–1987
Writer and Activist

2236. I did what I had to do.

Hattie McDaniel, 1895–1952
Actor

2237. I sell the shadow to support the substance.

Sojourner Truth, 1797?–1883
Abolitionist and Women's rights advocate

2238. I was a tough child. I was too large and too poor to fit, and I fought back.

Ethel Waters, 1896?–1977
Singer and Actor

2239. The major enemy of black survival in America has been and is neither oppression nor exploitation but rather the nihilistic threat—that is, loss of hope and absence of meaning. For as long as hope remains and meaning is preserved, the possibility of overcoming oppression stays alive.

Cornel West, 1954–
Philosopher and Activist

TALENTED TENTH

2240. The Negro race, like all races, is going to be saved by its exceptional men.

W.E.B. Du Bois, 1868–1963
Intellectual and Activist

THEATER

2241. The classic function of the theater is to project and illuminate the feelings and concerns of the community which sustains it.

Robert Abrahams, 1905–1971

2242. It is a sad fact that I have rarely seen a Negro actor really well used on the American stage or screen, or on television.

James Baldwin, 1924–1987
Writer and Activist

2243. My main concern is theater; and the theater does not reflect a universal society. It has been stingy and selfish and it has to do better.

Anna Deavere Smith, 1950–
Actor

2244. There are characteristics and natural tendencies in our people which make just as beautiful studies for the stage as to be found in the make-up of any other race, and perhaps far better.

Aida Overton Walker, 1880–1914
Singer and Dancer

2245. I was thinking about all the honors that are showered on me in the theater.... However, when I reach a hotel, I am refused permission to ride on the passenger elevator.

Bert Williams, 1876–1922
Entertainer

2246. If I could interpret in the theater [the] underlying tragedy of the race, I feel that we [African Americans] would be better known and better understood. Perhaps the time will come when that dream will come true.

Bert Williams, 1876–1922
Entertainer

355

THINKING

~~~~~~~~~

2247. Never be afraid to sit a while and think.

Lorraine Hansberry, 1930–1965
Dramatist

2248. His road of thought is what makes every man what he is.

Zora Neale Hurston, 1891–1960
Writer and Folklorist

TIME

2249. There is a way to look at the past. Don't hide from it. It will not catch you—if you don't repeat it.

Pearl Bailey, 1918–1990
Entertainer

2250. We've got to decide if it's going to be this generation or never.

Daisy Bates, 1920–
Civil rights activist

2251. Time is not a river. Time is a pendulum ... intricate patterns of recurrence in history.

Arna Bontemps, 1902–1973
Writer

2252. The past is a ghost, the future is a dream, and all we ever have is now.

Bill Cosby, 1937–
Actor

2253. There are years that ask questions and years that answer.

Zora Neale Hurston, 1891–1960
Writer and Folklorist

2254. We must use time creatively, and forever realize that the time is always ripe to do right.

Martin Luther King Jr., 1929–1968
Civil rights activist and Nobel laureate

TOKENISM

2255. All token blacks have the same experience. I have been pointed at as a solution to things that have not begun to be solved, because pointing at us token blacks eases the conscience of millions, and I think this is dreadfully wrong.

Leontyne Price, 1927–
Opera singer

TRAVEL

2256. Traveling round the world opened up my ears.

Ray Charles, 1930–
Singer

TROUBLE

2257. If a black person gets in trouble, he calls out two names: Jesus and the NAACP.

Joe Madison

2258. When I see trouble coming, I go on up ahead to meet it.

Bernice Johnson Reagon, 1942–
Singer

TRUTH

2259. You never find yourself until you face the truth.

Pearl Bailey, 1918–1990
Entertainer

2260. The greatest and most immediate danger of white culture is its fear of the truth, its childish belief in the efficacy of lies as a method of human uplift.

W.E.B. Du Bois, 1868–1963
Intellectual and Activist

2261. You've got to get the mind cleared out before you put the truth in it.

Louis Farrakhan, 1934–
Nation of Islam leader

2262. The truth should be told, though it kill.

T. Thomas Fortune, 1856–1928
Journalist

2263. If now isn't a good time for the truth, I don't see when we'll get to it.
Nikki Giovanni, 1943–
Poet

2264. It would have been more comfortable to remain silent. I took no initiative to inform anyone. But when I was asked by a representative of this committee to report my experience, I felt I had to tell the truth. I could not keep silent.
Anita Hill, 1956–
Law professor

2265. Truth is a letter from courage.
Zora Neale Hurston, 1891–1960
Writer and Folklorist

2266. If you raise up truth, it's magnetic. It has a way of drawing people.
Jesse Jackson, 1941–
Minister and Civil rights activist

2267. We have to undo the millions of little white lies that America told herself and the world about the American black man.
John O. Killens, 1916–1987
Novelist

2268. Truth is more than a mental exercise.
Thurgood Marshall, 1908–1993
U.S. Supreme Court Justice

2269. Truth burns up error.
Sojourner Truth, 1797?–1883
Abolitionist and Women's rights advocate

2270. Threats cannot suppress the truth.
Ida B. Wells, 1862–1931
Militant activist

2271. I am a threat to the degree that I am trying to tell the truth about America.
Cornel West, 1954–
Philosopher and Activist

2272. The quest for truth, the quest for the good, the quest for the beautiful, for me, presupposes allowing suffering to speak, allowing victims to be visible, and allowing social misery to be put on the agendas of those with power.

Cornel West, 1954–
Philosopher and Activist

2273. Truth knows no color; it appeals to intelligence.

Ralph Wiley, 1952–
Writer

2274. Truth could move multitudes with untutored language.

Carter G. Woodson, 1875–1950
Historian

2275. Truth must be dug up from the past and presented to the circle of scholastics in scientific form and then through stories and dramatizations that will permeate our educational system.

Carter G. Woodson, 1875–1950
Historian

2276. I'm for truth, no matter who tells it.

Malcolm X, 1925–1965
Nationalist leader

TWONESS

2277. One ever feels his twoness—an American, a Negro; two souls, two thoughts, two unreconciled strivings, two warring ideals in one dark body.

W.E.B. Du Bois, 1868–1963
Intellectual and Activist

UNDERGROUND RAILROAD

2278. Go and carry the news. One more soul got safe.

Attributed to Harriet Tubman, 1820?–1913
Abolitionist

2279. I never ran my train off the track. And I never lost a passenger.

Harriet Tubman, 1820?–1913
Abolitionist

UNITY

See also Solidarity

2280. We will never separate ourselves voluntarily from the slave population in this country; they are our brethren by the ties of consanguinity, of suffering and of wrong; and we feel there is more virtue in suffering privations with then than fancied advantage for a season.

Richard Allen, 1760–1831
AME Church founder

2281. I don't believe the accident of birth makes people sisters or brothers. It makes them siblings…. Sisterhood and brotherhood is a condition people have to work at.

Maya Angelou, 1928–
Novelist and Poet

2282. While I know myself as a creation of God, I am also obligated to realize and remember that everyone else and everything else are also God's creation.

Maya Angelou, 1928–
Novelist and Poet

2283. Lifting as we climb.

Anonymous
National Association of Colored Women motto

2284. If we have learned anything from the '50s and '60s, it is that we need an organized, collective response to our oppression.

Toni Cade Bambara, 1939–
Writer

2285. Two months ago I had a nice apartment in Chicago. I had a good job, I had a son. When something happened to the Negroes in the South I said, "That's their business, not mine." Now I know how wrong I was. The murder of my son has shown me that what happens to any of us, anywhere in the world, had better be the business of us all.

Mamie Bradley, 1929–
Mother of lynching victim Emmett Till

2286. I would unite with anybody to do right and with nobody to do wrong.

Frederick Douglass, 1817?–1895
Abolitionist and Autobiographer

2287. Remember that our cause is one and that we must help each other if we would succeed.

Frederick Douglass, 1817?–1895
Abolitionist and Autobiographer

2288. For the development of the Negro genius, of Negro literature and art, of Negro spirit, only Negroes bound and welded together, Negroes inspired by one vast ideal, can work out in its fullness the great message we have for humanity.

W.E.B. Du Bois, 1868–1963
Intellectual and Activist

2289. Never in the world should we fight against association with ourselves.

W.E.B. Du Bois, 1868–1963
Intellectual and Activist

2290. It is not culture which binds the people who are of partially African origin now scattered throughout the world, but an identity of passions. We share a hatred for the alienation forced upon us by Europeans during the process of colonization and empire, and we are bound more by our common suffering than by our pigmentation.

Ralph Ellison, 1914–1994
Novelist

2291. When we have someone in the White House like Mr. [Ronald] Reagan, he helps us, not because he wants to help us, but his wickedness helps us to find each other.

Louis Farrakhan, 1934–
Nation of Islam leader

2292. The thing to do is to get organized; keep separated and you will be exploited, you will be robbed, you will be killed. Get organized and you will compel the world to respect you.

Marcus Garvey, 1887–1940
Nationalist leader

2293. I hope you will … live in peace and love with your brothers.

Prince Hall, 1735–1807
Masonic founder

2294. The ethic of liberal individualism has so deeply permeated the psyches of blacks … of all classes that we have little support for a political ethnic of communalism that promotes the sharing of resources.

Bell Hooks, 1961–
Feminist and Critic

2295. Whites are beginning to realize that the entire culture is at stake if blacks and other minorities are not educated and included in this country's business community. It is all tied together: if blacks fail the whole culture will fail.

Coretta Scott King, 1927–
Civil rights activist

2296. One heart!

Bob Marley, 1946–?
Reggae singer

2297. Sometimes it appears that we should worry more about how we split among ourselves and less about how whites keep us divided.

Alvin Poussaint, 1934–
Psychiatrist

2298. A race, like an individual, lifts itself up by lifting others up.

Booker T. Washington, 1856–1915
Educator

2299. I lay awake amid sleeping Muslim brothers and I learned that pilgrims from every land—every color and class and rank—all snored in the same language.

Malcolm X, 1925–1965
Nationalist leader

VALUES

2300. It doesn't have to glitter to be gold.

Arthur Ashe, 1943–1993
Tennis champion

2301. America will destroy herself and revert to barbarism if she continues to cultivate things of the flesh and reject the higher virtues.

Nannie Burroughs, 1883–1961
Activist

2302. Teach your children the internals and the externals, rather than just the externals of clothing and money.

Nannie Burroughs, 1879–1961
Activist

2303. The most extraordinary characteristic of current American life is the attempt to reduce life to buying and selling.

W.E.B. Du Bois, 1868–1963
Intellectual and Activist

2304. Nobody ever asks what kind of car Ralph Bunche drove or what kind of designer suit Martin Luther King Jr. bought.

Marian Wright Edelman, 1939–
Children's Defense Fund official

2305. Any man can make money, but it takes a special kind of man to use it responsibly.

A.G. Gaston, 1892–1993
Businessperson

2306. Morality and values begin at home. If Black America is to continue its greatness, it must take care of its children.

Alvin Poussaint, 1934–
Psychiatrist

2307. The greatest gifts my parents gave to me and my sister were their unconditional love and a set of values, values they lived and didn't just lecture about.

Colin Powell, 1937–
U.S. General

2308. Do not think life consists of dress and show. Remember that everyone's life is measured by the power that that individual has to make the world better—this is all life is.

Booker T. Washington, 1856–1915
Educator

2309. Have you grown to the point where you can unflinchingly stand up for the right, for that which is honorable, honest, truthful, whether it makes you popular or unpopular? Have you grown to the point where absolutely and unreservedly you make truth and honor your standard of thinking and speaking?

Booker T. Washington, 1856–1915
Educator

2310. The individual is the instrument, national virtue the end.

Booker T. Washington, 1856–1915
Educator

2311. The true worth of any nation is determined by that nation's treatment of its most disadvantaged citizens.

Whitney M. Young Jr., 1921–1971
Civil rights activist

VICTORY

IOI IOIIOI IOIIOI IOIIOI IOI

2312. We have worked too long and too hard, made too many sacrifices, spent too much money, shed too much blood, lost too many lives fighting to vindicate our manhood as full participants in the American system, to allow our victories to be nullified by phony liberals, die-hard racists, discouraged and demoralized Negroes, and power-seeking politicians.

Benjamin Hooks, 1925–
NAACP official

2313. Our time has come. Suffering breeds character; character breeds faith; and in the end, faith will not disappoint. Our time has come. Our faith, hopes, and dreams will prevail. Our time has come. Weeping has endured for the night. And now joy cometh in the morning. Our time has come. No grave can hold our body down. Our time has come. No lie can live forever. Our time has come. We must leave the racial battleground and come to an economic common ground and a moral higher ground. America, our time has come. We've come from disgrace to Amazing Grace. Our time has come.

Jesse Jackson, 1941–
Minister and Civil rights activist

VIOLENCE

2314. It is not true, as so many commentators have said, that Nat Turner initiated a wave of violence in Southampton. The violence was already there. Slavery was violence.

Lerone Bennett, 1928–
Historian

2315. Violence is black children going to school for 12 years and receiving six years' worth of education.

Julian Bond, 1940–
Civil rights activist

2316. Violence is as American as cherry pie.

H. Rap Brown, 1943–
Militant activist

2317. We have never been involved in any kind of violence whatsoever. We have never initiated any violence against anyone, but we do believe that when violence is practiced against us we should be able to defend ourselves. We do not believe in turning the other cheek.

Malcolm X, 1925–1965
Nationalist leader

VIRTUE
See Morality

VISION

2318. A man is not a man until he is able and willing to accept his own vision of the world, no matter how radically this vision departs from that of others.

James Baldwin, 1924–1987
Writer and Activist

2319. Most people think I am a dreamer.... We need visions for larger things, for the unfolding and reviewing of worthwhile things.

Mary McLeod Bethune, 1875–1955
Educator

2320. The artist's technique, no matter how brilliant it is, should never obscure his vision.

Aaron Douglas, 1899–1979
Artist

2321. My eyes and my mind keep taking me where my old legs can't keep up.

Zora Neale Hurston, 1891–1960
Writer and Folklorist

2322. Very often when you try to see things in their largest form, you get discouraged, and you feel that it's impossible.

John H. Johnson, 1918–
Publisher

2323. Like anybody, I would like to live a long life. Longevity has its place. But I'm not concerned about that now. I just want to do God's will, and he's allowed me to go up to the mountain. And I've looked over. And I've seen the promised land.

Martin Luther King Jr., 1929–1968
Civil rights activist and Nobel laureate

VOTING
See Politics

WAR

2324. Three cheers for Massachusetts and seven dollars a month.

Anonymous
Massachusetts 54th regiment's Civil War slogan for equal pay

2325. [African American] blood is mingled with the soil of every battlefield, made glorious by revolutionary reminiscence, and [African American] bones have enriched the most productive lands of the country.

Alexander Crummell, 1819–1898
Minister and Scholar

2326. The destiny of the colored American, however this mighty [Civil] War shall terminate, is the destiny of America.

Frederick Douglass, 1817?–1895
Abolitionist and Autobiographer

2327. Men of Color, to arms!

Frederick Douglass, 1817?–1895
Abolitionist and Autobiographer

2328. A black man's got no place in the white man's army.

Cuba Gooding Jr.
Actor
Columbia's 1991 film *Boyz N the Hood*

2329. What a victory the black troops had lately won on the Georgian coast, and what a great good they had done the race in winning; they had proved to their enemies that the black man can and will fight for his freedom.

Charlotte Forten Grimke, 1837–1914
Abolitionist and Teacher

2330. The Negro soldier might just as well lay down his life here in defense of the principles of democracy as to go abroad to do so.

Francis J. Grimke, 1850–1937
Minister

2331. I speak out against this [Vietnam] war not in anger, but with sorrow in my heart and, above all, a passionate desire to see our beloved country stand as a moral example to the world.

Martin Luther King Jr., 1929–1968
Civil rights activist and Nobel laureate

2332. If we hadn't become soldiers, all might have gone back as it was before.

Thomas Long
Civil War soldier

2333. And then we saw the lightning, and that was the guns; and then we heard the thunder, and that was the big guns; and then we heard the rain falling, and that was the drops of blood falling; and when we came to get in the crops, it was dead men that we reaped.

Harriet Tubman, 1820?–1913
Abolitionist

WINNING

2334. You can't win unless you learn how to lose.

Kareem Abdul Jabbar, 1947–
Basketball star

2335. Win or lose, we win by raising the issues.

Charlotta Bass, 1880–1969
Newspaper publisher and Militant activist

2336. Most of us who aspire to be tops in our field don't really consider the amount of work required to stay tops.

Althea Gibson, 1927–
Tennis champion

2337. If you run, you might lose. If you don't run, you're guaranteed to lose.

Jesse Jackson, 1941–
Minister and Civil rights activist

WISDOM

2338. Black folks have been able to carve out of this hellish situation various ways of transmitting a moral wisdom.

Cornel West, 1954–
Philosopher and Activist

2339. Never confuse knowledge with wisdom. By wisdom I mean wrestling with how to live.

Cornel West, 1954–
Philosopher and Activist

WOMEN

See also Gender

2340. Black women whose ancestors were brought to the United States beginning in 1619 have lived through conditions of cruelty so horrible, so bizarre, the women had to reinvent themselves.

Maya Angelou, 1928–
Novelist and Poet

2341. We are the daughters of those who chose to survive.

Anonymous
Nina Poussaint in Julie Dash's film *Daughters of the Dust*

2342. My sisters-both blood and earth-have been the sole inspiration for all the truth I have ever learned. We as black women must understand the true power all of us bring to each other and to the struggle.

Belynda B. Bady, 1961–
Entrepreneur

2343. Let me state here and now that the black woman in America can justly be described as the slave of a slave.

Frances M. Beal, 1898–1953

2344. This is our moment. I honestly wouldn't be anyone but a black woman in America right now. I feel that this is our time to break new ground.

Halle Berry, 1968–
Actor

2345. Despite their achievements, the world has not been willing to accept the contributions women have made.

Mary McLeod Bethune, 1875–1955
Educator

2346. The true worth of a race must be measured by the character of its womanhood.

Mary McLeod Bethune, 1875–1955
Educator

2347. My mother made me strong. Watching her struggle to raise us and feed us made me want to be a stronger woman.

Mary J. Blige
Singer

2348. Artists do work with women, with the beauty of their bodies and the refinement of middle-class women, but I think there is a need to express something about the working-class black women and that's what I try to do.

Elizabeth Catlett, 1919–
Artist

2349. Black women are not here to compete or fight with you, brothers. If we have hang-ups about being male or female, we're not going to be able to use our talents to liberate all of our black people.

Shirley Chisholm, 1924–
Politician

2350. The next time a woman of whatever color, or a dark-skinned person of whatever sex aspires to be President, the way should be a little smoother because I helped pave it.

Shirley Chisholm, 1924–
Politician

2351. We have to help black men, but not at the expense of our own personalities as women.

Shirley Chisholm, 1924–
Politician

2352. If Rosa Parks' had not refused to move to the back of the bus, you and I might never have heard of Dr. Martin Luther King.

Ramsey Clark, 1927–
U.S. Attorney General

2353. The legacy of courage left by heroic black women was amassed, deed by deed, day by day, without praise or encouragement.

Johnnetta Cole, 1936–
Educator

2354. Only the black woman can say, "When and where I enter, in the quiet, undisputed dignity of my womanhood, without violence and without suing or special patronage, then and there the whole Negro race enters with me."

Anna Julia Cooper, 1858–1964
Educator

2355. To be a woman of the Negro race in America, and to be able to grasp the deep significance of the possibilities of the crisis, is to have a heritage, it seems to me, unique in the ages.

Anna Julia Cooper, 1858–1964
Educator

2356. In my world, black women can do anything.

Julie Dash, 1952–
Filmmaker

2357. It is sometimes assumed that the typical female slave was a house servant—either a cook, maid, or mammy.... As is so often the case, the reality is actually the diametrical opposite of the myth.... seven out of eight slaves, men and women alike, were field workers.

Angela Davis, 1944–
Militant activist

2358. We, the black women of today, must accept the full weight of a legacy wrought in blood by our mothers in chains ... heirs to a tradition of supreme perseverance and heroic resistance.

Angela Davis, 1944–
Militant activist

2359. All womanhood is hampered today because the world on which it is emerging is a world that tries to worship both virgins and mothers and in the end despises motherhood and despoils virgins.

W.E.B. Du Bois, 1868–1963
Intellectual and Activist

2360. I most sincerely doubt if any other race of women could have brought its fineness up through so devilish a fire.

W.E.B. Du Bois, 1868–1963
Intellectual and Activist

2361. I think black women have learned, more successfully than black men, to absorb the pain of their predicament and to keep stepping.

Michael Eric Dyson, 1958–
Scholar and Writer

2362. The race cannot succeed, nor build strong cottons, until we have a race of women competent to do more than bear a brood of negative men.

T. Thomas Fortune, 1856–1928
Journalist

2363. That the progenitor of the black literary tradition was a woman [Phillis Wheatley] means, in the most strictly literal sense, that all subsequent black writers have evolved in a matrilinear line of descent, and that each, consciously or unconsciously, has extended and revised a canon whose foundation was the poetry of a black woman.

Henry Louis Gates Jr., 1950–
Scholar and Critic

2364. The special role and plight of black women is not something that just happened three years ago. We've had a special plight for 350 years. My grandmother had it. My grandmother was a slave.

Fannie Lou Hamer, 1917–1977
Civil rights activist

2365. Obviously, the most oppressed of any oppressed group will be its women.

Lorraine Hansberry, 1930–1965
Dramatist

2366. If the fifteenth century discovered America to the Old World, the nineteenth is discovering woman to herself.

Frances Ellen Watkins Harper, 1825–1911
Writer and Orator

2367. While law and public opinion idealized motherhood and enforced the protection of white women's bodies, the opposite held true for black women's.

Evelyn Brooks Higginbotham, 1945–
Scholar

2368. Black women have the habit of survival.

Lena Horne, 1917–
Entertainer

2369. Now women forget all those things they don't want to remember, and remember everything they don't want to forget. The dream is the truth. Then they act and do things accordingly.

Zora Neale Hurston, 1891–1960
Writer and Folklorist

2370. So I was sold at last! A human being sold in the free city of New York! The bill of sale is on record, and future generations will learn from it that women were articles of traffic in New York, late in the nineteenth century of the Christian religion.

Harriet Jacobs, 1813–1897
Former slave autobiographer

2371. The heart of a woman goes forth with the dawn, / As a lone bird, soft winging, so restlessly on.

Georgia Douglas Johnson, 1877–1966
Writer

2372. Young women who need to know what they can do of enduring value should come and work with African women who are ensuring the future of the continent.

Florence Ladd, 1932–
Novelist and Educator

2373. For as unseemly as it may appear nowadays for a woman to preach, it should be remembered that nothing is impossible with God.

Jarena Lee, 1783–1853?
Minister

2374. Sisters have taught me that we should listen to the poetry within, capture and express our inner beauty as part of our political and social being.

Manning Marable, 1945–
Writer and Educator

2375. Mother came from a long line of black women from the South who thought they could create the world in their image.

Deborah E. McDowell, 1950–
Scholar

2376. It's good when you got a woman who is a friend of your mind.

Toni Morrison, 1931–
Novelist and Nobel laureate

2377. No man should be judged by the irrational criteria of race, religion, or national origin. And I assure you I use the word "man" in the generic sense, for the principle of nondiscrimination must be a reality for women as well.

Eleanor Holmes Norton, 1938–
Lawyer and Activist

2378. The worship of the black woman as the mother of the human race goes back to the dimmest antiquity.

J.A. Rogers, 1880–1966
Historian

2379. Any woman who has a great deal to offer the world is in trouble.

Hazel Scott, 1920–1981
Pianist

2380. Bein' alive & bein' a woman & bein' colored is a metaphysical dilemma I haven't yet conquered.

Ntozake Shange, 1948–
Poet and Dramatist

2381. I proudly love being a Negro woman. It's so involved and interesting. We are the problem—the great national game of taboo.

Anne Spencer, 1882–1975
Poet

2382. How long shall the fair daughters of Africa be compelled to bury their minds and talents beneath a load of iron pots and kettles?

Maria W. Stewart, 1803–1879
Lecturer

2383. O, ye daughters of Africa, awake! arise! no longer sleep nor slumber, but distinguish yourselves. Show forth to the world that ye are endowed with noble and exalted faculties.

Maria W. Stewart, 1803–1879
Lecturer

2384. A white woman has only one handicap to overcome, that of sex. I have two, both race and sex.

Mary Church Terrell, 1863–1954
Women's club leader

2385. Ain't I a woman? Look at me! Look at my arm! I have ploughed and planted and gathered into barns, and no man could head me. And ain't I a woman? I could work as much and eat as much as a man—when I could get it—and bear the lash as well. And ain't I a woman? I have borne 13 children and seen them most all sold off to slavery, and when I cried out with my mother's grief, none but Jesus heard me. And ain't I a woman?

Sojourner Truth, 1797?–1883
Abolitionist and Women's rights advocate

2386. I used to work in the fields and bind grain, keeping up with the cradler, but men doing no more, got twice as much pay.

Sojourner Truth, 1797?–1883
Abolitionist and Women's rights advocate

2387. I wanted to tell you a little might about women's rights, and so I come and said so. I'll be around again sometime. I'm watching things and I'll get up and tell you what time of night it is.

Sojourner Truth, 1797?–1883
Abolitionist and Women's rights advocate

2388. If the first woman God ever made was strong enough to turn the world upside down all alone, these women together ought to be able to turn it back, and get it right side up again!

Sojourner Truth, 1797?–1883
Abolitionist and Women's rights advocate

2389. That little man says women can't have as much rights as men 'cause Christ wasn't a woman! Where did your Christ come from? From God and a woman! Man had nothing to do with Him.

Sojourner Truth, 1797?–1883
Abolitionist and Women's rights advocate

2390. There is a great stir about colored men getting their rights but not a word about colored women; and if colored men get their rights and not colored women theirs, you see, colored men will be masters over the women.

Sojourner Truth, 1797?–1883
Abolitionist and Women's rights advocate

2391. Whatever good I have accomplished as an actress I believe came in direct proportion to my efforts to portray black women who have made positive contributions to my heritage.

Cecily Tyson, 1933–
Actor

2392. Black women were always imitating Harriet Tubman—escaping to become something unheard of.

Alice Walker, 1944–
Writer

2393. America be placed on notice. We know who we are. We understand our collective power. Following today we will act on that power.

Maxine Waters, 1938–
Politician
Million Woman March 1997

2394. Nothing had been promised us, and we didn't have even that to lose.

Sherley Anne Williams, 1944–
Writer

2395. I come here celebrating every African, every colored, black Negro American everywhere that ever cooked a meal, ever raised a child, ever worked in the fields, ever went to school, ever sang in a choir, ever loved a man or loved a woman, every corn-rowed, every Afroed, every wig-wearing, pigtailed, weave-wearing one of us. I come celebrating the journey, I come celebrating the little passage, the movement of our women people.

Oprah Winfrey, 1954–
Entertainer

2396. Women were part of our [Civil Rights] movement. It was women going door to door, speaking with their neighbors, meeting voter registration classes together, organizing through their churches, that gave the vital momentum and energy in the movement.

Andrew Young, 1932–
Civil rights activist

WORDS

2397. Cultivate the oratorical. Do it diligently and with purpose, remembering that it is by the exercise of this weapon perhaps more than any other that America is to be made a free land, not in name only, but in deed and truth.
William Grant Allen

2398. Transforming words were placed in the mouths of folk poets from the earliest times in America.
Molefi Asante, 1942–
Educator

2399. I cross out words so you will see them more. The fact that they are obscured makes you want to read them.
Jean-Michel Basquiat, 1960–1988
Graffiti-inspired artist

2400. I still do feel that a poet has a duty to words, and that words can do wonderful things, and it's too bad to just let them lie there without doing anything with and for them.
Gwendolyn Brooks, 1917–
Poet

2401. Words are your business, boy. Not just the Word. Words are everything. The key to the Rock, the answer to the Question.
Ralph Ellison, 1914–1994
Novelist

2402. One of the most effective ways to keep a people enslaved, in a scientific and technical state which is dependent upon a relatively high rate of literacy, is to create in that people a disrespect and fear of the written and spoken word.
Haki Madhubuti, 1942–
Poet

2403. We die. That may be the meaning of life. But we do have language. That may be the measure of our lives.

Toni Morrison, 1931–
Novelist and Nobel laureate

2404. We traded in our drums for respectability, so now it's just words.

George C. Wolfe, 1954–
Dramatist and Producer

2405. The novelist hasn't any right to inflict on the public his private ideas on politics, religion, or race. If he wants to preach he should go on the pulpit.

Frank Yerby, 1916–1991
Novelist

WORDS TO LIVE BY

2406. Float like a butterfly; sting like a bee.

Muhammad Ali, 1942–
Boxing champion

2407. Take a day to heal from the lies you've told yourself and the ones that have been told to you.

Maya Angelou, 1928–
Novelist and Poet

2408. Living a life is like constructing a building: if you start wrong, you'll end wrong.

Willie Bady Jr., 1955–
Businessperson and Builder and Developer

2409. The determination to outwit one's situation means that one has no models, only object lessons.

James Baldwin, 1924–1987
Writer and Activist

2410. If you don't live the only life you have, you won't live some other life, you won't live any life at all.

James Baldwin, 1924–1987
Writer and Activist

2411. You gotta whip up a storm and keep on blowin'.

Sidney Bechet, 1897–1959
Jazz musician

2412. I leave you love, I leave you hope, I leave you the charge of developing confidence in one another, I leave you a thirst for education. I leave you respect for the uses of power. I leave you faith. I leave you racial dignity.

Mary McLeod Bethune, 1875–1955
Educator

2413. If I'd known I was going to live this long, I'd have taken better care of myself.

Eubie Blake, 1883–1983
Pianist and Composer

2414. When life knocks you down, try to fall on your back because if you can look up, you can get up.

Les Brown, 1945–
Motivational speaker

2415. You go to school to find out what other people have done, and then you go in life to imitate them.

Melvin Chapman

2416. You're either part of the solution or part of the problem.

Eldridge Cleaver, 1935–1998
Black Panther Party leader

2417. One thing alone I charge you. As you live, believe in life! Always human beings will live and progress to greater, broader, and fuller life.

W.E.B. Du Bois, 1868–1963
Intellectual and Activist

2418. Life has two rules: number 1, never quit! number 2, always remember rule number 1.

Duke Ellington, 1899–1974
Composer and Band leader

2419. The end is in the beginning and lies far ahead.

Ralph Ellison, 1914–1994
Novelist

2420. Look at your life, man.

Louis Farrakhan, 1934–
Nation of Islam leader

2421. Whatever you do, do like a church steeple: aim high and go straight.

Rudolph Fischer, 1897–1934
Writer

2422. Just don't give up trying to do what you really want to do. Where there's love and inspiration, I don't think you can go wrong.

Ella Fitzgerald, 1918–1996?
Singer

2423. When I say "think small," I do not mean you to be small-minded or petty or parochial. I mean that you should focus your ambitions on those things that you can do something about, namely, about yourself and the things over which you have some degree of control: your temper, your manners, your morals, your habits, your soul.

Peter J. Gomes, 1942–
Minister

2424. [Y]ou must ... "act large." Another way of putting this is that you should live generously. Be extravagant in your expectations, lavish in your hopes, ambitious in your aspirations, especially for others, and you will have a hand in translating fantasies into facts.

Peter J. Gomes, 1942–
Minister

2425. Leave him some escape, for he will fight even more desperately if trapped.

Alex Haley, 1921–1992
Writer

2426. No, I do not weep at the world—I am too busy sharpening my oyster knife.

Zora Neale Hurston, 1891–1960
Writer and Folklorist

2427. No matter how far a person can go, the horizon is still way beyond you.

Zora Neale Hurston, 1891–1960
Writer and Folklorist

2428. Every day we live there is one step between triumph and tragedy.

Jesse Jackson, 1941–
Minister and Civil rights activist

2429. You may not be responsible for getting knocked down, but you're certainly responsible for getting back up.

Jesse Jackson, 1941–
Minister and Civil rights activist

2430. Be African!

Leonard Jeffries
Educator

2431. Your world is as big as you make it.

Georgia Douglas Johnson, 1877–1966
Writer

2432. I will not allow one prejudiced person or one million or one hundred million to blight my life.

James Weldon Johnson, 1871–1938
Writer and Activist

2433. Life is a grindstone, but whether it grinds you down or polishes you up depends on what you are made of.

Robert E. Johnson
Founder BET

2434. My job is to be resilient. That's why I call life a dance.

Bill T. Jones
Dancer

2435. On this day I will mend a quarrel, search for a forgotten friend, fight for a principle, show gratitude to God, and tell someone, "I love you."

Quincy Jones, 1933–
Musician and Business executive

2436. I pray hard, work hard, and leave the rest to God.

Florence Griffith Joyner, 1959–
Olympic track star

2437. There is nothing more tragic than to find an individual bogged down in the length of life, devoid of depth.

Martin Luther King Jr., 1929–1968
Civil rights activist and Nobel laureate

2438. Do the Right Thing.

Spike Lee, 1957–
Filmmaker

2439. It doesn't really matter what happens at the beginning; it's where you end up. And I think it's important that you know that today.

Spike Lee, 1957–
Filmmaker

2440. You can run, but you can't hide.

Joe Louis, 1914–1981
Boxing champion

2441. If you can take care of the internal, you can easily take care of the external. Then you can avoid the infernal and latch on to the eternal.

Joseph Lowery, 1924–
Civil rights activist

2442. We get what we deserve, and we live by the grace of God.

Benjamin Mays, 1895–1984
Educator

2443. You just ride to win.

Isaac Murphy, 1856?–1896
Thoroughbred jockey

2444. Life is accepting what is and working from that.

Gloria Naylor, 1950–
Writer

2445. Stand up for your rights, even if it kills you. That's all that life consists of.

Clarence Norris, 1913–?
Scottsboro victim

2446. Find the good. It's all around you. Find it, showcase it, and you'll start believing in it.

Jesse Owens, 1913–1980
Olympic track star

2447. Airplanes may kill you but they ain't likely to hurt you.

Satchel Paige, 1900?–1982
Baseball star

2448. Avoid fried meats, which angry up the blood. If your stomach disputes you, lie down and pacify it with cool thoughts. Keep the juices flowing by jangling around gently as you move. Go very light on the vices, such as carrying on in society—the social ramble ain't restful. Avoid running at all times. And don't look back; something might be gaining on you.

Satchel Paige, 1900?–1982
Baseball star

2449. Just take the ball and throw it where you want to.... Home plate don't move.

Satchel Paige, 1900?–1982
Baseball star

2450. Never give up and sit and grieve. Find another way.

Satchel Paige, 1900?–1982
Baseball star

2451. Be black, shine, aim high.

Leontyne Price, 1927–
Opera singer

2452. Look inside to find out where you're going, and it's better to do it before you get out of high school.

Prince, 1959–
Entertainer

2453. When I played, I went all out.

Wilma Rudolph, 1940–1994
Olympic track star

2454. Love yourself, appreciate yourself, see the good in you, see the God in you, and respect yourself.

Betty Shabazz, 1934?–1997
Educator

2455. Talk about it only enough to do it. Dream about it only enough to feel it. Think about it only enough to understand it. Contemplate it only enough to be it.

Jean Toomer, 1894–1967
Novelist

2456. I was a victim; I don't dwell on it.

Tina Turner, 1939–
Singer

2457. You asked me if I ever stood up for anything. Yeah, I stood up for my life.

Tina Turner, 1939–
Singer

2458. I am not a special person. I am a regular person who does special things.

Sarah Vaughan, 1924?–1990
Singer

2459. I got myself a start by giving myself a start.

Mme. C.J. Walker, 1867–1919
Entrepreneur

2460. We have lived in darker hours than those of today; we have seen American justice and fair play go through fire and death and devastation and come out purified by the faith that abides in the God of destiny.

Alexander Walters, 1858–1917
Minister

2461. Do a common thing in an uncommon way.

Booker T. Washington, 1856–1915
Educator

2462. Go out and be a center, a life-giving power, as it were, to a whole community, when an opportunity comes, when you may give life where there is no life, hope where there is no hope, power where there is no power. Begin in a humble way, and work to build up institutions that will put people on their feet. It is that kind of life that tells.

Booker T. Washington, 1856–1915
Educator

2463. No student is permitted to remain [at Tuskegee Institute] who does not keep and use a toothbrush.

Booker T. Washington, 1856–1915
Educator

2464. Fight hard and legally, and don't blow your top.

Robert C. Weaver, 1907–1997
U.S. Secretary of Housing

2465. Every day is borrowed time. You want to be able to use life as well as death as a form of service to something bigger than you; that makes life meaningful.

Cornel West, 1954–
Philosopher and Activist

2466. I was raised to believe that excellence is the best deterrent to racism or sexism, and that's how I operate my life.

Oprah Winfrey, 1954–
Entertainer

WORK

2467. [Mother] had to go wherever the work was, usually picking cotton or cleaning, washing, and cooking for white folks.

Alvin Ailey, 1926–1989
Dancer

2468. Just look around and you see the systematic disemployment of Black men that white America imposes on blacks.

Derrick Bell, 1930–
Law professor

2469. The job is so fantastic, you don't need a hobby. The hobby is going to work.

Guion S. Bluford Jr., 1942–
Astronaut

2470. I'm not divided and guilty about the fact that I want to work.

Diahann Carroll, 1935–
Singer

2471. If the unemployed could eat plans and promises, they would all be able to spend the winter on the Riviera.

W.E.B. Du Bois, 1868–1963
Intellectual and Activist

2472. People making a living doing something they don't enjoy wouldn't even be happy with a one-day work week.

Duke Ellington, 1899–1974
Composer and Band leader

2473. Caring for my orchids and creating conditions in which they can thrive is a great challenge, but it's the same in my work. I must be careful and thorough—I seek perfection in both.

John Hope Franklin, 1915–
Historian

2474. I never wanted to be a star, I just wanted to get work.

Gregory Hines, 1946–
Dancer and Actor

2475. I have come to know by experience that work is the nearest thing to happiness that I can find.

Zora Neale Hurston, 1891–1960
Writer and Folklorist

2476. [We] are demanding that this city [Memphis] respect the dignity of labor. So often we overlook the work and the significance of those who are not in professional jobs, of those who are not in the so-called big jobs. Let me say to you [sanitation workers] whenever you are engaged in work that serves humanity and is for the building up of humanity, it has dignity, it has worth.

Martin Luther King Jr., 1929–1968
Civil rights activist and Nobel laureate

2477. Hard work gives life meaning. everyone needs to work hard at something to feel good about themselves. Every job can be done well and every day has its satisfactions.

Osceola McCarthy, 1908–
Laundress and Philanthropist

2478. Employment is the big issue the government needs to be dealing with.

Della Simmons

2479. What works best is delegating authority, learning you cannot do everything, and some people can do it better.

Willi Smith, 1948–
Designer

2480. Black people [have] been denied an opportunity to acquire the necessary experience and [have] not been sufficiently motivated or had adequate access to training in fields where there was the greatest demand.

Leon Sullivan, 1922–
Minister and Entrepreneur

2481. Being worked meant degradation; working means civilization.

Booker T. Washington, 1856–1915
Educator

2482. No race can prosper until it learns that there is as much dignity in tilling a field as in writing a poem.

Booker T. Washington, 1856–1915
Educator

2483. Nothing ever comes to one that is worth having, except as a result of hard work.

Booker T. Washington, 1856–1915
Educator

2484. Many of today's problems in the inner-city—crime, dissolution of family, welfare—are fundamentally a consequence of the disappearance of work.

William Julius Wilson
Sociologist

WRITERS

2485. Where are the black writers who will dare to confront this racist nation? Who will illuminate the dream of the disenfranchised and sing the song of the voiceless?

Maya Angelou, 1928–
Novelist and Poet

2486. Any writer, I suppose, feels that the world into which he was born is nothing less than a conspiracy against the cultivation of his talent.
James Baldwin, 1924–1987
Writer and Activist

2487. Unless a writer is extremely old when he dies, in which case he has probably become a neglected institution, his death must always be seen as untimely. This is because a real writer is always shifting and changing and searching.
James Baldwin, 1924–1987
Writer and Activist

2488. If the writer exists for any social good, his role is that of preserving in art those human values which can endure by confronting change.
Ralph Ellison, 1914–1994
Novelist

2489. We can reveal to the Negro masses, from whence we came, our potential power to transform the now ugly face of the Southland into a region of peace and plenty.
Langston Hughes, 1902–1967
Poet and Writer

2490. We can reveal to the white masses those Negro qualities which go beyond the mere ability to laugh and sing and dance and make music, and which are a part of the useful heritage that we place at the disposal of a future free America.
Langston Hughes, 1902–1967
Poet and Writer

2491. But that's what makes you a writer; you keep writing until the noes become a yes. Writers are the ones who keep writing after all the other folks quit.
Ann Petry, 1909–1997
Writer

2492. A writer should not talk, a writer should write.
Ann Petry, 1909–1997
Writer

2493. Deliver me from writers who say the way they live doesn't matter. I'm not sure a bad person can write a good book. If art doesn't make us better, then what on earth is it for?

Alice Walker, 1944–
Writer

WRITING

2494. One writes out of one thing only—one's own experiences.

James Baldwin, 1924–1987
Writer and Activist

2495. The hand that holds the quill controls history.

Charles L. Blockson, 1933–
Book collector

2496. It is the dream of my life to be an author.

Charles W. Chesnutt, 1958–1932
Novelist

2497. I continue to create because writing is a labor of love and also an act of defiance, a way to light a candle in a gale wind.

Alice Childress, 1920–1994
Writer

2498. I have learned as much about writing about my people by listening to blues and jazz and spirituals as I have by reading novels.

Ernest J. Gaines, 1933–?
Novelist

2499. Learning to sing one's own songs, to trust the particular cadences of one's own voice, is also the goal of any writer.

Henry Louis Gates Jr., 1950–
Scholar and Critic

2500. My writing is a lens into the possibilities of the American experience.

Charles Johnson, 1948–
Novelist

2501. I have always tried to establish a voice in the work of the narrator which worked like a chorus, like what I think is going on in the black church, or in jazz, where people respond, where the reader is participating.

Toni Morrison, 1931–
Novelist and Nobel laureate

2502. I simply wanted to write literature that was irrevocably, indisputably black, not because its characters were, or because I was, but because it took as its creative task and sought as its credentials those recognized and verifiable principles of black art.

Toni Morrison, 1931–
Novelist and Nobel laureate

2503. I want to participate in developing a canon of black work ... where black people are talking to black people.

Toni Morrison, 1931–
Novelist and Nobel laureate

2504. A young black woman, struggling to find a mirror to her worth in the society, not only is [her] story worth telling, but it can be told in words so painstakingly eloquent that it becomes a song.

Gloria Naylor, 1950–
Writer

2505. It is difficult to beat making your living thinking and writing about subjects that matter to you.

Eleanor Holmes Norton, 1938–
Lawyer and Activist

2506. Writing travels so much farther than you could ever go. Something that was part of me gets to go places that I may never see.

Barbara Smith, 1946–
Writer and Publisher

YOUTH

2507. We have a powerful potential in our youth, and we must have the courage to change old ideas and practices so that we may direct their power towards good ends.

Mary McLeod Bethune, 1875–1955
Educator

2508. [Girls] want choices in life. They want to see themselves ... doing important things, being counted.

Julie Dash, 1952–
Filmmaker

2509. Youth are looking for something; it's up to adults to show them what's worth emulating.

Jesse Jackson, 1941–
Minister and Civil rights activist

2510. You are young, gifted, and black.

James Weldon Johnson, 1871–1938
Writer and Activist

2511. Denmark Vesey and Nat Turner were young men when they struck for freedom.

Paul Robeson, 1898–1976
Singer and Activist

2512. [Young African Americans are] a posse sent ahead to scout uncharted social and psychological domains. The posse may be killed, maimed, or wounded so that the rest of the society can occupy the social terrain that has been scouted with relative personal safety.

Timothy M. Simone
Writer

INDEXES

NAME INDEX

Numbers refer to entry numbers.

Aaron, Hank
Achievement, 1
Black Pride, 384
Children, 460
Community, 544
Abdul Jabbar, Kareem
Morality, 1451
Winning, 2334
Abernathy, Ralph
Church, 491
Abrahams, Robert
Theater, 2241
Adam, Andrea Thompson
Gender, 972
Adams, Charles G.
Education, 747
Adams, John Quincy
Slavery, 2013
Adams, Osceola
Race, 1656
Ailey, Alvin
Work, 2467
Alexander, Elizabeth
Language, 1282
Alexander, Sadie T.M.
Courage, 580
Ali, Muhammad
Achievement, 2
Action, 20
America, 134
Education, 748
Imagination, 1200
Integrity, 1223
Life, 1339
Purpose, 1650
Racism, 1693
Self-Realization, 1928, 1929, 1930
Sports, 2169
Words to Live By, 2406
Ali, Noble Drew
Change, 449
Names, 1493
Nationhood, 1499
Religion, 1769, 1770
Allen, Bonnie
Style, 2212, 2213
Allen, Paula Gunn
Oppression, 1518

Allen, Richard
America, 135
Church, 492
Religion, 1771
Slavery, 2014
Unity, 2280
Allen, Walter
Politics, 1565
Allen, William Grant
Words, 2397
Amlak, Elleni
Marriage, 1411
Amos, Wally
Poverty, 1599
Anderson, Marian
Achievement, 3
America, 136
Hate, 1070
Integrity, 1224
Money, 1443
Race, 1657
Race Relations, 1679
Angelou, Maya
Adolescence, 43
Africa, 65, 66, 67
Ancestors, 210
Courage, 581
Defeat, 657
Education, 749
Fear, 882
Healing, 1082
Heritage, 1088
Humanity, 1149
Love, 1372
Reality, 1743
Self-Reliance, 1947
Survival, 2233
Unity, 2281, 2282
Women, 2340
Words to Live By, 2407
Writers, 2485
Anonymous
Africa, 68
America, 137
Beauty of Blackness, 309
Blues, 413
Business, 434, 435
Church, 493

Color, 535
Education, 750, 751
Folk sayings, 895, 896, 897, 898, 899,
   900, 901, 902, 903
Freedom, 907, 908, 909, 910
History, 1095
Men, 1417
Segregation, 1843
Spirituals, 2080, 2081, 2082, 2083, 2084,
   2085, 2086, 2087, 2088, 2089, 2090,
   2091, 2092, 2093, 2094, 2095, 2096,
   2097, 2098, 2099, 2100, 2101, 2102,
   2103, 2104, 2105, 2106, 2107, 2108,
   2109, 2110, 2111, 2112, 2113, 2114,
   2115, 2116, 2117, 2118, 2119, 2120,
   2121, 2122, 2123, 2124, 2125, 2126,
   2127, 2128, 2129, 2130, 2131, 2132,
   2133, 2134, 2135, 2136, 2137, 2138,
   2139, 2140, 2141, 2142, 2143, 2144,
   2145, 2146, 2147, 2148, 2149, 2150,
   2151, 2152, 2153, 2154, 2155, 2156,
   2157, 2158, 2159, 2160, 2161, 2162,
   2163, 2164, 2165, 2166, 2167, 2168
Stress, 2180
Struggle, 2185
Unity, 2283
War, 2324
Women, 2341
Appiah, Anthony
   Africa, 69, 70
   Identity, 1182
   Politics, 1566
   Race, 1658, 1659, 1660
Aptheker, Herbert
   Resistance, 1797
Armstrong, Lil Hardin
   Music, 1461
Armstrong, Louis
   Authenticity, 307
   Jazz, 1241, 1242
   Music, 1462, 1463, 1464, 1465, 1466
Asante, Molefi
   Africa, 71
   Afrocentrism, 127
   Oppression, 1519
   Self-Expression, 1871
   Words, 2398
Ashe, Arthur
   Being Black in America, 325
   Goals, 991
   Racism, 1694
   Values, 2300
Bady, Barbara
   Life, 1340
Bady, Belynda B.
   Politics, 1567
   Women, 2342
Bady, Willie Jr.
   Words to Live By, 2408

Bailey, Pearl
   Action, 21
   Freedom, 911
   God, 1008
   Life, 1341
   Prejudice, 1619
   Self-Acceptance, 1847
   Self-Affirmation, 1859
   Survival, 2234
   Time, 2249
   Truth, 2259
Baker, Josephine
   Living, 1364
   Morality, 1452
   Paris, 1535, 1536
Baldwin, Alfred
   Religion, 1772
Baldwin, James
   Action, 22
   Africa, 72
   America, 138, 139, 140, 141, 142, 143,
      144
   Anger, 227
   Art, 230, 231, 232
   Being Black in America, 326, 327, 328
   Black Strength, 402
   Children, 461, 462
   Color, 536
   Daring, 638
   Dreams, 698, 699
   Drugs, 719
   Education, 752
   Evil, 849
   Experience, 857
   Family, 868
   Fear, 883
   Freedom, 912, 913
   Gender, 973
   Ghetto, 986
   God, 1009, 1010
   Hate, 1071, 1072, 1073, 1074
   History, 1096, 1097, 1098, 1099
   Humanism, 1147
   Humanity, 1150
   Identity, 1183
   Integration, 1213
   Islam, 1239
   Jazz, 1243, 1244, 1245
   Language, 1283, 1284, 1285
   Life, 1342, 1343
   Limitations, 1355
   Love, 1373, 1374
   Men, 1418
   Money, 1444
   Nonviolence, 1505
   Opportunity, 1508
   Oppression, 1520
   Paris, 1537, 1538
   Race Consciousness, 1672

Racism, 1695
Reality, 1744, 1745
Retribution, 1811
Self-Acceptance, 1848
Self-Hate, 1873, 1874
Self-Knowledge, 1885, 1886
Self-Reliance, 1948
Soul, 2063
Stress, 2181
Survival, 2235
Theater, 2242
Vision, 2318
Words to Live By, 2409, 2410
Writers, 2486, 2487
Writing, 2494
Ballard, Florence
Hope, 1131
Bambara, Toni Cade
Art, 233
Artists, 281
Dreams, 700
Language, 1286
Unity, 2284
Banks, Erin
Living, 1365
Banneker, Benjamin
Black Pride, 385
Intelligence, 1234
Peace, 1546
Bannister, Edward Mitchell
Art, 234
Baraka, Amiri
African Continuity, 124
America, 145
Artists, 282, 283
Freedom, 914
Hope, 1132
Nationhood, 1500
Poetry, 1556
Barnes, James B.
Artists, 284
Basquiat, Jean-Michel
Words, 2399
Bass, Charlotta
Winning, 2335
Bates, Daisy
Time, 2250
Beal, Frances M.
Women, 2343
Bearden, Romare
Art, 235, 236, 237, 238, 239, 240, 241, 242, 243, 244
Artists, 285, 286
Life, 1344
Love, 1375
Relationships, 1766
Spirit, 2068
Bechet, Sidney
Goals, 992

Paris, 1539
Words to Live By, 2411
Beckwourth, Jim
Direction, 681
Belafonte, Harry
Struggle, 2186
Bell, Derrick
Racism, 1696
Work, 2468
Beman, Jehiel C.
Slavery, 2015
Bennett, Gwendolyn
Love, 1376
Bennett, Lerone
Class, 523
Education, 753
Racism, 1697
Violence, 2314
Benson, Janice Hall
Education, 754
Family, 869
Bergreen, Laurence
Jazz, 1246
Berry, Halle
Women, 2344
Berry, Mary Frances
History, 1100
Bethune, Mary McLeod
Achievement, 4
Africa, 73
Artists, 287
Beauty of Blackness, 310
Black Pride, 386
Economics, 726
Ideals, 1170
Love, 1377
Soul, 2064
Vision, 2319
Women, 2345, 2346
Words to Live By, 2412
Youth, 2507
Bibb, Henry
Class, 524
Bierria, Alisa
Human Nature, 1145
Blackmun, Harry
Race Relations, 1680
Blackwell, Unita
Courage, 582
Blake, Bessie
Children, 463
Blake, Eubie
Words to Live By, 2413
Blige, Mary J.
Women, 2347
Blockson, Charles L.
Writing, 2495
Blue, Vida
Sports, 2170

Bluford, Guion S. Jr.
Work, 2469
Blyden, Edward Wilmot
Black Pride, 387
Bond, Julian
Economics, 727
Racism, 1698
Rock 'n' Roll, 1834
Violence, 2315
Bontemps, Arna
Time, 2251
Bowen, J.W.E.
Individuality, 1203
Boyd, Julia
Education, 755
Bradley, Crenner
Achievement, 5
Bradley, David
Being Black in America, 329
Bradley, Mamie
Unity, 2285
Bradley, Thomas
Government, 1035
Braithwaite, William Stanley
Literature, 1357
Brawley, Tawana
Fear, 884
Rape, 1730
Brennan, William J.
Affirmative Action, 49
Brewer, J. Mason
African Continuity, 125
Brinkley, Rhonda
Sex, 1989
Brooks, Gwendolyn
Beauty of Blackness, 311
Words, 2400
Brooks, Roy
Jazz, 1247
Brooks, Walter H.
Morality, 1453
Brown, Claude
America, 146
Community, 545
Brown, H. Rap
Racism, 1699
Violence, 2316
Brown, James
Being Black in America, 330
Black Pride, 388
Politics, 1568
Brown, Jim
Courage, 583
Brown, John
Action, 23
America, 147
Brown, Les
Expectations, 855
Words to Live By, 2414

Brown, Ronald H.
Ideas, 1175
Politics, 1569
Self-Confidence, 1865
Brown, Sterling A.
Men, 1419
Brown, Tony
Business, 436
Hair, 1048
Brown, William Wells
America, 148, 149, 150
Constitution, 569
Names, 1494, 1495
Self-Liberation, 1913
Self-Reliance, 1949
Slavery, 2016
Browne, Robert S.
Black Power, 377
Browne, Sir Thomas
Africa, 74
Broyard, Anatole
Sex, 1990
Bruce, Blanche K.
Black Strength, 403
Self-Liberation, 1914
Bruce, H.C.
Emancipation, 830
Bruce, John E.
Beauty of Blackness, 312
Identity, 1184
Buckley, Gail Lumet
Family, 870
Buick, Eliza
Rape, 1731
Bunche, Ralph
Black Strength, 404
Colonialism, 531
Freedom, 915
Peace, 1547
Race Relations, 1681
Struggle, 2187
Burke, Yvonne Brathwaite
Politics, 1570
Burroughs, Nannie
Achievement, 6
Leadership, 1309
Self-Reliance, 1950
Values, 2301, 2302
Burton, Jenny
Singing, 2004
Caesar, Julius
Africa, 75
Cain, Herman
Success, 2216
Campbell, Mary Schmidt
Art, 245
Campbell, Naomi
Role Models, 1835

Carmichael, Stokely
Africa, 76
Beauty of Blackness, 313
Black Power, 378, 379
Business, 437
Change, 450, 451
Community, 546
Integration, 1214
Politics, 1571
Carnesale, Albert
Affirmative Action, 50
Education, 756
Carney, William H.
Courage, 584
Carr, Johnnie
Civil Rights Movement, 509
Carroll, Diahann
Guilt, 1047
Work, 2470
Carson, Benjamin
Church, 494
Carson, Sonya
Education, 757
Carter, Betty
Jazz, 1248
Carver, George Washington
Achievement, 7
Education, 758
God, 1011
Hate, 1075
Opportunity, 1509
Slavery, 2017
Success, 2217
Catlett, Elizabeth
Art, 246
Community, 547
Creativity, 614
Liberation, 1327
Women, 2348
Chamberlain, Wilt
Sports, 2171
Chapman, Melvin
Words to Live By, 2415
Charles, Ray
America, 151
Courage, 585
Love, 1378
Soul, 2065
Travel, 2256
Charles, RuPaul
Identity, 1185, 1186
Men, 1420
Self-Realization, 1931
Chase, Henry
Living, 1366
Chavis, Benjamin Jr.
Community, 548
Prison, 1624

Cheatham, Michael J.
Faith, 863
Chesnutt, Charles W.
Action, 24
Fate, 880
Hope, 1133
Humanity, 1151
Justice, 1264
Prejudice, 1620
Writing, 2496
Childress, Alice
Education, 759
Racism, 1700, 1701
Reading, 1734
Self-Knowledge, 1887
Writing, 2497
Chipman, Charles P.
Education, 760
Chisholm, Shirley
Democracy, 659
Diversity, 688
Gender, 974, 975
Health, 1083
Integrity, 1225
Leadership, 1310
Politics, 1572, 1573
Service to the Community, 1983
Women, 2349, 2350, 2351
Cinque, Joseph
Courage, 586
Middle Passage, 1434
Clark, Joe
Defeat, 658
Clark, Kenneth B.
America, 152
Colonialism, 532
Destiny, 676
Clark, Ramsey
Women, 2352
Clark, Septima
Chaos, 459
Constitution, 570
Clarke, John Henrik
Africa, 77, 78, 79
Economics, 728
History, 1101, 1102
Integration, 1215
Literature, 1358
Racism, 1702
Revolution, 1814, 1815
Solidarity, 2055, 2056
Spirituality, 2073
Cleaver, Eldridge
America, 153
Hate, 1076
Heroes, 1093
Humanity, 1152
Rape, 1732
Words to Live By, 2416

Cleaver, Kathleen
  Colonialism, 533
  Race, 1661
Clifton, Lucille
  Drugs, 720
  Identity, 1187
  Slavery, 2018
Clinton, Bill
  Race Relations, 1682
  Separation, 1979
Cobb, Price
  Children, 469
Cochran, Johnnie J.
  Prison, 1625
Coffin, Frank M.
  Affirmative Action, 51
Cole, Johnnetta
  Education, 761, 762
  Family, 871
  Freedom, 916
  History, 1103
  Self-Confidence, 1866
  Slavery, 2019
  Women, 2353
Coleman, Bessie
  Courage, 587
Coleman, Ornette
  Spirituality, 2074
Colins, Janet
  Courage, 588
Collins, Marva
  Education, 763, 764
  Living, 1367
Coltrane, John
  Jazz, 1249
Colvin, Claudette
  Leadership, 1311
Comer, James P.
  Being Black in America, 331
Cone, James
  America, 154
  Being Black in America, 332
  Church, 495, 496
  Education, 765
  Endurance, 837
  Freedom, 917, 918
  Genocide, 985
  Justice, 1265
  Oppression, 1521
  Reality, 1746
  Religion, 1773
  Struggle, 2188
Cooke, Sam
  Change, 452
Cooper, Anna Julia
  Women, 2354, 2355
Coppin, Frances
  Failure, 859

Cosby, Bill
  Courage, 589
  Time, 2252
Cosby, Camille
  Economics, 729
  God, 1012
Cotter, Joseph S.
  Race, 1662
Cotton, Dorothy
  Civil Rights Movement, 510
Craft, Ellen
  Slavery, 2020
Crite, Allan Rohan
  Humanity, 1153
Crudup, Arthur
  Poverty, 1600
Crummell, Alexander
  Ancestors, 211
  Black Power, 380
  Democracy, 660
  Goals, 993
  War, 2325
Cruse, Harold
  America, 155
  History, 1104
  Identity, 1188
Cugoano, Ottaban
  Middle Passage, 1435
Cullen, Countee
  Africa, 80
  Poets, 1562
  Religion, 1774
D., Chuck
  Rap, 1725
Daggett, Janet
  Being Black in America, 333
Danky, James P.
  Race Relations, 1683
Danner, Margaret
  Ideas, 1176
Dash, Julie
  Women, 2356
  Youth, 2508
Davis, Angela
  Art, 247
  Capitalism, 444
  Politics, 1574
  Prison, 1626, 1627
  Racism, 1703, 1704
  Relationships, 1767
  Resistance, 1798
  Women, 2357, 2358
Davis, Anthony
  Music, 1467
Davis, Frank Marshall
  Ideas, 1177
Davis, Miles
  Artists, 288
  Creativity, 615

Jazz, 1250
Love, 1379
Music, 1468
Davis, Ossie
Beauty of Blackness, 314
Being Black in America, 334
Community, 549
Death, 640
Leadership, 1312
Davis, Sammy Jr.
Being Black in America, 335
Courage, 590
Silence, 2002
De Priest, Oscar
Sex, 1991
Solidarity, 2057
Debro, Sarah
America, 156
Dee, Ruby
Fear, 885
Self-Realization, 1932
DeFrantz, Anita
Future, 954
Delaney, Beauford
Self-Knowledge, 1888
Delaney, Joseph
Community, 550
Delany, Martin R.
Nationhood, 1501
Self-Reliance, 1951, 1952
Derricotte, Toi
Color, 537
Self-Acceptance, 1849
DeVore, Donald
History, 1105
Dinkins, David
America, 157
Dreams, 701
Freedom, 919
Politics, 1575
Progress, 1636
Donaldson, Greg
Children, 464
Douglas, Aaron
Artists, 289
Vision, 2320
Douglass, Frederick
Achievement, 8
Action, 25
Africa, 81
America, 158, 159, 160
Black Pride, 389
Christianity, 481
Class, 525
Color, 538
Education, 766, 767
Emancipation, 831, 832
Family, 872, 873
Fourth of July, 905

Freedom, 920
Gender, 976
Goals, 994
God, 1013
Government, 1036
Integrity, 1226
Justice, 1266
Liberty, 1334
Misery, 1439
Oppression, 1522
Politics, 1576, 1577
Racism, 1705
Rebellion, 1755, 1756
Resistance, 1799
Self-Affirmation, 1860
Slavery, 2021, 2022, 2023, 2024, 2025
Solidarity, 2058
Struggle, 2189
Unity, 2286, 2287
War, 2326, 2327
Dove, Rita
Books, 421
Dozier, Lamont
Love, 1384
Drake, St. Clair
Black Consciousness, 361
Drew, Charles R.
Struggle, 2190
Du Bois, W.E.B.
Action, 26
Africa, 82, 83
Ambition, 132
America, 161, 162, 163, 164
Art, 248
Beauty of Blackness, 315
Black Culture, 365
Black Power, 381
Black Pride, 390
Brotherhood, 429
Death, 641
Democracy, 661
Education, 768, 769, 770, 771
Emancipation, 833
Equality, 838
Freedom, 921, 922
Gender, 977
God, 1014
Hope, 1134
Humanity, 1154
Humor, 1163
Insight, 1208
Leadership, 1313
Liberation, 1328
Liberty, 1335
Love, 1380
Memory, 1414
Music, 1469
Oppression, 1523
Politics, 1578, 1579

Poverty, 1601
Race, 1663
Race Relations, 1684
Reconstruction, 1762
Resistance, 1800
Responsibility, 1809
Revolution, 1816
Sacrifice, 1840
Self-Knowledge, 1889, 1890
Self-Liberation, 1915
Self-Reliance, 1953, 1954
Talented Tenth, 2240
Truth, 2260
Twoness, 2277
Unity, 2288, 2289
Values, 2303
Women, 2359, 2360
Words to Live By, 2417
Work, 2471
Dunbar, Paul Laurence
Being Black in America, 336
Constitution, 571
Harlem, 1052
Money, 1445
Poets, 1563
Dunham, Katherine
Dance, 627
Purpose, 1651
Durr, Virginia
Change, 453
Civil Rights Movement, 511
Dvorak, Anton
Music, 1470
Dyson, Michael Eric
Authenticity, 308
Beauty of Blackness, 316
Children, 465
Dignity, 678
Faith, 864
Language, 1287
Prison, 1628, 1629
Self-Knowledge, 1891
Women, 2361
Edelin, Kenneth C.
Children, 466
Edelman, Marian Wright
Affirmative Action, 52
Change, 454
Children, 467
Family, 874
Solidarity, 2059
Values, 2304
Edmondson, William
Art, 249
Edwards, Audrey
Education, 772
Elders, Joycelyn
Education, 773
Gays and Lesbians, 965

Ellington, Duke
America, 165
Art, 250, 251
Artists, 290
Creativity, 616
Jazz, 1251, 1252, 1253
Love, 1381, 1382
Music, 1471, 1472, 1473
Opportunity, 1510
Prayer, 1612
Words to Live By, 2418
Work, 2472
Ellison, Ralph
America, 166, 167
Artists, 291
Black Culture, 366
Diversity, 689
Education, 774, 775
Fate, 881
Goals, 995
Growth, 1043
Humor, 1164
Invisibility, 1238
Reality, 1747
Slavery, 2026
Unity, 2290
Words, 2401
Words to Live By, 2419
Writers, 2488
Embry, James C.
Names, 1496
Emerson, Ralph Waldo
Slavery, 2027
Equiano, Olaudah
Black Culture, 367
Middle Passage, 1436
Reading, 1735
Essien-Udom, E.U.
Liberation, 1329
Evans, Mari
Beauty of Blackness, 317
Discipline, 684
Education, 776
Prison, 1630
Evans, Minnie
Artists, 292
Evers, Medgar
Ideas, 1178
Struggle, 2191
Evers-Williams, Myrlie
Language, 1288
Purpose, 1652
Resistance, 1801
Struggle, 2192
Fair, Brian
Affirmative Action, 53
Farajaje-Jones, Elias
Gays and Lesbians, 966

Farmer, James
Black Consciousness, 362
Farrakhan, Louis
America, 168, 169
Ancestors, 212
Atonement, 306
Economics, 730
Exploitation, 858
God, 1015
Growth, 1044
Hate, 1077
Leadership, 1314
Morality, 1454
Religion, 1775, 1776, 1777
Spirituality, 2075
Truth, 2261
Unity, 2291
Words to Live By, 2420
Father Divine
God, 1016, 1017
Peace, 1548
Religion, 1778
Fauset, Jessie
Equality, 839
Humor, 1165
Fischer, Rudolph
Words to Live By, 2421
Fitzgerald, Ella
Words to Live By, 2422
Flack, Roberta
Suffering, 2230
Flake, Floyd
Ghetto, 987
Foote, Julia A.J.
Preaching, 1616
Foreman, George
Dreams, 702
Forman, James
Revolution, 1817
Service to the Community, 1984
Forten, James
Brotherhood, 430
Race, 1664
Slavery, 2028
Fortune, T. Thomas
Africa, 84
America, 170
Courage, 591
Economics, 731
Lynching, 1403
Rights, 1828
Success, 2218
Truth, 2262
Women, 2362
Franklin, Aretha
Adolescence, 44
Christianity, 482
Singing, 2005

Franklin, C.L.
Faith, 865
Self-Knowledge, 1892
Franklin, John Hope
Declaration of Independence, 656
Education, 777
History, 1106, 1107
Racism, 1706
Slavery, 2029
Work, 2473
Frazier, E. Franklin
Class, 526
Education, 778
Justice, 1267
Self-Respect, 1969
Fuller, Solomon B.
Books, 422
Futrell, Mary
Dreams, 703
Education, 779
Gaines, Ernest J.
Writing, 2498
Gandhi, Mohandas K.
Integrity, 1227
Power, 1605
Self-Liberation, 1916
Slavery, 2030
Garnet, Henry Highland
Christianity, 483
Courage, 592
Liberty, 1336
Garvey, Amy Jacques
Freedom, 923
Lynching, 1404
Self-Reliance, 1955
Garvey, Marcus
Achievement, 9
Africa, 85, 86, 87, 88, 89, 90, 91
Ancestors, 213
Beauty of Blackness, 318
Community, 551
Courage, 593
Death, 642
Education, 780, 781
Freedom, 924
Goals, 996
God, 1018
Hate, 1078, 1079
Hell, 1087
Identity, 1189
Injustice, 1206
Inspiration, 1209
Integrity, 1228
Justice, 1268
Leadership, 1315, 1316
Men, 1421, 1422
Opportunity, 1511
Organization, 1532
Power, 1606

Purpose, 1653
Self-Confidence, 1867
Self-Liberation, 1917, 1918
Self-Realization, 1933
Self-Reliance, 1956
Slavery, 2031
Spirituality, 2076
Struggle, 2193
Unity, 2292
Gaston, A.G.
Business, 438
Money, 1446
Values, 2305
Gates, Henry Louis Jr.
Action, 27
Affirmative Action, 54
African American studies, 120, 121, 122
Art, 252
Black Culture, 368, 369
Black Experience, 376
Blackness, 409
Class, 527
Constitution, 572
Creativity, 617
Diversity, 690, 691, 692, 693
Ethnicity, 848
Harlem, 1053
Humanism, 1148
Identity, 1190, 1191, 1192
Integration, 1216
Language, 1289, 1290
Literature, 1359
Men, 1423
Racism, 1707
Rap, 1726
Reality, 1748
Self-Affirmation, 1861
Separation, 1980
Women, 2363
Writing, 2499
Gaye, Marvin
Art, 253
Artists, 293
Death, 643
Fear, 886
Peace, 1549
Self-Knowledge, 1893
Sex, 1992
Singing, 2006
Gayle, Addison Jr.
Black Consciousness, 363
Sanity, 1842
Gibson, Althea
Achievement, 10
Courage, 594
Sports, 2172
Winning, 2336
Gibson, Bob
Role Models, 1836

Giddings, Paula
Children, 468
Goals, 997
Gillespie, Dizzy
Freedom, 925
Music, 1474
Self-Acceptance, 1850
Gillespie, Marcia Ann
Self-Hate, 1875
Giovanni, Nikki
Death, 644
Democracy, 662
Identity, 1193, 1194
Life, 1345
Love, 1383
Mistakes, 1441
Revolution, 1818
Self-Respect, 1970
Truth, 2263
Golden, Marita
Creativity, 618
Hair, 1049
Gomes, Peter J.
Achievement, 11
Adversity, 47
Ambition, 133
Gays and Lesbians, 967
God, 1019, 1020
Identity, 1195
Life, 1346
Words to Live By, 2423, 2424
Gooding, Cuba Jr.
War, 2328
Goodman, James
Liberation, 1330
Goodman, Paul
Civil Rights Movement, 512
Gordy, Berry Jr.
Motown Sound, 1460
Gossett, Louis Jr.
Death, 645
Grace, Sweet Daddy
Religion, 1779, 1780, 1781
Graves, Earl G. Jr.
Failure, 860
Gray, Kimi
Dreams, 704
Gray, William H. III
Knowledge, 1276
Reality, 1749
Gregory, Dick
America, 171, 172
Blackness, 410
Civil Rights Movement, 513
Constitution, 573
Freedom, 926
Hate, 1080
History, 1108
Justice, 1269

Oppression, 1524
Self-Knowledge, 1894
Slavery, 2032
Grier, William
Children, 469
Self-Knowledge, 1895
Griffin, Judith
Education, 782
Griggs, Sutton E.
Reading, 1736
Slavery, 2033
Grimke, Charlotte Forten
War, 2329
Grimke, Francis J.
Slavery, 2034
War, 2330
Guinier, Lani
Affirmative Action, 55
Courage, 595
Democracy, 663
Leadership, 1317
Haley, Alex
Beauty of Blackness, 319
Education, 783
Family, 875
History, 1109
Words to Live By, 2425
Hall, Arsenio
Answers, 229
Hall, Prathia
Leadership, 1318
Hall, Prince
Color, 539
Education, 784
Unity, 2293
Hamer, Fannie Lou
America, 173
Being Black in America, 337
Law, 1302
Politics, 1580
Resistance, 1802
Self-Liberation, 1919
Sex, 1993
Women, 2364
Hampton, Fred
Revolution, 1819
Hampton, Lionel
Art, 254
Black Culture, 370
Music, 1475
Hancock, Gordon Blaine
Church, 497
Economics, 732, 733
Education, 785
Progress, 1637
Strategy, 2179
Handy, W.C.
Blues, 414, 415, 416

Hansberry, Lorraine
Africa, 92
Anger, 228
Art, 255
Creativity, 619
Intelligence, 1235
Revolution, 1820
Self-Knowledge, 1896
Sex, 1994
Struggle, 2194
Thinking, 2247
Women, 2365
Harding, Vincent
Constitution, 574
Hare, Nathan
Leadership, 1319
Harlan, John Marshall
Constitution, 575
Harper, Frances Ellen Watkins
Black Pride, 391
Economics, 734
Freedom, 927
Government, 1037, 1038
Race Consciousness, 1673
Racism, 1708
Retribution, 1812
Women, 2366
Harris, Patricia Roberts
Peace, 1550
Harrison, Richard B.
God, 1021
Hastie, William H.
Ancestors, 214
Evil, 850
Family, 876
Hawthorne, Nathaniel
Race Relations, 1685
Hayden, Palmer
Art, 256
Haynes, Lemuel
Faith, 866
Integrity, 1229
Religion, 1782
Self-Knowledge, 1897
Selfishness, 1977
Heber, Reginald
Africa, 93
Height, Dorothy
Goals, 998
Henderson, Stephen
Life, 1347
Henson, Matthew
Ideas, 1179
Hibbler, William
Children, 470
Higginbotham, Evelyn Brooks
Gender, 978, 979
Language, 1291
Women, 2367

Higginson, Thomas Wentworth
Religion, 1783
Hill, Anita
Gender, 980
Honesty, 1129
Men, 1424
Power, 1607
Reality, 1750
Truth, 2264
Himes, Chester
Prejudice, 1621
Purpose, 1654
Self-Knowledge, 1898
Hines, Gregory
Work, 2474
Hogan, Bessie
Education, 786
Self-Realization, 1934
Holiday, Billie
Children, 471
Drugs, 721
Fighting, 893
Marriage, 1412
Poverty, 1602
Holland, Brian
Love, 1384
Holland, Eddie
Love, 1384
Holmes, Larry
Sports, 2173
Holt, Thomas
Slavery, 2035
Holyfield, Evander
Courage, 596
Fear, 887
Hood, James Walker
Opportunity, 1512
Hooks, Bell
Language, 1292
Stress, 2182
Unity, 2294
Hooks, Benjamin
Business, 439
NAACP, 1492
Victory, 2312
Hope, John
Equality, 840
Horne, Lena
Hope, 1135
Self-Realization, 1935
Stress, 2183
Women, 2368
Horton, George M.
Slavery, 2036
Houston, Charles Hamilton
Black Strength, 405
Self-Reliance, 1957
Stress, 2184

Houston, Whitney
Singing, 2007
Huggins, Nathan
Harlem Renaissance, 1065
Slavery, 2037
Hughes, Dorothy Pitman
Business, 440
Hughes, Langston
America, 174
Art, 257
Beauty of Blackness, 320, 321
Books, 423
Economics, 735
Education, 787
Harlem, 1054, 1055, 1056
Harlem Renaissance, 1066
Humor, 1166
Jazz, 1254, 1255
Life, 1348
Self-Acceptance, 1851
Self-Expression, 1872
Soul, 2066
Writers, 2489, 2490
Hunter, Clementine
Art, 258
Hunter, Tera W.
Dance, 628
Hurston, Zora Neale
Color, 540, 541
Community, 552
Dreams, 705, 706
Education, 788
Fighting, 894
Folklore, 904
Freedom, 928
Future, 955
Hope, 1136
Ideals, 1171
Inspiration, 1210
Language, 1293
Memory, 1415
Segregation, 1844
Self-Knowledge, 1899
Self-Realization, 1936
Self-Respect, 1971
Thinking, 2248
Time, 2253
Truth, 2265
Vision, 2321
Women, 2369
Words to Live By, 2426, 2427
Work, 2475
Ice Cube
Rap, 1727
Jackson, George
Prison, 1631
Jackson, Jesse
Achievement, 12
America, 175, 176

Christianity, 484
Courage, 597
Diversity, 694
Dreams, 707
Hope, 1137, 1138
Integration, 1217
Justice, 1270
Morality, 1455
Politics, 1581, 1582
Poverty, 1603
Race, 1665
Role Models, 1837
Self-Acceptance, 1852
Success, 2219
Truth, 2266
Victory, 2313
Winning, 2337
Words to Live By, 2428, 2429
Youth, 2509
Jackson, Mahalia
Independence, 1201
Racism, 1709
Retribution, 1813
Jackson, Michael
Music, 1476
Jackson, Reggie
Sports, 2174
Jacob, John E.
Black Strength, 406
Jacobs, Harriet
America, 177
Gender, 981
Slavery, 2038
Women, 2370
Jacobs, John
Resistance, 1803
Jakes, T.D.
God, 1022
Names, 1497
Religion, 1784
Success, 2220, 2221
James, Chappie
Patriotism, 1542
Jamison, Judith
Dance, 629, 630
Self-Realization, 1937
Jeffries, Leonard
Words to Live By, 2430
Jemison, Mae
Gender, 982
Opportunity, 1513
Style, 2214
Jemison, T.J.
Hope, 1139
Joans, Ted
Creativity, 620
Johns, Vernon
God, 1023

Johnson, Charles
Writing, 2500
Johnson, Fenton
Black Pride, 392
Johnson, Georgia Douglas
Women, 2371
Words to Live By, 2431
Johnson, J. Rosamond
Singing, 2008
Johnson, Jack
Being Black in America, 338
Self-Confidence, 1868
Johnson, James Weldon
America, 178
Art, 259
Dance, 631
Future, 956
Harlem, 1057
Paris, 1540
Poets, 1564
Racism, 1710
Ragtime, 1723
Revolution, 1821
Self-Realization, 1938
Sex, 1995
Singing, 2008
Spirituality, 2077
Words to Live By, 2432
Youth, 2510
Johnson, John H.
Black Culture, 371
Business, 441
Success, 2222
Vision, 2322
Johnson, Lyndon B.
Civil Rights Movement, 514
Johnson, Magic
Sex, 1996
Johnson, Robert E.
Words to Live By, 2433
Johnson, Sargent
Art, 260
Johnson, William H.
Artists, 294
Black Pride, 393
Jones, Bessie
Ancestors, 215
Jones, Bill T.
Words to Live By, 2434
Jones, Joshua Henry
Responsibility, 1810
Jones, Lois Mailou
Art, 261
Artists, 295
Jones, Nettie
Self-Hate, 1876
Jones, Quincy
Drugs, 722
Service to the Community, 1985

Words to Live By, 2435
Joplin, Scott
Music, 1477
Jordan, Barbara
Achievement, 13
Action, 28
America, 179
Black Power, 382
Community, 553
Constitution, 576
Education, 789
Race Consciousness, 1674
Jordan, June
America, 180
Ancestors, 216
Faith, 867
Language, 1294
Love, 1385
Jordan, Michael
Courage, 598, 599
Expectations, 856
Joyner, Florence Griffith
Action, 29
Words to Live By, 2436
Joyner-Kersee, Jackie
Courage, 600
Goals, 999
Just, E.E.
Life, 1349
Karenga, Ron
Art, 262
Artists, 296
Civil Rights Movement, 515
Reality, 1751
Kennedy, Florynce
Men, 1425
Protest, 1646
Kennedy, Randall
Black Pride, 394
Race, 1666
Killens, John O.
America, 181
Black Pride, 395
Change, 455
Desegregation, 674
Harlem, 1058
History, 1110, 1111
Hope, 1140
Integration, 1218
Struggle, 2195
Truth, 2267
Kincaid, Jamaica
Peace, 1551
King, B.B.
Blues, 417
Creativity, 621
Education, 790
History, 1112
Language, 1295

King, Bernice
Church, 498
King, Coretta Scott
America, 182
Change, 456
Humanity, 1155
Politics, 1583
Segregation, 1845
Spirituality, 2078
Unity, 2295
King, Martin Luther Jr.
Action, 30, 31, 32
America, 183, 184, 185
Being Black in America, 339
Black Pride, 396
Black Strength, 407
Brotherhood, 431
Capitalism, 445, 446
Church, 499, 500
Civil Rights Movement, 516
Class, 528, 529
Community, 554
Courage, 601, 602, 603
Death, 646
Democracy, 664
Direction, 682
Dissent, 686, 687
Diversity, 695
Dreams, 708
Education, 791, 792
Freedom, 929, 930, 931, 932
Ghetto, 988
God, 1024
Heroes, 1094
Injustice, 1207
Law, 1303, 1304, 1305
Leadership, 1320, 1321
Love, 1386, 1387
Morality, 1456, 1457
Nonviolence, 1506, 1507
Peace, 1552
Politics, 1584
Power, 1608
Progress, 1638
Racism, 1711
Resistance, 1804
Rights, 1829
Self-Knowledge, 1900
Service to the Community, 1986
Suffering, 2231
Time, 2254
Vision, 2323
War, 2331
Words to Live By, 2437
Work, 2476
King, Melvin H.
Politics, 1585

King, Rodney
Race Relations, 1686
King, Yolanda
Living, 1368
Knight, Etheridge
Love, 1388
LaBelle, Patti
Self-Affirmation, 1862
Ladd, Florence
Women, 2372
Langston, John Mercer
Nationhood, 1502
Lawrence, Charles
Racism, 1712
Lawrence, Jacob
Art, 263
Artists, 297
Community, 555, 556
Creativity, 622
Heritage, 1089
Race Consciousness, 1675
Lawrence-Lightfoot, Sara
Education, 793
Ledbetter, Huddie
Music, 1478
Lee, Benjamin
Education, 794
Lee, Jarena
Preaching, 1617
Women, 2373
Lee, Spike
Dance, 632
Self-Reliance, 1958
Words to Live By, 2438, 2439
Lee-Smith, Hughie
Alienation, 130
Art, 264, 265
Artists, 298
Leonard, Buck
Sports, 2175
Leonard, Sugar Ray
Courage, 604
Lessing, Doris
Humanity, 1156
Lewis, Carl
Self-Confidence, 1869
Lewis, Elma
Self-Realization, 1939
Lewis, William Henry
Ideas, 1180
Lincoln, Abby
Artists, 299
Little Richard
Gays and Lesbians, 968
Locke, Alain
Africa, 94, 95, 96
African Continuity, 126
America, 186, 187
Art, 266

Beauty of Blackness, 322
Black Culture, 372
Creativity, 623
Dance, 633
Democracy, 665, 666
Future, 957
Harlem, 1059, 1060, 1061
Harlem Renaissance, 1067, 1068, 1069
Self-Realization, 1940
Spirituality, 2079
Long, Thomas
War, 2332
Lorde, Audre
Fear, 888
Gays and Lesbians, 969
Oppression, 1525
Poetry, 1557, 1558
Self-Affirmation, 1863
Louis, Joe
Achievement, 14
Goals, 1000
Mistakes, 1442
Money, 1447, 1448
Words to Live By, 2440
Love, Nat "Deadwood Dick, the cowboy adventurer"
Daring, 639
Death, 647
Education, 795
Freedom, 933
Men, 1426
Reading, 1737
Lowery, Joseph
Affirmative Action, 56
Being Black in America, 340
Death, 648
Drugs, 723
Preaching, 1618
Self-Hate, 1877
Struggle, 2196
Words to Live By, 2441
Luis, W.A.
Progress, 1639
Mabley, Moms
Love, 1389
Men, 1427, 1428
Progress, 1640
Macmillan, Harold
Africa, 97
Madhubuti, Haki
Self-Reliance, 1959
Words, 2402
Madison, Joe
Trouble, 2257
Makeba, Miriam
Education, 796, 797
Malvreaux, Julianne
Economics, 736

Manley, Michael
  Music, 1479
Marable, Manning
  Women, 2374
Markham, Pigmeat
  Humor, 1167
Marley, Bob
  Love, 1390
  Unity, 2296
Marrant, John
  Christianity, 485
  Misery, 1440
Mars, James N.
  Slavery, 2039
Marsalis, Wynton
  Art, 267
  Jazz, 1256
Marshall, Paule
  Art, 268
Marshall, Thurgood
  Affirmative Action, 57
  Constitution, 577, 578, 579
  Democracy, 667
  Equality, 841
  History, 1113
  Liberty, 1337
  Separation, 1981
  Sex, 1997
  Truth, 2268
Mason, Charles H.
  Religion, 1785
Matthews, Victoria Earle
  Literature, 1360
Mayfield, Curtis
  Education, 798
Mays, Benjamin
  Achievement, 15
  Ancestors, 217
  Dreams, 709
  Education, 799
  Encouragement, 836
  Goals, 1001
  Living, 1369
  Mind, 1437
  Service to the Community, 1987
  Words to Live By, 2442
McCall, Nathan
  Education, 800
McCarthy, Osceola
  Business, 442
  Work, 2477
McDaniel, Hattie
  Survival, 2236
McDowell, Deborah E.
  Women, 2375
McGriff, Deborah
  Failure, 861

McGuire, George Alexander
  Christianity, 486
  God, 1025
McHenry, Elizabeth
  Identity, 1196
  Self-Confidence, 1870
McKay, Claude
  Color, 542
  Dignity, 679
  Economics, 737
  Harlem, 1062
  Humor, 1168
  Individuality, 1204
  Progress, 1641
  Resistance, 1805
  Self-Knowledge, 1901
McMillan, Roslyn
  Self-Knowledge, 1902
Mfume, Kweisi
  Education, 801
  Struggle, 2197
Michaux, Solomon Lightfoot
  Religion, 1786
Miller, Kelly
  History, 1114
  Law, 1306
  Race Relations, 1687
  Revolution, 1822, 1823
  Self-Respect, 1972
Miller, Thomas E.
  America, 188
  Democracy, 668
Mitchell, Arthur
  Courage, 605
Monk, Thelonious
  Music, 1480, 1481
Monroe, Irene
  Church, 501
Moore, Melba
  Humanity, 1157
Morley, Jefferson
  Integration, 1219
Morrison, Toni
  Africa, 98
  Ancestors, 218
  Art, 269
  Education, 802
  Evil, 851, 852
  Harlem, 1063
  Language, 1296
  Liberation, 1331
  Love, 1391, 1392
  Oppression, 1526
  Racism, 1713
  Self-Liberation, 1920
  Women, 2376
  Words, 2403
  Writing, 2501, 2502, 2503

Moseley-Braun, Carol
  Change, 457
  Confederate Flag, 567
Moses, Bob
  Leadership, 1322
  Racism, 1714
Moses, Michael
  Children, 472
Mosley, Walter
  Blues, 418
  Colonialism, 534
Moss, Otis
  Christianity, 487
  Freedom, 934
Motley, Archibald Jr.
  Courage, 606
Motley, Constance Baker
  Politics, 1586
Moutoussamy-Ashe, Jeanne
  Adversity, 48
Muhammad, Elijah
  Education, 803, 804
  Independence, 1202
  Integration, 1220
  Self-Hate, 1878
  Self-Knowledge, 1903
  Self-Realization, 1941
  Self-Reliance, 1960
Muhammad, Herbert
  Evil, 853
Munroe, Roberta M.
  Gays and Lesbians, 970
Murphy, Isaac
  Honesty, 1130
  Words to Live By, 2443
Murray, Albert
  Jazz, 1257, 1258
Murray, Pauli
  Economics, 738
  Hope, 1141
  Self-Hate, 1879
Naylor, Gloria
  Life, 1350
  Men, 1429
  Words to Live By, 2444
  Writing, 2504
Neal, Larry
  Being Black in America, 341
  Church, 502
Nell, William C.
  Slavery, 2040
Nelson, Jill
  Diversity, 696
  Knowledge, 1277
Newman, Richard
  Africa, 99
Newton, Huey
  Black Power, 383
  Community, 557

Nixon, E.D.
  Civil Rights Movement, 517
  Segregation, 1846
Norris, Clarence
  Words to Live By, 2445
Northup, Solomon
  Black Culture, 373
  Slavery, 2041
Norton, Eleanor Holmes
  Being Black in America, 342
  Rights, 1830
  Struggle, 2198
  Women, 2377
  Writing, 2505
Nugent, Bruce
  Gays and Lesbians, 971
Nunez, Elizabeth
  Language, 1297
O'Neal, Shaquille
  Role Models, 1838
Owens, Jesse
  Being Black in America, 343
  Children, 473
  Life, 1351
  Opportunity, 1514
  Oppression, 1527
  Struggle, 2199
  Words to Live By, 2446
Paderewski, Ignacy
  Jazz, 1259
Paige, Satchel
  Age, 129
  Prayer, 1613
  Words to Live By, 2447, 2448, 2449,
    2450
Palmer, Aynim
  Education, 805
Parker, Charlie
  Art, 270
  Creativity, 624
  Music, 1482
  Religion, 1787
Parker-Smith, Bettye J.
  Love, 1393
Parks, Gordon
  Being Black in America, 344
  Self-Reliance, 1961
  Soul, 2067
  Success, 2223
Parks, Henry
  Dreams, 710
Parks, Rosa
  Action, 33
  Ancestors, 219
  Courage, 607, 608
  Freedom, 935, 936
  History, 1115
  Jazz, 1260
  Purpose, 1655

Parsons, Lucy
Revolution, 1824
Paul, Nathaniel
Being Black in America, 345
Payton, Benjamin
Education, 806
Pennington, James W.C.
America, 189
Education, 807
Perry, Richard
Self-Knowledge, 1904
Petry, Ann
Writers, 2491, 2492
Pickens, William
Democracy, 669
Rights, 1831
Self-Liberation, 1921
Sex, 1998
Success, 2224
Pinchback, Pinckney B.S.
Politics, 1587
Protest, 1647
Pinkney, Andrea D.
Success, 2225
Pippin, Horace
Art, 271, 272
Plato, Ann
Love, 1394
Pliny the Elder
Africa, 100
Polite, Craig K.
Education, 772
Polly
God, 1026
Porter, Dorothy
History, 1116
Poussaint, Alvin
Community, 558
Education, 808
Unity, 2297
Values, 2306
Powell, Adam Clayton Jr.
Community, 559
Courage, 609, 610
Economics, 739
Future, 958
Heaven, 1085
Ideas, 1181
Law, 1307
Religion, 1788
Self-Realization, 1942
Struggle, 2200
Powell, Colin
Affirmative Action, 58, 59
Future, 959, 960
Role Models, 1839
Success, 2226
Values, 2307

Pratt, Geronimo
Revolution, 1825
Preston, Douglas
Race, 1667
Price, Hugh
Children, 474
Poverty, 1604
Price, Leontyne
Black Pride, 397
Self-Respect, 1973
Tokenism, 2255
Words to Live By, 2451
Priestly, J.B.
Ragtime, 1724
Primus, Pearl
Dance, 634, 635
Prince
Words to Live By, 2452
Prochnow, Jurgen
Being Black in America, 346
Proctor, Samuel D.
Civil Rights Movement, 518
Prophet, Nancy Elizabeth
Artists, 300
Prosser, Gabriel
Rebellion, 1757
Pryor, Richard
Art, 273
Purvis, Robert
America, 190
Qualls, Schyleen
Poetry, 1559
Queen Mother Moore
Integrity, 1230
Race Consciousness, 1676
Reparations, 1794
Struggle, 2201
Ra, Sun
Heaven, 1086
Rains, Claude
Justice, 1271
Randolph, A. Philip
Action, 34
Equality, 842, 843
Freedom, 937
Labor, 1280, 1281
Organization, 1533, 1534
Politics, 1588
Revolution, 1826
Self-Liberation, 1922, 1923
Struggle, 2202, 2203
Ransom, Reverdy C.
God, 1027
Rawls, Lou
Music, 1483
Reagon, Bernice Johnson
Civil Rights Movement, 519
Singing, 2009
Trouble, 2258

Reed, Adolph
  Racism, 1715
Reed, Ishmael
  Artists, 301
  Being Black in America, 347
  Education, 809
  Reading, 1738
Reeves, Keith W.
  Affirmative Action, 60
Reeves, Ruby Lee
  Singing, 2010
Remond, Charles Lenox
  Radicalism, 1722
Reverend Ike
  Money, 1449, 1450
Reynolds, Mary
  Slavery, 2042
Rhodes, John
  Art, 274
Ridley, Elizabeth
  Being Black in America, 348
Riggs, Marlon
  Self-Knowledge, 1905
  Silence, 2003
Riley, Dorothy
  Drugs, 724
Rivers, Eugene
  Church, 503, 504
  Hope, 1142
Roach, Max
  Jazz, 1261
Robeson, Paul
  Africa, 101, 102, 103, 104, 105, 106
  America, 191
  Ancestors, 220, 221
  Artists, 302
  Capitalism, 447
  Community, 560
  Dance, 636
  Family, 877
  Freedom, 938, 939
  Future, 961, 962
  Giving, 990
  History, 1117
  Identity, 1197
  Music, 1484, 1485
  Oppression, 1528
  Racism, 1716
  Self-Acceptance, 1853
  Spirit, 2069
  Struggle, 2204, 2205
  Youth, 2511
Robinson, Bojangles
  Success, 2227
Robinson, Jackie
  Achievement, 16
  Fear, 889
  Respect, 1808
  Sports, 2176

Robinson, James H.
  Africa, 107
Robinson, Max
  Self-Acceptance, 1854
Robinson, Randall
  Africa, 108
  Politics, 1589
Robinson, Sugar Ray
  Sports, 2177
Rock, John S.
  Sex, 1999
Rodney, Muhammad
  Islam, 1240
Rogers, J.A.
  Music, 1486
  Women, 2378
Rollins, Sonny
  Black Culture, 374
Roman, Charles V.
  Democracy, 670
  Prejudice, 1622
Ross, Diana
  Dreams, 711
  Future, 963
Rudenstein, Neil L.
  Affirmative Action, 61
Rudolph, Wilma
  Discipline, 685
  Goals, 1002
  Self-Acceptance, 1855
  Words to Live By, 2453
Ruggles, David
  Prejudice, 1623
  Reform, 1764
Russell, Bill
  Love, 1395
  Self-Knowledge, 1906
Russwurm, John B.
  Being Black in America, 349
  Self-Reliance, 1962
Rustin, Bayard
  Equality, 844, 845
  Fear, 890
  Power, 1609
Sahibs, Abdulalim
  Education, 810
Sanchez, Sonia
  Adolescence, 45
  Art, 275
  Living, 1370
Savage, Augusta
  Being Black in America, 350
  Children, 475
Schomburg, Arthur
  Black Pride, 398
  Books, 424
  History, 1118, 1119, 1120, 1121
  Oral Tradition, 1531

Politics, 1590
Self-Respect, 1974
Schuyler, George
Harlem, 1064
Race Relations, 1688
Scott, Hazel
Art, 276
Freedom, 940
Women, 2379
Shabazz, Betty
Life, 1352
Love, 1396
Music, 1487
Peace, 1553
Self-Liberation, 1924
Words to Live By, 2454
Shakespeare, William
Africa, 109
Shakur, Assata
Politics, 1591
Prison, 1632
Shakur, Tupac
Integrity, 1231
Rap, 1728
Shange, Ntozake
America, 192
Women, 2380
Sharpton, Al
Action, 35
Diversity, 697
Government, 1039
Justice, 1272, 1273
Politics, 1592
Shaw, Nate
History, 1122
Sherman, William T.
Reparations, 1795
Shipler, David K.
Race, 1668
Shuttlesworth, Fred
Civil Rights Movement, 520
Simmons, Della
Work, 2478
Simmons, Judy
Race Relations, 1689
Simone, Nina
Jazz, 1262
Simone, Timothy M.
Black Culture, 375
Youth, 2512
Sister Souljah
Color, 543
Smith, Anna Deavere
Literature, 1361
Race Relations, 1690
Theater, 2243
Smith, Barbara
Gender, 983

Racism, 1717
Writing, 2506
Smith, Rose
Reading, 1739
Smith, Venture
Africa, 110
America, 193
Smith, Willi
Work, 2479
Smitherman, Geneva
Language, 1298, 1299
Snipes, Wesley
Relationships, 1768
Solomon, Charlene
Education, 811
Self-Realization, 1943
Sowell, Thomas
Adolescence, 46
Spencer, Anne
Women, 2381
Steele, Shelby
Opportunity, 1515
Stevens, Thaddeus
Politics, 1593
Steward, Rebecca
Ideals, 1172
Stewart, Maria W.
Action, 36
Africa, 111, 112
America, 194
Death, 649
Economics, 740
Self-Acceptance, 1856
Struggle, 2206
Women, 2382, 2383
Strawberry, Darryl
Sports, 2178
Strickland, William
Men, 1430
Politics, 1594
Sullivan, Leon
Integration, 1221
Reading, 1740
Work, 2480
Sundiata, Ibrahim K.
America, 195
History, 1123
Reparations, 1796
Slavery, 2043
Sutton, Percy
Creativity, 625
Dreams, 712
Tanner, Henry O.
Black Pride, 399
Taylor, Billy
Jazz, 1263
Taylor, Gardner C.
Christianity, 488

Taylor, Susan
Beauty of Blackness, 323
Dreams, 713
Leadership, 1323
Self-Hate, 1880
Spirit, 2070
Taylor, Susie King
Equality, 846
Teish, Luisah
Ancestors, 222
Terrell, Mary Church
Africa, 113
Morality, 1458
Solidarity, 2060
Women, 2384
Thomas, Clarence
Affirmative Action, 62
Lynching, 1405
Thurman, Howard
Children, 476
Dreams, 714, 715, 716
Family, 878, 879
Fear, 891
Growth, 1045
Hate, 1081
Life, 1353
Tillman, Dorothy
Politics, 1595
Tillman, Jane Irving
Books, 425
Toomer, Jean
Achievement, 17
Artists, 303
Education, 812
Fear, 892
Knowledge, 1278
Life, 1354
Limitations, 1356
Literature, 1362
Love, 1397
Race, 1669
Reform, 1765
Suffering, 2232
Words to Live By, 2455
Tourgee, Albion W.
Language, 1300
Trotter, William Monroe
Action, 37
Truth, Sojourner
Action, 38
Black Pride, 400
Courage, 611
Death, 650
God, 1028
Mind, 1438
Nationhood, 1503, 1504
Reading, 1741
Religion, 1789
Slavery, 2044

Solidarity, 2061
Survival, 2237
Truth, 2269
Women, 2385, 2386, 2387, 2388, 2389, 2390
Tubman, Harriet
Death, 651
Destiny, 677
Freedom, 941, 942
Liberty, 1338
Rights, 1832
Self-Knowledge, 1907
Slavery, 2045, 2046
Underground Railroad, 2279
War, 2333
Underground Railroad, 2278
Turnage, Jackie
Heritage, 1090
Turner, Darwin T.
Literature, 1363
Turner, Henry McNeal
Africa, 114
Emigration, 835
Fourth of July, 906
God, 1029, 1030
Humanity, 1158
Lynching, 1406, 1407
Patriotism, 1543, 1544
Rights, 1833
Turner, Lana
Books, 426
Turner, Nat
Rebellion, 1758, 1759
Slavery, 2047
Turner, Tina
Freedom, 943
Words to Live By, 2456, 2457
Tyson, Cecily
Women, 2391
Van Der Zee, James
Art, 277
Happiness, 1051
Vaughan, Sarah
Music, 1488
Singing, 2011
Words to Live By, 2458
Vernon, William T.
Books, 427
Vest, Hilda
Language, 1301
Vivian, C.T.
Being Black in America, 351
Wade-Gayles, Gloria
Community, 561
Walker, Aida Overton
Self-Respect, 1975
Theater, 2244
Walker, Alice
America, 196

Artists, 304
Creativity, 626
Freedom, 944
Friends, 952
God, 1031
Living, 1371
Men, 1431
Poetry, 1560
Self-Knowledge, 1908, 1909
Self-Liberation, 1925, 1926
Self-Realization, 1944
Self-Reliance, 1963
Struggle, 2207
Women, 2392
Writers, 2493
Walker, Charles T.
Men, 1432
Walker, David
America, 197, 198, 199
Beauty of Blackness, 324
Education, 813
Freedom, 945
Liberation, 1332
Men, 1433
Resistance, 1806
Sacrifice, 1841
Walker, Margaret
Love, 1398
Poetry, 1561
Walker, Mme. C.J.
Business, 443
Direction, 683
Opportunity, 1516
Words to Live By, 2459
Walker, Wyatt T.
Hope, 1143
Wallace, Michelle
Goals, 1003
Waller, Fats
Reality, 1752
Walters, Alexander
Words to Live By, 2460
Ward, Samuel Ringgold
Slavery, 2048
Warfield, William
Courage, 612
Washington, Augustus
America, 200
Washington, Booker T.
America, 201
Ancestors, 223
Black Strength, 408
Children, 477
Economics, 741, 742, 743
Education, 814, 815, 816, 817, 818, 819,
    820, 821, 822, 823
Emancipation, 834

Equality, 847
Freedom, 946
Health, 1084
Humanity, 1159
Integrity, 1232
Knowledge, 1279
Love, 1399
Morality, 1459
Opportunity, 1517
Oppression, 1529
Progress, 1642, 1643, 1644
Race, 1670
Religion, 1790
Self-Knowledge, 1910
Self-Reliance, 1964, 1965
Separation, 1982
Slavery, 2049, 2050, 2051, 2052, 2053
Unity, 2298
Values, 2308, 2309, 2310
Words to Live By, 2461, 2462, 2463
Work, 2481, 2482, 2483
Washington, Harold
Courage, 613
Struggle, 2208
Washington, James M.
Alienation, 131
Books, 428
Children, 478
Church, 505
Prayer, 1614, 1615
Racism, 1718
Religion, 1791, 1792
Waters, Ethel
Dignity, 680
Singing, 2012
Survival, 2238
Waters, Maxine
Rebellion, 1760
Women, 2393
Watkins, Frank
Affirmative Action, 63
Wattleton, Faye
Community, 562
Sex, 2000
Watts, Herman
God, 1032
Weaver, Robert C.
Government, 1040
Words to Live By, 2464
Weems, Renita
God, 1033
Love, 1400
Wells, Ida B.
America, 202
Education, 824
Law, 1308
Lynching, 1408, 1409, 1410

Rape, 1733
Reconstruction, 1763
Resistance, 1807
Self-Reliance, 1966
Sex, 2001
Truth, 2270
Welsing, Frances Cress
Children, 479
West, Cornel
Action, 39
Africa, 115
Afrocentrism, 128
Ancestors, 224
Art, 278
Being Black in America, 352, 353, 354
Blackness, 411
Blues, 419
Christianity, 489
Class, 530
Community, 563
Conservatives, 568
Democracy, 671, 672, 673
Despair, 675
Evil, 854
Goals, 1004
Government, 1041
Hope, 1144
Humanity, 1160
Ideals, 1173
Individuality, 1205
Intelligence, 1236
Leadership, 1324, 1325, 1326
Music, 1489
Names, 1498
Politics, 1596
Public Life, 1648
Race, 1671
Rap, 1729
Rebellion, 1761
Self-Acceptance, 1857
Self-Hate, 1881
Self-Knowledge, 1911
Self-Respect, 1976
Survival, 2239
Truth, 2271, 2272
Wisdom, 2338, 2339
Words to Live By, 2465
Weston, Randy
Music, 1490
Wheatley, Phillis
Death, 652
Freedom, 947
Heritage, 1091
Inspiration, 1211
Whipper, William S.
Integration, 1222
Power, 1610

Punishment, 1649
White, Charles
Art, 279
White, J.
Slavery, 2054
White, Walter
Economics, 744
Freedom, 948
Struggle, 2209
Wideman, John Edgar
Being Black in America, 355, 356
Ghetto, 989
Wiley, Ralph
Truth, 2273
Wilkerson, Dianne
Ideals, 1174
Wilkins, Roy
African American Studies, 123
History, 1124
Intelligence, 1237
Williams, Bert
Being Black in America, 357
Theater, 2245, 2246
Williams, Eddie N.
Economics, 745
Williams, John A.
Africa, 116
Williams, Patricia
Affirmative Action, 64
Williams, Robert
Civil Rights Movement, 521
Goals, 1005
Williams, Sherley Anne
Dreams, 717
Women, 2394
Williams, Tevis
Dance, 637
Wills, Frank
Government, 1042
Wilmore, Gayraud
Liberation, 1333
Wilson, August
Action, 40
Africa, 117
Community, 564
Freedom, 949
Wilson, Flip
Integrity, 1233
Reality, 1753
Wilson, Joseph
Racism, 1719
Wilson, Mary
Music, 1491
Wilson, William Julius
Race Relations, 1691
Work, 2484

Winfrey, Oprah
Ancestors, 225
Community, 565
Dreams, 718
Failure, 862
Freedom, 950
Friends, 953
Future, 964
Gender, 984
God, 1034
Marriage, 1413
Spirit, 2071
Women, 2395
Words to Live By, 2466
Wolfe, George C.
Style, 2215
Words, 2404
Wonder, Stevie
Achievement, 18
Self-Reliance, 1967
Woodard, Lynette
Self-Realization, 1945
Woodbey, George W.
Capitalism, 448
Woodruff, Hale
Goals, 1006
Woodson, Carter G.
Action, 41
Africa, 118
Ancestors, 226
Art, 280
Black Consciousness, 364
Black Pride, 401
Economics, 746
Education, 825, 826, 827, 828
Freedom, 951
History, 1125, 1126
Oppression, 1530
Peace, 1554
Politics, 1597
Selfishness, 1978
Service to the Community, 1988
Solidarity, 2062
Truth, 2274, 2275
Wright, Bruce
Politics, 1598
Wright, Richard
America, 203
Artists, 305
Being Black in America, 358
Blackness, 412
Blues, 420
Change, 458
Christianity, 490
Church, 506, 507, 508
Death, 653
Human Nature, 1146

Humanity, 1161
Justice, 1274
Paris, 1541
Prison, 1633
Race Consciousness, 1677
Reality, 1754
Religion, 1793
Self-Acceptance, 1858
Self-Hate, 1882
Self-Knowledge, 1912
Self-Realization, 1946
Wright, Richard R.
Self-Reliance, 1968
Wright, Sarah E.
Love, 1401
X, Malcolm
Action, 42
Africa, 119
America, 204, 205, 206, 207, 208
Being Black in America, 359, 360
Brotherhood, 432, 433
Community, 566
Death, 654
Drugs, 725
Education, 829
Goals, 1007
Growth, 1046
Hair, 1050
Heritage, 1092
History, 1127, 1128
Humanity, 1162
Humor, 1169
Identity, 1198, 1199
Justice, 1275
Love, 1402
Memory, 1416
Patriotism, 1545
Peace, 1555
Power, 1611
Prison, 1634
Progress, 1645
Race Consciousness, 1678
Race Relations, 1692
Racism, 1720
Reading, 1742
Revolution, 1827
Self-Affirmation, 1864
Self-Hate, 1883, 1884
Self-Liberation, 1927
Struggle, 2210
Success, 2228
Truth, 2276
Unity, 2299
Violence, 2317
Yarborough, Camille
Children, 480

Yerby, Frank
Words, 2405
Young, Andrew
Civil Rights Movement, 522
Death, 655
Prison, 1635
Spirit, 2072
Struggle, 2211
Women, 2396

Young, Coleman
Racism, 1721
Success, 2229
Young, Whitney M. Jr.
Achievement, 19
America, 209
Inspiration, 1212
Values, 2311

SUBJECT INDEX

Numbers refer to entry numbers.

Ability
Aaron, Hank, 1
Ali, Muhammad, 1928
Bruce, Blanche K., 403
Farrakhan, Louis, 1015
Hughes, Langston, 2490
Louis, Joe, 14
Mays, Benjamin, 15
Wonder, Stevie, 18
Young, Whitney M. Jr., 19

Abortion
Kennedy, Florynce, 1425

Abraham
Anonymous, 2147

Achievement
Aaron, Hank, 1, 384
Adams, Charles G., 747
Ali, Muhammad, 2
Anderson, Marian, 3
Baldwin, James, 883
Bethune, Mary McLeod, 4, 287, 2345
Bradley, Crenner, 5
Brown, Les, 2414
Burroughs, Nannie, 6
Carver, George Washington, 7
Colins, Janet, 588
Crummell, Alexander, 993
Dash, Julie, 2508
Douglass, Frederick, 8
Franklin, John Hope, 2473
Garvey, Marcus, 9, 996, 1933
Gates, Henry Louis Jr., 1748
Gibson, Althea, 10, 594
Gomes, Peter J., 11
Harper, Frances Ellen Watkins, 927
Holiday, Billie, 893
Jackson, Jesse, 12, 2428
Jakes, T.D., 2220
Johnson, James Weldon, 178
Johnson, John H., 2222
Jones, Lois Mailou, 295
Jordan, Barbara, 13
Jordan, Michael, 856
Kennedy, Randall, 394
King, Martin Luther Jr., 929

Lee, Benjamin, 794
Lee, Spike, 2439
Louis, Joe, 14
Mays, Benjamin, 15, 1987
McMillan, Roslyn, 1902
Miller, Kelly, 1114
Owens, Jesse, 473
Powell, Adam Clayton Jr., 1942
Randolph, A. Philip, 843, 937
Robinson, Jackie, 16
Rudolph, Wilma, 685, 1002
Stewart, Maria W., 2382, 2383
Strawberry, Darryl, 2178
Toomer, Jean, 17
Vaughan, Sarah, 2458
Washington, Booker T., 223, 2461
West, Cornel, 489
Williams, Eddie N., 745
Wonder, Stevie, 18
Woodson, Carter G., 826, 1125, 1126
Young, Whitney M. Jr., 19

Action
Ali, Muhammad, 20
Allen, William Grant, 2397
Bailey, Pearl, 21
Baldwin, James, 22
Bechet, Sidney, 2411
Brown, John, 23
Carver, George Washington, 1075
Chesnutt, Charles W., 24
Dee, Ruby, 885
Douglass, Frederick, 25, 920
Du Bois, W.E.B., 26
Ellison, Ralph, 881
Garvey, Marcus, 1078
Gates, Henry Louis Jr., 27
Gomes, Peter J., 2424
Holyfield, Evander, 887
Hurston, Zora Neale, 2369, 2426
Jackson, Jesse, 1582
Jamison, Judith, 1937
Jordan, Barbara, 28
Joyner, Florence Griffith, 29
Kennedy, Florynce, 1646
King, Martin Luther Jr., 30, 31, 32, 601
Lee, Spike, 2439

Lorde, Audre, 1557
Paige, Satchel, 2449, 2450
Parks, Rosa, 33
Powell, Colin, 960
Randolph, A. Philip, 34, 1533
Ross, Diana, 711, 963
Sharpton, Al, 35
Stewart, Maria W., 36, 2206
Toomer, Jean, 2455
Trotter, William Monroe, 37
Truth, Sojourner, 38
Washington, Booker T., 2461
Weaver, Robert C., 1040
West, Cornel, 39, 1325
Wilson, August, 40
Woodson, Carter G., 41, 1530
X, Malcolm, 42, 654

Adolescence *see also* **Youth**
Angelou, Maya, 43
Franklin, Aretha, 44
Sanchez, Sonia, 45
Sowell, Thomas, 46

Adversity
Douglass, Frederick, 8
Gomes, Peter J., 47
Moutoussamy-Ashe, Jeanne, 48

Aesthetics
Gates, Henry Louis Jr., 693
Hooks, Bell, 1292
Lawrence, Jacob, 263
Locke, Alain, 126

Affirmative action
Brennan, William J., 49
Carnesale, Albert, 50
Coffin, Frank M., 51
Edelman, Marian Wright, 52
Fair, Brian, 53
Gates, Henry Louis Jr., 54
Guinier, Lani, 55
Lowery, Joseph, 56
Marshall, Thurgood, 57
Powell, Colin, 58, 59
Reeves, Keith W., 60
Rudenstein, Neil L., 61
Thomas, Clarence, 62
Watkins, Frank, 63
Williams, Patricia, 64

Africa
Angelou, Maya, 65, 66, 67
Anonymous, 68

Appiah, Anthony, 69, 70, 1566
Armstrong, Louis, 1466
Asante, Molefi, 71
Baldwin, James, 72
Bethune, Mary McLeod, 73
Brown, Ronald H., 1865
Browne, Sir Thomas, 74
Bunche, Ralph, 531
Caesar, Julius, 75
Carmichael, Stokely, 76
Clarke, John Henrik, 77, 78, 79, 2055
Cullen, Countee, 80
Douglass, Frederick, 81
Du Bois, W.E.B., 82, 83, 1684
Ellington, Duke, 1252
Embry, James C., 1496
Essien-Udom, E.U., 1329
Fortune, T. Thomas, 84
Garvey, Marcus, 85, 86, 87, 88, 89, 90, 91, 1018
Gates, Henry Louis Jr., 368
Hansberry, Lorraine, 92
Harper, Frances Ellen Watkins, 391
Heber, Reginald, 93
Jeffries, Leonard, 2430
King, B.B., 1295
Lessing, Doris, 1156
Locke, Alain, 94, 95, 96
Macmillan, Harold, 97
Morrison, Toni, 98
Neal, Larry, 502
Newman, Richard, 99
Pliny the Elder, 100
Polly, 1026
Priestly, J.B., 1724
Robeson, Paul, 101, 102, 103, 104, 105, 106, 220, 636, 1197
Robinson, James H., 107
Robinson, Randall, 108, 1589
Schomburg, Arthur, 1531
Shakespeare, William, 109
Smith, Venture, 110, 193
Stewart, Maria W., 111, 112, 2382, 2383
Terrell, Mary Church, 113
Turner, Darwin T., 1363
Turner, Henry McNeal, 114
Walker, Alice, 196
West, Cornel, 115
Williams, John A., 116
Williams, Tevis, 637
Wilson, August, 117
Woodson, Carter G., 118
X, Malcolm, 119

African American studies
Gates, Henry Louis Jr., 120, 121, 122
Wilkins, Roy, 123

African art *see also* **Art**
Baldwin, James, 230
Ellington, Duke, 250
Gates, Henry Louis Jr., 252
Scott, Hazel, 276
Weston, Randy, 1490
Woodson, Carter G., 280

African continuity
Baraka, Amiri, 124
Brewer, J. Mason, 125
Clarke, John Henrik, 79
Ellison, Ralph, 2290
Garvey, Marcus, 85, 87
Locke, Alain, 126
Robeson, Paul, 106
Robinson, Randall, 108
Wilson, August, 117

Africanism
Morrison, Toni, 98

Afrocentrism
Asante, Molefi, 127
West, Cornel, 128

Age
Paige, Satchel, 129
Truth, Sojourner, 38

AIDS
Ashe, Arthur, 1694
Johnson, Magic, 1996

Alabama
Durr, Virginia, 453
King, Martin Luther Jr., 30
Owens, Jesse, 1527
Parks, Rosa, 936
Wilson, August, 564
X, Malcolm, 1827

Algeria
Cleaver, Kathleen, 533

Alienation
Baldwin, James, 2181
Ellison, Ralph, 2290
Lee-Smith, Hughie, 130
Washington, James M., 131

Allah
Farrakhan, Louis, 306

Ambition
Bailey, Pearl, 1341
Baldwin, James, 2409
Bradley, Thomas, 1035
Burroughs, Nannie, 6
Crummell, Alexander, 993
Dash, Julie, 2508
Douglass, Frederick, 25, 994
Du Bois, W.E.B., 132
Garvey, Marcus, 996
Gibson, Althea, 594, 2336
Gomes, Peter J., 133, 2423, 2424
Hines, Gregory, 2474
Houston, Charles Hamilton, 405
Jordan, Barbara, 13
Joyner, Florence Griffith, 29
Joyner-Kersee, Jackie, 999
Lee, Spike, 2439
Locke, Alain, 623
Louis, Joe, 14
Mays, Benjamin, 15
Motley, Archibald Jr., 606
Ross, Diana, 711
Rudolph, Wilma, 1002, 2453
Wallace, Michelle, 1003
Wilson, August, 40

America *see also* **Being Black in America**
Ali, Muhammad, 134, 1693
Allen, Richard, 135
Allen, William Grant, 2397
Anderson, Marian, 136
Angelou, Maya, 2340
Anonymous, 137
Asante, Molefi, 71, 2398
Ashe, Arthur, 325
Baldwin, James, 138, 139, 140, 141, 142,
143, 144, 326, 327, 328, 698, 1097,
1284, 1811, 1886, 2181, 2242
Baraka, Amiri, 145, 283
Barnes, James B., 284
Beal, Frances M., 2343
Bearden, Romare, 242
Bell, Derrick, 1696
Benson, Janice Hall, 754
Berry, Halle, 2344
Berry, Mary Frances, 1100
Bond, Julian, 1834
Bradley, David, 329
Brown, Claude, 146, 545
Brown, H. Rap, 2316
Brown, James, 330
Brown, John, 147

Brown, Ronald H., 1569
Brown, William Wells, 148, 149, 150, 1913, 1949
Bruce, H.C., 830
Bruce, John E., 1184
Bunche, Ralph, 531, 1681
Burroughs, Nannie, 2301
Carmichael, Stokely, 546
Charles, Ray, 151
Chesnutt, Charles W., 1264
Childress, Alice, 759, 1734
Chisholm, Shirley, 659, 688
Clark, Kenneth B., 152, 676
Cleaver, Eldridge, 153
Clinton, Bill, 1979
Cole, Johnnetta, 1103
Comer, James P., 331
Cone, James, 154, 332, 496
Cooper, Anna Julia, 2355
Craft, Ellen, 2020
Crummell, Alexander, 660
Cruse, Harold, 155, 1188
Daggett, Janet, 333
Davis, Ossie, 334
Davis, Sammy Jr., 335
Debro, Sarah, 156
DeVore, Donald, 1105
Dinkins, David, 157
Douglass, Frederick, 81, 158, 159, 160, 525, 831, 905, 2021, 2326
Du Bois, W.E.B., 161, 162, 163, 164, 661, 769, 771, 838, 1134, 1469, 1684, 1762, 1890, 2303
Dunbar, Paul Laurence, 336
Dvorak, Anton, 1470
Dyson, Michael Eric, 1287
Edelman, Marian Wright, 874
Ellington, Duke, 165, 616, 1252
Ellison, Ralph, 166, 167, 366
Embry, James C., 1496
Evers-Williams, Myrlie, 1288
Farmer, James, 362
Farrakhan, Louis, 168, 169, 306
Fauset, Jessie, 839
Fortune, T. Thomas, 170
Franklin, John Hope, 1107, 2029
Gates, Henry Louis Jr., 368, 690, 1191, 1423
Goodman, Paul, 512
Gregory, Dick, 171, 172, 1108
Griffin, Judith, 782
Guinier, Lani, 1317
Hamer, Fannie Lou, 173, 337

Hansberry, Lorraine, 228
Harper, Frances Ellen Watkins, 2366
Holt, Thomas, 2035
Hooks, Benjamin, 439, 2312
Hughes, Langston, 174, 735, 1255, 2490
Jackson, Jesse, 175, 176, 694, 1581, 1603, 2313
Jacobs, Harriet, 177
Johnson, Charles, 2500
Johnson, Jack, 338
Johnson, James Weldon, 178, 1710, 1723, 1995
Johnson, John H., 371
Jordan, Barbara, 179
Jordan, June, 180
Killens, John O., 181, 674, 2267
King, Coretta Scott, 182, 1155, 1583
King, Martin Luther Jr., 183, 184, 185, 339, 500, 664, 1608
Lawrence, Charles, 1712
Ledbetter, Huddie, 1478
Locke, Alain, 186, 187, 666, 957
Lowery, Joseph, 340
Luis, W.A., 1639
Marshall, Thurgood, 667
McHenry, Elizabeth, 1196
McKay, Claude, 737
Mfume, Kweisi, 2197
Miller, Thomas E., 188, 668
Morrison, Toni, 98
Moseley-Braun, Carol, 567
Neal, Larry, 341
Norton, Eleanor Holmes, 342
Owens, Jesse, 343
Parks, Gordon, 344
Parks, Rosa, 1260
Paul, Nathaniel, 345
Pennington, James W.C., 189
Pinchback, Pinckney B.S., 1647
Poussaint, Alvin, 2306
Powell, Colin, 959
Priestly, J.B., 1724
Prochnow, Jurgen, 346
Purvis, Robert, 190
Randolph, A. Philip, 2202
Reed, Ishmael, 301, 347
Ridley, Elizabeth, 348
Robeson, Paul, 106, 191, 221, 636
Robinson, James H., 107
Robinson, Randall, 108
Rollins, Sonny, 374
Russwurm, John B., 349
Sanchez, Sonia, 275

Savage, Augusta, 350
Schomburg, Arthur, 1118, 1120, 1590
Scott, Hazel, 276
Shange, Ntozake, 192
Shipler, David K., 1668
Simone, Nina, 1262
Simone, Timothy M., 375
Smith, Venture, 193
Solomon, Charlene, 811
Stewart, Maria W., 194
Strickland, William, 1430
Sundiata, Ibrahim K., 195
Thomas, Clarence, 1405
Turner, Henry McNeal, 835, 1406
Vivian, C.T., 351
Walker, Alice, 196, 2207
Walker, David, 197, 198, 199, 1332
Walters, Alexander, 2460
Washington, Augustus, 200
Washington, Booker T., 201, 816, 823
Washington, James M., 131
Waters, Maxine, 1760, 2393
Wells, Ida B., 202, 1409, 1410
West, Cornel, 352, 353, 354, 419, 568,
    675, 854, 1041, 1325, 1671, 1761,
    1881, 1976, 2239, 2271
White, Walter, 2209
Wideman, John Edgar, 355, 356
Williams, Bert, 357
Williams, Eddie N., 745
Williams, John A., 116
Williams, Tevis, 637
Wills, Frank, 1042
Wilson, William Julius, 1691
Wright, Richard, 203, 358, 1793
X, Malcolm, 204, 205, 206, 207, 208,
    359, 360, 1169, 1198, 1678, 1883
Young, Andrew, 2211
Young, Whitney M. Jr., 209

Americanism
X, Malcolm, 204

Ancestors *see also* **History**
Angelou, Maya, 210, 2340
Baldwin, James, 144
Brown, Claude, 146
Crummell, Alexander, 211
Davis, Angela, 2358
Dinkins, David, 1636
Du Bois, W.E.B., 164
Ellison, Ralph, 2026
Farrakhan, Louis, 212
Gandhi, Mohandas K., 2030

Garvey, Marcus, 213, 1079
Gates, Henry Louis Jr., 1190, 2363
Haley, Alex, 1109
Hamer, Fannie Lou, 2364
Hastie, William H., 214
Jackson, Jesse, 1581
Johnson, William H., 393
Jones, Bessie, 215
Jordan, June, 216
King, B.B., 1295
Lee-Smith, Hughie, 298
Mays, Benjamin, 217
Morrison, Toni, 218
Moseley-Braun, Carol, 457
Murray, Albert, 1257
Parks, Rosa, 219
Powell, Adam Clayton Jr., 559
Robeson, Paul, 191, 220, 221
Teish, Luisah, 222
Toomer, Jean, 1669
Turner, Henry McNeal, 114
Walker, David, 198
Walker, Margaret, 1561
Washington, Booker T., 223
Wells, Ida B., 1763
West, Cornel, 224
Winfrey, Oprah, 225
Woodson, Carter G., 226
X, Malcolm, 1199
Young, Andrew, 522, 2211

Anger
Baldwin, James, 227, 327
Brown, Claude, 146
Hansberry, Lorraine, 228
Hurston, Zora Neale, 1844
Weaver, Robert C., 2464
West, Cornel, 1324
Wilkins, Roy, 1237

Angola
Cleaver, Kathleen, 533

Answers
Cole, Johnnetta, 762
Ellison, Ralph, 2401
Hall, Arsenio, 229
Hansberry, Lorraine, 619
Hurston, Zora Neale, 2253
Jordan, Michael, 598
Walker, Alice, 1963
West, Cornel, 1236

Aristotle
Du Bois, W.E.B., 1890

Armenia
Wells, Ida B., 1410

Army
Gooding, Cuba Jr., 2328
Poussaint, Alvin, 808

Arrest *see* **Prison**

Art *see also* **Painting; Photography;**
Sculpture
Baldwin, James, 230, 231, 232
Bambara, Toni Cade, 233
Bannister, Edward Mitchell, 234
Bearden, Romare, 235, 236, 237, 238,
239, 240, 241, 242, 243, 244
Brewer, J. Mason, 125
Campbell, Mary Schmidt, 245
Catlett, Elizabeth, 246, 547, 614, 1327
Crite, Allan Rohan, 1153
Davis, Angela, 247
Davis, Miles, 615
Du Bois, W.E.B., 83, 248, 2288
Edmondson, William, 249
Ellington, Duke, 250, 251
Ellison, Ralph, 2488
Garvey, Marcus, 90
Gates, Henry Louis Jr., 252, 369
Gaye, Marvin, 253
Hampton, Lionel, 254
Hansberry, Lorraine, 255
Hayden, Palmer, 256
Houston, Whitney, 2007
Hughes, Langston, 257
Hunter, Clementine, 258
Johnson, James Weldon, 259, 631
Johnson, Sargent, 260
Jones, Lois Mailou, 261
Karenga, Ron, 262
Lawrence, Jacob, 263, 556
Lee-Smith, Hughie, 264, 265
Locke, Alain, 266, 322, 372
Marsalis, Wynton, 267
Marshall, Paule, 268
McKay, Claude, 1168
Morrison, Toni, 269, 2502
Parker, Charlie, 270
Pippin, Horace, 271, 272
Pryor, Richard, 273
Rhodes, John, 274
Sanchez, Sonia, 275
Savage, Augusta, 350
Scott, Hazel, 276
Shabazz, Betty, 1487

Van Der Zee, James, 277
West, Cornel, 278
White, Charles, 279
Woodson, Carter G., 280

Artists
Anderson, Marian, 136
Bambara, Toni Cade, 281
Baraka, Amiri, 282, 283
Barnes, James B., 284
Bearden, Romare, 241, 285, 286
Bethune, Mary McLeod, 287
Catlett, Elizabeth, 2348
Davis, Miles, 288
Davis, Ossie, 549
Douglas, Aaron, 289, 2320
Ellington, Duke, 290
Ellison, Ralph, 291
Evans, Minnie, 292
Gates, Henry Louis Jr., 1726
Gaye, Marvin, 293
Hooks, Bell, 1292
Hughes, Langston, 1872
Johnson, William H., 294
Jones, Lois Mailou, 295
Karenga, Ron, 296
Lawrence, Jacob, 297, 1675
Lee-Smith, Hughie, 298
Lincoln, Abby, 299
Locke, Alain, 623
Prophet, Nancy Elizabeth, 300
Reed, Ishmael, 301
Robeson, Paul, 302
Toomer, Jean, 303
Van Der Zee, James, 277
Walker, Alice, 304
Wright, Richard, 305

Asia
Du Bois, W.E.B., 1684

Astronauts
Jemison, Mae, 982

Atonement
Farrakhan, Louis, 306
Washington, Booker T., 2051

Attitude
Baldwin, James, 1885
Bergreen, Laurence, 1246
Bradley, Crenner, 5
Gregory, Dick, 410
Locke, Alain, 187
Muhammad, Herbert, 853

Schomburg, Arthur, 1121
Thurman, Howard, 1081
Williams, Robert, 1005
Wright, Richard, 490

Aurelius
Du Bois, W.E.B., 1890

Austria
Delany, Martin R., 1501

Authenticity
Armstrong, Louis, 307
Dyson, Michael Eric, 308

Average people
Baldwin, James, 1097
Cotton, Dorothy, 510
Davis, Sammy Jr., 335
Du Bois, W.E.B., 161
Jordan, Barbara, 13
Lee-Smith, Hughie, 130, 264
Vaughan, Sarah, 2458
West, Cornel, 39, 671

Aviation
Coleman, Bessie, 587
Jemison, Mae, 982
Paige, Satchel, 2447

Awareness *see* **Self-knowledge**

Bach, Johann Sebastian
Baldwin, James, 1885

Baggage
Sharpton, Al, 1592

Baldwin, James
Perry, Richard, 1904

Balzac, Honore de
Du Bois, W.E.B., 1890

Baptists
Washington, Booker T., 1790
Washington, James M., 505
X, Malcolm, 359

Beauty
Baldwin, James, 973
Bennett, Gwendolyn, 1376
Catlett, Elizabeth, 2348
Du Bois, W.E.B., 248, 390
Hooks, Bell, 1292
King, Martin Luther Jr., 695
Lawrence, Jacob, 263, 1089
Marable, Manning, 2374
Roach, Max, 1261

Savage, Augusta, 350
Walker, Alice, 1944
West, Cornel, 2272
Woodson, Carter G., 1126
Wright, Richard, 1541

Beauty of Blackness *see also* **Blackness**
Anonymous, 309
Bethune, Mary McLeod, 310
Brooks, Gwendolyn, 311
Bruce, John E., 312
Carmichael, Stokely, 313
Cone, James, 1521
Davis, Ossie, 314
Du Bois, W.E.B., 315
Dyson, Michael Eric, 316
Evans, Mari, 317
Garvey, Marcus, 318
Haley, Alex, 319
Hughes, Langston, 320, 321
Johnson, Sargent, 260
Locke, Alain, 322
Taylor, Susan, 323
Walker, Alice, 1925
Walker, David, 324

Being Black in America *see also* **America**
Ashe, Arthur, 325
Baldwin, James, 326, 327, 328
Bradley, David, 329
Brown, James, 330
Comer, James P., 331
Cone, James, 332
Daggett, Janet, 333
Davis, Ossie, 334
Davis, Sammy Jr., 335
Dunbar, Paul Laurence, 336
Hamer, Fannie Lou, 337
Johnson, Jack, 338
King, Martin Luther Jr., 339
Lowery, Joseph, 340
Neal, Larry, 341
Norton, Eleanor Holmes, 342
Owens, Jesse, 343
Parks, Gordon, 344
Paul, Nathaniel, 345
Prochnow, Jurgen, 346
Reed, Ishmael, 347
Ridley, Elizabeth, 348
Russwurm, John B., 349
Savage, Augusta, 350
Vivian, C.T., 351
West, Cornel, 352, 353, 354
Wideman, John Edgar, 355, 356

Williams, Bert, 357
Wright, Richard, 358
X, Malcolm, 359, 360

Beliefs *see also* **Faith; Religion**
Ali, Muhammad, 1693
Jordan, June, 216

Bible
Anonymous, 2099
Baldwin, James, 638
Taylor, Gardner C., 488
Turner, Henry McNeal, 1030
West, Cornel, 39

Birth
Ali, Muhammad, 1650
Angelou, Maya, 581, 2281
Anonymous, 907, 2100
Armstrong, Lil Hardin, 1461
Baldwin, James, 143, 328, 462
Bearden, Romare, 237
Brown, Ronald H., 1175
Charles, RuPaul, 1186
Cooke, Sam, 452
Crudup, Arthur, 1600
Ellington, Duke, 165
Evans, Mari, 317
Horton, George M., 2036
Jackson, Jesse, 597
Jones, Joshua Henry, 1810
Lawrence-Lightfoot, Sara, 793
Miller, Kelly, 1972
Moses, Michael, 472
Naylor, Gloria, 1429
Parker, Charlie, 624
Polly, 1026
Powell, Adam Clayton Jr., 1181
Reed, Adolph, 1715
Taylor, Susie King, 846
Walker, Alice, 1908
Washington, Augustus, 200

Bitterness
Clark, Joe, 658
Du Bois, W.E.B., 132
Himes, Chester, 1621
Johnson, Jack, 338
King, Martin Luther Jr., 407

Black consciousness *see also* **Race consciousness**
Drake, St. Clair, 361
Farmer, James, 362

Gayle, Addison Jr., 363
Woodson, Carter G., 364

Black culture *see also* **Culture**
Bond, Julian, 1834
Du Bois, W.E.B., 365
Dyson, Michael Eric, 308
Ellison, Ralph, 366
Equiano, Olaudah, 367
Gates, Henry Louis Jr., 368, 369, 1053
Hampton, Lionel, 370
Johnson, John H., 371
Locke, Alain, 372
Northup, Solomon, 373
Rollins, Sonny, 374
Simone, Timothy M., 375
Turner, Henry McNeal, 114

Black experience *see also* **Experience**
Angelou, Maya, 1149
Gates, Henry Louis Jr., 376
Lawrence, Jacob, 263
Parks, Rosa, 1260

Black nationalism
Delany, Martin R., 1951
West, Cornel, 128

Black Panther Party
Newton, Huey, 383

Black power *see also* **Power**
Browne, Robert S., 377
Carmichael, Stokely, 378
Crummell, Alexander, 380
Du Bois, W.E.B., 381
Jordan, Barbara, 382
Newton, Huey, 383

Black pride *see also* **Pride**
Aaron, Hank, 384
Baldwin, James, 1873
Banneker, Benjamin, 385
Bethune, Mary McLeod, 386
Blyden, Edward Wilmot, 387
Brown, James, 388, 1568
Brown, Ronald H., 1569
Douglass, Frederick, 389
Du Bois, W.E.B., 390
Harper, Frances Ellen Watkins, 391
Johnson, Fenton, 392
Johnson, William H., 393
Kennedy, Randall, 394
Killens, John O., 395
King, Martin Luther Jr., 396
Price, Leontyne, 397

Schomburg, Arthur, 398, 1590
Tanner, Henry O., 399
Truth, Sojourner, 400
Woodson, Carter G., 401
X, Malcolm, 359

Black strength
Baldwin, James, 402
Blige, Mary J., 2347
Bruce, Blanche K., 403
Bunche, Ralph, 404
Du Bois, W.E.B., 390
Houston, Charles Hamilton, 405
Jacob, John E., 406
King, Martin Luther Jr., 407
Newton, Huey, 557
Robinson, Randall, 1589
Washington, Booker T., 408

Blackness *see also* **Beauty of Blackness;
Being Black in America; Negroes;
Race**
Anonymous, 895, 896
Baraka, Amiri, 145
Bergreen, Laurence, 1246
Brown, William Wells, 150
Browne, Robert S., 377
Clarke, John Henrik, 77
Cone, James, 332
Davis, Angela, 1574
Ellison, Ralph, 167
Garvey, Marcus, 1316
Gates, Henry Louis Jr., 409, 1190
Gregory, Dick, 410
Jackson, Jesse, 12
Karenga, Ron, 1751
Lee, Spike, 632
Lee-Smith, Hughie, 130, 264
West, Cornel, 411
Wilson, August, 117
Wright, Richard, 412
X, Malcolm, 1198

Blood
Allen, Richard, 135, 2280
Angelou, Maya, 1088
Baldwin, James, 699
Brown, John, 147
Crummell, Alexander, 2325
Davis, Angela, 2358
Emerson, Ralph Waldo, 2027
Fortune, T. Thomas, 84
Garnet, Henry Highland, 592
Garvey, Marcus, 86, 1315

Harper, Frances Ellen Watkins, 391,
1708
Hawthorne, Nathaniel, 1685
Hooks, Benjamin, 2312
Hughes, Langston, 735
Miller, Thomas E., 188
Pickens, William, 1998
Prosser, Gabriel, 1757
Robeson, Paul, 102
Tanner, Henry O., 399
Toomer, Jean, 1669
Truth, Sojourner, 2044
Tubman, Harriet, 2046, 2333
Turner, Henry McNeal, 1833
Walker, David, 199
Washington, Booker T., 2051
Wilson, August, 117

Blues
Anonymous, 413
Baraka, Amiri, 124
Gaines, Ernest J., 2498
Handy, W.C., 414, 415, 416
King, B.B., 417, 790, 1295
Mosley, Walter, 418
West, Cornel, 419
Wright, Richard, 420

Boll weevil
Jackson, Mahalia, 1813

Books *see also* **Literature; Writers**
Anonymous, 1095
Baldwin, James, 1097
Cole, Johnnetta, 1866
Dove, Rita, 421
Equiano, Olaudah, 1735
Fuller, Solomon B., 422
Gates, Henry Louis Jr., 1192
Griggs, Sutton E., 1736
Hughes, Langston, 423
Lee, Benjamin, 794
Marshall, Thurgood, 578
Porter, Dorothy, 1116
Schomburg, Arthur, 424
Smith, Rose, 1739
Tillman, Jane Irving, 425
Truth, Sojourner, 1741
Turner, Lana, 426
Vernon, William T., 427
Washington, Booker T., 819
Washington, James M., 428
White, J., 2054

Boundaries
Baldwin, James, 1873
Garvey, Marcus, 87
Gates, Henry Louis Jr., 692
Parker, Charlie, 270
Washington, Booker T., 1159

Boycotts
Malvreaux, Julianne, 736

Braxton, Anthony
Davis, Anthony, 1467

Bridges
Brown, Ronald H., 1569
Ellison, Ralph, 775
Wilson, Mary, 1491
Winfrey, Oprah, 225

Brotherhood *see also* **Community;
  Solidarity; Unity**
Angelou, Maya, 2281
Anonymous, 1417, 2101
Baldwin, James, 699, 1520
Carmichael, Stokely, 546
Carson, Benjamin, 494
Clarke, John Henrik, 2055
D., Chuck, 1725
Douglass, Frederick, 1860, 2023
Du Bois, W.E.B., 429, 1523
Forten, James, 430, 1664
Gates, Henry Louis Jr., 691, 1148
Goodman, Paul, 512
Hall, Prince, 2293
Jakes, T.D., 2220
King, Martin Luther Jr., 431, 529, 708,
  1456
Robinson, Jackie, 16
Scott, Hazel, 940
Washington, Booker T., 1459
West, Cornel, 1857
Woodson, Carter G., 825
X, Malcolm, 432, 433

Brown, James
West, Cornel, 1004

Brown, John
Brown, John, 147
Douglass, Frederick, 1755

Brutality
Cone, James, 495
Johns, Vernon, 1023
King, Martin Luther Jr., 500
X, Malcolm, 359

Building
Anonymous, 2113
Bady, Willie Jr., 2408
Brown, William Wells, 569
Carmichael, Stokely, 437
Chisholm, Shirley, 659
Ellison, Ralph, 775
Farrakhan, Louis, 212
Garvey, Marcus, 551
King, Martin Luther Jr., 1457
Robeson, Paul, 191
Stewart, Maria W., 740
Turner, Henry McNeal, 1833

Bunche, Ralph
Edelman, Marian Wright, 2304

Burdens
Ashe, Arthur, 1694
Bennett, Lerone, 523
Franklin, Aretha, 482
Jackson, Jesse, 12
Jacobs, Harriet, 981
Jordan, Barbara, 28
King, Martin Luther Jr., 185
Washington, Booker T., 477
Wright, Richard, 420

Burns, Robert
Mays, Benjamin, 1369

Business *see also* **Economics**
Anonymous, 434, 435
Brown, Tony, 436
Carmichael, Stokely, 437
Carver, George Washington, 2017
Danky, James P., 1683
Gaston, A.G., 438
Hancock, Gordon Blaine, 732, 733
Hooks, Benjamin, 439
Hughes, Dorothy Pitman, 440
Johnson, John H., 441
Killens, John O., 2195
King, Coretta Scott, 2295
McKay, Claude, 737
Stewart, Maria W., 740
Walker, Mme. C.J., 443
Washington, Booker T., 820, 946, 1964

Byron, Lord
Mays, Benjamin, 1369

California
Himes, Chester, 1621
Waters, Maxine, 1760

Capitalism
Clarke, John Henrik, 728
Davis, Angela, 444
King, Martin Luther Jr., 445, 446
Robeson, Paul, 447
Woodbey, George W., 448

Caribbean
Robinson, Randall, 108, 1589

Catholics
King, Martin Luther Jr., 932
X, Malcolm, 359

Change
Ali, Noble Drew, 449
Anonymous, 902, 903
Bailey, Pearl, 2234
Baldwin, James, 2487
Bethune, Mary McLeod, 2507
Brown, William Wells, 1495
Carmichael, Stokely, 450, 451
Carver, George Washington, 1011
Cole, Johnnetta, 761
Cooke, Sam, 452
Douglass, Frederick, 1036
Durr, Virginia, 453
Edelman, Marian Wright, 454
Ellison, Ralph, 1043, 2488
Flake, Floyd, 987
Gillespie, Dizzy, 1474
Hill, Anita, 1607
Huggins, Nathan, 1065
Hughes, Langston, 2489
Jackson, Jesse, 1138
Jakes, T.D., 1497
Jordan, June, 1294
Killens, John O., 455
King, Coretta Scott, 456
Locke, Alain, 1067, 1068
Lorde, Audre, 1525, 1557
Macmillan, Harold, 97
Mfume, Kweisi, 801
Moseley-Braun, Carol, 457
Nelson, Jill, 1277
Nixon, E.D., 517
Parks, Rosa, 33
Powell, Adam Clayton Jr., 739
Ransom, Reverdy C., 1027
Robeson, Paul, 1117
Rodney, Muhammad, 1240
Simmons, Judy, 1689
Snipes, Wesley, 1768
Washington, Booker T., 834

Williams, Eddie N., 745
Wilson, Mary, 1491
Woodson, Carter G., 827
Wright, Richard, 412, 458, 1146
X, Malcolm, 829, 1742

Children *see also* **Education; Youth**
Aaron, Hank, 460
Angelou, Maya, 67
Anonymous, 899, 1843
Baldwin, James, 326, 461, 462, 868
Bethune, Mary McLeod, 73
Blackwell, Unita, 582
Blake, Bessie, 463
Bond, Julian, 2315
Brooks, Gwendolyn, 311
Brown, Claude, 146
Burroughs, Nannie, 2302
Carver, George Washington, 2017
Cole, Johnnetta, 871
Collins, Marva, 763
Donaldson, Greg, 464
Douglass, Frederick, 766
Dyson, Michael Eric, 465
Edelin, Kenneth C., 466
Edelman, Marian Wright, 467
Elders, Joycelyn, 965
Evers-Williams, Myrlie, 1652
Garvey, Marcus, 213
Gates, Henry Louis Jr., 1192
Gibson, Bob, 1836
Giddings, Paula, 468
Grier, William; Cobb, Price, 469
Haley, Alex, 875
Hawthorne, Nathaniel, 1685
Hibbler, William, 470
Hogan, Bessie, 786, 1934
Holiday, Billie, 471
Jemison, Mae, 982
Johnson, Magic, 1996
King, Coretta Scott, 1583
King, Martin Luther Jr., 932
Lawrence-Lightfoot, Sara, 793
Lee-Smith, Hughie, 298
Marshall, Thurgood, 1997
McGuire, George Alexander, 486
Moses, Michael, 472
Moutoussamy-Ashe, Jeanne, 48
Muhammad, Elijah, 803
Owens, Jesse, 473
Poussaint, Alvin, 558, 2306
Powell, Colin, 59, 960
Price, Hugh, 474

Ridley, Elizabeth, 348
Robeson, Paul, 106
Savage, Augusta, 475
Smitherman, Geneva, 1299
Solomon, Charlene, 1943
Thurman, Howard, 476
Truth, Sojourner, 2385
Turnage, Jackie, 1090
Walker, Alice, 2207
Walker, David, 1806
Washington, Booker T., 223, 477, 817
Washington, James M., 478
Waters, Ethel, 2238
Welsing, Frances Cress, 479
Yarborough, Camille, 480

China
Robeson, Paul, 103

Christ *see* **Jesus**

Christianity *see also* **Religion**
Baraka, Amiri, 124
Brown, William Wells, 2016
Bruce, H.C., 830
Cone, James, 154
Cullen, Countee, 1774
Douglass, Frederick, 481
Franklin, Aretha, 482
Garnet, Henry Highland, 483
Garvey, Marcus, 1087
Goodman, Paul, 512
Jackson, Jesse, 484
Jacobs, Harriet, 2370
Marrant, John, 485
McGuire, George Alexander, 486
Moss, Otis, 487
Taylor, Gardner C., 488
Washington, James M., 1615
West, Cornel, 489
Wright, Richard, 490

Church *see also* **Religion**
Abernathy, Ralph, 491
Allen, Richard, 492
Anonymous, 493, 2123
Armstrong, Louis, 1463
Baldwin, Alfred, 1772
Brown, William Wells, 2016
Carson, Benjamin, 494
Cone, James, 495, 496
Elders, Joycelyn, 965
Hancock, Gordon Blaine, 497
King, Bernice, 498
King, Martin Luther Jr., 499, 500

Mays, Benjamin, 836
McGuire, George Alexander, 1025
Monroe, Irene, 501
Morrison, Toni, 2501
Neal, Larry, 502
Powell, Adam Clayton Jr., 559
Rivers, Eugene, 503, 504
Smitherman, Geneva, 1298
Taylor, Susan, 2070
Washington, James M., 505
Whipper, William S., 1222
Wright, Richard, 506, 507, 508

Citizenship
Clark, Septima, 570
Douglass, Frederick, 1860
Harper, Frances Ellen Watkins, 1037
Russwurm, John B., 349
Walker, Charles T., 1432

Civil Rights Bill
Douglass, Frederick, 1577

Civil Rights Movement
Carr, Johnnie, 509
Cotton, Dorothy, 510
Durr, Virginia, 511
Goodman, Paul, 512
Gregory, Dick, 513
Hooks, Benjamin, 1492
Houston, Charles Hamilton, 1957
Johnson, Lyndon B., 514
Karenga, Ron, 515
King, Martin Luther Jr., 516
Nixon, E.D., 517
Proctor, Samuel D., 518
Reagon, Bernice Johnson, 519
Rustin, Bayard, 1609
Shuttlesworth, Fred, 520
Williams, Robert, 521
Young, Andrew, 522, 2072, 2396

Civil War
Anonymous, 2324
Douglass, Frederick, 2326
Fortune, T. Thomas, 1828
Marshall, Thurgood, 577, 579
Powell, Colin, 58
Washington, Booker T., 2051

Civilization
Du Bois, W.E.B., 161
Ellington, Duke, 616
Farrakhan, Louis, 212
King, Martin Luther Jr., 396, 1320

Locke, Alain, 94
Muhammad, Elijah, 803
Turner, Henry McNeal, 114, 1406
Washington, Booker T., 1459, 1910, 2481
Wells, Ida B., 202
West, Cornel, 115, 854
Weston, Randy, 1490
Woodson, Carter G., 1125
Wright, Richard, 506

Class
Bennett, Lerone, 523
Bibb, Henry, 524
Chisholm, Shirley, 688
Douglass, Frederick, 525
Frazier, E. Franklin, 526
Gates, Henry Louis Jr., 54, 527
Giovanni, Nikki, 662
Higginbotham, Evelyn Brooks, 979
King, Martin Luther Jr., 528, 529
Locke, Alain, 2079
Miller, Thomas E., 668
West, Cornel, 128, 530, 568, 1648

Clinton, Bill
Gates, Henry Louis Jr., 54
West, Cornel, 1041

Coleman, Steve
Davis, Anthony, 1467

Colonialism
Angelou, Maya, 67
Bunche, Ralph, 531
Clark, Kenneth B., 532
Cleaver, Kathleen, 533
Ellison, Ralph, 2290
Mosley, Walter, 534

Color *see also* **Beauty of Blackness; Blackness**
Anderson, Marian, 1224, 1657
Anonymous, 535
Baldwin, James, 536, 699, 1886
Banneker, Benjamin, 385
Bethune, Mary McLeod, 1377
Bruce, John E., 312
Chisholm, Shirley, 2350
Cone, James, 332
Davis, Ossie, 314
Derricotte, Toi, 537
Douglass, Frederick, 538, 2022
Du Bois, W.E.B., 1523, 1684, 1890
Ellison, Ralph, 2290

Embry, James C., 1496
Gates, Henry Louis Jr., 409, 848, 1190
Hall, Prince, 539
Houston, Whitney, 2007
Hughes, Langston, 735
Hurston, Zora Neale, 540, 541
Jackson, Jesse, 694
Jackson, Mahalia, 1709
McKay, Claude, 542
Motley, Archibald Jr., 606
Powell, Colin, 58
Robeson, Paul, 101
Sister Souljah, 543
Walker, Alice, 1031
Walker, David, 324
Washington, Booker T., 1159
Wiley, Ralph, 2273
Williams, Patricia, 64
Woodson, Carter G., 825
X, Malcolm, 1884

Commitment
Baldwin, James, 22
Ellison, Ralph, 1043
Futrell, Mary, 703
King, Martin Luther Jr., 1457
Shabazz, Betty, 1396
Taylor, Gardner C., 488

Common good *see also* **Goodness**
Goodman, Paul, 512
Jackson, Jesse, 2313
Randolph, A. Philip, 843
West, Cornel, 128

Common man *see* **Average people**

Communication *see also* **Language**
Gates, Henry Louis Jr., 1289
Hampton, Lionel, 254
Morrison, Toni, 2503
Rawls, Lou, 1483
Walker, Alice, 304

Community *see also* **Brotherhood; Service to the community; Solidarity; Unity**
Aaron, Hank, 544
Abrahams, Robert, 2241
Allen, Walter, 1565
Baldwin, James, 1150
Bambara, Toni Cade, 1286
Bechet, Sidney, 992
Brown, Claude, 545
Brown, Tony, 436
Campbell, Naomi, 1835

Carmichael, Stokely, 379, 437, 546
Catlett, Elizabeth, 547
Chavis, Benjamin Jr., 548
Cone, James, 1773
Davis, Ossie, 549
Delaney, Joseph, 550
Flake, Floyd, 987
Garvey, Marcus, 551
Gates, Henry Louis Jr., 1148
Hill, Anita, 980
Hurston, Zora Neale, 552
Jordan, Barbara, 553
King, B.B., 621
King, Martin Luther Jr., 554
Lawrence, Jacob, 555, 556, 1675
Locke, Alain, 1059
McKay, Claude, 737
Newton, Huey, 557
Parks, Rosa, 219
Poussaint, Alvin, 558
Powell, Adam Clayton Jr., 559
Powell, Colin, 960
Rivers, Eugene, 503
Roach, Max, 1261
Robeson, Paul, 560, 877
Rodney, Muhammad, 1240
Scott, Hazel, 940
Sharpton, Al, 697
Wade-Gayles, Gloria, 561
Walker, David, 197
Washington, James M., 1615
Wattleton, Faye, 562
West, Cornel, 563
White, Walter, 948
Wilson, August, 564
Winfrey, Oprah, 565, 953
X, Malcolm, 566

Confederate flag
Moseley-Braun, Carol, 567

Confidence *see* **Self-confidence**

Congo
Moses, Bob, 1714
X, Malcolm, 207

Congress
Chisholm, Shirley, 1572, 1573
Du Bois, W.E.B., 1578
Hill, Anita, 1129, 1750, 2264
Powell, Adam Clayton Jr., 609
Price, Hugh, 1604

Conscience
Chesnutt, Charles W., 1264
Garvey, Amy Jacques, 1404
Garvey, Marcus, 1228
Gomes, Peter J., 47
Price, Leontyne, 2255

Conservatives
Powell, Adam Clayton Jr., 1181
Shakur, Assata, 1591
West, Cornel, 568, 675

Constitution
Brown, William Wells, 569
Clark, Septima, 570
Dunbar, Paul Laurence, 571
Fortune, T. Thomas, 1828
Gates, Henry Louis Jr., 572
Gregory, Dick, 573
Harding, Vincent, 574
Harlan, John Marshall, 575
Johnson, James Weldon, 1821
Jordan, Barbara, 576
King, Martin Luther Jr., 1829
Marshall, Thurgood, 57, 577, 578, 579, 1337

Control *see* **Power**

Copeland, John A. Jr.
Douglass, Frederick, 1755

Courage *see also* **Daring; Perseverance**
Alexander, Sadie T.M., 580
Ali, Muhammad, 20
Angelou, Maya, 581
Bailey, Pearl, 21
Bearden, Romare, 240
Bethune, Mary McLeod, 2507
Blackwell, Unita, 582
Brown, Jim, 583
Carney, William H., 584
Charles, Ray, 585
Cinque, Joseph, 586
Cole, Johnnetta, 2353
Coleman, Bessie, 587
Colins, Janet, 588
Cosby, Bill, 589
Davis, Sammy Jr., 590
Evers-Williams, Myrlie, 1652
Fortune, T. Thomas, 591
Franklin, Aretha, 2005
Garnet, Henry Highland, 592
Garvey, Marcus, 593
Gibson, Althea, 594

Giddings, Paula, 997
Gordy, Berry Jr., 1460
Griggs, Sutton E., 1736
Guinier, Lani, 595
Holyfield, Evander, 596
Hurston, Zora Neale, 2265
Jackson, Jesse, 597
Jordan, Michael, 598, 599
Joyner-Kersee, Jackie, 600
King, Martin Luther Jr., 31, 407, 601,
    602, 603
Lee-Smith, Hughie, 298
Leonard, Sugar Ray, 604
Love, Nat "Deadwood Dick, the
    cowboy adventurer," 933
Mitchell, Arthur, 605
Motley, Archibald Jr., 606
Parks, Rosa, 607, 608
Powell, Adam Clayton Jr., 609, 610
Reagon, Bernice Johnson, 2258
Truth, Sojourner, 611
Warfield, William, 612
Washington, Harold, 613

Creativity see also Ideas; Imagination
Armstrong, Louis, 1466
Bearden, Romare, 239
Catlett, Elizabeth, 614
Childress, Alice, 2497
Davis, Miles, 615
Ellington, Duke, 616
Gates, Henry Louis Jr., 617
Golden, Marita, 618
Hansberry, Lorraine, 619
Joans, Ted, 620
Karenga, Ron, 296
King, B.B., 621
King, Martin Luther Jr., 686, 687, 2254
Lawrence, Jacob, 263, 622
Lee-Smith, Hughie, 130, 264
Locke, Alain, 623
Morrison, Toni, 2502
Parker, Charlie, 624
Prophet, Nancy Elizabeth, 300
Sutton, Percy, 625
Turner, Tina, 943
Walker, Alice, 626, 1963
Weaver, Robert C., 1040
West, Cornel, 530
Young, Whitney M. Jr., 19

Crime
Brown, John, 147
Douglass, Frederick, 2022, 2025

Dyson, Michael Eric, 1628
Hibbler, William, 470
Jackson, George, 1631
Lowery, Joseph, 1877
Taylor, Susan, 1880
Wilson, William Julius, 2484
X, Malcolm, 207, 725, 1883

Criticism
Baldwin, James, 139
Carson, Sonya, 757
Ellison, Ralph, 774
King, Martin Luther Jr., 1900
Wright, Richard, 1274
Young, Coleman, 1721, 2229

Culture see also African continuity; Black
    culture
Appiah, Anthony, 70
Asante, Molefi, 71
Baraka, Amiri, 124
Bearden, Romare, 238
Benson, Janice Hall, 754
Brewer, J. Mason, 125
Campbell, Mary Schmidt, 245
Cruse, Harold, 1188
Du Bois, W.E.B., 83, 161, 1154, 1208,
    2260
Ellison, Ralph, 366, 2290
Essien-Udom, E.U., 1329
Garvey, Marcus, 90
Gates, Henry Louis Jr., 617, 690, 1423
Hill, Anita, 980
Hurston, Zora Neale, 904
Jackson, Jesse, 484
Killens, John O., 674
King, Coretta Scott, 2295
King, Martin Luther Jr., 1320, 1321
Lawrence, Charles, 1712
Lewis, Elma, 1939
Locke, Alain, 126
Lorde, Audre, 1525
Madhubuti, Haki, 1959
Paderewski, Ignacy, 1259
Robeson, Paul, 103
Savage, Augusta, 350
Taylor, Billy, 1263
Turner, Darwin T., 1363
West, Cornel, 128, 224, 411
Wilmore, Gayraud, 1333
Wright, Richard, 1882

Czechoslovakia
Locke, Alain, 1061

Dance
Baker, Josephine, 1536
Baraka, Amiri, 124
Colins, Janet, 588
Du Bois, W.E.B., 248
Dunham, Katherine, 627
Ellison, Ralph, 366
Equiano, Olaudah, 367
Gates, Henry Louis Jr., 1726
Hughes, Langston, 257
Hunter, Tera W., 628
Jackson, Michael, 1476
Jamison, Judith, 629, 630
Johnson, James Weldon, 631
Jones, Bill T., 2434
Lee, Spike, 632
Locke, Alain, 633
Northup, Solomon, 373
Primus, Pearl, 634, 635
Robeson, Paul, 636
West, Cornel, 1004
Williams, Tevis, 637

Danger
Baldwin, James, 22, 1073, 1874
Davis, Angela, 1626, 1703
Douglass, Frederick, 767
Du Bois, W.E.B., 921, 2260
Garvey, Marcus, 551
Gates, Henry Louis Jr., 1289
Gregory, Dick, 573
Jemison, Mae, 1513
King, Martin Luther Jr., 792
Love, Nat "Deadwood Dick, the
    cowboy adventurer," 639
Strickland, William, 1430
West, Cornel, 1976

Daniel
Anonymous, 2084

Daring *see also* **Courage**
Baldwin, James, 638
Lorde, Audre, 888
Love, Nat "Deadwood Dick, the
    cowboy adventurer," 639

Death
Ali, Muhammad, 1223, 1339, 1693
Angelou, Maya, 43
Anonymous, 895, 2082, 2096, 2103
Bailey, Pearl, 1341
Baker, Josephine, 1364
Baldwin, James, 2487
Burroughs, Nannie, 1950

Childress, Alice, 1700
Cinque, Joseph, 586, 1434
Crudup, Arthur, 1600
Crummell, Alexander, 660
Cugoano, Ottaban, 1435
Davis, Frank Marshall, 1177
Davis, Ossie, 334, 640, 1312
Douglass, Frederick, 1755
Du Bois, W.E.B., 641, 771
Evans, Minnie, 292
Evers, Medgar, 1178
Farrakhan, Louis, 168
Foreman, George, 702
Fortune, T. Thomas, 591, 2262
Garvey, Marcus, 642, 1315, 1917
Gaye, Marvin, 643
Giovanni, Nikki, 644, 1818
Gomes, Peter J., 1195
Gossett, Louis Jr., 645
Haley, Alex, 783
Himes, Chester, 1654
Holiday, Billie, 721
Hooks, Benjamin, 2312
Hurston, Zora Neale, 955
Jackson, Jesse, 1270
Jones, Quincy, 722
Joplin, Scott, 1477
Kincaid, Jamaica, 1551
King, Coretta Scott, 182
King, Martin Luther Jr., 31, 601, 646,
    1711
Lawrence-Lightfoot, Sara, 793
Love, Nat "Deadwood Dick, the
    cowboy adventurer," 647, 1426
Lowery, Joseph, 648, 723
McKay, Claude, 1805
Morrison, Toni, 2403
Moses, Bob, 1714
Moss, Otis, 934
Muhammad, Elijah, 1220
Naylor, Gloria, 1429
Paige, Satchel, 2447
Parks, Gordon, 344
Pickens, William, 2224
Powell, Adam Clayton Jr., 1085
Randolph, A. Philip, 2203
Rivers, Eugene, 1142
Robeson, Paul, 191, 1197
Simone, Timothy M., 375
Stewart, Maria W., 649
Taylor, Gardner C., 488
Toomer, Jean, 892
Truth, Sojourner, 611, 650

Tubman, Harriet, 651, 1832, 2333
Walker, David, 198
Wells, Ida B., 1807
West, Cornel, 2465
Wheatley, Phillis, 652
Wright, Richard, 653
X, Malcolm, 654, 2210
Young, Andrew, 655

Declaration of Independence
Franklin, John Hope, 656

Defeat
Abdul Jabbar, Kareem, 1451
Angelou, Maya, 657
Benson, Janice Hall, 869
Burroughs, Nannie, 6
Clark, Joe, 658
Holiday, Billie, 893
Johnson, James Weldon, 2077
Robeson, Paul, 961
Waters, Ethel, 680
Wright, Richard, 420

Degradation
Franklin, John Hope, 1107
Robeson, Paul, 447
Washington, Booker T., 2481
West, Cornel, 411

Delany, Martin
Douglass, Frederick, 389

Democracy
Brown, William Wells, 1913
Chisholm, Shirley, 659
Crummell, Alexander, 660
Du Bois, W.E.B., 661, 1762
Giovanni, Nikki, 662
Grimke, Francis J., 2330
Guinier, Lani, 663
King, Martin Luther Jr., 664
King, Melvin H., 1585
Locke, Alain, 665, 666
Marshall, Thurgood, 667
Miller, Thomas E., 668
Pickens, William, 669
Randolph, A. Philip, 842, 2202
Roman, Charles V., 670
Washington, Booker T., 2051
West, Cornel, 354, 671, 672, 673, 1173, 1205
Woodson, Carter G., 226

Democratic Party
Brown, Ronald H., 1569

Du Bois, W.E.B., 1579
Hamer, Fannie Lou, 1580
King, Melvin H., 1585

Denial
Lessing, Doris, 1156
Lowery, Joseph, 340
Powell, Adam Clayton Jr., 958

Descendants
Ali, Muhammad, 134
Crummell, Alexander, 211
Garvey, Marcus, 213
Hawthorne, Nathaniel, 1685
Mays, Benjamin, 217
Washington, Booker T., 223

Desegregation
Killens, John O., 674
King, Martin Luther Jr., 1305

Despair
Chesnutt, Charles W., 1151
Moss, Otis, 487
West, Cornel, 675

Destination *see also* **Journeys; Travel**
Angelou, Maya, 66
Baldwin, James, 1355
Gomes, Peter J., 11
King, Martin Luther Jr., 682
Louis, Joe, 1000

Destiny *see also* **Fate**
Bailey, Pearl, 911
Baldwin, James, 141
Bruce, Blanche K., 403
Clark, Kenneth B., 676
Cone, James, 917
Delany, Martin R., 1952
Douglass, Frederick, 2326
Dunham, Katherine, 1651
Franklin, C.L., 1892
Garvey, Marcus, 1653
Gaye, Marvin, 253
Gregory, Dick, 171
Love, Nat "Deadwood Dick, the cowboy adventurer," 933
Tubman, Harriet, 677
Turner, Henry McNeal, 1029
Walters, Alexander, 2460

Destruction
Baldwin, James, 1071
Baraka, Amiri, 283
Brown, William Wells, 569

Burroughs, Nannie, 2301
Cleaver, Eldridge, 153
Du Bois, W.E.B., 769
Ellison, Ralph, 291
Fortune, T. Thomas, 84
Garvey, Marcus, 551, 1189
Jackson, Jesse, 1455
Muhammad, Elijah, 1220
Schomburg, Arthur, 1119
Thurman, Howard, 891
Wilson, Joseph, 1719

Dignity
Anonymous, 907
Bethune, Mary McLeod, 2412
Cooper, Anna Julia, 2354
Dunbar, Paul Laurence, 1445
Dyson, Michael Eric, 678
Johnson, Sargent, 260
King, Martin Luther Jr., 396, 2476
McKay, Claude, 679
Murray, Pauli, 738
Robeson, Paul, 1528
Washington, Booker T., 2482
Waters, Ethel, 680

Direction
Beckwourth, Jim, 681
Clarke, John Henrik, 1101
Ellington, Duke, 1252
King, Martin Luther Jr., 682
Walker, Mme. C.J., 683

Discipline
Evans, Mari, 684
Rudolph, Wilma, 685

Discrimination
Appiah, Anthony, 1659
Clinton, Bill, 1979
Coffin, Frank M., 51
Edelman, Marian Wright, 52
Franklin, John Hope, 1107, 1706
Hampton, Lionel, 370
Hastie, William H., 214
Hurston, Zora Neale, 1844
Marshall, Thurgood, 57
Reeves, Keith W., 60
Strickland, William, 1430
Washington, Booker T., 1644
Williams, Bert, 2245

Dissent *see also* **Protest**
King, Martin Luther Jr., 686, 687

Diversity
Benson, Janice Hall, 754
Berry, Mary Frances, 1100
Carnesale, Albert, 50
Chisholm, Shirley, 688
Cole, Johnnetta, 871
Cotter, Joseph S., 1662
Crite, Allan Rohan, 1153
Dyson, Michael Eric, 308
Ellison, Ralph, 689
Gates, Henry Louis Jr., 690, 691, 692, 693, 1148
Jackson, Jesse, 175, 176, 694
King, Martin Luther Jr., 695
Nelson, Jill, 696
Sharpton, Al, 697
Toomer, Jean, 1669

Dominant society
Guinier, Lani, 663
Miller, Thomas E., 668
Roman, Charles V., 670
Woodson, Carter G., 364

Double standard
Terrell, Mary Church, 1458

Douglass, Frederick
Chipman, Charles P., 760
Taylor, Susan, 1323

Dreams *see also* **Hope**
Ali, Muhammad, 1928
Angelou, Maya, 210, 1149, 2485
Baldwin, James, 144, 698, 699
Ballard, Florence, 1131
Bambara, Toni Cade, 700
Bethune, Mary McLeod, 2319
Carver, George Washington, 2217
Chesnutt, Charles W., 2496
Danky, James P., 1683
Dinkins, David, 701
Du Bois, W.E.B., 1414
Foreman, George, 702
Futrell, Mary, 703
Garvey, Marcus, 9
Gomes, Peter J., 2424
Gray, Kimi, 704
Gray, William H. III, 1749
Harding, Vincent, 574
Himes, Chester, 1898
Hughes, Langston, 1056
Hurston, Zora Neale, 705, 706, 1136, 2369
Jackson, Jesse, 707, 2313

Johnson, John H., 2222
King, Martin Luther Jr., 184, 708
Lorde, Audre, 1557
Mays, Benjamin, 709
Parks, Henry, 710
Robeson, Paul, 220
Ross, Diana, 711
Sutton, Percy, 625, 712
Taylor, Susan, 713
Thurman, Howard, 714, 715, 716
Toomer, Jean, 2455
Williams, Bert, 2246
Williams, Sherley Anne, 717
Winfrey, Oprah, 718

Drugs
Baldwin, James, 719
Clifton, Lucille, 720
Holiday, Billie, 721
Jones, Quincy, 722
Lowery, Joseph, 723
Morley, Jefferson, 1219
Riley, Dorothy, 724
X, Malcolm, 725

Du Bois, W.E.B.
Gates, Henry Louis Jr., 848

Dukakis, Michael
Jackson, Jesse, 1581

Dumas, Alexandre
Du Bois, W.E.B., 1890

Dunbar, Paul
Mays, Benjamin, 1369

Duty see **Responsibility**

Economics
Bethune, Mary McLeod, 726
Bond, Julian, 727
Chisholm, Shirley, 688
Clark, Kenneth B., 532, 676
Clarke, John Henrik, 728
Cosby, Camille, 729
Davis, Angela, 1703
Du Bois, W.E.B., 770, 977, 1762, 2303
Farrakhan, Louis, 730
Fortune, T. Thomas, 731
Garvey, Marcus, 1606
Hancock, Gordon Blaine, 732, 733
Harper, Frances Ellen Watkins, 734
Hughes, Langston, 735
Jackson, Jesse, 2313
Jordan, Barbara, 789

Malvreaux, Julianne, 736
McKay, Claude, 737
Murray, Pauli, 738
Powell, Adam Clayton Jr., 739, 1307
Randolph, A. Philip, 2202
Stewart, Maria W., 740
Sundiata, Ibrahim K., 1796
Truth, Sojourner, 2386
Washington, Booker T., 741, 742, 743,
    815, 820, 946, 2053
White, Walter, 744
Williams, Eddie N., 745
Woodson, Carter G., 746

Education
Adams, Charles G., 747
Ali, Muhammad, 748
Angelou, Maya, 749
Anonymous, 750, 751, 1843
Baldwin, James, 752, 1097, 1213
Bennett, Lerone, 753
Benson, Janice Hall, 754
Berry, Mary Frances, 1100
Bethune, Mary McLeod, 2412
Bond, Julian, 2315
Bowen, J.W.E., 1203
Boyd, Julia, 755
Carnesale, Albert, 756
Carson, Sonya, 757
Carver, George Washington, 758
Chapman, Melvin, 2415
Childress, Alice, 759, 1701
Chipman, Charles P., 760
Cleaver, Eldridge, 1152
Cochran, Johnnie J., 1625
Cole, Johnnetta, 761, 762
Collins, Marva, 763, 764
Cone, James, 765
Douglass, Frederick, 766, 767, 1705
Du Bois, W.E.B., 768, 769, 770, 771
Edwards, Audrey; Polite, Craig K., 772
Elders, Joycelyn, 773
Ellison, Ralph, 774, 775
Evans, Mari, 776
Flake, Floyd, 987
Fortune, T. Thomas, 84
Franklin, John Hope, 777
Frazier, E. Franklin, 778
Futrell, Mary, 779
Garvey, Marcus, 780, 781, 2076
Gates, Henry Louis Jr., 120, 693
Gayle, Addison Jr., 363
Griffin, Judith, 782

Guinier, Lani, 55
Haley, Alex, 783
Hall, Prince, 784
Hancock, Gordon Blaine, 785
Hogan, Bessie, 786
Hughes, Langston, 787
Hurston, Zora Neale, 788
Jackson, Jesse, 2219
Jordan, Barbara, 789
Killens, John O., 674
King, B.B., 790
King, Coretta Scott, 2295
King, Martin Luther Jr., 791, 792
Lawrence-Lightfoot, Sara, 793
Lee, Benjamin, 794
Love, Nat "Deadwood Dick, the
    cowboy adventurer," 795, 1737
Makeba, Miriam, 796, 797
Mayfield, Curtis, 798
Mays, Benjamin, 799, 836
McCall, Nathan, 800
Mfume, Kweisi, 801
Morrison, Toni, 802
Moutoussamy-Ashe, Jeanne, 48
Muhammad, Elijah, 803, 804, 1941
Palmer, Aynim, 805
Parks, Gordon, 1961
Parks, Rosa, 608
Paul, Nathaniel, 345
Payton, Benjamin, 806
Pennington, James W.C., 807
Poussaint, Alvin, 808
Queen Mother Moore, 1230
Reed, Ishmael, 809
Rudenstein, Neil L., 61
Ruggles, David, 1623
Rustin, Bayard, 844
Sahibs, Abdulalim, 810
Schomburg, Arthur, 1531
Shipler, David K., 1668
Smitherman, Geneva, 1299
Solomon, Charlene, 811, 1943
Stewart, Maria W., 111
Sullivan, Leon, 1740
Terrell, Mary Church, 113
Toomer, Jean, 812
Walker, David, 813
Washington, Booker T., 741, 814, 815,
    816, 817, 818, 819, 820, 821, 822,
    823, 1964, 2463
Wells, Ida B., 824
Whipper, William S., 1222
White, Walter, 744

Woodson, Carter G., 364, 825, 826, 827,
    828, 1530, 2062, 2275
X, Malcolm, 829, 1046

Egypt
Anonymous, 68, 2092, 2103
Asante, Molefi, 71
Douglass, Frederick, 81
Johns, Vernon, 1023
Truth, Sojourner, 1504
Wheatley, Phillis, 947

Elections *see* **Voting**

Emancipation *see also* **Liberation**
Bruce, Blanche K., 1914
Bruce, H.C., 830
Douglass, Frederick, 831, 832
Du Bois, W.E.B., 833, 1328, 1915
Hurston, Zora Neale, 928
Owens, Jesse, 1527
Washington, Booker T., 834

Emotion
Alexander, Elizabeth, 1282
Chisholm, Shirley, 974
Douglas, Aaron, 289
Handy, W.C., 416
Locke, Alain, 126, 623, 2079
Robinson, Jackie, 2176
Wright, Richard, 458

Employment *see* **Jobs**

Encouragement
Bibb, Henry, 524
Brown, William Wells, 1913
Carmichael, Stokely, 546
Cole, Johnnetta, 2353
Coleman, Bessie, 587
Hansberry, Lorraine, 1820
King, Martin Luther Jr., 687
Lawrence, Jacob, 556
Mays, Benjamin, 836
Washington, Booker T., 223

Endurance *see also* **Perseverance**
Bruce, Blanche K., 403
Cone, James, 837

Energy
Baldwin, James, 230
Bearden, Romare, 240
Harper, Frances Ellen Watkins, 927
Lorde, Audre, 1525
Neal, Larry, 502

Nunez, Elizabeth, 1297
Young, Andrew, 2396

England
Craft, Ellen, 2020
Terrell, Mary Church, 113

Entertainment
Baker, Josephine, 1364
Hampton, Lionel, 370
Mayfield, Curtis, 798
Waters, Ethel, 2012

Entrepreneurship *see* **Business**

Environment
Brewer, J. Mason, 125
Cole, Johnnetta, 871
Ellison, Ralph, 774
Grier, William; Cobb, Price, 469
Lawrence, Jacob, 263

Envy
Marrant, John, 1440
West, Cornel, 563
X, Malcolm, 2228

Equal opportunity
Anonymous, 1843
Bethune, Mary McLeod, 73
Carnesale, Albert, 756
Coffin, Frank M., 51
Rudenstein, Neil L., 61
West, Cornel, 489

Equality *see also* **Inequality**
Ali, Muhammad, 1693
Anonymous, 907
Bell, Derrick, 1696
Bunche, Ralph, 404
Chisholm, Shirley, 688
Douglass, Frederick, 976, 1266
Du Bois, W.E.B., 838
Fauset, Jessie, 839
Franklin, John Hope, 777
Hope, John, 840
Jackson, Jesse, 12
Johnson, Lyndon B., 514
Mars, James N., 2039
Marshall, Thurgood, 667, 841
Parks, Rosa, 936
Powell, Colin, 58
Randolph, A. Philip, 842, 843, 2202
Rustin, Bayard, 844, 845
Taylor, Susie King, 846
Truth, Sojourner, 38

Walker, Alice, 2207
Washington, Booker T., 847
West, Cornel, 1173
Woodson, Carter G., 825

Ethiopia
Anonymous, 68, 535
Du Bois, W.E.B., 163
Garvey, Marcus, 88, 1018

Ethnicity *see also* **Race**
Brown, Ronald H., 1569
Gates, Henry Louis Jr., 848, 1191

Eurocentrism
Asante, Molefi, 127

Europe
Anderson, Marian, 136
Appiah, Anthony, 69
Baldwin, James, 1243, 1245
Bearden, Romare, 237
Clarke, John Henrik, 1702
Du Bois, W.E.B., 661
Ellington, Duke, 250
Ellison, Ralph, 2290
Garvey, Marcus, 90
Johnson, William H., 393
Priestly, J.B., 1724
Turner, Darwin T., 1363
Wells, Ida B., 1410
West, Cornel, 115
Wilson, Joseph, 1719

Everyday people *see* **Average people**

Evil
Baldwin, James, 849
Brown, William Wells, 148
Chesnutt, Charles W., 24, 1620
Du Bois, W.E.B., 1889
Grace, Sweet Daddy, 1781
Gregory, Dick, 171
Hancock, Gordon Blaine, 497
Hastie, William H., 850
King, Martin Luther Jr., 1386, 1457
Morrison, Toni, 851, 852
Muhammad, Herbert, 853
Reverend Ike, 1449
Turner, Nat, 1758
West, Cornel, 854
Whipper, William S., 1649

Excuses
Ashe, Arthur, 991
Douglass, Frederick, 2025

Hill, Anita, 980
Jordan, Michael, 599

Expectations
Brown, Les, 855
Cone, James, 1746
Gomes, Peter J., 2424
Grier, William; Cobb, Price, 469
Jordan, Michael, 856
Wonder, Stevie, 1967

Experience *see also* **Black experience**
Angelou, Maya, 657
Baldwin, James, 141, 857, 2494
Cone, James, 765
Forman, James, 1817
Himes, Chester, 1898
Johnson, Charles, 2500
Lawrence, Jacob, 297, 622
Lee-Smith, Hughie, 265
Locke, Alain, 1059, 2079
Murray, Albert, 1258
Parker, Charlie, 1482
Shipler, David K., 1668
Smith, Barbara, 1717
Sowell, Thomas, 46
Sullivan, Leon, 2480
Toomer, Jean, 1397
Tubman, Harriet, 941
Walker, Alice, 1926
Wilkins, Roy, 1124

Exploitation
Farrakhan, Louis, 858
Garvey, Marcus, 1228, 2292
King, Martin Luther Jr., 446
Queen Mother Moore, 1794
West, Cornel, 2239
White, Walter, 744
Woodson, Carter G., 1978

Ezekiel
Anonymous, 2089

Failure
Angelou, Maya, 1149
Bambara, Toni Cade, 700
Coppin, Frances, 859
Du Bois, W.E.B., 1313
Edelman, Marian Wright, 2059
Gates, Henry Louis Jr., 121
Graves, Earl G. Jr., 860
Jordan, Michael, 598
McGriff, Deborah, 861
Parks, Gordon, 2223

Powell, Colin, 2226
Solomon, Charlene, 811
Thurman, Howard, 1045
Winfrey, Oprah, 862

Faith *see also* **Beliefs; Religion**
Bethune, Mary McLeod, 1170, 2412
Cheatham, Michael J., 863
Du Bois, W.E.B., 2417
Dyson, Michael Eric, 864
Farrakhan, Louis, 1776
Franklin, C.L., 865
Garvey, Marcus, 593
Gates, Henry Louis Jr., 572
Haynes, Lemuel, 866
Jackson, Jesse, 2313
James, Chappie, 1542
Jordan, Barbara, 576
Jordan, June, 867
Joyner, Florence Griffith, 2436
Owens, Jesse, 2446
Polly, 1026
Powell, Adam Clayton Jr., 610, 1788
Powell, Colin, 959
Walker, Alice, 1031
Walters, Alexander, 2460
Washington, Harold, 2208
Winfrey, Oprah, 950

Family *see also* **Children**
Ailey, Alvin, 2467
Angelou, Maya, 749
Anonymous, 899
Baldwin, James, 868
Benson, Janice Hall, 869
Blige, Mary J., 2347
Boyd, Julia, 755
Buckley, Gail Lumet, 870
Carson, Benjamin, 494
Cole, Johnnetta, 871
Douglass, Frederick, 872, 873, 2058
Edelman, Marian Wright, 874
Gates, Henry Louis Jr., 1190
Haley, Alex, 875
Hamer, Fannie Lou, 1993
Hastie, William H., 876
Holiday, Billie, 1412
Johnson, William H., 393
LaBelle, Patti, 1862
Lee-Smith, Hughie, 298
Love, Nat "Deadwood Dick, the
    cowboy adventurer," 1737
McDowell, Deborah E., 2375
Parks, Rosa, 936

Powell, Adam Clayton Jr., 559, 1942
Powell, Colin, 2307
Queen Mother Moore, 1794
Robeson, Paul, 877
Sherman, William T., 1795
Solomon, Charlene, 811, 1943
Thurman, Howard, 878, 879
Walker, Alice, 626, 1944
Walker, David, 198, 1806
Washington, Booker T., 1279
Washington, James M., 428, 1615
Wilson, William Julius, 2484
X, Malcolm, 1199

Fate *see also* **Destiny**
Chesnutt, Charles W., 880
Ellison, Ralph, 166, 881

Fathers *see* **Family**

Faulkner, William
West, Cornel, 419

Fear
Angelou, Maya, 882
Baldwin, James, 698, 883, 1074
Brawley, Tawana, 884
Clark, Kenneth B., 532
Clarke, John Henrik, 77
Cosby, Bill, 589
Dee, Ruby, 885
Du Bois, W.E.B., 2260
Durr, Virginia, 511
Farrakhan, Louis, 1454
Garvey, Amy Jacques, 1404
Gaye, Marvin, 886
Gregory, Dick, 926
Hancock, Gordon Blaine, 1637
Holyfield, Evander, 887
Hughes, Langston, 1872
Jacobs, Harriet, 177, 2038
Jakes, T.D., 2221
Johnson, Jack, 338
Lorde, Audre, 888, 1863
Madhubuti, Haki, 2402
Miller, Thomas E., 668
Parks, Gordon, 344, 2223
Parks, Rosa, 608
Robinson, Jackie, 889
Rustin, Bayard, 890
Stewart, Maria W., 1856
Thurman, Howard, 891
Toomer, Jean, 892

Walker, Alice, 944
Walker, David, 813
Washington, Booker T., 821

Fellowship
Baraka, Amiri, 282
Bethune, Mary McLeod, 1377
Brown, William Wells, 149
Ellison, Ralph, 166
Parks, Rosa, 219
Walker, David, 197

Feminism
Smith, Barbara, 983

Fighting
Ali, Muhammad, 134, 1693
Anderson, Marian, 1443
Bethune, Mary McLeod, 386
Carmichael, Stokely, 450
Chisholm, Shirley, 1225
Du Bois, W.E.B., 771, 2289
Fauset, Jessie, 839
Fortune, T. Thomas, 2218
Garvey, Amy Jacques, 1955
Griggs, Sutton E., 1736
Grimke, Charlotte Forten, 2329
Haley, Alex, 2425
Henderson, Stephen, 1347
Holiday, Billie, 893
Hooks, Benjamin, 2312
Hurston, Zora Neale, 894
Jones, Quincy, 2435
Killens, John O., 395, 674
Primus, Pearl, 635
Queen Mother Moore, 1794
Randolph, A. Philip, 2202
Robeson, Paul, 302, 1528
Robinson, Jackie, 1808
Robinson, Sugar Ray, 2177
Steele, Shelby, 1515
Tubman, Harriet, 1338
Walker, Alice, 1908
Waters, Ethel, 2238
Weaver, Robert C., 2464
Wells, Ida B., 1807
West, Cornel, 1004
X, Malcolm, 1162, 2210

Films
Baldwin, James, 2242
Marshall, Thurgood, 578
Robeson, Paul, 105, 1197

First Amendment
Gates, Henry Louis Jr., 572, 1290
Marshall, Thurgood, 578

Flags
Carney, William H., 584
Jackson, Jesse, 694
Moseley-Braun, Carol, 567
Turner, Henry McNeal, 906

Folklore
Hurston, Zora Neale, 904

Fourth of July
Douglass, Frederick, 905
Turner, Henry McNeal, 906

France *see also* **Paris**
Baldwin, James, 1885
Cleaver, Kathleen, 533
Du Bois, W.E.B., 1816
Johnson, James Weldon, 1540

Franklin, Aretha
West, Cornel, 1004

Freedom *see also* **Liberation; Liberty**
Ali, Muhammad, 1650, 1693, 1929
Allen, Richard, 135
Anonymous, 907, 908, 909, 910, 2090, 2096, 2105, 2120, 2137
Bailey, Pearl, 911
Baldwin, James, 143, 328, 912, 913, 1537
Baraka, Amiri, 914
Brown, H. Rap, 1699
Brown, John, 23
Brown, William Wells, 569
Bunche, Ralph, 915
Carver, George Washington, 758
Charles, RuPaul, 1931
Cinque, Joseph, 1434
Cole, Johnnetta, 916
Coleman, Ornette, 2074
Cone, James, 837, 917, 918, 1265
Craft, Ellen, 2020
Davis, Angela, 1798
Davis, Miles, 1468
Debro, Sarah, 156
Dinkins, David, 919, 1636
Douglass, Frederick, 920, 1756, 2025
Dove, Rita, 421
Du Bois, W.E.B., 833, 921, 922, 1134, 1154
Ellington, Duke, 1251
Forten, James, 1664
Fortune, T. Thomas, 591

Futrell, Mary, 779
Gandhi, Mohandas K., 1916
Garnet, Henry Highland, 592
Garvey, Amy Jacques, 923
Garvey, Marcus, 87, 924, 1917, 1956, 2193
Gates, Henry Louis Jr., 1359
Giddings, Paula, 997
Gillespie, Dizzy, 925
Giovanni, Nikki, 644
Gomes, Peter J., 133
Gregory, Dick, 926
Grimke, Charlotte Forten, 2329
Harding, Vincent, 574
Harper, Frances Ellen Watkins, 927
Hooks, Benjamin, 1492
Hurston, Zora Neale, 928
King, Coretta Scott, 182
King, Martin Luther Jr., 31, 516, 601, 646, 929, 930, 931, 932
Locke, Alain, 1069
Love, Nat "Deadwood Dick, the cowboy adventurer," 933
Mars, James N., 2039
Marshall, Thurgood, 577
Mays, Benjamin, 217
Mosley, Walter, 418
Moss, Otis, 934
Owens, Jesse, 1527
Parks, Rosa, 33, 935, 936, 1260, 1655
Prosser, Gabriel, 1757
Randolph, A. Philip, 842, 937, 1826, 1923, 2202
Robeson, Paul, 302, 938, 939, 2069, 2204, 2205, 2511
Scott, Hazel, 940
Shabazz, Betty, 1924
Shuttlesworth, Fred, 520
Smith, Barbara, 983
Smith, Venture, 193
Taylor, Susie King, 846
Truth, Sojourner, 38
Tubman, Harriet, 941, 942, 2046, 2278
Turner, Henry McNeal, 835
Turner, Nat, 1759
Turner, Tina, 943
Walker, Alice, 196, 944
Walker, David, 945
Washington, Booker T., 820, 834, 946, 2049
Watts, Herman, 1032
Wells, Ida B., 1408
West, Cornel, 1173, 1976

Wheatley, Phillis, 947
White, Walter, 948
Wilson, August, 949
Winfrey, Oprah, 950
Woodbey, George W., 448
Woodson, Carter G., 951
Wright, Richard, 653
X, Malcolm, 1162, 1555, 1611, 1634

Friends
Anonymous, 901
Bambara, Toni Cade, 700
Jones, Quincy, 2435
Morrison, Toni, 2376
Stewart, Maria W., 1856
Walker, Alice, 952
Washington, Booker T., 1965
Winfrey, Oprah, 953

Future
Baldwin, James, 699, 1096, 1505
Buckley, Gail Lumet, 870
Cheatham, Michael J., 863
Cone, James, 1746
Cosby, Bill, 2252
DeFrantz, Anita, 954
Donaldson, Greg, 464
Du Bois, W.E.B., 381, 977
Dvorak, Anton, 1470
Edelin, Kenneth C., 466
Edelman, Marian Wright, 874, 2059
Ellison, Ralph, 2419
Evans, Mari, 776
Flake, Floyd, 987
Hughes, Langston, 1851
Hurston, Zora Neale, 955
Jackson, Jesse, 694
Johnson, James Weldon, 956
King, Martin Luther Jr., 396, 1024
Ladd, Florence, 2372
Locke, Alain, 957
Love, Nat "Deadwood Dick, the
   cowboy adventurer," 933
Moses, Michael, 472
Powell, Adam Clayton Jr., 958
Powell, Colin, 959, 960
Robeson, Paul, 961, 962
Ross, Diana, 963
Schomburg, Arthur, 1118
Simone, Timothy M., 2512
Walker, Alice, 944, 2207
Welsing, Frances Cress, 479
West, Cornel, 1326
Winfrey, Oprah, 964

Wright, Richard, 1677
X, Malcolm, 829

Gays and lesbians
Elders, Joycelyn, 965
Farajaje-Jones, Elias, 966
Gates, Henry Louis Jr., 1191
Gomes, Peter J., 967
Johnson, Magic, 1996
Little Richard, 968
Lorde, Audre, 969
Monroe, Irene, 501
Munroe, Roberta M., 970
Nugent, Bruce, 971
Smith, Barbara, 983
West, Cornel, 128

Gender see also **Men; Women**
Adam, Andrea Thompson, 972
Baldwin, James, 973
Chisholm, Shirley, 974, 975, 2349
Douglass, Frederick, 976
Du Bois, W.E.B., 977
Edelman, Marian Wright, 52
Gates, Henry Louis Jr., 691, 1191
Higginbotham, Evelyn Brooks, 978, 979
Hill, Anita, 980
Jacobs, Harriet, 981
Jemison, Mae, 982
Lee, Jarena, 1617
Monroe, Irene, 501
Smith, Barbara, 983
Winfrey, Oprah, 984

Genocide
Baldwin, James, 719
Cone, James, 985
Jones, Nettie, 1876

Geography
Appiah, Anthony, 69
Baldwin, James, 72
Clarke, John Henrik, 78, 1101

Georgia
King, Martin Luther Jr., 708, 1804
Wilson, August, 564

Ghettos
Baldwin, James, 227, 719, 986, 1948
Bunche, Ralph, 531
Clark, Kenneth B., 532
Flake, Floyd, 987
Gates, Henry Louis Jr., 122
Jackson, Jesse, 597
King, Martin Luther Jr., 988

Wideman, John Edgar, 989
Woodson, Carter G., 1988
X, Malcolm, 1007

Giuliani, Rudolph
Sharpton, Al, 1039

Giving
Campbell, Naomi, 1835
Jamison, Judith, 629
Queen Mother Moore, 1230
Robeson, Paul, 990

Goals *see also* **Purpose**
Ashe, Arthur, 991
Bechet, Sidney, 992
Carnesale, Albert, 756
Collins, Marva, 1367
Crummell, Alexander, 993
Douglass, Frederick, 994
Ellison, Ralph, 995
Fischer, Rudolph, 2421
Garvey, Marcus, 996, 1653
Gates, Henry Louis Jr., 1216, 2499
Giddings, Paula, 997
Height, Dorothy, 998
Hurston, Zora Neale, 2427
Johnson, John H., 2222
Joyner-Kersee, Jackie, 999
King, Martin Luther Jr., 791
Louis, Joe, 1000
Mays, Benjamin, 1001
Price, Leontyne, 2451
Randolph, A. Philip, 2203
Rudolph, Wilma, 1002
Steward, Rebecca, 1172
Wallace, Michelle, 1003
West, Cornel, 1004
Williams, Robert, 1005
Winfrey, Oprah, 2071
Woodruff, Hale, 1006
X, Malcolm, 1007

God *see also* **Lord**
Ali, Muhammad, 2
Ali, Noble Drew, 1499
Angelou, Maya, 2282
Anonymous, 68, 493, 2090, 2149, 2151,
    2162, 2166
Bailey, Pearl, 1008
Baldwin, Alfred, 1772
Baldwin, James, 638, 1009, 1010
Banneker, Benjamin, 385
Bethune, Mary McLeod, 1170
Brown, William Wells, 2016

Carson, Benjamin, 494
Carver, George Washington, 1011
Charles, Ray, 585
Chesnutt, Charles W., 1151
Cone, James, 837
Cosby, Camille, 1012
Douglass, Frederick, 389, 1013, 2022
Du Bois, W.E.B., 1014, 1134, 1380
Edmondson, William, 249
Ellington, Duke, 1612
Farrakhan, Louis, 1015, 1077
Father Divine, 1016, 1017
Forten, James, 1664
Franklin, C.L., 865
Garnet, Henry Highland, 1336
Garvey, Marcus, 318, 1018, 1189, 1228,
    1421, 1653
Gomes, Peter J., 1019, 1020, 1346
Grace, Sweet Daddy, 1779, 1780
Griggs, Sutton E., 2033
Hall, Prince, 539
Harper, Frances Ellen Watkins, 927,
    1812
Harrison, Richard B., 1021
Haynes, Lemuel, 1897
Jackson, Jesse, 1455
Jackson, Mahalia, 1813
Jakes, T.D., 1022, 1497
Johns, Vernon, 1023
Jones, Nettie, 1876
Jones, Quincy, 2435
Joyner, Florence Griffith, 2436
King, Martin Luther Jr., 407, 499, 932,
    1024, 1829, 2323
Lee, Jarena, 2373
Mason, Charles H., 1785
Mays, Benjamin, 2442
McGuire, George Alexander, 1025
Moore, Melba, 1157
Polly, 1026
Ransom, Reverdy C., 1027
Shabazz, Betty, 2454
Stewart, Maria W., 1856
Taylor, Susie King, 846
Toomer, Jean, 2232
Truth, Sojourner, 400, 1028, 2388, 2389
Turner, Henry McNeal, 1029, 1030
Walker, Alice, 1031
Walker, Charles T., 1432
Walker, David, 324, 945, 1332, 1841
Walters, Alexander, 2460
Washington, James M., 1615
Watts, Herman, 1032

Weems, Renita, 1033
Wheatley, Phillis, 947
Winfrey, Oprah, 1034
Wolfe, George C., 2215
X, Malcolm, 1050, 1199
Young, Andrew, 522

Goodness
Brown, William Wells, 148
Douglass, Frederick, 158
Father Divine, 1016
Jordan, Barbara, 179
King, Martin Luther Jr., 1457
Owens, Jesse, 2446
Washington, Harold, 2208
West, Cornel, 2272

Government
Bradley, Thomas, 1035
Brennan, William J., 49
Chesnutt, Charles W., 1264
Douglass, Frederick, 832, 1036
Flake, Floyd, 987
Harper, Frances Ellen Watkins, 1037,
   1038
Johnson, James Weldon, 1821
Lowery, Joseph, 56
Marshall, Thurgood, 577
Sharpton, Al, 1039
Simmons, Della, 2478
Waters, Maxine, 1760
Weaver, Robert C., 1040
West, Cornel, 1041, 1761
Wills, Frank, 1042

Grace
Anonymous, 901, 2080, 2100
Ellington, Duke, 616
Grace, Sweet Daddy, 1780
Jackson, Jesse, 2313
Locke, Alain, 266
Mays, Benjamin, 2442
Morrison, Toni, 1296

Great Britain
Delany, Martin R., 1501

Greatness
Ali, Muhammad, 2169
Baldwin, James, 232
Davis, Miles, 615
Douglass, Frederick, 81
Garvey, Marcus, 213, 1422
Gaye, Marvin, 293
Height, Dorothy, 998

Hood, James Walker, 1512
Johnson, James Weldon, 259
Jordan, Michael, 598
King, Martin Luther Jr., 183, 396, 1986
Mays, Benjamin, 1987
Poussaint, Alvin, 2306
Stewart, Maria W., 194
Winfrey, Oprah, 862

Greece
Asante, Molefi, 71
Robeson, Paul, 103
Stewart, Maria W., 111

Greed
Baldwin, James, 699
Clark, Kenneth B., 532
Fortune, T. Thomas, 84
Pennington, James W.C., 189

Green, Shields
Douglass, Frederick, 1755

Growth
Anonymous, 899, 902
Baldwin, James, 1373
Du Bois, W.E.B., 429
Ellison, Ralph, 1043
Farrakhan, Louis, 1044, 1077
Franklin, Aretha, 44
Garvey, Marcus, 2031
Holiday, Billie, 1602
Hughes, Langston, 2066
King, Martin Luther Jr., 1900
Macmillan, Harold, 97
Parks, Rosa, 1655
Sanchez, Sonia, 45
Thurman, Howard, 1045
Walker, Alice, 952
Washington, Booker T., 2309
West, Cornel, 278, 1881
X, Malcolm, 1046

Guilt
Baldwin, James, 699
Brown, John, 147
Carroll, Diahann, 1047, 2470
Clark, Kenneth B., 532
Garvey, Amy Jacques, 1404
Lessing, Doris, 1156
Turner, Henry McNeal, 1407

Hair
Brown, Tony, 1048
Davis, Miles, 1379
Davis, Ossie, 314

Equiano, Olaudah, 1436
Garvey, Marcus, 2031
Golden, Marita, 1049
Johnson, Sargent, 260
Muhammad, Elijah, 1878
X, Malcolm, 1050, 1884

Hamer, Fannie Lou
Winfrey, Oprah, 225

Hamilton, Alexander
Jordan, Barbara, 576

Happiness
Cain, Herman, 2216
Douglass, Frederick, 1439
Du Bois, W.E.B., 1840
Father Divine, 1548
Franklin, Aretha, 2005
Hurston, Zora Neale, 2475
King, Coretta Scott, 2078
King, Martin Luther Jr., 183
Michaux, Solomon Lightfoot, 1786
Northup, Solomon, 373
Van Der Zee, James, 1051
Walker, David, 1433
Wright, Richard, 1912

Hard work *see also* **Work**
Bunche, Ralph, 404
Charles, Ray, 2065
Davis, Sammy Jr., 590
Gibson, Althea, 594, 2336
Hughes, Langston, 1255
Hurston, Zora Neale, 788
Joyner, Florence Griffith, 2436
Love, Nat "Deadwood Dick, the
     cowboy adventurer," 1737
McCall, Nathan, 800
McCarthy, Osceola, 2477
McKay, Claude, 1641
Motley, Archibald Jr., 606
Muhammad, Elijah, 804
Powell, Colin, 2226
Robinson, Bojangles, 2227
Rudolph, Wilma, 2453
Sahibs, Abdulalim, 810
Truth, Sojourner, 2385
Washington, Booker T., 2483
West, Cornel, 568
Wilson, August, 949

Harlem
Baldwin, James, 227, 1150
Bearden, Romare, 238

Dunbar, Paul Laurence, 1052
Gates, Henry Louis Jr., 1053
Hughes, Dorothy Pitman, 440
Hughes, Langston, 1054, 1055, 1056,
     1254
Johnson, James Weldon, 1057
Killens, John O., 1058
Locke, Alain, 1059, 1060, 1061
McKay, Claude, 1062
Morrison, Toni, 1063
Schuyler, George, 1064
X, Malcolm, 1827

Harlem Renaissance
Huggins, Nathan, 1065
Hughes, Langston, 1066
Locke, Alain, 1067, 1068, 1069

Harmony
Bannister, Edward Mitchell, 234
Bruce, John E., 1184
Jones, Quincy, 1985
Parker, Charlie, 624
Robeson, Paul, 1485
Sharpton, Al, 1273

Harvard University
Mays, Benjamin, 799

Hate *see also* **Self-hate**
Anderson, Marian, 1070
Baldwin, James, 699, 1071, 1072, 1073,
     1074
Bethune, Mary McLeod, 1377
Carver, George Washington, 1075
Cleaver, Eldridge, 1076
Douglass, Frederick, 481
Ellison, Ralph, 2290
Farrakhan, Louis, 1077
Frazier, E. Franklin, 1969
Garvey, Marcus, 1078, 1079
Gregory, Dick, 1080
Himes, Chester, 1621
Jacobs, Harriet, 2038
King, Martin Luther Jr., 1457
Miller, Kelly, 1687
Moss, Otis, 487
Parks, Gordon, 344
Russell, Bill, 1395
Strickland, William, 1430, 1594
Thurman, Howard, 476, 1081
Turner, Henry McNeal, 1544
Walker, Alice, 1909
Woodson, Carter G., 401

Wright, Richard, 1882
X, Malcolm, 119, 1720

Haves and have nots *see also* **Poverty**
Edelman, Marian Wright, 2059

Healing
Alexander, Elizabeth, 1282
Angelou, Maya, 1082, 2407
Baldwin, James, 1239
Bethune, Mary McLeod, 1377
Evers-Williams, Myrlie, 1652
Jones, Quincy, 2435
King, Martin Luther Jr., 1506, 2231
X, Malcolm, 1645

Health
Chisholm, Shirley, 1083
Edelin, Kenneth C., 466
Evers-Williams, Myrlie, 1652
McCall, Nathan, 800
Washington, Booker T., 1084

Heaven
Allen, Richard, 1771
Anonymous, 2088, 2125, 2139
Farrakhan, Louis, 169
Johnson, James Weldon; Johnson, J.
    Rosamond, 2008
Powell, Adam Clayton Jr., 1085
Ra, Sun, 1086
Ransom, Reverdy C., 1027

Hell
Carver, George Washington, 1075
Davis, Ossie, 640
Farrakhan, Louis, 169
Garvey, Marcus, 1087
Johnson, James Weldon, 1938
Powell, Adam Clayton Jr., 1085
Tubman, Harriet, 2045

Help
Bailey, Pearl, 21
Drake, St. Clair, 361
Garvey, Marcus, 89
Gibson, Althea, 10
Jakes, T.D., 2220
Owens, Jesse, 473
Robinson, Jackie, 16
Trotter, William Monroe, 37
Washington, Booker T., 1459, 2298
Winfrey, Oprah, 953

Henry, Patrick
Moss, Otis, 934

Heritage
Angelou, Maya, 1088
Baldwin, James, 1885
Carmichael, Stokely, 379
Cinque, Joseph, 586
Clarke, John Henrik, 1814
Cooper, Anna Julia, 2355
Du Bois, W.E.B., 390
Embry, James C., 1496
Gates, Henry Louis Jr., 1423, 2363
Gregory, Dick, 1894
Hughes, Langston, 2490
Lawrence, Jacob, 263, 1089
Locke, Alain, 126
Robeson, Paul, 636
Terrell, Mary Church, 113
Turnage, Jackie, 1090
Tyson, Cecily, 2391
Walker, Alice, 1944
Washington, Booker T., 1279
Wells, Ida B., 1763
Wheatley, Phillis, 1091
X, Malcolm, 1092, 1927

Heroes
Cleaver, Eldridge, 1093
King, Martin Luther Jr., 1094

Heroism
Baldwin, James, 402
Benson, Janice Hall, 869
Cole, Johnnetta, 2353
Davis, Angela, 2358
Paul, Nathaniel, 345
Pickens, William, 1921

History *see also* **Ancestors**
Angelou, Maya, 66, 67
Anonymous, 751, 903, 1095
Aptheker, Herbert, 1797
Baldwin, James, 140, 141, 1096, 1097,
    1098, 1099
Bell, Derrick, 1696
Bennett, Lerone, 523
Benson, Janice Hall, 754
Berry, Mary Frances, 1100
Blockson, Charles L., 2495
Bontemps, Arna, 2251
Charles, Ray, 151
Clark, Kenneth B., 676
Clarke, John Henrik, 1101, 1102
Cole, Johnnetta, 1103, 2019
Cone, James, 154
Cruse, Harold, 1104

DeVore, Donald, 1105
Du Bois, W.E.B., 164, 1663
Ellington, Duke, 1253
Fortune, T. Thomas, 2218
Franklin, C.L., 1892
Franklin, John Hope, 1106, 1107
Garvey, Marcus, 91, 1079
Gates, Henry Louis Jr., 1359
Gregory, Dick, 1108
Haley, Alex, 1109
Hastie, William H., 850
Hawthorne, Nathaniel, 1685
Holt, Thomas, 2035
Hooks, Bell, 2182
Ice Cube, 1727
Killens, John O., 1110, 1111
King, B.B., 1112
King, Coretta Scott, 456
King, Martin Luther Jr., 183, 396, 500, 528
Luis, W.A., 1639
Marshall, Thurgood, 57, 1113, 1337
Matthews, Victoria Earle, 1360
Miller, Kelly, 1114
Miller, Thomas E., 188
Moseley-Braun, Carol, 567
Muhammad, Elijah, 803
Parks, Rosa, 935, 1115, 1260
Porter, Dorothy, 1116
Robeson, Paul, 101, 447, 1117
Savage, Augusta, 350
Schomburg, Arthur, 1118, 1119, 1120, 1121, 1974
Shaw, Nate, 1122
Stewart, Maria W., 111
Sundiata, Ibrahim K., 1123
Terrell, Mary Church, 113
Turner, Henry McNeal, 906
Walker, Wyatt T., 1143
Washington, Booker T., 817
Wells, Ida B., 824
West, Cornel, 115, 419, 1326, 1671
Wilkins, Roy, 123, 1124
Woodson, Carter G., 118, 825, 1125, 1126
Wright, Richard, 358
X, Malcolm, 1127, 1128, 1198, 1416
Young, Andrew, 2211

HIV *see* **AIDS**

Honesty *see also* **Integrity**
Du Bois, W.E.B., 1313
Franklin, John Hope, 656

Hill, Anita, 1129
Murphy, Isaac, 1130
Robinson, Jackie, 1808
Washington, Booker T., 2309

Hope *see also* **Dreams**
Aaron, Hank, 460
Baldwin, James, 144, 973
Ballard, Florence, 1131
Baraka, Amiri, 1132
Bearden, Romare, 240
Bethune, Mary McLeod, 2412
Brown, Claude, 146
Carver, George Washington, 1509
Chesnutt, Charles W., 1133
Cone, James, 1773
Cruse, Harold, 1104
Du Bois, W.E.B., 381, 641, 1134
Durr, Virginia, 453, 511
Garvey, Marcus, 1209
Gomes, Peter J., 2424
Hall, Prince, 2293
Himes, Chester, 1898
Horne, Lena, 1135
Hurston, Zora Neale, 1136
Jackson, Jesse, 1137, 1138, 2313
Jemison, T.J., 1139
Killens, John O., 1140
Kincaid, Jamaica, 1551
King, Martin Luther Jr., 339
Lorde, Audre, 1557
Morrison, Toni, 218
Moss, Otis, 487
Murray, Pauli, 1141
Paige, Satchel, 2450
Rivers, Eugene, 1142
Thurman, Howard, 715
Walker, Wyatt T., 1143
Washington, Booker T., 816, 2462
West, Cornel, 224, 1144, 2239
Winfrey, Oprah, 964
Wright, Richard, 420

Housing
Baldwin, James, 1239
Danky, James P., 1683
Evers-Williams, Myrlie, 1652
Rustin, Bayard, 844

Hughes, Langston
Lawrence, Jacob, 555

Human nature
Bierria, Alisa, 1145

Douglass, Frederick, 1036
Wright, Richard, 1146

Humanism
Baldwin, James, 1147
Gates, Henry Louis Jr., 1148
West, Cornel, 115

Humanities
Rollins, Sonny, 374

Humanity
Adam, Andrea Thompson, 972
Adams, Osceola, 1656
Angelou, Maya, 1149
Anonymous, 907
Baldwin, James, 1150
Chesnutt, Charles W., 1151
Clarke, John Henrik, 728
Cleaver, Eldridge, 1152
Crite, Allan Rohan, 1153
Du Bois, W.E.B., 163, 381, 1154, 2288
Gates, Henry Louis Jr., 1148
Henson, Matthew, 1179
Johnson, James Weldon, 1540
Karenga, Ron, 515
Killens, John O., 1111
King, Coretta Scott, 1155
King, Martin Luther Jr., 2476
Lessing, Doris, 1156
McHenry, Elizabeth, 1196
Miller, Kelly, 1306
Moore, Melba, 1157
Preston, Douglas, 1667
Rogers, J.A., 2378
Truth, Sojourner, 1789
Turner, Henry McNeal, 1158
Walker, Alice, 1431
Washington, Booker T., 1159
Wells, Ida B., 1410
West, Cornel, 530, 1160, 1498, 1596
Whipper, William S., 1649
Woodson, Carter G., 41
Wright, Richard, 508, 1161
X, Malcolm, 1162

Humor
Du Bois, W.E.B., 1163
Ellison, Ralph, 1164
Fauset, Jessie, 1165
Hughes, Langston, 1166
Markham, Pigmeat, 1167
McKay, Claude, 1168
Rollins, Sonny, 374
X, Malcolm, 1169

Hungarians
Delany, Martin R., 1501

Hypocrisy
Douglass, Frederick, 159, 481, 905
Garnet, Henry Highland, 483
X, Malcolm, 1169

Ice Cube
Hooks, Bell, 1292

Ideals
Bannister, Edward Mitchell, 234
Bethune, Mary McLeod, 1170
Du Bois, W.E.B., 163, 2277
Higginbotham, Evelyn Brooks, 2367
Hurston, Zora Neale, 1171
Randolph, A. Philip, 1588
Robeson, Paul, 1197
Steward, Rebecca, 1172
West, Cornel, 673, 1173
Wilkerson, Dianne, 1174
X, Malcolm, 1092, 1927

Ideas *see also* **Creativity; Imagination**
Brown, Ronald H., 1175
Danner, Margaret, 1176
Davis, Frank Marshall, 1177
Davis, Miles, 1250
Douglass, Frederick, 1334
Du Bois, W.E.B., 1154
Elders, Joycelyn, 965
Evers, Medgar, 1178
Forman, James, 1817
Forten, James, 2028
Hampton, Lionel, 254, 1475
Henson, Matthew, 1179
Lewis, William Henry, 1180
Lorde, Audre, 1557
McHenry, Elizabeth, 1196
Morrison, Toni, 1063
Powell, Adam Clayton Jr., 1181
Robeson, Paul, 1197
Sutton, Percy, 625
Turner, Henry McNeal, 1029
Yerby, Frank, 2405

Identity *see also* **Self-knowledge**
Appiah, Anthony, 1182, 1658
Baldwin, James, 144, 1183
Bearden, Romare, 239
Brown, William Wells, 149
Bruce, John E., 1184
Charles, RuPaul, 1185, 1186
Clifton, Lucille, 1187

Cruse, Harold, 1188
Garvey, Marcus, 1189
Gates, Henry Louis Jr., 692, 1148, 1190, 1191, 1192
Giovanni, Nikki, 1193, 1194
Gomes, Peter J., 1195
Higginbotham, Evelyn Brooks, 978
McHenry, Elizabeth, 1196
Robeson, Paul, 1197
Smitherman, Geneva, 1299
Steele, Shelby, 1515
West, Cornel, 1596, 1911
X, Malcolm, 1198, 1199

Ideology
Gates, Henry Louis Jr., 27
Strickland, William, 1594
West, Cornel, 1160

Ignorance
Angelou, Maya, 749
Bailey, Pearl, 1619
Brawley, Tawana, 884
Brown, William Wells, 148
Douglass, Frederick, 525
Du Bois, W.E.B., 769, 1523
Hooks, Bell, 1292
King, Martin Luther Jr., 792
Primus, Pearl, 635
Roman, Charles V., 1622
Simmons, Judy, 1689
Taylor, Susan, 1880
Toomer, Jean, 1278
Washington, Booker T., 815, 821

Illinois
Robinson, Bojangles, 2227

Imagination see also **Creativity; Ideas**
Ali, Muhammad, 1200
Gates, Henry Louis Jr., 1423
Houston, Charles Hamilton, 405
Joans, Ted, 620
Morrison, Toni, 98
Nixon, E.D., 1846
Washington, James M., 478
Winfrey, Oprah, 1034

Imitation
Baldwin, James, 461
Brown, H. Rap, 1699
Chapman, Melvin, 2415
Jackson, Jesse, 1837, 2509
Johnson, John H., 371
King, Martin Luther Jr., 1321

Walker, Aida Overton, 1975
Walker, Alice, 2392

Impact
Angelou, Maya, 1743
Banks, Erin, 1365
Dyson, Michael Eric, 1629
Edelman, Marian Wright, 874
Houston, Charles Hamilton, 1957
Jackson, Jesse, 1582
Johnson, James Weldon, 178
Locke, Alain, 372
Lowery, Joseph, 2441
Parks, Rosa, 33
Stewart, Maria W., 36
Trotter, William Monroe, 37

Impatience see also **Patience**
Bunche, Ralph, 915
Gates, Henry Louis Jr., 27
Robinson, Jackie, 1808
Sanchez, Sonia, 45
Wheatley, Phillis, 947

Independence
Du Bois, W.E.B., 977
Jackson, Mahalia, 1201
Macmillan, Harold, 97
Muhammad, Elijah, 1202
Turner, Henry McNeal, 906
Washington, Booker T., 741, 742
Woodson, Carter G., 746

India
Wells, Ida B., 1410

Indians see also **Native Americans**
Cone, James, 154
Wilson, Joseph, 1719

Individuality
Bowen, J.W.E., 1203
Matthews, Victoria Earle, 1360
McKay, Claude, 1204
West, Cornel, 673, 1205

Inequality see also **Equality**
Anonymous, 137
Coffin, Frank M., 51
Gates, Henry Louis Jr., 1980
King, Martin Luther Jr., 1608
White, Walter, 744
Wilson, William Julius, 1691
Woodson, Carter G., 825

Injustice see also **Justice**
Cone, James, 154

Douglass, Frederick, 905
Du Bois, W.E.B., 390
Garvey, Marcus, 1018, 1206, 1606
Harris, Patricia Roberts, 1550
Jackson, George, 1631
Johnson, James Weldon, 2077
King, Martin Luther Jr., 1207, 1304
Washington, Booker T., 1644
Wright, Richard, 1274, 1633

Insight
Du Bois, W.E.B., 1208
Walker, Alice, 1431

Inspiration
Bady, Belynda B., 2342
Blyden, Edward Wilmot, 387
Catlett, Elizabeth, 547
Du Bois, W.E.B., 2288
Fitzgerald, Ella, 2422
Frazier, E. Franklin, 778
Garvey, Marcus, 1209
Hurston, Zora Neale, 1210
Lawrence, Jacob, 263
Savage, Augusta, 475
Wheatley, Phillis, 1211
Woodson, Carter G., 827, 828, 1126
Young, Whitney M. Jr., 1212

Integration
Baldwin, James, 1213
Benson, Janice Hall, 754
Bond, Julian, 727
Carmichael, Stokely, 1214
Clarke, John Henrik, 1215
Gates, Henry Louis Jr., 1216
Hamer, Fannie Lou, 1993
Hughes, Langston, 320
Jackson, Jesse, 1217
Killens, John O., 1218
King, Martin Luther Jr., 695, 1305
Morley, Jefferson, 1219
Muhammad, Elijah, 1220, 1878
Sullivan, Leon, 1221
Whipper, William S., 1222
White, Walter, 2209
X, Malcolm, 1162

Integrity *see also* **Honesty**
Ali, Muhammad, 1223
Anderson, Marian, 1224
Chisholm, Shirley, 1225
Crummell, Alexander, 211
Douglass, Frederick, 1226
Gandhi, Mohandas K., 1227

Garvey, Marcus, 1228
Harding, Vincent, 574
Haynes, Lemuel, 1229
Jackson, Jesse, 1582
Johnson, James Weldon, 1938
Queen Mother Moore, 1230
Shakur, Tupac, 1231
Washington, Booker T., 1232
Wilson, Flip, 1233

Intelligence
Gates, Henry Louis Jr., 1707
Hansberry, Lorraine, 1235
Jordan, Barbara, 382
King, Martin Luther Jr., 791
Plato, Ann, 1394
Simmons, Judy, 1689
Washington, Booker T., 743, 815
West, Cornel, 1236
Wiley, Ralph, 2273
Wilkins, Roy, 1237

Intimacy
Baldwin, James, 1744
Dyson, Michael Eric, 864
Schuyler, George, 1688
Weems, Renita, 1033

Inventions
Appiah, Anthony, 69
Jordan, Michael, 598
Killens, John O., 181
King, B.B., 1295
Young, Whitney M. Jr., 19

Inventiveness
Carver, George Washington, 7
Hampton, Lionel, 1475
Hansberry, Lorraine, 619
Parks, Gordon, 1961
Simone, Nina, 1262

Invisibility
Du Bois, W.E.B., 1163
Ellison, Ralph, 1238
Louis, Joe, 2440
Owens, Jesse, 2199
Powell, Adam Clayton Jr., 1788
Wideman, John Edgar, 356

Ireland
Locke, Alain, 1061

Irish
Delany, Martin R., 1501

Iron work
Terrell, Mary Church, 113

Islam
Baldwin, James, 1239
Rodney, Muhammad, 1240
X, Malcolm, 359, 1199, 2299

Jacob
Anonymous, 2163

Jail *see* **Prison**

Japanese
Cosby, Camille, 729

Jazz
Armstrong, Louis, 1241, 1242
Baldwin, James, 1243, 1244, 1245
Baraka, Amiri, 124
Bearden, Romare, 244
Bergreen, Laurence, 1246
Brooks, Roy, 1247
Carter, Betty, 1248
Coltrane, John, 1249
Davis, Anthony, 1467
Davis, Miles, 1250
Ellington, Duke, 1251, 1252, 1253
Gaines, Ernest J., 2498
Hughes, Langston, 1056, 1254, 1255
Marsalis, Wynton, 1256
Morrison, Toni, 2501
Murray, Albert, 1257, 1258
Paderewski, Ignacy, 1259
Parks, Rosa, 1260
Roach, Max, 1261
Simone, Nina, 1262
Taylor, Billy, 1263
Walker, Alice, 1560

Jemison, Mae
Jemison, Mae, 982

Jesus
Anonymous, 898, 2093, 2096, 2108,
   2109, 2121, 2122, 2126, 2130, 2135,
   2146, 2148, 2152, 2164
Haynes, Lemuel, 866
Lee, Jarena, 1617
Madison, Joe, 2257
Mays, Benjamin, 1369
Truth, Sojourner, 2385, 2389
Turner, Nat, 1758

Jews
Edelman, Marian Wright, 52

King, Martin Luther Jr., 932
Wells, Ida B., 1410

Joan of Arc
Mays, Benjamin, 1369

Jobs *see also* **Labor; Work**
Anonymous, 434, 435
Ashe, Arthur, 325
Bluford, Guion S. Jr., 2469
Edelman, Marian Wright, 52
Evers-Williams, Myrlie, 1288
Gates, Henry Louis Jr., 1192
Hancock, Gordon Blaine, 733
Holiday, Billie, 471
King, Martin Luther Jr., 2476
McCarthy, Osceola, 2477
Owens, Jesse, 343
Parks, Rosa, 608
Pinkney, Andrea D., 2225
Randolph, A. Philip, 1826
Rustin, Bayard, 844
Vest, Hilda, 1301

John
Anonymous, 2104, 2118

Johnson, Magic
Johnson, Magic, 1996

Joshua
Anonymous, 2119

Journeys *see also* **Travel**
Angelou, Maya, 66
Anonymous, 909, 2161
Bearden, Romare, 241, 1766
Beckwourth, Jim, 681
Brown, William Wells, 148
Charles, Ray, 2256
Cinque, Joseph, 1434
Clarke, John Henrik, 78
Cugoano, Ottaban, 1435
Dinkins, David, 157, 1636
Douglass, Frederick, 159
Ellington, Duke, 1510
Equiano, Olaudah, 1436
Gates, Henry Louis Jr., 368
Giovanni, Nikki, 1345
Gomes, Peter J., 11
Haley, Alex, 875
Hamer, Fannie Lou, 337
Harris, Patricia Roberts, 1550
Hawthorne, Nathaniel, 1685
Jackson, Jesse, 1581
Johnson, Jack, 338

Nunez, Elizabeth, 1297
Smith, Barbara, 2506
Truth, Sojourner, 1504
Tubman, Harriet, 2279, 2278
Turner, Henry McNeal, 835
Winfrey, Oprah, 2395
X, Malcolm, 1678

Joyce, James
Wright, Richard, 1677

Justice *see also* **Injustice**
Ali, Muhammad, 1693
Anonymous, 908
Bethune, Mary McLeod, 1377
Chesnutt, Charles W., 1264
Cone, James, 1265
Davis, Angela, 1627
Dinkins, David, 1636
Douglass, Frederick, 525, 1266
Franklin, John Hope, 777
Frazier, E. Franklin, 1267
Garvey, Marcus, 1268, 1532
Gregory, Dick, 1269
Harding, Vincent, 574
Harris, Patricia Roberts, 1550
Jackson, Jesse, 1270
King, Martin Luther Jr., 407, 1207, 1506, 1552
Markham, Pigmeat, 1167
McHenry, Elizabeth, 1196
Monroe, Irene, 501
Rains, Claude, 1271
Randolph, A. Philip, 842, 1923
Sharpton, Al, 1272, 1273
Walters, Alexander, 2460
Wells, Ida B., 1308
West, Cornel, 1004
Wright, Richard, 1274
X, Malcolm, 1275

Kentucky
Gates, Henry Louis Jr., 1216

King, Martin Luther Jr.
Clark, Ramsey, 2352
Danky, James P., 1683
Edelman, Marian Wright, 2304
Gray, William H. III, 1749
Horne, Lena, 1135
Mays, Benjamin, 1369
Taylor, Susan, 1323

Knowledge *see also* **Self-knowledge**
Ali, Muhammad, 748

Baldwin, James, 1744
Bethune, Mary McLeod, 386
Douglass, Frederick, 766, 1705
Du Bois, W.E.B., 26
Frazier, E. Franklin, 778
Fuller, Solomon B., 422
Garvey, Marcus, 780
Gray, William H. III, 1276
Himes, Chester, 1654
Makeba, Miriam, 797
Muhammad, Elijah, 803
Nelson, Jill, 1277
Payton, Benjamin, 806
Shipler, David K., 1668
Toomer, Jean, 812, 1278
Walker, Alice, 1371
Washington, Booker T., 821, 1279
West, Cornel, 673, 2339

Labor *see also* **Jobs; Work**
King, Martin Luther Jr., 2476
Randolph, A. Philip, 1280, 1281
Ward, Samuel Ringgold, 2048
Young, Andrew, 2211

Lamar, Hedy
Horne, Lena, 1935

Language *see also* **Oral tradition; Talk; Words**
Alexander, Elizabeth, 1282
Appiah, Anthony, 70
Asante, Molefi, 1519, 1871
Baldwin, James, 1283, 1284, 1285
Bambara, Toni Cade, 1286
Brewer, J. Mason, 125
Charles, Ray, 1378
Davis, Ossie, 314
Dyson, Michael Eric, 864, 1287
Ellington, Duke, 290, 1612
Evers-Williams, Myrlie, 1288
Gates, Henry Louis Jr., 1289, 1290
Harper, Frances Ellen Watkins, 1708
Higginbotham, Evelyn Brooks, 1291
Hooks, Bell, 1292
Hurston, Zora Neale, 1293
Jordan, June, 1294
King, B.B., 1295
Locke, Alain, 266, 623
Lorde, Audre, 1557
Morrison, Toni, 1296, 1713, 2403
Nunez, Elizabeth, 1297
Rawls, Lou, 1483
Simone, Nina, 1262

Smitherman, Geneva, 1298, 1299
Tourgee, Albion W., 1300
Turner, Henry McNeal, 1029
Vest, Hilda, 1301
Walker, Alice, 1431
Washington, Booker T., 1159, 2309
West, Cornel, 1160
Woodson, Carter G., 2274
X, Malcolm, 2299

Latinos
Donaldson, Greg, 464
Rudenstein, Neil L., 61

Laughter
Fauset, Jessie, 1165
Hughes, Langston, 1166, 1255, 2490

Law
Childress, Alice, 759, 1734
De Priest, Oscar, 1991
Forten, James, 1664
Fortune, T. Thomas, 1403
Hamer, Fannie Lou, 1302
Harlan, John Marshall, 575
Higginbotham, Evelyn Brooks, 2367
Jacobs, Harriet, 2038
Jacobs, John, 1803
Johnson, James Weldon, 1821
Johnson, Lyndon B., 514
King, Martin Luther Jr., 1303, 1304, 1305
Miller, Kelly, 1306
Morley, Jefferson, 1219
Powell, Adam Clayton Jr., 1307
Shuttlesworth, Fred, 520
Stewart, Maria W., 111
Terrell, Mary Church, 2060
Thomas, Clarence, 62
Turner, Henry McNeal, 114
Wells, Ida B., 1308
Williams, Robert, 521

Leadership
Bailey, Pearl, 21
Burroughs, Nannie, 1309
Chisholm, Shirley, 1310
Colvin, Claudette, 1311
Davis, Ossie, 1312
DeFrantz, Anita, 954
Du Bois, W.E.B., 1313
Farrakhan, Louis, 1314
Garvey, Marcus, 1315, 1316
Guinier, Lani, 1317
Hall, Prathia, 1318

Hancock, Gordon Blaine, 1637
Hare, Nathan, 1319
Jackson, Jesse, 694
King, Martin Luther Jr., 1320, 1321
Moses, Bob, 1322
Rivers, Eugene, 504
Taylor, Susan, 1323
West, Cornel, 673, 1324, 1325, 1326
Woodson, Carter G., 1988

Learning see **Education**

Lesbians see **Gays and lesbians**

Lessons
Baldwin, James, 2409
Cosby, Camille, 729
Douglass, Frederick, 158
King, Yolanda, 1368
Parks, Rosa, 935, 1260
Wideman, John Edgar, 355

Liberals
Bady, Belynda B., 1567
Baldwin, James, 699
Carmichael, Stokely, 451
Hansberry, Lorraine, 1820
Hooks, Bell, 2294
Hooks, Benjamin, 2312
Powell, Adam Clayton Jr., 1181
Rivers, Eugene, 1142
West, Cornel, 675

Liberation see also **Emancipation;**
Freedom; Liberty; Self-liberation
Baldwin, James, 1009
Catlett, Elizabeth, 1327
Clarke, John Henrik, 1215
Cleaver, Kathleen, 533
Cone, James, 1521
Drake, St. Clair, 361
Du Bois, W.E.B., 1328
Edwards, Audrey; Polite, Craig K., 772
Essien-Udom, E.U., 1329
Goodman, James, 1330
Gray, William H. III, 1276
Hamer, Fannie Lou, 1919
Killens, John O., 1218
Morrison, Toni, 1331
Queen Mother Moore, 2201
Randolph, A. Philip, 1534
Robeson, Paul, 2205
Robinson, Max, 1854
Walker, David, 1332

Wilmore, Gayraud, 1333
X, Malcolm, 1092

Liberty *see also* **Freedom; Liberation**
Brown, William Wells, 569, 1494
Cleaver, Eldridge, 153
Cone, James, 837
Dinkins, David, 1636
Douglass, Frederick, 832, 905, 1334, 1860
Du Bois, W.E.B., 1154, 1335
Forten, James, 1664, 2028
Futrell, Mary, 779
Garnet, Henry Highland, 1336
Garvey, Marcus, 2193
Harris, Patricia Roberts, 1550
Johnson, Jack, 338
King, Martin Luther Jr., 183
Marshall, Thurgood, 1337
Mays, Benjamin, 217
McHenry, Elizabeth, 1196
Miller, Thomas E., 188
Moss, Otis, 934
Prosser, Gabriel, 1757
Tubman, Harriet, 941, 1338, 1832
Woodson, Carter G., 951

Libraries
Childress, Alice, 1701
Dove, Rita, 421
Haley, Alex, 783

Lies
Angelou, Maya, 2407
Baldwin, James, 143, 328, 1147
Cruse, Harold, 155
Du Bois, W.E.B., 2260
Dunbar, Paul Laurence, 336
Killens, John O., 2267
Muhammad, Herbert, 853
Vivian, C.T., 351

Life
Ali, Muhammad, 1339, 1930
Anonymous, 2165, 2167
Bady, Barbara, 1340
Bady, Willie Jr., 2408
Bailey, Pearl, 1341
Baldwin, James, 1073, 1284, 1342, 1343, 1873, 1874, 2410
Bearden, Romare, 1344
Brown, Les, 2414
Carver, George Washington, 1509
Catlett, Elizabeth, 1327
Chapman, Melvin, 2415

Charles, Ray, 2065
Crite, Allan Rohan, 1153
Cugoano, Ottaban, 1435
Du Bois, W.E.B., 641, 768, 1890, 2417
Dyson, Michael Eric, 1287
Ellington, Duke, 1510, 2418
Farrakhan, Louis, 2420
Garvey, Marcus, 642, 2193
Gaye, Marvin, 2006
Giovanni, Nikki, 1345, 1441
Gomes, Peter J., 133, 1020, 1195, 1346
Hansberry, Lorraine, 619
Henderson, Stephen, 1347
Himes, Chester, 1654
Hughes, Langston, 1348
Hurston, Zora Neale, 1936
Jackson, Jesse, 1138, 2428
Jemison, Mae, 2214
Johnson, James Weldon, 1057, 1938, 2432
Johnson, Robert E., 2433
Jones, Bill T., 2434
Jones, Joshua Henry, 1810
Just, E.E., 1349
Kincaid, Jamaica, 1551
King, Martin Luther Jr., 183, 1456, 2323, 2437
Lawrence, Jacob, 1089
Locke, Alain, 1068, 1069
Love, Nat "Deadwood Dick, the cowboy adventurer," 1426
Madhubuti, Haki, 1959
Mays, Benjamin, 1001
McCarthy, Osceola, 442, 2477
Morrison, Toni, 2403
Moutoussamy-Ashe, Jeanne, 48
Naylor, Gloria, 1350, 2444
Norris, Clarence, 2445
Owens, Jesse, 1351
Paige, Satchel, 2448
Parks, Gordon, 2067
Shabazz, Betty, 1352
Thurman, Howard, 1353
Toomer, Jean, 1354
Turner, Tina, 2457
Walker, David, 1841
Washington, Booker T., 2308, 2462
Wells, Ida B., 1807
West, Cornel, 1489, 2339, 2465
White, J., 2054
Williams, Eddie N., 745
Winfrey, Oprah, 718, 2071, 2466
Wonder, Stevie, 1967

Woodson, Carter G., 827
Wright, Richard, 1858
X, Malcolm, 1007, 1742

Limitations
Baldwin, James, 1355
Gaye, Marvin, 886
Houston, Charles Hamilton, 405
Jackson, Jesse, 484
Norton, Eleanor Holmes, 342
Reagon, Bernice Johnson, 519
Robinson, Max, 1854
Simone, Timothy M., 375
Toomer, Jean, 1356
Turner, Henry McNeal, 1158
Wideman, John Edgar, 356
Woodson, Carter G., 1554

Lincoln, Abraham
West, Cornel, 1325
Woodbey, George W., 448

Literature *see also* **Books; Writers**
Ali, Noble Drew, 449
Braithwaite, William Stanley, 1357
Brewer, J. Mason, 125
Clarke, John Henrik, 1358
Du Bois, W.E.B., 2288
Ellison, Ralph, 366
Equiano, Olaudah, 367
Garvey, Marcus, 90
Gates, Henry Louis Jr., 693, 1359
Hurston, Zora Neale, 904
Johnson, James Weldon, 259
Matthews, Victoria Earle, 1360
McHenry, Elizabeth, 1870
Morrison, Toni, 98, 2502
Smith, Anna Deavere, 1361
Toomer, Jean, 1362
Turner, Darwin T., 1363
Washington, Booker T., 817

Living
Bady, Willie Jr., 2408
Baker, Josephine, 1364
Banks, Erin, 1365
Chase, Henry, 1366
Collins, Marva, 1367
Ellison, Ralph, 774
Flack, Roberta, 2230
Fortune, T. Thomas, 591
Gomes, Peter J., 2424
King, Martin Luther Jr., 1024
King, Yolanda, 1368
Locke, Alain, 2079

Mays, Benjamin, 1369, 2442
Parker, Charlie, 1482
Parks, Rosa, 1655
Pickens, William, 2224
Powell, Colin, 2307
Robeson, Paul, 1197
Sanchez, Sonia, 1370
Simone, Nina, 1262
Thurman, Howard, 714
Walker, Alice, 1371, 2493

Lobbying
Chisholm, Shirley, 1572

Loneliness
Anonymous, 2144
Gomes, Peter J., 1020
Hansberry, Lorraine, 1896
Mitchell, Arthur, 605
Parker-Smith, Bettye J., 1393
Robinson, Jackie, 1808
Walker, Alice, 944
X, Malcolm, 1634

Longevity
Blake, Eubie, 2413
King, Martin Luther Jr., 1024, 2323
Mays, Benjamin, 1369

Lord *see also* **God; Jesus**
Anonymous, 2081, 2084, 2085, 2086,
    2099, 2113, 2115, 2127, 2128, 2133,
    2137, 2138, 2164
Baldwin, James, 868, 1010
Beman, Jehiel C., 2015
Du Bois, W.E.B., 1014
Hunter, Clementine, 258
Jackson, Mahalia, 1201
Truth, Sojourner, 1504
Tubman, Harriet, 677, 1338
Walker, Mme. C.J., 683

Louisiana
Armstrong, Louis, 1463
Northup, Solomon, 373

Love
Angelou, Maya, 1372
Anonymous, 2100
Bailey, Pearl, 1341
Baker, Josephine, 1535
Baldwin, James, 139, 232, 1074, 1373,
    1374
Bearden, Romare, 1375
Bennett, Gwendolyn, 1376
Bethune, Mary McLeod, 1377, 2412

Brinkley, Rhonda, 1989
Brown, William Wells, 149
Cain, Herman, 2216
Carmichael, Stokely, 437, 546
Charles, Ray, 1378
Childress, Alice, 2497
Cleaver, Eldridge, 1076
Davis, Miles, 1379
Davis, Ossie, 1312
Douglass, Frederick, 481
Du Bois, W.E.B., 922, 1380
Ellington, Duke, 1381, 1382
Fitzgerald, Ella, 2422
Frazier, E. Franklin, 1267
Gates, Henry Louis Jr., 1192
Giovanni, Nikki, 1383
Gordy, Berry Jr., 1460
Hall, Prince, 2293
Hayden, Palmer, 256
Holland, Brian; Dozier, Lamont;
    Holland, Eddie, 1384
Jamison, Judith, 629
Jones, Quincy, 2435
Jordan, June, 180, 1385
King, Martin Luther Jr., 1303, 1305,
    1386, 1387, 1457
Knight, Etheridge, 1388
Mabley, Moms, 1389
Marley, Bob, 1390
Morrison, Toni, 1391, 1392
Moss, Otis, 487
Parker-Smith, Bettye J., 1393
Pippin, Horace, 271
Plato, Ann, 1394
Powell, Colin, 2307
Qualls, Schyleen, 1559
Robinson, Max, 1854
Russell, Bill, 1395
Shabazz, Betty, 1352, 1396
Thurman, Howard, 476
Toomer, Jean, 1397
Turner, Henry McNeal, 1544
Walker, Alice, 1431
Walker, Margaret, 1398
Washington, Booker T., 1399
Weems, Renita, 1400
West, Cornel, 224, 1857
Wheatley, Phillis, 947
Whipper, William S., 1610
Woodson, Carter G., 401
Wright, Richard, 420
Wright, Sarah E., 1401
X, Malcolm, 1050, 1402

Loyalty
Davis, Ossie, 314
Dunbar, Paul Laurence, 571
Franklin, C.L., 865
McKay, Claude, 1204
Powell, Colin, 2226

Lynching
Bradley, Mamie, 2285
Brown, William Wells, 148
Fortune, T. Thomas, 1403
Garvey, Amy Jacques, 1404
Hansberry, Lorraine, 228
King, Martin Luther Jr., 1303, 1305
Lowery, Joseph, 723
Parks, Gordon, 344
Randolph, A. Philip, 2202
Reed, Ishmael, 347
Thomas, Clarence, 1405
Turner, Henry McNeal, 1406, 1407
Wells, Ida B., 1408, 1409, 1410, 1807
White, Walter, 744
X, Malcolm, 1883

Maps
Baldwin, James, 72
Hurston, Zora Neale, 1293

Marches
Dinkins, David, 919
Johnson, James Weldon, 956
King, Martin Luther Jr., 516
Proctor, Samuel D., 518
Robeson, Paul, 2069

Marriage
Amlak, Elleni, 1411
Giddings, Paula, 468
Holiday, Billie, 1412
Winfrey, Oprah, 1413

Marsalis, Wynton
Davis, Anthony, 1467

Martha
Anonymous, 2129

Marxism
King, Martin Luther Jr., 445

Mary
Anonymous, 2129, 2130, 2140

Massachusetts
Anonymous, 2324
Powell, Colin, 58

Mayflower
Brown, William Wells, 148
Hawthorne, Nathaniel, 1685
X, Malcolm, 1678

Meaning
Banks, Erin, 1365
Ellington, Duke, 1251
Flack, Roberta, 2230
Himes, Chester, 1898
King, Martin Luther Jr., 396
Lee-Smith, Hughie, 265
Shabazz, Betty, 1352
Washington, James M., 131
Waters, Ethel, 2012
West, Cornel, 224, 2239
Wilkins, Roy, 123
Wright, Richard, 1912

Melting pot
Evers-Williams, Myrlie, 1288
Hughes, Langston, 1056
Jackson, Jesse, 1217

Melville, Herman
West, Cornel, 419

Memory
Allen, Paula Gunn, 1518
Baldwin, James, 2063
Du Bois, W.E.B., 1414
Haley, Alex, 1109
Himes, Chester, 1898
Hurston, Zora Neale, 1415, 2369
Neal, Larry, 502
Walker, Margaret, 1561
X, Malcolm, 1127, 1416

Men see also **Gender**
Anonymous, 1417
Baldwin, James, 1418
Brown, Sterling A., 1419
Charles, RuPaul, 1420
Chisholm, Shirley, 2349, 2351
Davis, Angela, 1767
Dyson, Michael Eric, 2361
Edelman, Marian Wright, 52
Fortune, T. Thomas, 2362
Garvey, Marcus, 1421, 1422
Gates, Henry Louis Jr., 691, 1423
Hill, Anita, 1424
Jacobs, Harriet, 981
Jemison, Mae, 982
Kennedy, Florynce, 1425
Lee, Jarena, 1617

Little Richard, 968
Love, Nat "Deadwood Dick, the
    cowboy adventurer," 1426
Mabley, Moms, 1427, 1428
Naylor, Gloria, 1429
Paul, Nathaniel, 345
Strickland, William, 1430
Truth, Sojourner, 2386, 2389, 2390
Walker, Alice, 1431
Walker, Charles T., 1432
Walker, David, 1433

Methodists
Allen, Richard, 1771
Washington, Booker T., 1790
X, Malcolm, 359

Michael
Anonymous, 2132

Middle Passage
Cinque, Joseph, 1434
Cugoano, Ottaban, 1435
Equiano, Olaudah, 1436
Strickland, William, 1430

Militancy
Hastie, William H., 214
Huggins, Nathan, 1065
Jordan, Barbara, 1674
Powell, Adam Clayton Jr., 559

Mind see also **Thinking**
Angelou, Maya, 1088
Anonymous, 750
Asante, Molefi, 1519, 1871
Banneker, Benjamin, 1234
Clarke, John Henrik, 1815
Cone, James, 332
Douglass, Frederick, 538
Ellison, Ralph, 1238
Farrakhan, Louis, 2261
Father Divine, 1778
Gandhi, Mohandas K., 1916
Garvey, Amy Jacques, 923
Garvey, Marcus, 781, 2031
Hansberry, Lorraine, 619
Harper, Frances Ellen Watkins, 927
Hurston, Zora Neale, 2321
Jordan, Barbara, 382
Killens, John O., 674
Makeba, Miriam, 797
Mays, Benjamin, 1437
McCall, Nathan, 800
Morrison, Toni, 2376

Muhammad, Elijah, 1878
Pippin, Horace, 271
Prophet, Nancy Elizabeth, 300
Robinson, Sugar Ray, 2177
Rodney, Muhammad, 1240
Schomburg, Arthur, 1531
Stewart, Maria W., 2382
Taylor, Susan, 1880
Teish, Luisah, 222
Truth, Sojourner, 1438
Woodson, Carter G., 1530
Young, Whitney M. Jr., 1212

Minorities
Anonymous, 1843
Ashe, Arthur, 1694
Brennan, William J., 49
Cruse, Harold, 155
Edelman, Marian Wright, 52
Gates, Henry Louis Jr., 693
Hancock, Gordon Blaine, 2179
King, Coretta Scott, 2295
Locke, Alain, 372
Rudenstein, Neil L., 61
Sharpton, Al, 697

Misery
Armstrong, Louis, 1466
Brown, Claude, 146
Delaney, Beauford, 1888
Douglass, Frederick, 1439
Marrant, John, 1440
Marshall, Thurgood, 1997
Naylor, Gloria, 1350
Walker, David, 945
West, Cornel, 2272

Missionaries
Baldwin, James, 144
Locke, Alain, 96
Woodson, Carter G., 118

Mississippi
Anonymous, 908
Hamer, Fannie Lou, 337, 1580
Johnson, James Weldon, 1821
Marshall, Thurgood, 667
Moses, Bob, 1714
Walker, Alice, 196
Wilson, August, 564
X, Malcolm, 1827

Mistakes
Franklin, Aretha, 44
Giovanni, Nikki, 1441

Jemison, Mae, 1513
Johnson, Jack, 1868
Jordan, Barbara, 576
Locke, Alain, 96
Louis, Joe, 1442
Monk, Thelonious, 1481
Truth, Sojourner, 2269

Mitford, Jessica
Durr, Virginia, 511

Money
Ali, Muhammad, 1223
Anderson, Marian, 1443
Anonymous, 900
Baldwin, James, 1444
Bethune, Mary McLeod, 1170
Burroughs, Nannie, 2302
Chavis, Benjamin Jr., 548
Chisholm, Shirley, 1573
Douglass, Frederick, 1577
Dunbar, Paul Laurence, 1445
Farrakhan, Louis, 730
Gaston, A.G., 1446, 2305
Gates, Henry Louis Jr., 1192
Hooks, Benjamin, 2312
Hughes, Langston, 1056
Hurston, Zora Neale, 788
Jackson, Mahalia, 1201
Jackson, Reggie, 2174
Johnson, John H., 441
King, Coretta Scott, 2078
King, Martin Luther Jr., 30
Louis, Joe, 1447, 1448
McCarthy, Osceola, 442
Reverend Ike, 1449, 1450
Shakur, Assata, 1591
Stewart, Maria W., 740
Walker, Mme. C.J., 443

Moors
Ali, Noble Drew, 1769

Morality *see also* **Values**
Abdul Jabbar, Kareem, 1451
Baker, Josephine, 1452
Baldwin, James, 1537
Bannister, Edward Mitchell, 234
Brooks, Walter H., 1453
Douglass, Frederick, 1577, 2286
Farrakhan, Louis, 1454
Frazier, E. Franklin, 1969
Gates, Henry Louis Jr., 1192
Gomes, Peter J., 2423
Guinier, Lani, 1317

Hughes, Langston, 787
Jackson, Jesse, 1455, 2313
Karenga, Ron, 515
King, Martin Luther Jr., 1304, 1305, 1456, 1457, 2331
Lee, Spike, 2438
Pickens, William, 1998
Poussaint, Alvin, 2306
Randolph, A. Philip, 1826, 2202
Rustin, Bayard, 1609
Terrell, Mary Church, 1458
Washington, Booker T., 1459, 2050
Wells, Ida B., 1733
West, Cornel, 2338
White, Walter, 2209

Morehouse College
Mays, Benjamin, 799

Moses
Anonymous, 2092
Burroughs, Nannie, 1950
Johns, Vernon, 1023

Motherhood
Angelou, Maya, 65
Bethune, Mary McLeod, 73
Du Bois, W.E.B., 2359
Higginbotham, Evelyn Brooks, 2367
Locke, Alain, 94
Rogers, J.A., 2378

Mothers *see* **Family**

Motown sound
Gordy, Berry Jr., 1460

Movies *see* **Films**

Muhammad, Elijah
Baldwin, James, 1239
Rodney, Muhammad, 1240
X, Malcolm, 1199

Multiculturalism *see* **Diversity**

Murder
Angelou, Maya, 43
Bradley, Mamie, 2285
Garvey, Marcus, 2292
Love, Nat "Deadwood Dick, the cowboy adventurer," 647
Moses, Bob, 1714
Turner, Henry McNeal, 1407
Walker, David, 198
Wells, Ida B., 202, 1408
X, Malcolm, 654

Museums
Bearden, Romare, 243

Music *see also* **Blues; Jazz; Rap; Rock 'n' roll; Singing; Spirituals**
Anonymous, 413
Armstrong, Lil Hardin, 1461
Armstrong, Louis, 1462, 1463, 1464, 1465, 1466
Baldwin, James, 1245
Baraka, Amiri, 124, 1556
Bergreen, Laurence, 1246
Brewer, J. Mason, 125
Davis, Anthony, 1467
Davis, Miles, 615, 1468
Du Bois, W.E.B., 83, 248, 1469
Dvorak, Anton, 1470
Ellington, Duke, 1253, 1471, 1472, 1473
Ellison, Ralph, 366
Equiano, Olaudah, 367
Gates, Henry Louis Jr., 1290
Gillespie, Dizzy, 925, 1474
Golden, Marita, 618
Gordy, Berry Jr., 1460
Hampton, Lionel, 1475
Handy, W.C., 414, 415, 416
Holiday, Billie, 721
Houston, Whitney, 2007
Hughes, Langston, 2490
Jackson, Michael, 1476
Joplin, Scott, 1477
Just, E.E., 1349
King, B.B., 417
Ledbetter, Huddie, 1478
Locke, Alain, 623, 633
Manley, Michael, 1479
Monk, Thelonious, 1480, 1481
Mosley, Walter, 418
Parker, Charlie, 270, 624, 1482, 1787
Rawls, Lou, 1483
Roach, Max, 1261
Robeson, Paul, 104, 105, 1197, 1484, 1485
Rogers, J.A., 1486
Rollins, Sonny, 374
Shabazz, Betty, 1487
Simone, Nina, 1262
Vaughan, Sarah, 1488
West, Cornel, 352, 419, 1489
Weston, Randy, 1490
Wheatley, Phillis, 652
Wilson, Mary, 1491

Muslims *see* **Islam**

Names
Ali, Noble Drew, 1493
Allen, Richard, 1771
Anonymous, 2080, 2098, 2139
Armstrong, Louis, 1463
Brown, William Wells, 1494, 1495
Carver, George Washington, 1011
Embry, James C., 1496
Farrakhan, Louis, 1776
Jackson, Jesse, 1665
Jakes, T.D., 1497
Johns, Vernon, 1023
Lorde, Audre, 1558
Queen Mother Moore, 1676, 1794
Riggs, Marlon, 1905
Truth, Sojourner, 1504
West, Cornel, 1498
X, Malcolm, 1199

Nationhood
Ali, Noble Drew, 1499
Baraka, Amiri, 1500
Delany, Martin R., 1501
Du Bois, W.E.B., 1154
Garvey, Marcus, 9, 88
Langston, John Mercer, 1502
Truth, Sojourner, 1503, 1504
Turner, Henry McNeal, 114, 835

Native Americans *see also* **Indians**
Childress, Alice, 1701
Purvis, Robert, 190
Rudenstein, Neil L., 61
West, Cornel, 354

Negroes *see also* **Blackness**
Gates, Henry Louis Jr., 1190
Hughes, Langston, 1066
Johnson, William H., 393
Killens, John O., 181
Queen Mother Moore, 1230
Wright, Richard, 203
X, Malcolm, 42, 1198

New York *see also* **Harlem**
Baldwin, James, 1885
Dunbar, Paul Laurence, 1052
Gates, Henry Louis Jr., 1053, 1216
Jacobs, Harriet, 2370
Robinson, Bojangles, 2227
Sharpton, Al, 1039

Nihilism
Rivers, Eugene, 503
West, Cornel, 2239

Nixon, Richard
Shakur, Assata, 1591

Nonviolence
Baldwin, James, 1505
Cooper, Anna Julia, 2354
Houston, Charles Hamilton, 1957
King, Martin Luther Jr., 499, 1506, 1507

North and South *see also* **Civil War**
Debro, Sarah, 156
Gregory, Dick, 172
Hamer, Fannie Lou, 337
Washington, Booker T., 2051

North Carolina
Wilson, August, 564

Obscenity
Gates, Henry Louis Jr., 1290

Opportunity
Baldwin, James, 1508
Carver, George Washington, 1509
Du Bois, W.E.B., 429
Ellington, Duke, 1510
Flake, Floyd, 987
Garvey, Marcus, 1511
Hood, James Walker, 1512
Hurston, Zora Neale, 928
Jemison, Mae, 1513
King, Martin Luther Jr., 695
Owens, Jesse, 1514
Steele, Shelby, 1515
Sullivan, Leon, 2480
Walker, Mme. C.J., 1516
Washington, Booker T., 946, 1517, 2462

Oppression
Allen, Paula Gunn, 1518
Angelou, Maya, 210
Asante, Molefi, 1519
Baldwin, James, 1520
Bambara, Toni Cade, 281, 2284
Bennett, Lerone, 753
Clarke, John Henrik, 1358
Cone, James, 1521
Douglass, Frederick, 525, 1013, 1522
Du Bois, W.E.B., 1154, 1328, 1523, 1800, 1915
Gregory, Dick, 573, 1524
Hansberry, Lorraine, 2365
Harris, Patricia Roberts, 1550
Haynes, Lemuel, 1897
Height, Dorothy, 998
Higginson, Thomas Wentworth, 1783

Karenga, Ron, 515
King, Martin Luther Jr., 931
Locke, Alain, 372
Lorde, Audre, 1525
Lowery, Joseph, 1877
Mfume, Kweisi, 801
Monroe, Irene, 501
Morrison, Toni, 1526
Murray, Pauli, 738, 1879
Owens, Jesse, 1527
Randolph, A. Philip, 1923
Reed, Ishmael, 301
Remond, Charles Lenox, 1722
Robeson, Paul, 1528
Shakur, Assata, 1591
Simmons, Judy, 1689
Stewart, Maria W., 112
Terrell, Mary Church, 2060
Walker, David, 1332
Washington, Booker T., 1529, 1644
West, Cornel, 2239
Wheatley, Phillis, 947
Wilson, Joseph, 1719
Woodson, Carter G., 828, 1530
X, Malcolm, 433

Oral tradition *see also* **Language; Talk**
Schomburg, Arthur, 1531
Smitherman, Geneva, 1298

Ordinary people *see* **Average people**

Organization
Bambara, Toni Cade, 2284
Crummell, Alexander, 380
Garvey, Marcus, 1532, 2292
Gillespie, Dizzy, 925
Houston, Charles Hamilton, 1957
Randolph, A. Philip, 1281, 1533, 1534

Pain
Baldwin, James, 1072
Dyson, Michael Eric, 2361
Franklin, Aretha, 44
Garvey, Marcus, 1315
Joyner-Kersee, Jackie, 600
Proctor, Samuel D., 518
Weems, Renita, 1033, 1400

Painting *see also* **Art**
Bearden, Romare, 240, 242
Gates, Henry Louis Jr., 252, 1192
Golden, Marita, 618
Hunter, Clementine, 258
Jones, Lois Mailou, 261

Karenga, Ron, 296
Lawrence, Jacob, 297
Lee-Smith, Hughie, 265
McGuire, George Alexander, 486
Pippin, Horace, 271
Turner, Henry McNeal, 1029
White, Charles, 279

Parents *see* **Family**

Paris
Baker, Josephine, 1535, 1536
Baldwin, James, 1537, 1538, 1885
Bechet, Sidney, 1539
Johnson, James Weldon, 1540, 1723
Wright, Richard, 1541

Parker, Charlie
Carter, Betty, 1248

Parks, Rosa
Clark, Ramsey, 2352
Dyson, Michael Eric, 678

Patience *see also* **Impatience**
Ransom, Reverdy C., 1027
Washington, Harold, 613

Patriotism
Dunbar, Paul Laurence, 571
James, Chappie, 1542
Turner, Henry McNeal, 1543, 1544
X, Malcolm, 1545

Peace
Banneker, Benjamin, 1546
Bunche, Ralph, 1547
Douglass, Frederick, 481
Du Bois, W.E.B., 833
Father Divine, 1548
Garvey, Marcus, 2076
Gaye, Marvin, 886, 1549
Hall, Prince, 2293
Harris, Patricia Roberts, 1550
Hughes, Langston, 2489
Kincaid, Jamaica, 1551
King, Coretta Scott, 182
King, Martin Luther Jr., 1552
Moss, Otis, 487
Shabazz, Betty, 1553
Sharpton, Al, 1272
Walker, David, 1433
Williams, Robert, 521
Woodson, Carter G., 1554
X, Malcolm, 1555

Perseverance *see also* **Courage; Endurance**
Alexander, Sadie T.M., 580
Ali, Muhammad, 1928
Angelou, Maya, 657, 1149
Baldwin, James, 1343
Bunche, Ralph, 404
Burroughs, Nannie, 6
Charles, Ray, 585
Davis, Angela, 2358
Davis, Sammy Jr., 590
Douglass, Frederick, 8
Ellison, Ralph, 995
Fortune, T. Thomas, 2218
Holyfield, Evander, 596
Jackson, Jesse, 597
Lee-Smith, Hughie, 298
Leonard, Sugar Ray, 604
Petry, Ann, 2491
Powell, Adam Clayton Jr., 2200
Powell, Colin, 2226
Robeson, Paul, 2069
Truth, Sojourner, 2044
Walker, David, 945
Warfield, William, 612
Washington, Booker T., 1644
Woodard, Lynette, 1945

Photography
Van Der Zee, James, 277

Picasso, Pablo
Ellington, Duke, 250
Gates, Henry Louis Jr., 252, 1861

Pilgrims
Du Bois, W.E.B., 164
Gates, Henry Louis Jr., 1053
Gomes, Peter J., 1019
Hawthorne, Nathaniel, 1685
X, Malcolm, 2299

Plays
Robeson, Paul, 105, 1197
Woodson, Carter G., 2275

Pluralism *see* **Diversity**

Plymouth Rock
Brown, William Wells, 148
Hawthorne, Nathaniel, 1685
X, Malcolm, 208

Poetry
Baraka, Amiri, 1556
Gates, Henry Louis Jr., 369, 2363
Jordan, June, 1294

Locke, Alain, 266
Lorde, Audre, 1557, 1558
Marable, Manning, 2374
Qualls, Schyleen, 1559
Walker, Alice, 1560
Walker, Margaret, 1561
Washington, Booker T., 2482

Poets
Asante, Molefi, 2398
Brooks, Gwendolyn, 2400
Cullen, Countee, 1562
Dunbar, Paul Laurence, 1563
Equiano, Olaudah, 367
Johnson, James Weldon, 1564
Locke, Alain, 1940

Poles
Delany, Martin R., 1501

Politics
Allen, Walter, 1565
Appiah, Anthony, 1566
Bady, Belynda B., 1567
Baldwin, James, 536
Brown, James, 1568
Brown, Ronald H., 1569
Burke, Yvonne Brathwaite, 1570
Carmichael, Stokely, 1571
Charles, RuPaul, 1931
Chisholm, Shirley, 688, 1572, 1573, 2350
Clark, Kenneth B., 676
Davis, Angela, 1574
Dinkins, David, 1575
Douglass, Frederick, 976, 1576, 1577, 2021
Du Bois, W.E.B., 838, 1578, 1579, 1762
Gates, Henry Louis Jr., 693
Goodman, Paul, 512
Hamer, Fannie Lou, 1580
Hooks, Bell, 2294
Hooks, Benjamin, 2312
Jackson, Jesse, 1581, 1582, 1665
Jordan, Barbara, 789
King, Coretta Scott, 1583
King, Martin Luther Jr., 1584
King, Melvin H., 1585
Locke, Alain, 1061
Macmillan, Harold, 97
Marable, Manning, 2374
Motley, Constance Baker, 1586
Pinchback, Pinckney B.S., 1587
Randolph, A. Philip, 1588, 2202
Robinson, Randall, 1589

Schomburg, Arthur, 1590
Shakur, Assata, 1591
Sharpton, Al, 1592
Smith, Barbara, 983
Stevens, Thaddeus, 1593
Strickland, William, 1594
Tillman, Dorothy, 1595
Tillman, Jane Irving, 425
Washington, Booker T., 741, 1159
West, Cornel, 1596, 1911
Wilmore, Gayraud, 1333
Woodson, Carter G., 1597
Wright, Bruce, 1598
Yerby, Frank, 2405
Young, Andrew, 1635

Portugal
Cleaver, Kathleen, 533

Poverty
Amos, Wally, 1599
Armstrong, Louis, 1465
Baldwin, James, 2235
Brown, William Wells, 148
Chavis, Benjamin Jr., 1624
Cone, James, 154
Crudup, Arthur, 1600
Douglass, Frederick, 525
Du Bois, W.E.B., 1523, 1601, 1889
Edelman, Marian Wright, 467
Evers-Williams, Myrlie, 1652
Fair, Brian, 53
Fortune, T. Thomas, 731
Gates, Henry Louis Jr., 1748
Gray, Kimi, 704
Gregory, Dick, 573
Higginbotham, Evelyn Brooks, 1291
Holiday, Billie, 1602
Holmes, Larry, 2173
Hughes, Langston, 735
Jackson, Jesse, 1603
Jemison, T.J., 1139
Jordan, Barbara, 553
King, Coretta Scott, 1155
Louis, Joe, 1447
Marshall, Thurgood, 1997
Price, Hugh, 1604
Randolph, A. Philip, 1280
Reverend Ike, 1449
Robeson, Paul, 938
Taylor, Susan, 1880
Tillman, Dorothy, 1595
Washington, Booker T., 819
West, Cornel, 1041

Powell, Adam Clayton
Taylor, Susan, 1323

Power see also **Black power**
Angelou, Maya, 657
Bady, Belynda B., 2342
Baldwin, James, 1285
Bambara, Toni Cade, 1286
Bannister, Edward Mitchell, 234
Bethune, Mary McLeod, 2412, 2507
Brinkley, Rhonda, 1989
Chisholm, Shirley, 1310
Cole, Johnnetta, 761
Cone, James, 495
Douglas, Aaron, 289
Douglass, Frederick, 158
Du Bois, W.E.B., 922
Forten, James, 1664
Fortune, T. Thomas, 84
Franklin, John Hope, 777
Gandhi, Mohandas K., 1605
Garvey, Marcus, 1606
Gray, William H. III, 1276
Harper, Frances Ellen Watkins, 1038
Hill, Anita, 1424, 1607
Hooks, Benjamin, 2312
Hughes, Langston, 735, 2489
Hurston, Zora Neale, 540
Johnson, James Weldon, 178
Jordan, Barbara, 789
Karenga, Ron, 515
King, Martin Luther Jr., 1387, 1506, 1608
Lorde, Audre, 1525
Moore, Melba, 1157
Neal, Larry, 502
Nelson, Jill, 1277
Parsons, Lucy, 1824
Pinkney, Andrea D., 2225
Randolph, A. Philip, 1534
Reagon, Bernice Johnson, 519
Robinson, Randall, 108, 1589
Rustin, Bayard, 1609
Washington, Booker T., 820, 1642, 2308, 2462
Waters, Maxine, 2393
Wells, Ida B., 1763, 2001
West, Cornel, 1236, 2272
Whipper, William S., 1610
Woodson, Carter G., 746
X, Malcolm, 1611, 1827

Prayer see also **Religion**
Anonymous, 2087, 2110, 2115, 2117

Ellington, Duke, 1612
Franklin, C.L., 865
Joyner, Florence Griffith, 2436
Mason, Charles H., 1785
Paige, Satchel, 1613
Qualls, Schyleen, 1559
Smith, Rose, 1739
Walker, Alice, 1908
Washington, James M., 1614, 1615
Young, Andrew, 522

Preaching
Foote, Julia A.J., 1616
Lee, Jarena, 1617, 2373
Lowery, Joseph, 1618
Smitherman, Geneva, 1298
Washington, James M., 505
West, Cornel, 1729
Yerby, Frank, 2405

Prejudice
Bailey, Pearl, 1619
Bethune, Mary McLeod, 726
Brennan, William J., 49
Bruce, John E., 1184
Chesnutt, Charles W., 1620
Gregory, Dick, 1269
Himes, Chester, 1621
Johnson, James Weldon, 2077, 2432
Locke, Alain, 322
Primus, Pearl, 635
Roman, Charles V., 1622
Ruggles, David, 1623
Schomburg, Arthur, 398, 1590
Washington, Booker T., 1644
White, Walter, 744

Pressure
Angelou, Maya, 43
Locke, Alain, 2079
Randolph, A. Philip, 34

Pride *see also* **Black pride**
Blue, Vida, 2170
Browne, Robert S., 377
Bruce, John E., 312
Dyson, Michael Eric, 678
Garvey, Marcus, 213
Hastie, William H., 876
Jackson, Mahalia, 1813
Kennedy, Randall, 394
Marrant, John, 1440
Muhammad, Herbert, 853
Russell, Bill, 1906
Schomburg, Arthur, 1974

Spencer, Anne, 2381
Washington, Booker T., 223
Wells, Ida B., 1763

Principles
Bunche, Ralph, 404
Chesnutt, Charles W., 1264
Delany, Martin R., 1951
Ellington, Duke, 165
Farrakhan, Louis, 1776
Grimke, Francis J., 2330
Harris, Patricia Roberts, 1550
Jones, Quincy, 2435
Morrison, Toni, 2502
Queen Mother Moore, 1230
Randolph, A. Philip, 1588
Wheatley, Phillis, 947

Prison
Chavis, Benjamin Jr., 1624
Cochran, Johnnie J., 1625
Daggett, Janet, 333
Davis, Angela, 1626, 1627
Dyson, Michael Eric, 1628, 1629
Evans, Mari, 1630
Hampton, Fred, 1819
Jackson, George, 1631
Jackson, Jesse, 1603
King, Martin Luther Jr., 30, 1584
Neal, Larry, 341
Paul, Nathaniel, 345
Randolph, A. Philip, 2203
Robeson, Paul, 2205
Rodney, Muhammad, 1240
Shakur, Assata, 1632
Washington, Booker T., 815
Wright, Richard, 1633
X, Malcolm, 1634
Young, Andrew, 1635

Problem solving
Cleaver, Eldridge, 2416
Flake, Floyd, 987
Guinier, Lani, 1317
King, Martin Luther Jr., 603
Price, Leontyne, 2255
Washington, Booker T., 818
Washington, Harold, 613
Weaver, Robert C., 1040

Progress
Bell, Derrick, 1696
Brown, William Wells, 1949
Cole, Johnnetta, 1103
Dinkins, David, 1636

Douglass, Frederick, 2189
Du Bois, W.E.B., 2417
Gates, Henry Louis Jr., 1053, 1748
Hancock, Gordon Blaine, 1637
King, Martin Luther Jr., 1638
Luis, W.A., 1639
Mabley, Moms, 1640
McKay, Claude, 1641
Terrell, Mary Church, 2060
Washington, Booker T., 1642, 1643,
    1644, 1982
Woodson, Carter G., 1125
X, Malcolm, 1645

Promised land
Anonymous, 2142, 2143
Brown, Claude, 146
Burroughs, Nannie, 1950
Du Bois, W.E.B., 833
King, Martin Luther Jr., 1024, 2323
West, Cornel, 353

Promises
Baldwin, James, 638
Charles, Ray, 151
Cole, Johnnetta, 1103
Danky, James P., 1683
Du Bois, W.E.B., 2471
Edwards, Audrey; Polite, Craig K., 772
Jordan, Barbara, 179
Locke, Alain, 623
Williams, Sherley Anne, 2394
Wright, Richard, 1161

Protest
Bearden, Romare, 239
Kennedy, Florynce, 1646
King, Martin Luther Jr., 516
Pinchback, Pinckney B.S., 1647
Powell, Adam Clayton Jr., 559

Protestants
Berry, Mary Frances, 1100
Cruse, Harold, 155
King, Martin Luther Jr., 932

Psychology
Chisholm, Shirley, 974
Clark, Kenneth B., 152
Drake, St. Clair, 361
Gates, Henry Louis Jr., 1423
Hooks, Bell, 2182
Houston, Charles Hamilton, 1957
McHenry, Elizabeth, 1870

Poussaint, Alvin, 558
Simone, Timothy M., 2512

Public life *see also* **Politics**
West, Cornel, 1648

Punishment
Whipper, William S., 1649

Puppets
Chesnutt, Charles W., 880

Purpose *see also* **Goals**
Ali, Muhammad, 1650
Burroughs, Nannie, 1309
Dunham, Katherine, 1651
Evers-Williams, Myrlie, 1652
Garvey, Marcus, 1189, 1653
Himes, Chester, 1654
Jordan, June, 1385
King, Martin Luther Jr., 32
Mayfield, Curtis, 798
Morrison, Toni, 852
Moss, Otis, 487
Parks, Rosa, 1655
Ruggles, David, 1764
White, Walter, 744

Questions
Cole, Johnnetta, 762
Dee, Ruby, 1932
Ellison, Ralph, 2401
Hall, Arsenio, 229
Hill, Anita, 1129
Hurston, Zora Neale, 2253
King, Martin Luther Jr., 1456
Lewis, William Henry, 1180
Locke, Alain, 666
Walker, Alice, 1963
Washington, Booker T., 821
West, Cornel, 1236

Quickness
Ali, Muhammad, 2, 1928
Holyfield, Evander, 887
Rudolph, Wilma, 1855
Wideman, John Edgar, 356

Race *see also* **Blackness; Ethnicity**
Adams, Osceola, 1656
Anderson, Marian, 1657
Anonymous, 1843
Appiah, Anthony, 69, 70, 1182, 1658,
    1659, 1660
Bearden, Romare, 239
Brennan, William J., 49

Brown, Ronald H., 1569
Chavis, Benjamin Jr., 1624
Chesnutt, Charles W., 1620
Chisholm, Shirley, 688
Cleaver, Kathleen, 1661
Cotter, Joseph S., 1662
Douglass, Frederick, 81
Du Bois, W.E.B., 390, 1154, 1523, 1663
Edelman, Marian Wright, 52
Embry, James C., 1496
Fair, Brian, 53
Forten, James, 1664
·Gates, Henry Louis Jr., 54, 1191
Guinier, Lani, 663, 1317
Hastie, William H., 214
Higginbotham, Evelyn Brooks, 978, 979
Himes, Chester, 1621
Jackson, Jesse, 1665
Johnson, James Weldon, 1995
Kennedy, Randall, 394, 1666
Matthews, Victoria Earle, 1360
Norton, Eleanor Holmes, 2377
Preston, Douglas, 1667
Reeves, Keith W., 60
Schomburg, Arthur, 1121
Shakur, Assata, 1591
Shipler, David K., 1668
Sundiata, Ibrahim K., 195
Terrell, Mary Church, 2384
Toomer, Jean, 1669
Truth, Sojourner, 400
Washington, Booker T., 1159, 1670
West, Cornel, 128, 354, 672, 1648, 1671
White, Walter, 744
Wilkins, Roy, 123
Winfrey, Oprah, 984
Woodson, Carter G., 825
Yerby, Frank, 2405

Race consciousness
Baldwin, James, 1672
Harper, Frances Ellen Watkins, 1673
Jordan, Barbara, 1674
Lawrence, Jacob, 1675
Queen Mother Moore, 1676
Wright, Richard, 1677
X, Malcolm, 1678

Race relations
Anderson, Marian, 1679
Baldwin, James, 912, 1183, 1285, 1695
Bell, Derrick, 1696, 2468
Blackmun, Harry, 1680
Bond, Julian, 1834

Bunche, Ralph, 1681
Cleaver, Eldridge, 1732
Clinton, Bill, 1682
Cone, James, 495
Danky, James P., 1683
Douglass, Frederick, 1439
Du Bois, W.E.B., 1684
Fauset, Jessie, 839
Franklin, John Hope, 777
Gates, Henry Louis Jr., 691
Gooding, Cuba Jr., 2328
Hawthorne, Nathaniel, 1685
Hughes, Langston, 1872
Jackson, Mahalia, 1709
Johnson, James Weldon, 1710, 1821
Johnson, John H., 371
Karenga, Ron, 515
King, Coretta Scott, 1845, 2295
King, Martin Luther Jr., 932, 1321
King, Rodney, 1686
Miller, Kelly, 1687
Moses, Bob, 1714
Mosley, Walter, 534
Paderewski, Ignacy, 1259
Parks, Gordon, 344
Poussaint, Alvin, 2297
Powell, Colin, 1839
Randolph, A. Philip, 1922
Reeves, Keith W., 60
Schuyler, George, 1688
Simmons, Judy, 1689
Smith, Anna Deavere, 1690
Smith, Rose, 1739
Walker, David, 199
Washington, Booker T., 1790, 1965
Wells, Ida B., 1733
West, Cornel, 128, 568
Wilson, Mary, 1491
Wilson, William Julius, 1691
X, Malcolm, 1692

Racism
Ali, Muhammad, 1693
Angelou, Maya, 2485
Appiah, Anthony, 1182
Ashe, Arthur, 991, 1694
Baldwin, James, 1695
Bell, Derrick, 1696
Bennett, Lerone, 1697
Blackmun, Harry, 1680
Bond, Julian, 1698
Brown, H. Rap, 1699
Childress, Alice, 1700, 1701

Clarke, John Henrik, 1702
Cone, James, 985
Davis, Angela, 444, 1703, 1704
Douglass, Frederick, 1705
Franklin, John Hope, 1706
Gates, Henry Louis Jr., 527, 1707
Gray, William H. III, 1749
Harper, Frances Ellen Watkins, 1708
Hooks, Benjamin, 2312
Jackson, Mahalia, 1709
Jamison, Judith, 1937
Johnson, James Weldon, 1710
Jones, Nettie, 1876
King, Martin Luther Jr., 1711
Lawrence, Charles, 1712
Monroe, Irene, 501
Morrison, Toni, 1713
Moses, Bob, 1714
Norton, Eleanor Holmes, 2198
Pinkney, Andrea D., 2225
Reed, Adolph, 1715
Robeson, Paul, 1716
Smith, Barbara, 1717
Strickland, William, 1594
Washington, James M., 131, 1718, 1791
West, Cornel, 352, 568
Wilson, Joseph, 1719
Winfrey, Oprah, 2466
X, Malcolm, 1720
Young, Coleman, 1721

Radicalism
Garvey, Marcus, 924
Hansberry, Lorraine, 1820
Johnson, James Weldon, 1821
Powell, Adam Clayton Jr., 1181
Remond, Charles Lenox, 1722
Robeson, Paul, 2204
Rustin, Bayard, 844, 845

Rage *see* **Anger**

Ragtime
Armstrong, Louis, 1463
Johnson, James Weldon, 1723
Priestly, J.B., 1724

Rap
D., Chuck, 1725
Gates, Henry Louis Jr., 1290, 1726
Ice Cube, 1727
Shabazz, Betty, 1487
Shakur, Tupac, 1728
West, Cornel, 1729

Rape
Brawley, Tawana, 1730
Buick, Eliza, 1731
Cleaver, Eldridge, 1732
Wells, Ida B., 1733

Reading *see also* **Books**
Basquiat, Jean-Michel, 2399
Childress, Alice, 759, 1734
Collins, Marva, 764
Dove, Rita, 421
Equiano, Olaudah, 1735
Fuller, Solomon B., 422
Gaines, Ernest J., 2498
Griggs, Sutton E., 1736
Love, Nat "Deadwood Dick, the
    cowboy adventurer," 1737
Marshall, Thurgood, 578
McHenry, Elizabeth, 1196
Morrison, Toni, 802, 2501
Reed, Ishmael, 1738
Smith, Rose, 1739
Sullivan, Leon, 1740
Tillman, Jane Irving, 425
Truth, Sojourner, 1741
Turner, Lana, 426
West, Cornel, 854, 1004
X, Malcolm, 1742

Reagan, Ronald
Farrakhan, Louis, 2291
Shakur, Assata, 1591

Reality
Ali, Muhammad, 1930
Angelou, Maya, 1743
Anonymous, 897
Aptheker, Herbert, 1797
Baldwin, James, 536, 1744, 1745
Catlett, Elizabeth, 246
Clark, Kenneth B., 152
Cole, Johnnetta, 2019
Cone, James, 495, 1746, 2188
Davis, Angela, 2357
Ellison, Ralph, 1747
Farrakhan, Louis, 1777
Gates, Henry Louis Jr., 1748
Gray, William H. III, 1749
Hill, Anita, 1424, 1750
Himes, Chester, 1898
Jackson, Jesse, 1270
Karenga, Ron, 1751
Norton, Eleanor Holmes, 2377
Parks, Rosa, 936

Rustin, Bayard, 845
Toomer, Jean, 1397
Waller, Fats, 1752
Wilson, Flip, 1753
Wright, Richard, 305, 1754
X, Malcolm, 206, 1545

Rebellion
Douglass, Frederick, 1755, 1756
Prosser, Gabriel, 1757
Turner, Nat, 1758, 1759
Waters, Maxine, 1760
West, Cornel, 1761

Reconstruction
Du Bois, W.E.B., 661, 1762
Wells, Ida B., 1763

Records
Brown, Jim, 583

Redemption
Garvey, Marcus, 86, 88
Hansberry, Lorraine, 92
Heber, Reginald, 93
King, Martin Luther Jr., 646, 2231

Reform
Miller, Kelly, 1823
Ruggles, David, 1764
Toomer, Jean, 1765

Reggae
Manley, Michael, 1479

Relationships
Bearden, Romare, 1766
Davis, Angela, 1767
Locke, Alain, 1067
Muhammad, Elijah, 1903
Snipes, Wesley, 1768
Winfrey, Oprah, 1413

Religion *see also* **Catholics; Christianity; Islam; Jews; Methodists; Protestants**
Ali, Muhammad, 1693
Ali, Noble Drew, 1769, 1770
Allen, Richard, 1771
Anonymous, 2091
Appiah, Anthony, 70
Baldwin, Alfred, 1772
Baraka, Amiri, 124
Bethune, Mary McLeod, 1377
Brown, Ronald H., 1569
Brown, William Wells, 1913
Clarke, John Henrik, 2073

Cone, James, 1773
Cullen, Countee, 1774
Douglass, Frederick, 905, 2021
Farrakhan, Louis, 1775, 1776, 1777
Father Divine, 1778
Grace, Sweet Daddy, 1779, 1780, 1781
Harper, Frances Ellen Watkins, 1708
Haynes, Lemuel, 1782
Higginson, Thomas Wentworth, 1783
Jakes, T.D., 1784
King, Martin Luther Jr., 932
Marrant, John, 485
Mason, Charles H., 1785
Michaux, Solomon Lightfoot, 1786
Norton, Eleanor Holmes, 2377
Parker, Charlie, 1787
Powell, Adam Clayton Jr., 1788
Truth, Sojourner, 1789
Washington, Booker T., 741, 1159, 1790
Washington, James M., 1791, 1792
West, Cornel, 352
Wilmore, Gayraud, 1333
Woodson, Carter G., 825
Wright, Richard, 1793
X, Malcolm, 359
Yerby, Frank, 2405

Rembrandt
Baldwin, James, 1885

Reparations
Queen Mother Moore, 1794
Sherman, William T., 1795
Sundiata, Ibrahim K., 1796
Turner, Henry McNeal, 1833

Repression
Du Bois, W.E.B., 1335
Dyson, Michael Eric, 465
Rollins, Sonny, 374

Republican Party
Douglass, Frederick, 1576, 1577
Du Bois, W.E.B., 1579
King, Melvin H., 1585

Research
Cone, James, 765
Gates, Henry Louis Jr., 120
Jones, Lois Mailou, 261
X, Malcolm, 1128

Resistance
Aptheker, Herbert, 1797
Bambara, Toni Cade, 1286
Davis, Angela, 1798, 2358

Douglass, Frederick, 1799
Du Bois, W.E.B., 1800
Evers-Williams, Myrlie, 1801
Hamer, Fannie Lou, 1802
Hunter, Tera W., 628
Jacobs, John, 1803
King, Martin Luther Jr., 1507, 1804
McKay, Claude, 1805
Reeves, Keith W., 60
Walker, David, 1806
Wells, Ida B., 1807

Respect *see also* **Self-respect**
Adam, Andrea Thompson, 972
Chisholm, Shirley, 688
Garvey, Marcus, 9, 2292
King, Martin Luther Jr., 2476
Powell, Adam Clayton Jr., 1307
Robinson, Jackie, 1808
Stewart, Maria W., 2206
Turner, Henry McNeal, 1407
Walker, Alice, 1944
Walker, Mme. C.J., 443
Wells, Ida B., 2001
Wolfe, George C., 2404

Responsibility
Baldwin, James, 1342
Brooks, Walter H., 1453
Carmichael, Stokely, 450
Coleman, Bessie, 587
Cone, James, 496
Davis, Miles, 288
Du Bois, W.E.B., 1809
Edelin, Kenneth C., 466
Edelman, Marian Wright, 874
Gaston, A.G., 2305
Jackson, Jesse, 2429
Jones, Joshua Henry, 1810
King, Martin Luther Jr., 1304
Lowery, Joseph, 56
Toomer, Jean, 303
Turner, Henry McNeal, 1158
Weaver, Robert C., 1040
Wells, Ida B., 202

Retribution
Baldwin, James, 1811
Garvey, Amy Jacques, 1404
Harper, Frances Ellen Watkins, 1812
Jackson, Mahalia, 1813

Revolution
Bambara, Toni Cade, 281
Bennett, Lerone, 753

Bowen, J.W.E., 1203
Chisholm, Shirley, 1310
Clarke, John Henrik, 1814, 1815
Cone, James, 1521
Crummell, Alexander, 2325
Davis, Anthony, 1467
Du Bois, W.E.B., 1816
Forman, James, 1817
Giovanni, Nikki, 1818
Gregory, Dick, 513
Hampton, Fred, 1819
Hansberry, Lorraine, 1820
Hughes, Langston, 1255
Johnson, James Weldon, 1821
Jordan, June, 1294
Manley, Michael, 1479
Miller, Kelly, 1822, 1823
Parsons, Lucy, 1824
Pratt, Geronimo, 1825
Randolph, A. Philip, 1826
Washington, James M., 505
X, Malcolm, 1092, 1827, 1927

Right to life
Marshall, Thurgood, 1997

Rights
Anonymous, 907
Brown, William Wells, 1495
Douglass, Frederick, 976, 1036
Fortune, T. Thomas, 1828
Higginbotham, Evelyn Brooks, 1291
Johnson, James Weldon, 1821
Johnson, Lyndon B., 514
King, Martin Luther Jr., 1829
Marshall, Thurgood, 577, 667, 1337
Norris, Clarence, 2445
Norton, Eleanor Holmes, 1830
Pickens, William, 1831
Pinchback, Pinckney B.S., 1647
Randolph, A. Philip, 2202
Robeson, Paul, 2205
Sharpton, Al, 697
Truth, Sojourner, 38, 2387, 2389, 2390
Tubman, Harriet, 1832
Turner, Henry McNeal, 1833
Wattleton, Faye, 2000
West, Cornel, 671
Woodson, Carter G., 746

Risk
Ali, Muhammad, 20
Coleman, Bessie, 587
Thurman, Howard, 1045

Robinson, Jackie
Aaron, Hank, 384, 544

Rock 'n' roll
Bond, Julian, 1834

Role models
Aaron, Hank, 460
Campbell, Naomi, 1835
Gibson, Bob, 1836
Jackson, Jesse, 1837
O'Neal, Shaquille, 1838
Powell, Colin, 1839

Romance
Anonymous, 900

Russia
Delany, Martin R., 1501
Douglass, Frederick, 832
Wells, Ida B., 1410

Sacrifice
Du Bois, W.E.B., 1840
Hooks, Benjamin, 2312
Parks, Rosa, 935, 1260
Prosser, Gabriel, 1757
Randolph, A. Philip, 2203
Walker, David, 1841
West, Cornel, 568
Woodson, Carter G., 1978

Safety
Douglass, Frederick, 525
Johnson, Magic, 1996
Shange, Ntozake, 192
Simone, Timothy M., 2512
Tubman, Harriet, 2278

Saints
Anonymous, 898, 2128
Bearden, Romare, 1375
Du Bois, W.E.B., 1313
West, Cornel, 1326

Sanity
Gayle, Addison Jr., 1842

Santo Domingo
Moses, Bob, 1714

Schools *see* **Education**

Science
Garvey, Marcus, 90, 1606
Locke, Alain, 94, 95
Madhubuti, Haki, 2402
Muhammad, Elijah, 803

Parsons, Lucy, 1824
Schomburg, Arthur, 1121
Stewart, Maria W., 111
Woodson, Carter G., 2275
Wright, Richard, 305

Scotch
Delany, Martin R., 1501

Sculpture
Catlett, Elizabeth, 246
Du Bois, W.E.B., 83
Edmondson, William, 249
Gates, Henry Louis Jr., 252
Turner, Henry McNeal, 1029

Security
Clarke, John Henrik, 77
James, Chappie, 1542
Robeson, Paul, 877

Segregation
Anonymous, 1843
Bond, Julian, 1698
Childress, Alice, 1701
Clinton, Bill, 1979
Evers-Williams, Myrlie, 2192
Franklin, John Hope, 1107
Gates, Henry Louis Jr., 122
Gray, William H. III, 1749
Hancock, Gordon Blaine, 732
Hurston, Zora Neale, 1844
King, Coretta Scott, 1845
Nixon, E.D., 1846
Randolph, A. Philip, 2202
Sutton, Percy, 712
White, Walter, 2209
Wilkins, Roy, 123

Self-acceptance
Bailey, Pearl, 1847
Baldwin, James, 1848, 2318
Derricotte, Toi, 1849
Gillespie, Dizzy, 1850
Hughes, Langston, 1851
Jackson, Jesse, 1852
Louis, Joe, 2440
Naylor, Gloria, 2444
Robeson, Paul, 1853
Robinson, Max, 1854
Rudolph, Wilma, 1855
Shabazz, Betty, 2454
Stewart, Maria W., 1856
West, Cornel, 1857
Wright, Richard, 1858

Self-actualization *see* **Self-realization**

Self-affirmation
Bailey, Pearl, 1859
Douglass, Frederick, 1860
Gates, Henry Louis Jr., 1861
LaBelle, Patti, 1862
Lorde, Audre, 1863
X, Malcolm, 1864

Self-awareness *see* **Self-knowledge**

Self-confidence
Bethune, Mary McLeod, 386, 1170
Brown, Ronald H., 1865
Cole, Johnnetta, 1866
Garvey, Marcus, 1867
Johnson, Jack, 1868
Johnson, John H., 2222
Jones, Nettie, 1876
Lewis, Carl, 1869
Locke, Alain, 186
McHenry, Elizabeth, 1870
Palmer, Aynim, 805

Self-consciousness *see* **Self-knowledge**

Self-definition *see* **Self-confidence**

Self-determination *see* **Self-liberation**

Self-expression *see also* **Self-realization**
Allen, Richard, 492
Asante, Molefi, 1871
Baldwin, James, 231
Ellington, Duke, 251, 1251
Garvey, Marcus, 1511
Hughes, Langston, 1872
Jakes, T.D., 1784
Johnson, William H., 294
Karenga, Ron, 296
Locke, Alain, 1069, 1940
Marable, Manning, 2374
Marsalis, Wynton, 267
McDowell, Deborah E., 2375
Monk, Thelonious, 1480
Pryor, Richard, 273
Robeson, Paul, 962
Smith, Anna Deavere, 1361
Turner, Tina, 943
Walker, Alice, 1560
Walker, Mme. C.J., 1516
Wright, Richard, 507

Self-fulfillment *see* **Self-realization**

Self-hate
Baldwin, James, 1873, 1874
Gillespie, Marcia Ann, 1875
Grier, William, 1895
Jones, Nettie, 1876
Lowery, Joseph, 1877
Muhammad, Elijah, 1878
Murray, Pauli, 1879
Taylor, Susan, 1880
West, Cornel, 1881
Wright, Richard, 1882
X, Malcolm, 1883, 1884

Self-help *see* **Self-realization**

Self-identity *see* **Self-knowledge**

Self-knowledge
Bailey, Pearl, 2259
Baldwin, James, 1150, 1538, 1885, 1886
Carmichael, Stokely, 1571
Carver, George Washington, 2217
Childress, Alice, 1887
Collins, Marva, 1367
Cone, James, 918
Delaney, Beauford, 1888
Douglass, Frederick, 1226
Du Bois, W.E.B., 1889, 1890
Dyson, Michael Eric, 316, 1891
Franklin, C.L., 1892
Garvey, Marcus, 2076
Gaye, Marvin, 1549, 1893
Giovanni, Nikki, 1193, 1194
Golden, Marita, 1049
Gregory, Dick, 1894
Grier, William, 1895
Hansberry, Lorraine, 1896
Haynes, Lemuel, 1897
Himes, Chester, 1898
Hurston, Zora Neale, 1899
King, Martin Luther Jr., 1900
Lee, Spike, 1958
Locke, Alain, 186
Marable, Manning, 2374
McKay, Claude, 1901
McMillan, Roslyn, 1902
Muhammad, Elijah, 1903
Paige, Satchel, 2448
Perry, Richard, 1904
Prince, 2452
Riggs, Marlon, 1905
Russell, Bill, 1906
Shabazz, Betty, 1352
Smith, Willi, 2479

Thurman, Howard, 878
Tubman, Harriet, 1907
Walker, Alice, 1908, 1909
Washington, Booker T., 1910
Waters, Maxine, 2393
West, Cornel, 1671, 1911
Winfrey, Oprah, 718, 984
Woodruff, Hale, 1006
Wright, Richard, 1912

Self-liberation
Brown, William Wells, 1913
Bruce, Blanche K., 1914
Du Bois, W.E.B., 1915
Gandhi, Mohandas K., 1916
Garvey, Marcus, 1917, 1918
Hamer, Fannie Lou, 1919
Lowery, Joseph, 2441
Morrison, Toni, 1920
Pickens, William, 1921
Randolph, A. Philip, 1922, 1923
Shabazz, Betty, 1924
Sundiata, Ibrahim K., 2043
Walker, Alice, 1925, 1926
West, Cornel, 1976
X, Malcolm, 1927

Self-realization *see also* **Self-expression**
Ali, Muhammad, 1928, 1929, 1930
Angelou, Maya, 2340
Charles, RuPaul, 1931
Cleaver, Kathleen, 533
Dee, Ruby, 1932
Garvey, Marcus, 1933
Gomes, Peter J., 2423
Hogan, Bessie, 1934
Horne, Lena, 1935
Hurston, Zora Neale, 1936
Jamison, Judith, 1937
Johnson, James Weldon, 1938
Johnson, Robert E., 2433
Lewis, Elma, 1939
Locke, Alain, 1067, 1069, 1940
Muhammad, Elijah, 1941
Powell, Adam Clayton Jr., 1942
Solomon, Charlene, 1943
Walker, Alice, 1944
West, Cornel, 673
Woodard, Lynette, 1945
Wright, Richard, 1946

Self-reliance
Adams, Charles G., 747
Angelou, Maya, 1947

Baldwin, James, 1948
Bearden, Romare, 240
Brown, Les, 2414
Brown, William Wells, 1949
Burroughs, Nannie, 1950
Delany, Martin R., 1951, 1952
Du Bois, W.E.B., 1953, 1954
Garvey, Amy Jacques, 1955
Garvey, Marcus, 1956
Houston, Charles Hamilton, 1957
Jackson, Jesse, 2429
Johnson, Georgia Douglas, 2431
Lee, Spike, 1958
Madhubuti, Haki, 1959
McDaniel, Hattie, 2236
Muhammad, Elijah, 1202, 1960
Parks, Gordon, 1961
Russwurm, John B., 1962
Walker, Alice, 1963
Walker, Mme. C.J., 2459
Washington, Booker T., 1964, 1965
Wells, Ida B., 1966
Wonder, Stevie, 1967
Wright, Richard R., 1968

Self-respect *see also* **Respect**
Frazier, E. Franklin, 1969
Giovanni, Nikki, 1970
Hurston, Zora Neale, 1971
Killens, John O., 395
Miller, Kelly, 1972
Price, Leontyne, 1973
Schomburg, Arthur, 1974
Shabazz, Betty, 2454
Stewart, Maria W., 2206
Walker, Aida Overton, 1975
West, Cornel, 1976

Self-understanding *see* **Self-knowledge**

Selfishness
Haynes, Lemuel, 1977
Smith, Anna Deavere, 2243
Woodson, Carter G., 1978

Separation
Allen, Richard, 2280
Anonymous, 137
Bunche, Ralph, 531
Clarke, John Henrik, 78
Clinton, Bill, 1979
Garvey, Marcus, 2292
Gates, Henry Louis Jr., 1980
Hansberry, Lorraine, 1235
Jones, Quincy, 722

Lee-Smith, Hughie, 130, 264
Locke, Alain, 1059
Marshall, Thurgood, 1981
Randolph, A. Philip, 1281
Robinson, Randall, 108, 1589
Sahibs, Abdulalim, 810
Washington, Booker T., 1982
X, Malcolm, 1162

Service to the community *see also*
    Community
Blue, Vida, 2170
Catlett, Elizabeth, 246
Chisholm, Shirley, 1983
Forman, James, 1984
Jones, Quincy, 1985
King, Martin Luther Jr., 1986, 2476
Mays, Benjamin, 1987
Washington, Booker T., 2462
Woodson, Carter G., 1988

Sex
Baldwin, James, 1444
Brinkley, Rhonda, 1989
Broyard, Anatole, 1990
Chisholm, Shirley, 974
De Priest, Oscar, 1991
Gates, Henry Louis Jr., 1726
Gaye, Marvin, 1992
Hamer, Fannie Lou, 1993
Hansberry, Lorraine, 1994
Johnson, James Weldon, 1995
Johnson, Magic, 1996
Marshall, Thurgood, 1997
Pickens, William, 1998
Rock, John S., 1999
Terrell, Mary Church, 2384
Wattleton, Faye, 2000
Wells, Ida B., 2001
Wright, Richard, 420

Sexism
Norton, Eleanor Holmes, 2198
Winfrey, Oprah, 2466

Sexual orientation
Charles, RuPaul, 1931
Elders, Joycelyn, 965
Farajaje-Jones, Elias, 966
Gates, Henry Louis Jr., 1191
Gaye, Marvin, 1992
Gomes, Peter J., 967
Hansberry, Lorraine, 1994
Little Richard, 968
Lorde, Audre, 969

Monroe, Irene, 501
Munroe, Roberta M., 970
Nugent, Bruce, 971
West, Cornel, 128

Shakespeare, William
Baldwin, James, 1885
Du Bois, W.E.B., 1890

Siblings *see* **Family**

Silence
Davis, Sammy Jr., 2002
Douglass, Frederick, 1705
Dyson, Michael Eric, 465
Equiano, Olaudah, 1735
Guinier, Lani, 595
Hill, Anita, 2264
Johnson, James Weldon, 178
Morrison, Toni, 1331
Nunez, Elizabeth, 1297
Powell, Adam Clayton Jr., 609
Riggs, Marlon, 2003
Shaw, Nate, 1122
Walker, Alice, 952
Washington, James M., 1792
Wells, Ida B., 1410
West, Cornel, 128
Wright, Richard, 1274

Singing *see also* **Spirituals**
Angelou, Maya, 2485
Baldwin, James, 638
Burton, Jenny, 2004
Cullen, Countee, 1562
Du Bois, W.E.B., 365
Dunbar, Paul Laurence, 1563
Franklin, Aretha, 2005
Gates, Henry Louis Jr., 1290, 2499
Gaye, Marvin, 2006
Holiday, Billie, 721
Horne, Lena, 1935
Houston, Whitney, 2007
Hughes, Langston, 174, 257, 2490
Jackson, Mahalia, 1709
Jackson, Michael, 1476
Johnson, James Weldon; Johnson, J.
    Rosamond, 2008
King, B.B., 417
King, Martin Luther Jr., 932
LaBelle, Patti, 1862
Locke, Alain, 266
Murray, Pauli, 1141
Naylor, Gloria, 2504
Primus, Pearl, 634

Rawls, Lou, 1483
Reagon, Bernice Johnson, 2009
Reeves, Ruby Lee, 2010
Robeson, Paul, 104, 939, 1485, 2205
Vaughan, Sarah, 2011
Waters, Ethel, 2012
West, Cornel, 1004

Skin color *see* **Color**

Slavery
Adams, John Quincy, 2013
Ali, Muhammad, 134
Allen, Richard, 2014, 2280
Angelou, Maya, 67, 210
Anonymous, 2134, 2137, 2149, 2158
Aptheker, Herbert, 1797
Armstrong, Louis, 1466
Baldwin, James, 638
Beal, Frances M., 2343
Beman, Jehiel C., 2015
Bennett, Lerone, 2314
Bibb, Henry, 524
Brewer, J. Mason, 125
Brown, James, 330
Brown, John, 23
Brown, William Wells, 148, 149, 569,
    1495, 1913, 2016
Bruce, H.C., 830
Buick, Eliza, 1731
Carver, George Washington, 2017
Cinque, Joseph, 586
Clark, Kenneth B., 676
Clarke, John Henrik, 78, 1702
Clifton, Lucille, 720, 2018
Cole, Johnnetta, 2019
Craft, Ellen, 2020
Davis, Angela, 2357
Debro, Sarah, 156
Dinkins, David, 157, 1636
Douglass, Frederick, 481, 831, 873, 905,
    994, 1755, 1799, 1860, 2021, 2022,
    2023, 2024, 2025
Du Bois, W.E.B., 1469
Durr, Virginia, 453, 511
Edwards, Audrey; Polite, Craig K., 772
Ellington, Duke, 616
Ellison, Ralph, 2026
Emerson, Ralph Waldo, 2027
Equiano, Olaudah, 1735
Forten, James, 430, 2028
Fortune, T. Thomas, 591, 1828
Franklin, John Hope, 2029
Gandhi, Mohandas K., 1916, 2030

Garnet, Henry Highland, 592
Garvey, Marcus, 2031
Gates, Henry Louis Jr., 368, 1359
Giovanni, Nikki, 644
Gray, William H. III, 1749
Gregory, Dick, 2032
Griggs, Sutton E., 2033
Grimke, Francis J., 2034
Hamer, Fannie Lou, 2364
Harding, Vincent, 574
Harper, Frances Ellen Watkins, 734
Haynes, Lemuel, 1897
Holt, Thomas, 2035
Horton, George M., 2036
Huggins, Nathan, 1065, 2037
Jackson, Jesse, 1581
Jacobs, Harriet, 981, 2038, 2370
Johns, Vernon, 1023
Killens, John O., 1218
King, Martin Luther Jr., 183, 446, 708
Locke, Alain, 126, 266
Love, Nat "Deadwood Dick, the
    cowboy adventurer," 795
Lowery, Joseph, 648
Luis, W.A., 1639
Madhubuti, Haki, 2402
Mars, James N., 2039
Mason, Charles H., 1785
Moseley-Braun, Carol, 567
Moss, Otis, 934
Muhammad, Elijah, 1903
Nell, William C., 2040
Northup, Solomon, 373, 2041
Owens, Jesse, 1527
Pennington, James W.C., 807
Powell, Adam Clayton Jr., 739
Reynolds, Mary, 2042
Robeson, Paul, 191, 302, 961
Schomburg, Arthur, 1119
Smith, Venture, 193
Stewart, Maria W., 194
Strickland, William, 1430
Sundiata, Ibrahim K., 1123, 2043
Taylor, Susan, 1880
Tourgee, Albion W., 1300
Trotter, William Monroe, 37
Truth, Sojourner, 38, 400, 2044, 2061,
    2385
Tubman, Harriet, 941, 1907, 2045, 2046
Turner, Nat, 2047
Walker, David, 198, 199, 324, 1806
Ward, Samuel Ringgold, 2048

Washington, Booker T., 814, 1279, 2049, 2050, 2051, 2052, 2053
Washington, James M., 131, 505
Wells, Ida B., 824, 1408
Whipper, William S., 1610
White, J., 2054
Woodbey, George W., 448
X, Malcolm, 1199, 1883
Young, Andrew, 522, 2211

Sleep
Anonymous, 897
Du Bois, W.E.B., 1953
Garvey, Marcus, 91
Stewart, Maria W., 2383
X, Malcolm, 2299

Snoop Doggy Dog
Hooks, Bell, 1292

Solidarity *see also* **Brotherhood; Community; Unity**
Clarke, John Henrik, 2055, 2056
De Priest, Oscar, 2057
Douglass, Frederick, 2058
Du Bois, W.E.B., 1154
Edelman, Marian Wright, 2059
Frazier, E. Franklin, 526
Randolph, A. Philip, 1281
Terrell, Mary Church, 2060
Truth, Sojourner, 2061
Woodson, Carter G., 2062

Soul *see also* **Spirit**
Adams, John Quincy, 2013
Aptheker, Herbert, 1797
Armstrong, Louis, 1466
Baldwin, James, 2063
Baraka, Amiri, 282
Bearden, Romare, 235
Bethune, Mary McLeod, 2064
Charles, Ray, 2065
Cone, James, 332
Du Bois, W.E.B., 248, 315, 390, 429, 1328, 1890, 1915, 1953, 2277
Ellington, Duke, 1252
Father Divine, 1778
Gandhi, Mohandas K., 1605
Gomes, Peter J., 2423
Hughes, Langston, 1255, 2066
Jones, Quincy, 722
King, Martin Luther Jr., 185
Locke, Alain, 1068
Parks, Gordon, 2067
Prophet, Nancy Elizabeth, 300

Riggs, Marlon, 2003
Robeson, Paul, 102, 1485, 2069
Shabazz, Betty, 1352, 1553
Stewart, Maria W., 194
Toomer, Jean, 1397
Truth, Sojourner, 2044
Tubman, Harriet, 2278
Vaughan, Sarah, 2011
Washington, James M., 1614

South Africa
Bunche, Ralph, 531

South and North *see* **North and South**

South Carolina
Wilson, August, 564

Soviet Union
Robeson, Paul, 1528

Speech *see* **Language; Oral tradition; Talk; Words**

Spirit *see also* **Soul**
Anonymous, 2087
Bearden, Romare, 2068
Du Bois, W.E.B., 248, 2288
Father Divine, 1016
Garnet, Henry Highland, 1336
Gaye, Marvin, 886
Gomes, Peter J., 1195
Hampton, Lionel, 1475
Hansberry, Lorraine, 619
Huggins, Nathan, 2037
Jones, Bessie, 215
King, Martin Luther Jr., 646
Neal, Larry, 341
Primus, Pearl, 634
Robeson, Paul, 2069
Taylor, Susan, 2070
Turner, Nat, 1758
Winfrey, Oprah, 2071
Young, Andrew, 2072

Spirituality
Anonymous, 898
Burroughs, Nannie, 1309
Clarke, John Henrik, 2073
Coleman, Ornette, 2074
Du Bois, W.E.B., 922
Edelman, Marian Wright, 467
Farrakhan, Louis, 2075
Garvey, Marcus, 2076
Johnson, James Weldon, 2077
Johnson, William H., 294

King, Bernice, 498
King, Coretta Scott, 456, 2078
Locke, Alain, 2079
Miller, Kelly, 1114
Poussaint, Alvin, 558
Powell, Adam Clayton Jr., 1788
Randolph, A. Philip, 2202
West, Cornel, 352
White, Walter, 2209

Spirituals
Anonymous, 2080, 2081, 2082, 2083,
2084, 2085, 2086, 2087, 2088, 2089,
2090, 2091, 2092, 2093, 2094, 2095,
2096, 2097, 2098, 2099, 2100, 2101,
2102, 2103, 2104, 2105, 2106, 2107,
2108, 2109, 2110, 2111, 2112, 2113,
2114, 2115, 2116, 2117, 2118, 2119,
2120, 2121, 2122, 2123, 2124, 2125,
2126, 2127, 2128, 2129, 2130, 2131,
2132, 2133, 2134, 2135, 2136, 2137,
2138, 2139, 2140, 2141, 2142, 2143,
2144, 2145, 2146, 2147, 2148, 2149,
2150, 2151, 2152, 2153, 2154, 2155,
2156, 2157, 2158, 2159, 2160, 2161,
2162, 2163, 2164, 2165, 2166, 2167,
2168
Gaines, Ernest J., 2498
King, Martin Luther Jr., 932

Sports
Aaron, Hank, 384
Ali, Muhammad, 1928, 2169, 2406
Blue, Vida, 2170
Brown, Jim, 583
Chamberlain, Wilt, 2171
Gibson, Althea, 2172
Holmes, Larry, 2173
Jackson, Reggie, 2174
Leonard, Buck, 2175
Leonard, Sugar Ray, 604
Louis, Joe, 14
Robinson, Jackie, 2176
Robinson, Sugar Ray, 2177
Rudolph, Wilma, 2453
Strawberry, Darryl, 2178

Stevens, Thaddeous
Du Bois, W.E.B., 1762

Storytelling
Brewer, J. Mason, 125
Crite, Allan Rohan, 1153
Du Bois, W.E.B., 365
Woodson, Carter G., 2275

Strangers
Gomes, Peter J., 1020
Smith, Anna Deavere, 1690
Tubman, Harriet, 942

Strategy
Ali, Muhammad, 2406
Hancock, Gordon Blaine, 2179

Strength *see* **Black strength**

Stress
Anonymous, 2180
Baldwin, James, 2181
Hooks, Bell, 2182
Horne, Lena, 2183
Houston, Charles Hamilton, 2184

Struggle
Anonymous, 2185
Bady, Belynda B., 2342
Baldwin, James, 1373
Belafonte, Harry, 2186
Benson, Janice Hall, 869
Bunche, Ralph, 2187
Burroughs, Nannie, 6
Clarke, John Henrik, 1702
Cleaver, Kathleen, 533
Cone, James, 2188
Davis, Angela, 1704
Douglass, Frederick, 1860, 2189
Drew, Charles R., 2190
Du Bois, W.E.B., 771
Evers, Medgar, 2191
Evers-Williams, Myrlie, 2192
Farajaje-Jones, Elias, 966
Forman, James, 1817
Garvey, Marcus, 2193
Gordy, Berry Jr., 1460
Haley, Alex, 875
Hancock, Gordon Blaine, 785
Hansberry, Lorraine, 2194
Hooks, Benjamin, 1492
Hope, John, 840
Killens, John O., 2195
King, Martin Luther Jr., 31, 407, 499,
529, 601, 664, 1638
Lowery, Joseph, 2196
Mfume, Kweisi, 2197
Murray, Pauli, 738
Naylor, Gloria, 2504
Norton, Eleanor Holmes, 2198
Owens, Jesse, 2199
Pickens, William, 1921
Powell, Adam Clayton Jr., 2200

Queen Mother Moore, 2201
Randolph, A. Philip, 1923, 2202, 2203
Robeson, Paul, 2204, 2205
Rustin, Bayard, 844
Smith, Barbara, 983
Stewart, Maria W., 2206
Turner, Nat, 1759
Walker, Alice, 2207
Washington, Harold, 2208
West, Cornel, 854, 1911
Whipper, William S., 1222
White, Walter, 2209
X, Malcolm, 2210
Young, Andrew, 2211

Style
Allen, Bonnie, 2212, 2213
Baldwin, James, 1695
Cone, James, 917
Edmondson, William, 249
Ellison, Ralph, 366
Jemison, Mae, 2214
King, Martin Luther Jr., 1321
Turner, Darwin T., 1363
West, Cornel, 1729
Wolfe, George C., 2215

Submission
Bell, Derrick, 1696
Douglass, Frederick, 1799
Du Bois, W.E.B., 1800
Trotter, William Monroe, 37
Wells, Ida B., 1408

Success
Bell, Derrick, 1696
Cain, Herman, 2216
Carver, George Washington, 1509, 2217
Douglass, Frederick, 2287
Dyson, Michael Eric, 2361
Fortune, T. Thomas, 2218, 2362
Gaston, A.G., 438
Gates, Henry Louis Jr., 121, 369
Jackson, Jesse, 2219
Jakes, T.D., 2220, 2221
Johnson, John H., 2222
Killens, John O., 2195
Lawrence, Jacob, 263
Murphy, Isaac, 1130
Parks, Gordon, 2223
Pickens, William, 2224
Pinkney, Andrea D., 2225
Powell, Colin, 2226
Robinson, Bojangles, 2227

Washington, Booker T., 477, 1084
X, Malcolm, 2228
Young, Coleman, 2229

Suffering
Allen, Richard, 2280
Armstrong, Louis, 1466
Baraka, Amiri, 1132
Douglass, Frederick, 1860
Ellison, Ralph, 2290
Flack, Roberta, 2230
Forten, James, 430
Gaye, Marvin, 293
Jackson, Jesse, 2313
Jacobs, Harriet, 981
King, Martin Luther Jr., 2231
Marrant, John, 1440
Muhammad, Elijah, 1960
Purvis, Robert, 190
Randolph, A. Philip, 2203
Remond, Charles Lenox, 1722
Toomer, Jean, 2232
Walker, David, 1332
West, Cornel, 854, 2272

Sumner, Charles
Du Bois, W.E.B., 1762

Supreme Court
Douglass, Frederick, 1577
Hill, Anita, 1129
Marshall, Thurgood, 57
Reeves, Keith W., 60

Survival
Angelou, Maya, 43, 1149, 2233
Anonymous, 2341
Bailey, Pearl, 2234
Baldwin, James, 986, 2235
Clarke, John Henrik, 1358
Collins, Marva, 1367
Flack, Roberta, 2230
Hancock, Gordon Blaine, 2179
Horne, Lena, 2368
Lorde, Audre, 1557
Marshall, Thurgood, 579
McDaniel, Hattie, 2236
Morrison, Toni, 852
Robeson, Paul, 220
Strickland, William, 1430
Truth, Sojourner, 2237
Walker, Alice, 1909, 2207
Waters, Ethel, 2238
West, Cornel, 2239
X, Malcolm, 1007

Talented tenth
Du Bois, W.E.B., 2240

Talk *see also* **Language; Oral tradition; Words**
Anonymous, 2088, 2116
Brown, John, 23
Clinton, Bill, 1682
Equiano, Olaudah, 1735
Garvey, Marcus, 1018
Guinier, Lani, 595
Jakes, T.D., 1022
Johnson, Lyndon B., 514
Jordan, Barbara, 28
Morrison, Toni, 2503
Petry, Ann, 2492
Russwurm, John B., 349
Stewart, Maria W., 36
Toomer, Jean, 2455
Woodson, Carter G., 41

Teaching *see* **Education**

Tears
Allen, Richard, 135
Baldwin, James, 1010
Farajaje-Jones, Elias, 966
Franklin, Aretha, 2005
Miller, Thomas E., 188
Tubman, Harriet, 2046
Turner, Henry McNeal, 1833
Walker, David, 199
Washington, Booker T., 2051

Television
Baldwin, James, 2242
Gates, Henry Louis Jr., 369
West, Cornel, 1326

Tennessee
Chase, Henry, 1366
King, Martin Luther Jr., 2476
Wilson, August, 564

Testimony
Cone, James, 1773
Gates, Henry Louis Jr., 1359

Tests
Griffin, Judith, 782

Theater
Abrahams, Robert, 2241
Baldwin, James, 2242
Childress, Alice, 1701
De Priest, Oscar, 1991
Robinson, Bojangles, 2227

Smith, Anna Deavere, 2243
Walker, Aida Overton, 2244
Williams, Bert, 2245, 2246

Theology
Cone, James, 496

Thinking *see also* **Mind**
Amos, Wally, 1599
Clark, Septima, 459
Cole, Johnnetta, 1866
Garvey, Marcus, 1078, 2031
Gomes, Peter J., 2423
Hansberry, Lorraine, 2247
Hill, Anita, 1607
Hurston, Zora Neale, 2248
Johnson, John H., 2222
Marsalis, Wynton, 267
Norton, Eleanor Holmes, 2505
Robinson, Sugar Ray, 2177
Simone, Nina, 1262
Toomer, Jean, 2455
Turner, Tina, 2456
Washington, Booker T., 2309
Woodson, Carter G., 1530

Third World
Moses, Bob, 1714
Rivers, Eugene, 504

Thomas, Clarence
Hill, Anita, 1129

Time *see also* **Future; History**
Anderson, Marian, 1070
Anonymous, 2117
Bailey, Pearl, 2249
Baldwin, James, 1096, 1505
Bates, Daisy, 2250
Berry, Halle, 2344
Bethune, Mary McLeod, 386
Bontemps, Arna, 2251
Bradley, David, 329
Brown, Ronald H., 1865
Buckley, Gail Lumet, 870
Clarke, John Henrik, 1101
Clinton, Bill, 1682
Cosby, Bill, 2252
Davis, Ossie, 314
Du Bois, W.E.B., 429, 1134
Evers-Williams, Myrlie, 1652
Gates, Henry Louis Jr., 27
Giovanni, Nikki, 2263
Hare, Nathan, 1319
Harper, Frances Ellen Watkins, 927

Hurston, Zora Neale, 2253
Jackson, Jesse, 2313
King, Martin Luther Jr., 2254
Lowery, Joseph, 648
Morrison, Toni, 269
Ross, Diana, 963
Turner, Henry McNeal, 1029
West, Cornel, 2465
Woodson, Carter G., 2275
X, Malcolm, 2210

Tocqueville, Alexis de
West, Cornel, 354

Tokenism
Price, Leontyne, 2255

Traditions
Bambara, Toni Cade, 1286
Bearden, Romare, 237
Cone, James, 1773
Gayle, Addison Jr., 363
Johnson, William H., 294
Schomburg, Arthur, 398
West, Cornel, 39, 673, 1160
Woodson, Carter G., 226

Travel *see also* **Journeys**
Charles, Ray, 2256
Douglass, Frederick, 159
Smith, Barbara, 2506
Truth, Sojourner, 1504

Trouble
Anonymous, 2135, 2151, 2162
Farrakhan, Louis, 306
Madison, Joe, 2257
O'Neal, Shaquille, 1838
Reagon, Bernice Johnson, 2258
Yarborough, Camille, 480

Truth
Allen, William Grant, 2397
Angelou, Maya, 66
Bady, Belynda B., 2342
Bailey, Pearl, 2259
Baldwin, James, 1283
Bearden, Romare, 238
Cone, James, 2188
Du Bois, W.E.B., 661, 1890, 2260
Farrakhan, Louis, 2261
Fortune, T. Thomas, 2262
Giovanni, Nikki, 2263
Hill, Anita, 2264
Hurston, Zora Neale, 705, 2265, 2369
Jackson, Jesse, 2266

Killens, John O., 2267
Marshall, Thurgood, 2268
Pryor, Richard, 273
Rustin, Bayard, 890
Sanchez, Sonia, 275
Truth, Sojourner, 1504, 2269
Turner, Henry McNeal, 1406
Walker, Alice, 1926
Washington, Booker T., 2309
Wells, Ida B., 2270
West, Cornel, 1976, 2271, 2272
Wiley, Ralph, 2273
Woodson, Carter G., 2274, 2275
X, Malcolm, 205, 2276

Truth, Sojourner
Higginbotham, Evelyn Brooks, 979
Truth, Sojourner, 1504
Winfrey, Oprah, 225

Tubman, Harriet
Walker, Alice, 2392
Winfrey, Oprah, 225

Turner, Nat
Bennett, Lerone, 2314
Douglass, Frederick, 1755
Robeson, Paul, 2511

Tuskegee Institute
Trotter, William Monroe, 37
Washington, Booker T., 2463

Twain, Mark
West, Cornel, 419

Twoness
Du Bois, W.E.B., 2277

U.S. Congress *see* **Congress**

U.S. Constitution *see* **Constitution**

U.S. Supreme Court *see* **Supreme Court**

Ugliness
Baldwin, James, 1744
Hughes, Langston, 2489
King, Martin Luther Jr., 1457
West, Cornel, 411

Uncle Toms
Hughes, Langston, 787

Underground railroad
Tubman, Harriet, 2279, 2278

Uniqueness
Cooper, Anna Julia, 2355

Ellison, Ralph, 291
King, Martin Luther Jr., 1506
Price, Leontyne, 397

United Kingdom
Delany, Martin R., 1501

United Nations
Bunche, Ralph, 1547

United States *see* **America**

Unity *see also* **Brotherhood; Community; Solidarity**
Allen, Richard, 2280
Angelou, Maya, 2281, 2282
Anonymous, 2283
Appiah, Anthony, 1658
Bambara, Toni Cade, 2284
Baraka, Amiri, 282
Bethune, Mary McLeod, 726
Bradley, Mamie, 2285
Bruce, John E., 1184
Clarke, John Henrik, 79
Crummell, Alexander, 380
Douglass, Frederick, 2286, 2287
Du Bois, W.E.B., 2288, 2289
Ellison, Ralph, 2290
Farrakhan, Louis, 2291
Forten, James, 430
Garvey, Marcus, 2292
Hall, Prince, 2293
Hooks, Bell, 2294
King, Coretta Scott, 2295
Marley, Bob, 2296
Poussaint, Alvin, 2297
Robeson, Paul, 2205
Scott, Hazel, 940
Washington, Booker T., 2298
White, Walter, 948
Woodson, Carter G., 1554
X, Malcolm, 2299

Values
Ashe, Arthur, 2300
Burroughs, Nannie, 2301, 2302
Carmichael, Stokely, 76
Du Bois, W.E.B., 2303
Edelman, Marian Wright, 2304
Ellison, Ralph, 2488
Gaston, A.G., 2305
Gates, Henry Louis Jr., 693
Karenga, Ron, 262
Lee, Spike, 2438
Paige, Satchel, 2448

Poussaint, Alvin, 2306
Powell, Colin, 2307
Schomburg, Arthur, 1974
Washington, Booker T., 2308, 2309, 2310
Woodson, Carter G., 226
Young, Whitney M. Jr., 209, 2311

Vesey, Denmark
Douglass, Frederick, 1755
Robeson, Paul, 2511

Victory *see also* **Winning**
Bell, Derrick, 1696
Burroughs, Nannie, 6
Giddings, Paula, 997
Grimke, Charlotte Forten, 2329
Hooks, Benjamin, 2312
Jackson, Jesse, 2313
Johnson, James Weldon, 956

Vietnam
Moses, Bob, 1714

Vietnam War
Baldwin, James, 138
King, Martin Luther Jr., 2331

Villages
Du Bois, W.E.B., 83
Edelin, Kenneth C., 466

Violence
Baldwin, James, 1074
Bennett, Lerone, 523, 2314
Bond, Julian, 2315
Brown, H. Rap, 2316
Douglass, Frederick, 1799
King, Martin Luther Jr., 500
Thurman, Howard, 1081
White, Walter, 744
X, Malcolm, 2317

Virgins
Du Bois, W.E.B., 2359

Virtue *see* **Morality; Values**

Vision
Ali, Muhammad, 1928
Baldwin, James, 2318
Bethune, Mary McLeod, 2319
Douglas, Aaron, 2320
Du Bois, W.E.B., 661
Garvey, Marcus, 781
Hurston, Zora Neale, 2321
Johnson, John H., 2322

King, Martin Luther Jr., 2323
Miller, Kelly, 1114
Rustin, Bayard, 845
Smith, Barbara, 983
West, Cornel, 1325
Winfrey, Oprah, 718

Voting
Carmichael, Stokely, 1571
Chisholm, Shirley, 1573
Du Bois, W.E.B., 1578
Hamer, Fannie Lou, 1580
Jackson, Jesse, 1582
King, Coretta Scott, 1583
King, Martin Luther Jr., 1584
Pickens, William, 669
Reeves, Keith W., 60
Stevens, Thaddeus, 1593
Tillman, Dorothy, 1595
White, Walter, 744
Wright, Bruce, 1598

Walker, C. J.
Winfrey, Oprah, 225

War
Anonymous, 2324
Baldwin, James, 1373
Crummell, Alexander, 2325
Douglass, Frederick, 2326, 2327
Gooding, Cuba Jr., 2328
Grimke, Charlotte Forten, 2329
Grimke, Francis J., 2330
King, Martin Luther Jr., 2331
Long, Thomas, 2332
Nell, William C., 2040
Parsons, Lucy, 1824
Price, Hugh, 1604
Randolph, A. Philip, 2202
Tubman, Harriet, 2333
Turner, Nat, 1759
Washington, Booker T., 2051

Washington, George
Jordan, Barbara, 576
Prosser, Gabriel, 1757

Waste
Anonymous, 750
Powell, Colin, 2226
Russwurm, John B., 349

Wealth
Baldwin, James, 142
Brown, Tony, 436
Hughes, Langston, 735

Marshall, Thurgood, 667
Mays, Benjamin, 1987

Welfare
Baldwin, James, 1239
Flake, Floyd, 987
Rivers, Eugene, 504
Wilson, William Julius, 2484

Wells, Ida B.
Winfrey, Oprah, 225

Welsh
Delany, Martin R., 1501

West Indies
Du Bois, W.E.B., 1816

Wheatley, Phillis
Gates, Henry Louis Jr., 2363

White supremacy
Cleaver, Kathleen, 1661
West, Cornel, 411, 854, 1881
X, Malcolm, 1092, 1927

Whites *see also* **Race relations**
Ali, Muhammad, 1223
Asante, Molefi, 71
Baldwin, James, 698, 1508, 1672
Bergreen, Laurence, 1246
Berry, Mary Frances, 1100
Bethune, Mary McLeod, 4
Clarke, John Henrik, 77
Cleaver, Eldridge, 1093
Cruse, Harold, 155, 1188
Dinkins, David, 1575
Douglass, Frederick, 81
Du Bois, W.E.B., 1014, 1328, 2260
Edelman, Marian Wright, 52
Edwards, Audrey; Polite, Craig K., 772
Elders, Joycelyn, 773
Ellison, Ralph, 366
Farrakhan, Louis, 169
Fortune, T. Thomas, 84
Gregory, Dick, 573
Hamer, Fannie Lou, 1580
Hancock, Gordon Blaine, 1637
Hansberry, Lorraine, 1820
Higginbotham, Evelyn Brooks, 2367
Hooks, Bell, 1292
Hughes, Langston, 2490
Jackson, Jesse, 484, 1603
King, Martin Luther Jr., 646
Lessing, Doris, 1156
McGuire, George Alexander, 1025

Muhammad, Elijah, 1878
Munroe, Roberta M., 970
Parks, Rosa, 607
Pickens, William, 1998
Savage, Augusta, 350
Shakur, Assata, 1632
Sharpton, Al, 1039
Terrell, Mary Church, 2384
Turner, Henry McNeal, 1030
Walker, David, 324
Washington, Booker T., 201, 946, 1670
Wells, Ida B., 824, 2001
X, Malcolm, 1007, 1402

Winning *see also* **Victory**
Abdul Jabbar, Kareem, 1451, 2334
Bass, Charlotta, 2335
Gibson, Althea, 2336
Grimke, Charlotte Forten, 2329
Jackson, Jesse, 2337
Murphy, Isaac, 2443

Wisdom
Allen, Richard, 135
Douglass, Frederick, 158
Edmondson, William, 249
Parker, Charlie, 1482
Reed, Ishmael, 1738
Walker, Alice, 1431
Washington, Booker T., 847
West, Cornel, 2338, 2339
Young, Whitney M. Jr., 19

Women *see also* **Gender**
Alexander, Elizabeth, 1282
Allen, Bonnie, 2213
Angelou, Maya, 2340
Anonymous, 2341
Bady, Belynda B., 2342
Beal, Frances M., 2343
Berry, Halle, 2344
Bethune, Mary McLeod, 2345, 2346
Blige, Mary J., 2347
Brawley, Tawana, 1730
Buick, Eliza, 1731
Catlett, Elizabeth, 2348
Charles, RuPaul, 1420
Chisholm, Shirley, 974, 975, 2349, 2350, 2351
Clark, Ramsey, 2352
Clifton, Lucille, 1187
Cole, Johnnetta, 1866, 2353
Cooper, Anna Julia, 2354, 2355
Craft, Ellen, 2020

Dash, Julie, 2356, 2508
Davis, Angela, 1767, 2357, 2358
Douglass, Frederick, 976
Du Bois, W.E.B., 977, 2359, 2360
Dyson, Michael Eric, 2361
Edelman, Marian Wright, 52
Fortune, T. Thomas, 2362
Gates, Henry Louis Jr., 691, 693, 1191, 2363
Giddings, Paula, 468
Haley, Alex, 319
Hamer, Fannie Lou, 1993, 2364
Hansberry, Lorraine, 2365
Harper, Frances Ellen Watkins, 2366
Higginbotham, Evelyn Brooks, 979, 2367
Hill, Anita, 1424, 1607
Horne, Lena, 1935, 2368
Hughes, Dorothy Pitman, 440
Hurston, Zora Neale, 2369
Jacobs, Harriet, 981, 2370
Jemison, Mae, 982
Johnson, Georgia Douglas, 2371
King, Coretta Scott, 1583
Ladd, Florence, 2372
Lee, Jarena, 1617, 2373
Mabley, Moms, 1428
Marable, Manning, 2374
Marshall, Thurgood, 1997
McDowell, Deborah E., 2375
Monroe, Irene, 501
Morrison, Toni, 2376
Motley, Constance Baker, 1586
Norton, Eleanor Holmes, 2198, 2377
Paul, Nathaniel, 345
Rogers, J.A., 2378
Scott, Hazel, 2379
Shange, Ntozake, 2380
Smith, Barbara, 983
Spencer, Anne, 2381
Stewart, Maria W., 2382, 2383
Terrell, Mary Church, 2384
Truth, Sojourner, 2385, 2386, 2387, 2388, 2389, 2390
Tyson, Cecily, 2391
Walker, Alice, 1925, 1963, 2392
Waters, Maxine, 2393
Wells, Ida B., 1410, 2001
West, Cornel, 128
Williams, Sherley Anne, 2394
Winfrey, Oprah, 2395
Young, Andrew, 2396

Wonders
  Browne, Sir Thomas, 74
  Chase, Henry, 1366

Words *see also* **Language; Oral tradition; Talk**
  Allen, William Grant, 2397
  Angelou, Maya, 1088
  Asante, Molefi, 2398
  Basquiat, Jean-Michel, 2399
  Brooks, Gwendolyn, 2400
  Ellison, Ralph, 2401
  Gates, Henry Louis Jr., 1289
  King, Martin Luther Jr., 1457
  Madhubuti, Haki, 2402
  Morrison, Toni, 2403
  Norton, Eleanor Holmes, 2377
  Nugent, Bruce, 971
  Russwurm, John B., 349
  Simone, Nina, 1262
  Turner, Henry McNeal, 1029
  Turner, Lana, 426
  Walker, Alice, 1431
  Wolfe, George C., 2404

Work *see also* **Hard work; Jobs; Labor**
  Ailey, Alvin, 2467
  Anonymous, 435
  Bell, Derrick, 2468
  Bluford, Guion S. Jr., 2469
  Carroll, Diahann, 2470
  Du Bois, W.E.B., 768, 1380, 2471
  Ellington, Duke, 2472
  Franklin, John Hope, 2473
  Gates, Henry Louis Jr., 1192
  Gomes, Peter J., 1020
  Hines, Gregory, 2474
  Hughes, Langston, 1255
  Hurston, Zora Neale, 2475
  King, Martin Luther Jr., 2476
  Love, Nat "Deadwood Dick, the
    cowboy adventurer," 1426
  McCarthy, Osceola, 2477
  Owens, Jesse, 1527
  Rustin, Bayard, 844
  Simmons, Della, 2478
  Sullivan, Leon, 2480
  Washington, Booker T., 2481, 2482
  Wilson, William Julius, 2484

Writers *see also* **Literature**
  Angelou, Maya, 2485
  Baldwin, James, 2486, 2487
  Chesnutt, Charles W., 2496

  Childress, Alice, 1734
  Douglass, Frederick, 81
  Ellison, Ralph, 2488
  Evans, Mari, 684
  Gates, Henry Louis Jr., 369, 2363, 2499
  Gayle, Addison Jr., 363
  Golden, Marita, 618
  Hughes, Langston, 2489, 2490
  Killens, John O., 455
  Petry, Ann, 2491, 2492
  Turner, Lana, 426
  Walker, Alice, 2493
  West, Cornel, 1004
  Wright, Richard, 1677
  Yerby, Frank, 2405

Writing
  Baldwin, James, 2494
  Blockson, Charles L., 2495
  Chesnutt, Charles W., 2496
  Childress, Alice, 2497
  Du Bois, W.E.B., 1208
  Gaines, Ernest J., 2498
  Gates, Henry Louis Jr., 2499
  Johnson, Charles, 2500
  McHenry, Elizabeth, 1196
  Morrison, Toni, 2501, 2502, 2503
  Naylor, Gloria, 2504
  Norton, Eleanor Holmes, 2505
  Smith, Barbara, 2506
  West, Cornel, 854

X, Malcolm
  Davis, Ossie, 1312
  Horne, Lena, 1135
  Shabazz, Betty, 1396
  Taylor, Susan, 1323
  X, Malcolm, 1199

Yale University
  Jackson, Jesse, 1603

Youth *see also* **Adolescence; Children**
  Angelou, Maya, 43
  Baldwin, James, 1508
  Bethune, Mary McLeod, 2507
  Bond, Julian, 1834
  Brown, William Wells, 2016
  Cochran, Johnnie J., 1625
  Dash, Julie, 2508
  Donaldson, Greg, 464
  Ice Cube, 1727
  Jackson, Jesse, 1837, 2509
  Johnson, James Weldon, 2510
  Johnson, Magic, 1996

King, Bernice, 498
Ladd, Florence, 2372
McCall, Nathan, 800
Naylor, Gloria, 2504
Powell, Colin, 959

Robeson, Paul, 2511
Shabazz, Betty, 1487
Simone, Timothy M., 375, 2512
Washington, Booker T., 1964

OCCUPATION INDEX

Numbers refer to entry numbers.

Abolition Movement

Douglass, Frederick, 8, 25, 81, 158, 159, 160, 389, 481, 525, 538, 766, 767, 831, 832, 872, 873, 905, 920, 976, 994, 1013, 1036, 1226, 1266, 1334, 1439, 1522, 1576, 1577, 1705, 1755, 1756, 1799, 1860, 2021, 2022, 2023, 2024, 2025, 2058, 2189, 2286, 2287, 2326, 2327

Forten, James, 430, 1664, 2028

Garnet, Henry Highland, 483, 592, 1336

Grimke, Charlotte Forten, 2329

Higginson, Thomas Wentworth, 1783

Nell, William C., 2040

Purvis, Robert, 190

Remond, Charles Lenox, 1722

Ruggles, David, 1623, 1764

Russwurm, John B., 349, 1962

Truth, Sojourner, 38, 400, 611, 650, 1028, 1438, 1503, 1504, 1741, 1789, 2044, 2061, 2237, 2269, 2385, 2386, 2387, 2388, 2389, 2390

Tubman, Harriet, 651, 677, 941, 942, 1338, 1832, 1907, 2045, 2046 , 2278, 2279, 2333

Walker, David, 197, 198, 199, 324 , 813, 945, 1332, 1433, 1806, 1841

Ward, Samuel Ringgold, 2048

Whipper, William S., 1222, 1610, 1649,

Activism *see also* Government and Politics; Organization Leaders

Alexander, Sadie T.M., 580

Baldwin, James, 22, 72, 138, 139, 140, 141, 142, 143, 144, 227, 230, 231, 232, 326, 327, 328, 402, 461, 462, 536, 638, 698, 699, 719, 752, 849, 857, 868, 883, 912, 913, 973, 986, 1009, 1010, 1071, 1072, 1073, 1074, 1096, 1097, 1098, 1099, 1147, 1150, 1183, 1213, 1239, 1243, 1244, 1245, 1283, 1284, 1285, 1342, 1343, 1355,

1373, 1374, 1418, 1444, 1505, 1508, 1520, 1537, 1538, 1672, 1695, 1744, 1745, 1811, 1848, 1873, 1874, 1885, 1886, 1948, 2063, 2181, 2235, 2242, 2318, 2409, 2410, 2486, 2487, 2494

Burroughs, Nannie, 6, 1309, 1950, 2301, 2302

Carmichael, Stokely, 76, 313, 378, 379, 437, 450, 451, 546, 1214, 1571

Carr, Johnnie, 509

Chavis, Benjamin Jr., 548, 1624

Du Bois, W.E.B., 26, 82, 83, 132, 161, 162, 163, 164, 248, 315 , 365, 381, 390, 429, 641, 661 , 768, 769, 770, 771, 833, 838, 921, 922, 977, 1014, 1134, 1154, 1163, 1208, 1313, 1328, 1335, 1380, 1414, 1469, 1523, 1578, 1579, 1601, 1663, 1684, 1762, 1800, 1809, 1816, 1840, 1889, 1890, 1915, 1953, 1954, 2240, 2260, 2277, 2288, 2289, 2303, 2359, 2360, 2417 , 2471

Goodman, Paul, 512

Gregory, Dick, 171, 172, 410, 513 , 573, 926, 1080, 1108, 1269, 1524, 1894, 2032

Jackson, George, 1631

Johnson, James Weldon, 178, 259, 631, 956, 1057, 1540, 1564, 1710, 1723, 1821, 1938, 1995, 2008, 2077, 2432

King, Melvin H., 1585

Norton, Eleanor Holmes, 342, 1830, 2198 , 2377, 2505

Robeson, Paul, 101, 102, 103, 104 , 105, 106, 191, 220, 221, 302, 447, 560, 636, 877, 938, 939, 961, 962, 990, 1117, 1197 , 1484, 1485, 1528, 1716, 1853, 2069, 2204, 2205, 2511

Sharpton, Al, 35, 697, 1039, 1272, 1273, 1592

Shuttlesworth, Fred, 520

West, Cornel, 39, 115, 128, 224 , 278, 352, 353, 354, 411, 419, 488, 530, 563, 568, 671, 672, 673, 675, 854,

1004, 1041 , 1144, 1160, 1173, 1205,
1236, 1324, 1325, 1326, 1489, 1498,
1596 , 1648, 1671, 1729, 1761, 1857,
1881, 1911, 1976, 2239, 2271, 2272,
2338, 2339, 2465

Anarchist
Parsons, Lucy, 1824

Black Panther Party leader
Cleaver, Eldridge, 153, 1076, 1093,
1152, 1732, 2416
Hampton, Fred, 1819
Newton, Huey, 383, 557

Civil Rights activist
Abernathy, Ralph, 491
Bates, Daisy, 2250
Belafonte, Harry, 2186
Blackwell, Unita, 582
Bond, Julian, 727, 1698, 1834, 2315
Clark, Septima, 459, 570
Colvin, Claudette, 1311
Cotton, Dorothy, 510
Durr, Virginia, 453, 511
Evers, Medgar, 1178, 2191
Farmer, James, 362
Forman, James, 1817, 1984
Hamer, Fannie Lou, 173, 337, 1302,
1580, 1802, 1919, 1993, 2364
Houston, Charles Hamilton, 405,
1957, 2184
Jackson, Jesse, 12, 175, 176, 484, 597,
694, 707, 1137, 1138, 1217, 1270,
1455, 1581, 1582, 1603, 1665, 1837,
1852, 2219, 2266, 2313, 2337, 2428,
2429, 2509
King, Coretta Scott, 182, 456, 1155,
1583, 1845, 2078, 2295
King, Martin Luther Jr., 30, 31, 32,
183, 184, 185, 339, 396, 407, 431,
445, 446, 499, 500, 516, 528, 529,
554, 601, 602, 603, 646, 664, 682,
686, 687, 695, 708, 791, 792, 929,
930, 931, 932, 988, 1024, 1094,
1207, 1303, 1304, 1305, 1320, 1321,
1386, 1387, 1456, 1457, 1506, 1507,
1552, 1584 , 1608, 1638, 1711,
1804, 1829, 1900, 1985, 2231, 2254,
2323, 2331, 2437, 2476
Lowery, Joseph, 56, 340, 648, 723,
1618, 1877, 2196, 2441
Moses, Bob, 1322, 1714
Nixon, E.D., 517, 1846
Parks, Rosa, 33, 219, 607, 608, 935,
936, 1115, 1260, 1655

Pickens, William, 669, 1831, 1921,
1998, 2224
Rustin, Bayard, 844, 845, 890, 1609
Tillman, Dorothy, 1595
Trotter, William Monroe, 37
Vivian, C.T., 351
Walker, Wyatt T., 1143
White, Walter, 744, 948, 2209
Wilkins, Roy, 123, 1124, 1237
Young, Andrew, 522, 655, 1635, 2072,
2211, 2396
Young, Whitney M. Jr., 19, 209, 1212,
2311

Insurrectionist
Brown, John, 23, 147
Cinque, Joseph, 586, 1434
Prosser, Gabriel, 1757
Turner, Nat, 1758, 1759, 2047

Lesbian activist
Smith, Barbara, 983, 1717, 2506

Militant activist
Bass, Charlotta, 2335
Brown, H. Rap, 1699, 2316
Davis, Angela, 247, 444, 1574, 1626 ,
1627, 1703, 1704, 1767, 1798, 2357,
2358
Pratt, Geronimo, 1825
Turner, Henry McNeal, 114, 835,
906, 1029, 1030, 1158, 1406, 1407,
1543, 1544, 1833
Wells, Ida B., 202, 824, 1308, 1408,
1409, 1410, 1733, 1763, 1807, 1966,
2001, 2270
Williams, Robert, 521, 1005
X, Malcolm, 42,119, 204, 205, 206,
207, 208, 359, 360, 432, 433, 566,
654, 725, 829, 1007, 1046, 1050,
1092, 1127, 1128, 1162, 1169, 1198,
1199, 1275, 1402, 1416, 1545, 1555,
1611, 1634, 1645, 1678, 1692, 1720,
1742, 1827, 1864, 1883, 1884, 1927,
2210, 2228, 2276, 2299, 2317

Women's Rights activist
Truth, Sojourner, 38, 400, 611, 650,
1028, 1438, 1503, 1504, 1741, 1789,
2044, 2061, 2237, 2269, 2385, 2386,
2387, 2388, 2389, 2390

Actor see **Entertainment**

Art see also **Photography**
Bearden, Romare, 235, 236, 237, 238,
  239, 240, 241, 242, 243, 244, 285,
  286, 1344, 1375, 1766, 2068
Catlett, Elizabeth, 246, 547, 614, 1327,
  2348
Crite, Allan Rohan, 1153
Douglas, Aaron, 289, 2320
Evans, Minnie, 292
Hunter, Clementine, 258
Jones, Lois Mailou, 261, 295
Motley, Archibald Jr., 606
Nugent, Bruce, 971
Arts administrator
  Campbell, Mary Schmidt, 245
  Lewis, Elma, 1939
Graffiti-inspired artist
  Basquiat, Jean-Michel, 2399
Painter
  Banister, Edward Mitchell, 234
  Bennett, Gwendolyn, 1376
  Delaney, Beauford, 1888
  Delaney, Joseph, 550
  Hayden, Palmer, 256
  Johnson, William H., 294, 393
  Lawrence, Jacob, 263, 297, 555, 556,
    622, 1089, 1675
  Lee-Smith, Hughie, 130, 264, 265, 298
  Pippin, Horace, 271, 272
  Tanner, Henry O., 399
  White, Charles, 279
  Woodruff, Hale, 1006
Sculptor
  Edmondson, William, 249
  Johnson, Sargent, 260
  Prophet, Nancy Elizabeth, 300
  Savage, Augusta, 350, 475

Astronaut see **Aerospace,**
  Astronaut

Athletics
Amos, Wally, 1599
Brown, Jim, 583
DeFrantz, Anita, 954
Lewis, William Henry, 1180
Baseball star
  Aaron, Hank, 1, 384, 460, 544
  Blue, Vida, 2170
  Gibson, Bob, 1836
  Jackson, Reggie, 2174

Leonard, Buck, 2175
Paige, Satchel, 129, 1613, 2447, 2448,
  2449, 2450
Robinson, Jackie, 16, 889, 1808, 2176
Strawberry, Darryl, 2178
Basketball star
  Abdul Jabbar, Kareem, 1451, 2334
  Chamberlain, Wilt, 2171
  Johnson, Magic, 1996
  Jordan, Michael, 598, 599, 856
  O'Neal, Shaquille, 1838
  Russell, Bill, 1395, 1906
  Woodard, Lynette, 1945
Boxer
  Ali, Muhammad, 2, 20, 134, 748,
    1200, 1223, 1339, 1650, 1693, 1928,
    1929, 1930, 2169, 2406
  Foreman, George, 702
  Holmes, Larry, 2173
  Holyfield, Evander, 596, 887
  Johnson, Jack, 338, 1868
  Leonard, Sugar Ray, 604
  Louis, Joe, 14, 1000, 1442, 1447, 1448,
    2440
  Robinson, Sugar Ray, 2177
Jockey
  Murphy, Isaac, 1130, 2443
Tennis champion
  Ashe, Arthur, 325, 991, 1694, 2300
  Gibson, Althea, 10, 594, 2172, 2336
Track star
  Joyner, Florence Griffith, 29, 2436
  Joyner-Kersee, Jackie, 600, 999
  Lewis, Carl, 1869
  Owens, Jesse, 343, 473, 1351, 1514,
    1527, 2199, 2446
  Rudolph, Wilma, 685, 1002, 1855,
    2453

Aerospace
Astronaut
  Bluford, Guion S. Jr., 2469
  Jemison, Mae, 982, 1513, 2214
Aviator
  Coleman, Bessie, 587

Book Collecting
Blockson, Charles L., 2495
Schomburg, Arthur, 398, 424, 1118,
  1119, 1120, 1121, 1531, 1590, 1974

Business and Economics
Bady, Willie Jr, 2408

Cain, Herman, 2216
Forten, James, 430, 1664, 2028
Gaston, A.G., 438, 1446, 2305
Parks, Henry, 710
BET founder
  Johnson, Robert E., 2433
Economist
  Browne, Robert S., 377
  Malvreaux, Julianne, 736
  Sowell, Thomas, 46
Entrepreneur
  Amos, Wally, 1599
  Bady, Belynda B., 1567, 2342
  Fuller, Solomon B., 422
  Hughes, Dorothy Pitman, 440
  Sullivan, Leon, 1221, 1740, 2480
  Walker, Mme. C.J., 443, 683, 1516,
    2459
  Wright, Richard R., 1968
Music executive
  Gordy, Berry Jr., 1460
  Jones, Quincy, 722, 1985, 2435

Comedian *see* **Entertainment**

Cowboy
Love, Nat, 639, 647, 795, 933, 1426, 1737

Dance *see* **Entertainment**

Doctor *see* **Health and Medicine,**
  Physician

Economics *see* **Business and**
  Economics

Education
Asante, Molefi, 71, 127, 1519, 1871 ,
  2398
Barnes, James B., 284
Bethune, Mary McLeod, 4, 73, 287, 310,
  386, 726, 1170, 1377, 2064, 2319,
  2345, 2346, 2412, 2507
Clark, Joe, 658
Clark, Septima, 459, 570
Cole, Johnnetta, 761, 762, 871, 916,
  1103, 1866, 2019, 2353
Collins, Marva, 763, 764, 1367
Cooper, Anna Julia, 2354, 2355
Coppin, Frances, 859
Futrell, Mary, 703, 779
Giddings, Paula, 468, 997
Golden, Marita, 618, 1049

Henderson, Stephen, 1347
Hope, John, 840
Houston, Charles Hamilton, 405, 1957,
  2184
Jeffries, Leonard, 2430
Karenga, Ron, 262, 296, 515, 1751
Ladd, Florence, 2372
Langston, John Mercer, 1502
Lee, Benjamin, 794
Luis, W.A., 1639
Marable, Manning, 2374
Mays, Benjamin, 15, 217, 709, 799, 836,
  1001, 1369, 1437, 1987, 2442
McGriff, Deborah, 861
Miller, Kelly, 1114, 1306, 1687, 1822,
  1823, 1972
Payton, Benjamin, 806
Proctor, Samuel D., 518
Ridley, Elizabeth, 348
Riley, Dorothy, 724
Rudenstein, Neil L., 61
Shabazz, Betty, 1352, 1396, 1487, 1553,
  1924, 2454
Vernon, William T., 427
Vest, Hilda, 1301
Washington, Booker T., 201, 223, 408,
  477, 741, 742, 743, 814, 815, 816,
  817, 818, 819, 820, 821, 822, 823,
  834, 847, 946, 1084, 1159, 1232,
  1279, 1399, 1459, 1517, 1529, 1642,
  1643, 1644, 1670, 1790, 1910, 1964,
  1965, 1982, 2049, 2050, 2051, 2052,
  2053, 2298, 2308, 2309, 2310, 2461,
  2462, 2463, 2481, 2482, 2483
Washington, James M., 131, 478, 505,
  1614, 1615, 1718, 1791, 1792
Wright, Richard R., 1968
Scholar
  Blyden, Edward Wilmot, 387
  Brown, Sterling A., 1419
  Crummell, Alexander, 211, 380, 660,
    993, 2325
  Cruse, Harold, 155, 1104, 1188
  Du Bois, W.E.B., 26, 82, 83, 132, 161,
    162, 163, 164, 248, 315, 365, 381,
    390, 429, 641, 661, 768, 769, 770,
    771, 833, 838, 921, 922, 977, 1014,
    1134, 1154, 1163, 1208, 1313, 1328,
    1335, 1380, 1414, 1469, 1523, 1578,
    1579, 1601, 1663, 1684, 1762, 1800,
    1809, 1816, 1840, 1889, 1890, 1915,
    1953, 1954, 2240, 2260, 2277, 2288,
    2289, 2303, 2359, 2360, 2417 , 2471

Dyson, Michael Eric, 308, 316, 465, 678, 864, 1287, 1628, 1629, 1891, 2361
Gates, Henry Louis Jr., 27, 54, 120, 121, 122, 252, 368, 369, 376, 409, 527, 572, 617, 690, 691, 692, 693, 848, 1053, 1148, 1190, 1191, 1192, 1216, 1289, 1290, 1359, 1423 , 1707, 1726, 1748, 1861, 1980, 2363, 2499
Goodman, James, 1330
Harding, Vincent, 574
Higginbotham, Evelyn Brooks, 978, 979, 1291, 2367
Holt, Thomas, 2035
Lawrence-Lightfoot, Sara, 793
Locke, Alain, 94, 95, 96, 126, 186, 187, 266, 322, 372, 623, 633, 665, 666, 957, 1059, 1060 , 1061, 1067, 1068, 1069, 1940, 2079
McDowell, Deborah E., 2375
McHenry, Elizabeth, 1196, 1870
Pennington, James W.C., 189, 807
Pliny the Elder, 100
Sundiata, Ibrahim K., 195, 1123, 1796, 2043
Turner, Darwin T., 1363
Teacher
Cotter, Joseph S., 1662
Grimke, Charlotte Forten, 2329
University chancellor
Carnesale, Albert, 50, 756

Emigration
Bibb, Henry, 524
Delany, Martin R., 1501, 1951, 1952

Entertainment
Bailey, Pearl, 21, 911, 1008, 1341, 1619, 1847, 1859, 2234, 2249, 2259
Baker, Josephine, 1364, 1451, 1535, 1536
Charles, RuPaul, 1185, 1186, 1420, 1931
Davis, Sammy Jr., 335, 590, 2002
Hall, Arsenio, 229
Horne, Lena, 1135, 1935, 2183, 2368
Jackson, Michael, 1476
Little Richard, 968
Prince, 2452
Riggs, Marlon, 1905, 2003
Williams, Bert, 357, 2245, 2246
Winfrey, Oprah, 225, 565, 718, 862, 950, 953, 964, 984, 1034, 1413, 2071, 2395, 2466

Actor
Adams, Osceola, 1656
Berry, Halle, 2344
Brown, Jim, 583
Cosby, Bill, 589, 2252
Davis, Ossie, 314, 334, 549, 640, 1312
Dee, Ruby, 885, 1932
Gooding, Cuba Jr., 2328
Gossett, Louis Jr., 645
Harrison, Richard B., 1021
Hines, Gregory, 2474
King, Yolanda, 1368
Lincoln, Abby, 299
McDaniel, Hattie, 2236
Prochnow, Jurgen, 346
Qualls, Schyleen, 1559
Rains, Claude, 1271
Scott, Hazel, 276
Smith, Anna Deavere, 1361, 1690, 2243
Snipes, Wesley, 1768
Tyson, Cecily, 2391
Waters, Ethel, 680, 2012, 2238
Yarborough, Camille, 480
BET founder
Johnson, Robert E., 2433
Comedian
Gregory, Dick, 171, 172, 410, 513, 573, 926, 1080, 1108, 1269, 1524, 1894, 2032
Mabley, Moms, 1389, 1427, 1428, 1640
Markham, Pigmeat, 1167
Pryor, Richard, 273
Wilson, Flip, 1233, 1753
Dancer
Ailey, Alvin, 2467
Colins, Janet, 588
Dunham, Katherine, 627, 1651
Hines, Gregory, 2474
Jamison, Judith, 629, 630, 1937
Jones, Bill T., 2434
Primus, Pearl, 634, 635
Robinson, Bojangles, 2227
Walker, Aida Overton, 1975, 2244
Filmmaker
Dash, Julie, 2356, 2508
Lee, Spike, 632, 1958, 2438, 2439
Producer
Brown, Tony, 436, 1048
Wolfe, George C., 2215, 2404

Exploration
Explorer
  Henson, Matthew, 1179

Fashion
Designer
  Amlak, Elleni, 1411
  Smith, Willi, 2479
Editor
  Allen, Bonnie, 2212, 2213
Model
  Campbell, Naomi, 1835

Feminist *see* **Writing**

Filmmaker *see* **Entertainment**

Folklorist *see* **Writing**

Government and Politics
British Prime Minister
  Macmillan, Harold, 97
Diplomat
  Blyden, Edward Wilmot, 387
Indian nationalist leader
  Gandhi, Mohandas K., 1227, 1605,
    1916 , 2030
Jamaican political leader
  Manley, Michael, 1479
Nationalist leader
  Garvey, Amy Jacques, 923, 1404, 1955
  Garvey, Marcus, 9, 85, 86, 87, 88, 89 ,
    90, 91, 213, 318, 551, 593, 642, 780,
    781, 924, 996, 1018, 1078, 1079,
    1087, 1189, 1206, 1209, 1228, 1268,
    1315, 1316, 1421, 1422, 1511, 1532,
    1606, 1653 , 1867, 1917, 1918,
    1933, 1956, 2031, 2076, 2193, 2292
  Moore, Queen Mother, 1230, 1676,
    1794, 2201
  X, Malcolm, 42, 119, 204, 205, 206,
    207, 208, 359, 360, 432, 433, 566,
    654, 725, 829, 1007, 1046, 1050,
    1092, 1127, 1128, 1162 , 1169,
    1198, 1199, 1275, 1402, 1416, 1545,
    1555, 1611, 1634, 1645, 1678, 1692,
    1720, 1742, 1827, 1864, 1883, 1884,
    1927, 2210, 2228 , 2276, 2299, 2317
Political scientist
  Reeves, Keith W., 60
Politician
  Bradley, Thomas, 1035
  Brown, Ronald H., 1175, 1569, 1865

  Bunche, Ralph, 404, 531, 915, 1547,
    1681, 2187
  Burke, Yvonne Brathwaite, 1570
  Chisholm, Shirley, 659, 688, 974, 975,
    1083, 1225, 1310, 1572, 1573, 1983,
    2349, 2350, 2351
  Dinkins, David, 156, 700, 919, 1575,
    1636
  King, Melvin H., 1585
  Sutton, Percy, 625, 712
  Washington, Harold, 613, 2208
  Waters, Maxine, 1760, 2393
  Wilkerson, Diane, 1174
  Young, Coleman, 1721, 2229
Socialist
  Woodbey, George W., 448
U.S. Attorney General
  Clark, Ramsey, 2352
U.S. Congressperson
  Bruce, Blanche K., 403, 1914
  De Priest, Oscar, 1998, 2057
  Gray, William H. III, 1276, 1749
  Jordan, Barbara, 13, 28, 179, 382, 553,
    576, 789, 1674
  Langston, John Mercer, 1502
  Miller, Thomas E., 188, 668
  Mitchell, Arthur, 605
  Moseley-Braun, Carol, 457, 567
  Powell, Adam Clayton Jr., 559, 609,
    610 , 739, 958, 1085, 1181, 1307,
    1788, 1942, 2200
  Pinchback, Pinckney B.S., 1587, 1647
U.S. President
  Adams, John Quincy, 2013
  Clinton, Bill, 1682, 1979
  Johnson, Lyndon B., 514
U.S. Secretary of Health, Education,
  and Welfare
  Harris, Patricia Roberts, 1550
U.S. Secretary of Housing
  Weaver, Robert C., 1040, 2464

Health and Medicine
Nurse
  Taylor, Susie King, 846
Physician
  Browne, Sir Thomas, 74
  Drew, Charles R., 2190
  Grier, William, 469, 1895
  Rock, John S., 1999
  Roman, Charles V., 670, 1622

Mental health
Psychiatrist
Cobb, Price, 469
Comer, James P., 331
Poussaint, Alvin, 558, 808, 2297, 2306
Welsing, Frances Cress, 479
Psychotherapist
Benson, Janice Hall, 754, 869
Boyd, Julia, 755
Social psychologist
Clark, Kenneth B., 151, 532, 676
Surgeon
Carson, Benjamin, 494
U.S. Surgeon General
Elders, Joycelyn, 773, 965

History
Historian
Aptheker, Herbert, 1797
Bennett, Lerone, 523, 753, 1697, 2314
Berry, Mary Frances, 1100
Clarke, John Henrik, 77, 78, 79, 728, 1101, 1102, 1215, 1358, 1702, 1814, 1815, 2055, 2056, 2073
Franklin, John Hope, 656, 777, 1106, 1107, 1706, 2029, 2473
Huggins, Nathan, 1065, 2037
Nell, William C., 2040
Rogers, J.A., 1486, 2378
Wilson, Joseph, 1719
Woodson, Carter G., 41, 118, 226, 280, 364, 401, 746, 825, 826, 827, 828, 951, 1125, 1126, 1530, 1554, 1597, 1978, 1988, 2062, 2274, 2275

Insurrectionist *see* Activism

Intellectual *see* Education, Scholar

Inventor *see* Scientist, Inventor

Labor
Labor leader
Randolph, A. Philip, 34, 842, 843, 937, 1280, 1281, 1533, 1534, 1588, 1826, 1922, 1923, 2202, 2203

Laundry Industry
Laundress
McCarty, Osceola, 442, 2477

Law
Judge
Hastie, William H., 214, 850, 876
Hibbler, William, 470
Motley, Constance Baker, 1586
Wright, Bruce, 1598
Lawyer
Alexander, Sadie T.M., 580
Cochran, Johnnie J., 1625
De Frantz, Anita, 954
Hastie, William H., 214, 850, 876
Houston, Charles Hamilton, 405, 1957, 2184
Jordan, Barbara, 13, 28, 179, 382 , 553, 576, 789, 1674
Kennedy, Florynce, 1425, 1646
Lewis, William Henry, 1180
Motley, Constance Baker, 1586
Murray, Pauli, 738, 1141, 1879
Norton, Eleanor Holmes, 342, 1830, 2198 , 2377, 2505
Rock, John S., 1998
Law professor
Bell, Derrick, 1696, 2468
Cleaver, Kathleen, 533, 1661
Guinier, Lani, 55, 595, 663, 1317
Hill, Anita, 980, 1129, 1424, 1607, 1749, 2264
Kennedy, Randall, 394, 1666
Williams, Patricia, 64
Security guard (Watergate)
Wills, Frank, 1042
U.S. Supreme Court Justice
Blackmun, Harry, 1680
Brennan, William J., 49
Harlan, John Marshall, 575
Marshall, Thurgood, 57, 577, 578, 579, 667, 841, 1113, 1337, 1981, 1996, 2268
Thomas, Clarence, 62, 1405

Libraries
Librarian
Danky, James P., 1683
Porter, Dorothy, 1116
Schomburg, Arthur, 398, 424, 1118, 1119, 1120, 1121, 1531, 1590, 1974

Linguistics
Linguist
Smitherman, Geneva, 1298, 1299

Medicine *see* **Health and Medicine**

Military
Civil War
  Carney, William H., 584
  Higginson, Thomas Wentworth, 1783
  Long, Thomas, 2332
Roman General
  Caesar, Julius, 75
U.S. General
  James, Chappie, 1542
  Powell, Colin, 58, 59, 959, 960, 1839, 2226, 2307
  Sherman, William T., 1795

Music
Band Leader
  Ellington, Duke, 165, 250, 251, 290 , 616, 1251, 1252, 1253, 1381, 1382, 1471, 1472, 1473, 1510, 1612, 2418, 2472
  Hampton, Lionel, 254, 370, 1475
Blues Musician
  Crudup, Arthur, 1600
  Handy, W.C., 414, 415, 416
  King, B.B., 417, 621, 790, 1112, 1295
Composer
  Blake, Eubie, 2413
  Brown, James, 330, 388, 1568
  Davis, Anthony, 1467
  Ellington, Duke, 165, 250, 251, 290, 616, 1251, 1252, 1253, 1381, 1382, 1471, 1472, 1473, 1510, 1612, 2418, 2472
  Gaye, Marvin, 253, 293, 643, 886, 1549, 1893, 1992, 2006
  Johnson, Rosamond J., 2008
  Joplin, Scott, 1477
  Waller, Fats, 1752
  Bebop
    Monk, Thelonious, 1480, 1481
  Classical
    Dvorak, Anton, 1470
    Paderewski, Ignacy, 1259
Drummer
  Roach, Max, 1261
Jazz Musician
  Armstrong, Lil Hardin, 1461
  Armstrong, Louis, 307, 1241, 1242, 1462, 1463, 1464, 1465, 1466
  Bechet, Sidney, 992, 1539, 2411
  Coleman, Ornette, 2074

  Coltrane, John, 1249
  Davis, Miles, 288, 615, 1250, 1379, 1468
  Gillespie, Dizzy, 925, 1474, 1850
  Marsalis, Wynton, 267, 1256
  Parker, Charlie, 270, 624, 1482, 1787
  Ra, Sun, 1086
  Rollins, Sonny, 374
  Taylor, Billy, 1263
Music Executive
  Gordy, Berry Jr., 1460
  Jones, Quincy, 722, 1985, 2435
Pianist
  Blake, Eubie, 2413
  Joplin, Scott, 1477
  Monk, Thelonious, 1480, 1481
  Paderewski, Ignacy, 1259
  Scott, Hazel, 276, 940, 2379
  Simone, Nina, 1262
  Waller, Fats, 1752
  Weston, Randy, 1490
Rap
  D., Chuck, 1725
  Ice Cube, 1727
  Shakur, Tupac, 1231, 1728
  Sister Souljah, 543
Singer
  Anderson, Marian, 3, 136, 1070, 1224, 1443, 1657, 1679
  Ballard, Florence, 1131
  Belafonte, Harry, 2186
  Blige, Mary J., 2347
  Brown, James, 330, 388, 1568
  Carroll, Diahann, 1047, 2470
  Carter, Betty, 1248
  Charles, Ray, 151, 585, 1378, 2065, 2256
  Cooke, Sam, 452
  Fitzgerald, Ella, 2422
  Flack, Roberta, 2230
  Franklin, Aretha, 44, 482, 2005
  Gaye, Marvin, 253, 293, 643, 886, 1549, 1893, 1992, 2006
  Houston, Whitney, 2007
  LaBelle, Patti, 1862
  Lincoln, Abby, 299
  Makeba, Miriam, 796, 797
  Mayfield, Curtis, 798
  Moore, Melba, 1157
  Rawls, Lou, 1483
  Reagon, Beatrice Johnson, 519, 2009, 2258

Robeson, Paul, 101, 102, 103, 104 , 105, 106, 191, 220, 221, 302, 447, 560, 636, 877, 938, 939, 961, 962, 990, 1117, 1197, 1484, 1485, 1528, 1716, 1853, 2069, 2204, 2205, 2511
Ross, Diana, 711, 963
Simone, Nina, 1262
Turner, Tina, 943, 2456, 2457
Vaughan, Sarah, 1488, 2011, 2458
Walker, Aida Overton, 1975, 2244
Warfield, William, 612
Waters, Ethel, 680, 2012, 2238
Wonder, Stevie, 18, 1967
  Blues Singer
    Holiday, Billie, 471, 721, 893, 1412, 1602
    Ledbetter, Huddie, 1478
  Gospel Singer
    Jackson, Mahalia, 1201, 1709, 1813
  Opera Singer
    Price, Leontyne, 397, 1973, 2255, 2451
  Reggae Singer
    Marley, Bob, 1390, 2296
Songwriter
  Dozier, Lamont, 1384
  Holland, Brian, 1384
  Holland, Eddie, 1384
  Mayfield, Curtis, 798

NAACP Leader *see* **Organizations**

Nationalist Leader *see* **Government and Politics**

News Media *see also* **Entertainment; Publishing**
Newspaper publisher
  Bass, Charlotta, 2335
Newspaper reporter
  Jones, Joshua Henry, 1810
  Morley, Jefferson, 1219
Television reporter
  Tillman, Jane Irving, 425

Nobel Prize
Laureate
  King, Martin Luther Jr., 30, 31, 32, 183, 184, 185, 339, 396, 407, 431, 445, 446, 499, 500, 516, 528, 529, 554, 601, 602, 603, 646, 664, 682, 686, 687, 695, 708, 791, 792, 929,

930, 931, 932, 988, 1024, 1094, 1207, 1303 , 1304, 1305, 1320, 1321, 1386, 1387, 1456, 1457, 1506, 1507, 1552 , 1584, 1608, 1638, 1711, 1804, 1829, 1900, 1986, 2231, 2254, 2323 , 2331, 2437, 2476
Morrison, Toni, 98, 218, 269, 802, 851, 852, 1063, 1296, 1331, 1391, 1392, 1526, 1713, 1920, 2376 , 2403, 2501, 2502, 2503

Orator *see* **Speaking**

Organizations
Arts administrator
  Campbell, Mary Schmidt, 245
Arts director
  Lewis, Elma, 1939
Amistad Research Center official
  DeVore, Donald, 1105
Black Panther Party leader
  Cleaver, Eldridge, 153, 1076, 1093, 1152, 1732, 2416
  Hampton, Fred, 1819
  Newton, Huey, 383, 557
Book Club founder
  Turner, Lana, 426
Children's Defense Fund official
  Edelman, Marian Wright, 52, 454, 467, 874, 2059, 2304
Civic leader
  Coppin, Frances, 859
Comprehensive Community Health Center official
  Edelin, Kenneth C., 466
Crossroads Africa official
  Robinson, James H., 107
DC Coalition of Black Gay Men representative
  Farajaje-Jones, Elias, 966
Joint Center for Political and Economic Studies official
  Williams, Eddie N., 745
Los Angeles Commission on Assaults against Women official
  Adam, Andrea Thompson, 972
Masonic leader
  Hall, Prince, 539, 784, 2293
NAACP official
  Evers-Williams, Myrlie, 1288, 1652, 1801, 2192
  Hooks, Benjamin, 439, 1492, 2312
  Mfume, Kweisi, 801, 2197

National Council of Negro Women official
Height, Dorothy, 998
National Urban League official
Jacob, John E., 406, 1803
Price, Hugh, 474, 1604
Planned Parenthood president
Wattleton, Faye, 562, 2000
Rosa Parks Sexual Assault Crisis Center, LA, representative
Brinkley, Rhonda, 1989
Trans Africa official
Robinson, Randall, 108, 1589
Women's club leader
Terrell, Mary Church, 113, 1458, 2060, 2384

Philanthropy
Cosby, Camille, 729, 1012
McCarty, Osceola, 442, 2477

Philosophy
Appiah, Anthony, 69, 70, 1182, 1566, 1658, 1659, 1660
Bierria, Alisa, 1145
Emerson, Ralph Waldo, 2027
West, Cornel, 39, 115, 128, 224, 278, 352, 353, 354, 411, 419, 489, 530, 563, 568, 671, 672, 673, 675, 854, 1004, 1041, 1144 , 1160, 1173, 1205, 1236, 1324, 1325, 1326, 1489, 1498, 1596, 1648 , 1671, 1729, 1761, 1857, 1881, 1911, 1976, 2239, 2271, 2272, 2338, 2339, 2465

Photography *see also* Art
Moutoussamy-Ashe, Jeanne, 48
Parks, Gordon, 344, 1961, 2067, 2223
Van Der Zee, James, 277, 1051

Poet *see* Writing

Politics *see* Government and Politics

Publishing *see also* News Media
Editor
Gillespie, Marcia Ann, 1875
Pickens, William, 669, 1831, 1921, 1998, 2224
Taylor, Susan, 323, 713, 1323, 1880, 2070
Executive
Graves, Earl G. Jr., 860

Publisher
Edwards, Audrey, 772
Johnson, John H., 371, 441, 2222, 2322
Polite, Craig K., 772
Smith, Barbara, 983, 1717, 2506

Religion
African Orthodox Church founder
McGuire, George Alexander, 486, 1025
AME Church Founder
Allen, Richard, 135, 492, 1771, 2014, 2280
AME Zion bishop
Hood, James Walker, 1512
Church of God in Christ founder
Mason, Charles H., 1785
Clergy
Adams, Charles G., 747
Beman, Jehiel C., 2015
Bowen, J.W.E., 1203
Brooks, Walter H., 1453
Crummell, Alexander, 211, 380, 660, 993, 2325
Father Divine, 1016, 1017, 1548, 1778
Flake, Floyd, 987
Foote, Julia A.J., 1616
Franklin, C.L., 865, 1892
Garnet, Henry Highland, 483, 592, 1336
Gomes, Peter J., 11, 47, 133, 967, 1019, 1020, 1195, 1346, 2423, 2424
Grace, Sweet Daddy, 1779, 1780, 1781
Griggs, Sutton E., 1736, 2033
Grimke, Francis J., 2034, 2330
Hancock, Gordon Blaine, 497, 732, 733, 785, 1637, 2179
Haynes, Lemuel, 866, 1229, 1782, 1897, 1977
Heber, Reginald, 95
Jackson, Jesse, 12, 175, 176, 484, 597, 694, 707, 1137, 1138, 1217, 1270, 1455, 1581, 1582, 1603, 1665, 1837, 1852, 2219, 2266, 2313, 2337, 2428, 2429, 2509
Jemison, T.J., 1139
Johns, Vernon, 1023
King, Bernice, 498
Lee, Jarena, 1617, 2373
Moss, Otis, 487, 934
Murray, Pauli, 738, 1141, 1879
Paul, Nathaniel, 345
Pennington, James W.C., 189, 807

Powell, Adam Clayton Jr., 559, 609, 610 , 739, 958, 1085, 1181, 1307, 1788, 1942, 2200
Proctor, Samuel D., 518
Ransom, Reverdy C., 1027
Reverend Ike, 1449, 1450
Rivers, Eugene, 503, 504, 1142
Sharpton, Al, 35, 697, 1039, 1272, 1273, 1592
Shuttlesworth, Fred, 520
Sullivan, Leon, 1221, 1740, 2480
Taylor, Gardner C., 488
Thurman, Howard, 476, 714, 715, 716, 878, 879, 891, 1045, 1081, 1353
Turner, Henry McNeal, 114, 835, 906, 1029, 1030, 1158, 1406, 1407, 1543, 1544, 1833
Vivian, C.T., 351
Walker, Charles T., 1432
Walker, Wyatt T., 1143
Walters, Alexander, 2460
Washington, James M., 131, 428, 478, 505, 1614, 1615, 1718, 1791, 1792
Watts, Herman, 1032
Wilmore, Gayraud, 1333
Woodbey, George W., 448

Evangelist
Jakes, T.D., 1022, 1497, 1784, 2220, 2221
Michaux, Solomon Lightfoot, 1786

Islamic leader
Ali, Noble Drew, 449, 1493, 1499, 1769, 1770

Missionary
Marrant, John, 485, 1440

Nation of Islam leader
Farrakhan, Louis, 168, 169, 212, 306, 730, 858, 1015, 1044, 1077, 1314, 1454, 1775, 1776, 1777, 2075, 2261, 2291, 2420
Muhammad, Elijah, 803, 804, 1202, 1220, 1878, 1903, 1941, 1960
Muhammad, Herbert, 853

New Orleans Yoruba priest
Teish, Luisah, 222

Prophet
Turner, Nat, 1758, 1759, 2047

Seminary professor
Weems, Renita, 1033, 1400

Theologian
Cone, James, 154, 332, 495, 496, 765, 837, 917, 918, 985, 1265, 1521, 1746, 1773, 2188

Monroe, Irene, 501

Scholar see **Education**

Science
Inventor
Banneker, Benjamin, 385, 1234, 1546
Carver, George Washington, 7, 758, 1011, 1075, 1509, 2017, 2217
Drew, Charles R., 2190
Marine biologist
Just, E.E., 1349

Singer see **Music, Singer**

Slavery
Enslaved free man
Northrup, Solomon, 373
Escaped slave
Craft, Ellen, 2020
Former slave
Debro, Sarah, 155
Jacobs, Harriet, 177, 981, 2038, 2370
Mars, James N., 2039
Reynolds, Mary, 2042
Taylor, Susie King, 846
White, J., 2054
Slave
Polly, 1026

Slave writer see **Slavery**

Sociology
Social psychologist
Clark, Kenneth B., 152, 532, 676
Sociologist
Drake, St. Clair, 361
Frazier, E. Franklin, 526, 778, 1267, 1969
Hancock, Gordon Blaine, 497, 732, 733, 785, 1637, 2179
Hare, Nathan, 1319
Wilson, William Julius, 1691, 2484

Speaking
Lecturer
Stewart, Maria W., 36, 111, 112, 194, 649, 740, 1856, 2206, 2382, 2383
Motivational speaker
Brown, Les, 855, 2414
Orator
Harper, Frances Ellen Watkins, 391, 734, 927, 1037, 1038, 1673, 1708, 1812, 2366

Writing *see also* **Publishing**
Browne, Sir Thomas, 74
Fair, Brian, 53
Anthologist
Braithwaite, William Stanley, 1357
Autobiographer
Douglass, Frederick, 8, 25, 81, 158,
159, 160, 389, 481, 525, 538, 766,
767, 831, 832, 872, 873, 905, 920,
976, 994, 1013, 1036, 1226, 1266,
1334, 1439, 1522, 1576, 1577, 1705,
1755, 1756, 1799, 1860, 2021, 2022,
2023, 2024, 2025, 2058, 2189, 2286,
2287, 2326, 2327
Critic
Gates, Henry Louis Jr., 27, 54, 120,
121, 122, 252, 368, 369, 376, 409,
527, 572, 617, 690, 691, 692, 693,
848, 1053, 1148, 1190, 1191, 1192,
1216, 1289, 1290, 1359, 1423, 1707,
1726, 1748, 1861, 1980, 2363, 2499
Hooks, Bell, 1292, 2182, 2294
Locke, Alain, 94, 95, 96, 126, 186, 187,
266, 322, 372, 623, 633, 665, 666,
957, 1059, 1060, 1061, 1067, 1068,
1069, 1940, 2079
Murray, Albert, 1257, 1258
Neal, Larry, 341, 502
Reed, Adolph, 1715
Literary
Broyard, Anatole, 1990
Gayle, Addison Jr., 363, 1842
Dramatist
Hansberry, Lorraine, 92, 228, 255,
619, 1235, 1820, 1896, 1994, 2194,
2247, 2365
Neal, Larry, 341, 502
Shakespeare, William, 109
Shange, Ntozake, 192, 2380
Wilson, August, 40, 117, 564, 949
Wolfe, George C., 2215, 2404
Essayist
Jordan, June, 180, 216, 867, 1294, 1385
Feminist
Hooks, Bell, 1292, 2182, 2294
Kennedy, Florynce, 1425, 1646
Folklorist
Brewer, J. Mason, 125
Hurston, Zora Neale, 540, 541, 552,
705, 706, 788, 894, 904, 928, 955,
1136, 1171, 1210, 1293, 1415, 1844,
1899, 1936, 1971, 2248, 2253, 2265,
2321, 2369, 2426, 2427, 2475

Journalist
Davis, Frank Marshall, 1177
Fortune, T. Thomas, 84, 170, 590,
731, 1403, 1828, 2218, 2262, 2362
Munroe, Roberta M., 970
Robinson, Max, 1854
Ruggles, David, 1623, 1764
Russwurm, John B., 349, 1962
Schuyler, George, 1064, 1688
Simmons, Judy, 1689
Trotter, William Monroe, 37
Wallace, Michelle, 1003
Williams, Tevis, 637
Novelist
Angelou, Maya, 43, 65, 66, 67, 210,
581, 657, 749, 882, 1082, 1088,
1149, 1372, 1743, 1947, 2233, 2281,
2282, 2340, 2407, 2485
Baldwin, James, 22, 72, 138, 139, 140,
141, 142, 143, 144, 227, 230, 231,
232, 326, 327, 328, 402, 461, 462,
536, 638, 698, 699, 719, 752, 849,
857, 868, 883, 912, 913, 973, 986,
1009, 1010, 1071, 1072, 1073, 1074,
1096, 1097, 1098, 1099, 1147, 1150,
1183, 1213, 1239, 1243, 1244, 1245,
1283, 1284, 1285, 1342, 1343, 1355,
1373, 1374, 1418, 1444, 1505, 1508,
1520, 1537, 1538, 1672, 1695, 1744,
1745, 1811, 1848, 1873, 1874, 1885,
1886, 1948, 2063, 2181, 2235, 2242,
2318, 2409, 2410, 2486, 2487, 2494
Chesnutt, Charles W., 24, 880, 1133,
1151, 1264, 1620, 2496
Ellison, Ralph, 166, 167, 291, 366,
689, 774, 775, 881, 995, 1043, 1164,
1238, 1747, 2026, 2290, 2401, 2419,
2488
Gaines, Ernest J., 2498
Griggs, Sutton E., 1736, 2033
Hawthorne, Nathaniel, 1685
Johnson, Charles, 2500
Jones, Joshua Henry, 1810
Killens, John O., 181, 395, 455, 674,
1058, 1110, 1111, 1140, 1218, 2195,
2267
Ladd, Florence, 2372
Lessing, Doris, 1156
Marshall, Paule, 268
Morrison, Toni, 98, 218, 269, 802,
851, 852, 1063, 1296, 1331, 1391,
1392, 1526, 1713, 1920, 2376, 2403,
2501, 2502, 2503

Toomer, Jean, 17, 303, 811, 892, 1278, 1354, 1356, 1362, 1397, 1669, 1765, 2232, 2455

Tourgee, Albion W., 1300

Walker, Alice, 196, 304, 626, 944, 952, 1031, 1371, 1431, 1560, 1908, 1909, 1925, 1926, 1944, 1963, 2207, 2392, 2493

Wideman, John Edgar, 355, 356, 989

Wright, Richard, 203, 305, 358, 412, 420, 458, 490, 506, 507, 508, 653, 1146, 1161, 1274, 1541, 1633, 1677, 1754, 1793, 1858, 1882, 1912, 1946

Yerby, Frank, 2405

Poet

Alexander, Elizabeth, 1282

Angelou, Maya, 43, 65, 66, 67, 210, 581, 657, 749, 882, 1082, 1088, 1149, 1372, 1743, 1947, 2233, 2281, 2282, 2340, 2407, 2485

Bady, Barbara, 1340

Baraka, Amiri, 124, 145, 282, 283, 914, 1132, 1500, 1556

Braithwaite, William Stanley, 1357

Brooks, Gwendolyn, 311, 2400

Clifton, Lucille, 720, 1187, 2018

Cullen, Countee, 80, 1562, 1774

Danner, Margaret, 1176

Davis, Frank Marshall, 1177

Dove, Rita, 421

Dunbar, Paul Laurence, 336, 571, 1052, 1445, 1563

Evans, Mari, 317, 684, 776, 1630

Giovanni, Nikki, 644, 662, 1193, 1194, 1345, 1383, 1441, 1818, 1970, 2263

Hughes, Langston, 174, 257, 320, 321, 423, 735, 787, 1054, 1055, 1056, 1066, 1166, 1254, 1255, 1348, 1851, 1872, 2066, 2489, 2490

Joans, Ted, 620

Johnson, Fenton, 392

Jordan, June, 180, 216, 867, 1294, 1385

Knight, Etheridge, 1388

Madhubuti, Haki, 1959, 2402

Neal, Larry, 341, 502

Plato, Ann, 1394

Qualls, Schyleen, 1559

Sanchez, Sonia, 45, 275, 1370

Shange, Ntozake, 192, 2380

Spencer, Anne, 2381

Wheatley, Phillis, 652, 947, 1091, 1211

Slavery

Equiano, Olaudah, 367, 1436, 1735

Horton, George M., 2036

Jacobs, Harriet, 177, 981, 2038, 2370

Smith, Venture, 110, 193

Writers

Bambara, Toni Cade, 233, 281, 700, 1286, 2284

Baraka, Amiri, 124, 145, 282, 283, 914, 1132, 1500, 1556

Bergreen, Laurence, 1246

Bontemps, Arna, 2251

Bradley, David, 329

Brown, Claude, 146, 545

Brown, Sterling A., 1419

Brown, William Wells, 148, 149, 150, 569, 1494, 1495, 1913, 1949, 2016

Bruce, H.C., 830

Bruce, John E., 312, 1184

Buckley, Gail Lumet, 870

Childress, Alice, 759, 1700, 1701, 1734, 1887, 2497

Chipman, Charles P., 760

Cotter, Joseph S., 1662

Cullen, Countee, 80

Derricotte, Toi, 537, 1849

Donaldson, Greg, 464

Dyson, Michael Eric, 308, 316, 465, 678, 864, 1287, 1628, 1629, 1891, 2361

Fair, Brian, 53

Faucet, Jessie, 839, 1165

Fischer, Rudolph, 2421

Giddings, Paula, 468, 997

Golden, Marita, 618, 1049

Haley, Alex, 319, 783, 875, 1109, 2425

Harding, Vincent, 574

Harper, Frances Ellen Watkins, 391, 734, 927, 1037, 1038, 1673, 1708, 1812, 2366

Haynes, Lemuel, 866, 1229, 1782, 1897, 1977

Himes, Chester, 1621, 1654, 1898

Hunter, Tera W., 628

Hurston, Zora Neale, 540, 541, 552, 705, 706, 788, 894, 904, 928, 955, 1137, 1171, 1210, 1293, 1415, 1844, 1899, 1936, 1971, 2248, 2253, 2265, 2321, 2369, 2426, 2427, 2475

Johnson, Georgia Douglas, 2371, 2431

Johnson, James Weldon, 178, 259, 631, 956, 1057, 1540, 1564, 1710, 1723, 1821, 1938, 1995, 2008, 2077, 2432

Jones, Bessie, 215

Jones, Nettie, 1876
Kincaid, Jamaica, 1551
Lawrence-Lightfoot, Sara, 793
Lorde, Audre, 888, 969, 1525, 1557,
    1558, 1863
Marable, Manning, 2374
Matthews, Victoria Earle, 1360
McKay, Claude, 542, 679, 737, 1062,
    1168, 1204, 1641, 1805, 1901
McMillan, Roslyn, 1902
Moseley, Walter, 418, 534
Murray, Albert, 1257, 1258
Naylor, Gloria, 1350, 1429, 2444, 2504
Neal, Larry, 341, 502
Nelson, Jill, 696, 1277
Newman, Richard, 99

Nugent, Bruce, 971
Perry, Richard, 1904
Petry, Ann, 2492
Priestly, J.B., 1724
Shipler, David K., 1668
Simone, Timothy M., 375, 2512
Smith, Barbara, 983, 1717, 2506
Steele, Shelby, 1515
Taylor, Susan, 323, 713, 1323, 1880,
    2070
Walker, Margaret, 1398, 1561
Wiley, Ralph, 2273
Williams, John A., 116
Williams, Sherley Anne, 717, 2394
Wright, Sarah E., 1401